ROUTLEDGE LIBRARY EDITIONS:
TAXATION

Volume 5

THE INCOME TAX AND THE PROGRESSIVE ERA

THE INCOME TAX AND THE PROGRESSIVE ERA

JOHN D. BUENKER

Routledge
Taylor & Francis Group
LONDON AND NEW YORK

First published in 1985 by Garland Publishing, Inc.

This edition first published in 2019
by Routledge
2 Park Square, Milton Park, Abingdon, Oxon OX14 4RN

and by Routledge
711 Third Avenue, New York, NY 10017

Routledge is an imprint of the Taylor & Francis Group, an informa business

British Library Cataloguing in Publication Data
A catalogue record for this book is available from the British Library

ISBN: 978-1-138-56291-2 (Set)
ISBN: 978-0-429-48988-4 (Set) (ebk)
ISBN: 978-1-138-59148-6 (Volume 5) (hbk)
ISBN: 978-1-138-59163-9 (Volume 5) (pbk)
ISBN: 978-0-429-49040-8 (Volume 5) (ebk)

Publisher's Note
The publisher has gone to great lengths to ensure the quality of this reprint but points out that some imperfections in the original copies may be apparent.

Disclaimer
The publisher has made every effort to trace copyright holders and would welcome correspondence from those they have been unable to trace.

THE INCOME TAX
AND
THE PROGRESSIVE ERA

John D. Buenker

Garland Publishing, Inc.
New York & London ★ 1985

Library of Congress Cataloging in Publication Data

Buenker, John D.
The income tax and the Progressive era.

(Modern American history)
Bibliography: p.
Includes index.
1. Income tax—United States—History.
2. Progressivism (United States politics)—History.
3. United States—Politics and government—1901–1953.
I. Title. II. Series.
HJ4652.B89 1985 336.24'0973 85-16252
ISBN 0-8240-5665-5

All volumes in this series are printed on acid-free, 250-year-life paper.

Printed in the United States of America

The Income Tax

and

The Progressive Era

John D. Buenker

To the Memory of

J. Joseph Huthmacher
1929-1982

With deepest gratitude and affection

TABLE OF CONTENTS

PREFACE

The present study began over twenty years ago as a doctoral dissertation designed to investigate the enactment of the federal income tax as a case study of an important Progressive Era reform. It was undertaken during the height of the historiographical debate over the origins of Progressive reform in the hope that the study would shed some light on the relative merits of the conflicting interpretations. The income tax was chosen because it was a truly nationwide reform, not one that occurred in a single city, state, or region. It was also a critical issue that seemed likely to have divided people fairly sharply along socioeconomic lines, thus helping to provide insight into the debate that was ranging over the "class origins" of the reformist impulse.

In the ensuing twenty years, our knowledge of the Era has been deepened and broadened by the work of a number of scholars and the debate has moved far beyond the controversies of the 1960s. That is apparent to anyone who reads such recent publications as John Whiteclay Chambers, The Tyranny of Change: America in the Progressive Era, (New York, 1980); Arthur S. Link and Richard L. McCormick, Progressivism, (Arlington Heights, Illinois, 1983) and Daniel T. Rodgers, "In Search of Progressivism," Reviews in American History, 10(December, 1982); 113-132. Despite important differences of emphasis and conceptualization, these three excellent studies all take for granted certain propositions that were once regarded as radical: that the reformist activities of the Era were too complex and diverse to be subsumed under the aegis of a single movement or "progressive" ideology, that many segments of society outside of the amorphous "middle class," however defined, made significant contributions to the enactment of major reforms, that a new issue-oriented, candidate-centered, weak party politics facilitated many of these activities, and that the Progressive Era was, at bottom, a broad-based response on the part of Americans from nearly every socioeconomic, ethnocultural, and geographic segment of society to the emergence of the United States as a modern, urban, industrial, multicultural world power. Over the years, my interpretation of the origins of the federal income tax has been significantly altered by the establishment of these propositions and it is my hope and belief that the present manuscript reflects the current state of historiography as faithfully as humanly possible. My debt to all of the outstanding scholars who have contributed to this intellectual evolution is enormous and I trust that it is accurately reflected in the notes and bibliography.

The idea for this study originated, as did my interest in the Progressive Era itself, with my mentor, the late J. Joseph Huthmacher, Richards Professor of American History at the University of Delaware. In his pathbreaking essay "Urban Liberalism and Progressive Reform" (Mississippi Valley Historical Review, 44(September, 1962): 231-141), he challenged the prevailing view that reform was essentially the contribution of the articulate, activist, urban middle class, and suggested that it "seems to have depended upon constructive collaboration between elements of the new stock lower class and the urban middle class, with the further cooperation, at times, of organized labor." What was needed to establish the validity of that perspective, he asserted, was to shift the focus of the Era's historians from investigations of reputedly progressive groups and organizations to analyses of the origins of the period's landmark legislation. This perspective, urban liberalism, coalition politics, and an issue-focused approach, along with Joe's constant insistence upon viewing the Progressive Era as a multifaceted, variegated response to the emergence of modern America, was the one with which I began my own research. Despite important alterations and modifications, it still remains the foundation of my interpretation of the Progressive Era.

More than an historical perspective, however, what Joe Huthmacher gave me was a model of a scholar who was unwilling to compromise his own intellectual integrity and who was not afraid to challenge conventional wisdom or the historical establishment. With incisive wit, but generally with good humor, he regularly pricked the pretensions of the pompous and often turned that same weapon on his students and on himself,just in order to keep us all from gaining exaggerated opinions of our own brilliance. When a fellow historian mentioned, in an article, that I had made a certain argument in a more developed and convincing manner than had Joe, he photocopied the page and sent it to me with the marginal notation "uppity graduate student." Whatever kind of a historian I am or may become I owe am primarily to his teaching and example. His untimely death robbed the profession and those of us who loved him of a brilliant historian and a first-rate human being. It is my sincere wish that this book might serve as a modest repayment to Joe for all that he gave to me and might serve as a statement that scholars of his calibre live on in those they teach.

In the late 1960s, I was fortunate enough to have three chapters of my dissertation published in historical journals: 1) "The Western States and the Federal Income Tax Amendment," Rocky Mountain Review,

IV(1967): 35-58; 2) "Progressivism in Practice: New York State And The Federal Income Tax Amendment," The New York Historical Society Quarterly, LII(April, 1968): 139-160; and 3) "Urban Liberalism and the Federal Income Tax Amendment," Pennsylvania History, XXVI(April, 1969): 192-215. These were the remote, in some cases very remote, ancestors of Chapters IV, VI, and VII. In April of 1980, I was an invited participant in a national conference on taxation at the University of Chicago sponsored by the CATO Foundation. I gave a paper entitled "The Ratification of the Federal Income Tax Amendment" that was later published in The CATO Journal: An Interdisciplinary Journal of Applied Public Policy, 1(Spring, 1981): 183-224. Preparing that paper, which was essentially a reassessment of the material in Chapters IV through VII, reawakened my interest in the topic that had lain dormant while I pursued other research avenues. I am grateful to the editors of these four journals for permission to reprint portions of those original articles.

I am particularly indebted to two of the finest Progressive Era scholars in the nation for their assistance in the preparation of the final manuscript, Professors David P. Thelen of the University of Missouri-Columbia and Lewis L. Gould of the University of Texas-Austin. Both read earlier versions of the manuscript and made many cogent and insightful, sometimes painful, comments and suggestions. They are largely responsible for whatever improvement that I have made and in no way culpable for the problems that remain. I would also like to express my sincere gratitude to Professor Frank Freidel of the University of Washington, editor of Garland Publishing Company's Modern American History series, and to his associate, Professor Robert E. Burke of the University of Washington, for their encouragement and aid in completing the project. Being associated with a series edited by such distinguished scholars is gratifying.

I would also like to thank the University of Wisconsin-Parkside Committee on Research and Creative Activity for providing me with released time in which to revise the manuscript. I am also deeply grateful to Parkside Chancellor Alan E. Guskin for his support of all my work and for his assistance in getting the manuscripted typed. Josephine McCool and Carla Thomas, who did the actual typing, deserve my highest praise and thanks, especially for the good will with which they tolerated my sometimes illegible handwriting and prolix writing style. The staff of the U.W. Parkside Library, and especially the Interlibrary Loan Department, were invaluable to me in completing my research. I would like to pay especial homage to B.J. Nielsen, the director of the Interlibrary Loan Department, for her indefatigueable and resourceful efforts at tracking down exotic publications and documents. My colleague, Nicholas C. Burckel, Parkside's Archivist and Area Research Center director, is also deserving of many plaudits for his help in locating research materials, for sharing his own insights into the Progressive Era, and for allowing me to vent my frustrations on him on the tennis court. My colleague and friend Professor Gerald Michael Greenfield also deserves my undying gratitude for the intellectual stimulation, common sense advice, and bolstering encouragement with which he always provides me. I would also like to thank Carol Amendola Hannes for her invaluable assistance in preparing the index during her "spare time," apart from her activities as full time mother, businesswoman, and science student. A special debt of gratitude is owed to Marge Rowley and Carol Trolle for their editorial assistance in the hectic last minute preparation of the manuscript.

Finally, I would like to thank my children, Jeannie, Cathy, Eileen, Tom, and Joe, for putting up with their father's frequent immersion in the nether-world of research and writing and with his occasional outbursts of frustration. This project is older than all of them, and, as proud as I am of its completion, I am more proud of being my children's father. Rearing them is an infinitely more complex and time-consuming task than deciphering the mysteries of the Progressive Era, but the stakes, and the rewards, are much greater. We may never entirely close the generation gap, but working at the task has proven to be mutually enhancing.

John D. Buenker
Kenosha, Wisconsin
30 June 1984

CHAPTER 1

BUILDING A NATIONAL CONSENSUS

The enactment of a federal income tax in 1913 was the culmination of nearly a century of effort. Over the years, its sponsors ranged all the way from agrarian radicals to sophisticated political economists, and the arguments ranged widely from the need for increased revenue to the desire for a fundamental redistribution of wealth. Twice before, during the Civil War and in 1894, its advocates achieved success, only to see their handiwork undone. Even in the reformist euphoria of the Populist-Progressive Era, the obstacles remained formidable enough to postpone its adoption for nearly two decades. In the end, though, the conditions demanding the enactment of the tax led to the creation of a broad-based coalition from nearly all walks of life, who saw in it at least a partial solution to their economic problems. The notion of an income tax was anything but a novelty by the onset of the Progressive Era. Beginning with Massachusetts Bay in 1634, numerous colonies had employed a rough form of income levy known as the faculty tax. Since most colonial revenue was derived from imposts on real and personal property, the faculty tax was designed to reach "those persons who derived their incomes from other sources." It sought to tax the "returns and gains" of tradesmen, artificers, and handicraftsmen "according to his estate and with considerations of all his other abilities whatsoever," and "proportionate unto other men for the produce of their estates." The faculty tax was not, strictly speaking, an income tax as it was levied on a person's assumed income, but it did establish two significant precedents -- that taxes could be assessed on something other than tangible property and that their weight should be determined as far as possible by the ability to pay. In the opinion of Randolph Paul, long-time Treasury Department counsel, the faculty tax "went a considerable distance in the direction of modern income taxation." Although several colonies abandoned the attempt, South Carolina and Massachusetts retained the levy after the American Revolution and developed it into something closer to a real income tax. An estimated one-third of the states partially financed the costs of the Revolutionary War through some variation of the faculty tax.[1]

Numerous states experimented with an actual income tax at various periods. The severe depression of the 1840s led several states, especially in the South, to resort to income taxation as a fiscal measure. Nearly all that region's states resorted to an income tax during the Civil War. Although there was a brief hiatus in its use during the next two decades, at least seventeen states had utilized it at some point by 1895; four of these -- Massachusetts, Virginia, North Carolina and Louisiana -- still retained it. During the next three decades, there was a dramatic renewal of interest in state income taxes. By 1910 twenty states, mostly east of the Mississippi, had enacted income levies of some type, and such important states as Wisconsin, New York, Massachusetts and Missouri adopted the levy in the next decade. The income tax was also a worldwide phenomenon, having been adopted in such diverse nations as Switzerland, England, Austria, Italy, New Zealand, Tasmania, Japan, Prussia, and the Netherlands by 1910.[2]

Proposals for a federal income tax dated back to 1815. The revenue demands of the War of 1812 led Jeffersonian Secretary of the Treasury Alexander Dallas to call for an income levy. Given his political affiliation, it is also likely that Dallas was motivated by a desire to shift the burden of financing the war onto manufacturers and financiers. The Peace of Ghent removed the most compelling argument for the levy, however, and Congress made no effort to act upon Dallas' recommendation. The staggering cost of the Civil War finally forced the enactment of the nation's first income tax law in 1862. The eastern leadership of the Republican Party originally proposed to meet the need for increased revenue by the issuance of bonds, raising tariff rates, and additional excise taxes. When these proved insufficient, Thaddeus Stevens of Pennsylvania, chairman of the House Ways and Means Committee, sponsored a direct tax upon land. The objection of agrarian representatives, though, was so intense that Stevens was forced to resort to an income tax instead. Establishing a pattern that still persisted in 1913, the Civil War income tax was one of moderate rates levied upon a very small percentage of the nation's income receivers. After the experience of those years, there could be no doubt that a federal income tax was a levy only upon the nation's most affluent citizens. For the duration of the war, most such taxpayers were disposed to acquiesce in the necessity for the income tax, despite periodic debates over rates, administration, and the principle of graduation. The cessation of hostilities, however, touched off a seven year debate over the retention of the tax in peacetime that generally pitted the representatives of the Northeast against those of the South and West. In the end the former won out; the tax was repealed in 1872.[3]

During the next two decades, income tax bills were introduced in almost every session of Congress, nearly all by the representatives of the South and West. Finally, the measure was sponsored by Democrats of both houses in the depression year of 1893. Presenting the income tax primarily as an alternative source of revenue that would allow for the reduction of tariff receipts, the majority party was finally able to mandate its inclusion in the Wilson-Gorman Tariff of 1894. True to the Civil War pattern, the new tax was a flat two percent levy on incomes over $4,000. The collection machinery had scarcely been established, however, before Charles Pollock, a stockholder in the Farmer's Loan and Trust Company of New York, successfully challenged the case in court. In one of the most controversial and precedent breaking decisions in history, the Supreme Court overturned the 1894 income tax on a 5-4 decision. The Pollock Decision seemed to take the steam out of the pro-income tax forces for a decade or so, but the mounting pressure was intense enough to cause both President Theodore Roosevelt and the national Democratic Party to advocate its adoption by 1908. Clearly, the notion of a federal income tax was a familiar one to most Americans by the height of the Progressive Era.[4]

Yet this familiarity by no means guaranteed the enactment of a federal income tax, even in an era when Roosevelt achieved popularity by verbally flaying the "malefactors of great wealth." For one thing, the previous operation of the tax, on both the state and federal level, inspired no great confidence that it would actually reach the people that it was designed to affect. In Louisiana, in 1899, only two of the fifty-nine parishes returned any revenue yield at all. In South Carolina, in 1896, only thirty-nine of ninety-six counties did so. The amount of revenue raised in most states was described, even by such pro-income tax experts as E.R.A. Seligman, K.K. Kennan, and Delos R. Kinsman, as "insignificant" and "ludicrously" inadequate. Assessment was generally left to the individual taxpayer, and collection was usually in the hands of local, elected tax assessors. Excessive zeal in collecting revenue ticketed for the state capital was not the best platform for continuation in office. Many state tax commissions conceded the essential justice of tax, while recommending against adoption because of the formidable enforcement problem. Not until the enactment of a centralized system of administration by Wisconsin in 1911 did most of the onus of bad administration in state income taxes disappear. Actually the operation of state income tax was a mixed bag so far as the chances of a federal income tax were concerned. Besides the drawbacks already noted, the existence of a state tax often provided opponents of a federal measure with the argument that it would preclude a source of revenue that rightfully belonged to the state. On the other hand, the dismal record of failure in the states gave pro-income tax people the claim that only the federal government could do an effective job of taxing incomes. "If an income tax is to be utilized at all in the United States," E.R.A. Seligman contended, "it must be a national income tax." The sentiment was echoed by the Chautauquan which pronounced state income taxes a "melancholy failure" and concluded that only a "federal income tax could be uniform, fair, and evasion-proof." Conversely, as Yearley has demonstrated, the adoption and operation of the federal tax provided a strong impetus to the enactment of state income taxes. Despite the efforts of income tax opponents in several states to obfuscate the issue, the sources of support and opposition to both state and federal income taxation were essentially the same.[5]

The operation of the Civil War income tax did not hold out much promise that federal income taxation would be much more equitable or productive. Once the patriotic fervor subsided, there was, according to Internal Revenue Service Commissioner David Wells, a "considerable falling off in the revenue to be derived from the income tax." The number of taxpayers declined from 460,170 in 1866 to only 72,949 in 1872. The latter figure was .06 percent of the nation's population, and an estimated ten percent of its eligible taxpayers. The revenue yield similarly declined from 24.8 percent of total federal income to a mere 4.4 percent. By the time of repeal, Senator Justin Morrill of Vermont claimed, with a good deal of justification, that the income tax "had become little more than the sum each man chose to pay on his own estimate of his income." Harry Smith, the most thorough student of the Civil War tax, later concluded that "it would seem that the greatest weakness of the system was the incapacity of the lower officers and the dishonesty of the higher ones." In any case, the open evasion of the income tax in the post-war years earned it the reputation of being easily circumvented and unevenly administered.[6]

In addition, the income tax faced the heavy burden of its popular association with political radicalism. Despite its endorsement by respectable academics, such upright middle class groups as the National Tax Association, and such mainstream politicians as Roosevelt and the Democratic Party, a large portion of the American public understandably connected it with the agitation of less established segments of society. The 1894 tax materialized contemporaneously with, and partly in response to, Populism.

The Anti-Monopoly, Greenback, Union Labor, and United Labor Parties also advocated income taxation, as did the rapidly growing Socialist Party of Eugene Debs. An increasing number of newspapers, especially in the industrial Northeast, regularly stigmatized the tax as "class legislation", while the Philadelphia Public Ledger strongly questioned the notion that the rich should pay taxes "solely because they are rich." The New York Sun branded an income levy as "taxation of the few for the benefit of the many," while the New York Herald seriously suggested that "instead of taxing income, [the government] ought to pay premiums to men for achieving financial success."[7]

Its 1894 Congressional opponents labeled the tax variously as anarchism, communism, socialism, and populism, sentiments echoed by the plaintiff's attorneys in the Pollock Case, and even by some of the justices who concurred in the majority opinion. Whether these views represented sincere conviction or constituted rationalizations contrived to mislead the middle and lower classes is impossible to determine with certitude. Like most people, the nation's rich probably experienced little difficulty in convincing themselves that an attack upon their well-being was an assault against the foundations of national society. In any case, their contentions apparently helped to frighten large numbers of people away from support of a tax that would not even affect them. The income tax, as C.K. Yearley has put it, "unquestionably suffered as well from the company it kept." Allegations of class legislation, as a Nashville, Tennessee paper observed, totally missed the point that those whose incomes were too meager to be reached by a federal income tax would have gladly changed places with those whose incomes would be so burdened. The playwright George Fitch characterized potential taxpayers as members of "an exclusive club" which "the ordinary wage earning man cannot hope to enter" and suggested they "organize the Sons of Simoleons with a golden ribbon on the coat lapel for a badge."[8]

The true nature of the income tax issue was also obscured by several other misconceptions on the part of many who logically should have had a stake in its enactment. The notion of taxing citizens at different rates, based upon their varying incomes, seemed inherently undemocratic, especially since so many would not be taxed at all. Its opponents eagerly rallied behind the argument because it enabled them to pose as defenders of the cherished notion of democracy, and to claim that all men should bear the burden of financing government equally. W.D. Guthrie, one of Pollock's attorneys, stressed that concept with telling effectiveness in his opening remarks; anti-income tax newspapers and legislators frequently advanced it. A more sophisticated appreciation of the socioeconomic base of a democracy, as Yearley has demonstrated, has led to an understanding that tax burdens can only be equalized by taking into account what portion of a man's worth the levy is, rather than insisting upon strict mathematical parity. This was a lesson that people were slow to learn, however, and the "pseudo-democratic" contention of strict dollar for dollar equality died hard.[9]

The waters were further muddied by the spectre of sectionalism. It was clearly understood that the major impetus for a federal income tax emanated from the West and the South. Nearly all the bills introduced in Congress from the Civil War on came from representatives of those regions, while the delegates from the industrial Northeast, regardless of party, formed a nearly solid phalanx of opposition. This was a natural function of the fact that those individuals with sufficient incomes to be effected by the proposed tax were heavily concentrated in the Northeast. Almost seventy-two percent of the revenue from the Civil War income taxes came from the northeastern states, while the whole region west of the Mississippi paid only about twenty-two percent; the entire South yielded but 5.6 percent. This geographical circumstance made it possible for opponents of the tax to fuzz over the fact that the tax was to be paid by individuals, no matter where they lived, and to animate the resistance of those northeasterners without sufficient income to be affected by styling the tax a sectional plot. This was especially effective in an era when the South was still associated with secession and the West with agrarian radicalism. Ironically, some southern opponents of tax tried to stigmatize it as a northern plot to despoil the region of what little it had been able to recoup from the ravages of war and Reconstruction. As a concomitant of the sectional argument, bitter debates often raged over which region would benefit most by the increased revenue that a federal income tax might bring. Anti-income tax forces in the Northeast were extremely vocal in insisting that the revenue would be expended to develop the West at the expense of eastern taxpayers.[10]

This tendency to obscure the fact that the income tax was a levy upon individuals was also present in the frequent reminders that the bulk of the burden would fall upon only a few states. Approximately eighty percent of the Civil War tax had been paid by the residents of eight states -- New York, Pennsylvania, Massachusetts, Ohio, Illinois, California, New Jersey, and Maryland. The first three alone had produced almost sixty percent of the revenue, with New York accounting for one-third the national total. In 1916 these top eight states still accounted for three-fourths of the total personal and corporate income tax paid, with New York alone producing more than thirty-five percent. Beyond those states, there were only eight others -- Connecticut, Delaware, Michigan, Minnesota, Missouri, Oklahoma, Texas and Wisconsin -- that accounted for more than one percent of the national total. It was easy enough to portray the tax as a scheme of the forty or so "have-not" states to raid the "haves". In the South, consideration of the issue on a state-against--state basis caused many to view a federal income tax as a threat to the hallowed tradition of state rights.[11]

This tendency to think of the income tax as a levy upon states rather than upon individuals was given tremendous impetus by the interpretations of the direct tax clause of the U.S. Constitution. That highly controversial provision required that direct taxes had to be apportioned among the states on the basis of population. This was the clause that had been insisted upon by Southern slaveholders to ameliorate any possible federal taxation of their two most valuable assets -- land and slaves. They had added to it the "Three-Fifths Clause" that provided for the counting of three slaves for each five for the purposes of both representation and taxation. Unfortunately, no one had ever determined what the Founding Fathers considered direct taxes. According to James Madison's Journal of the Constitutional Convention, Rufus King "asked what was the precise meaning of direct taxation," and "no one answered." A century of Supreme Court decisions had established only that capitation and land levies fell into that elusive category. The Pollock Decision flew in the face of all previous precedents by declaring the 1894 income tax a direct one, and voiding it because it was not apportioned among the states on the basis of population. Had it been so apportioned, it was estimated that South Carolina would have been assessed three times as much as Massachusetts in relation to the income of its citizens, Mississippi four times as much as Rhode Island, and North Carolina four times as much as New York. In 1875 the New England states paid about $4,000,000 in federal taxes. If these had been apportioned by population, their bill would have been $9,350,000 and if by wealth, ballooned to $14,000,000. The northwestern states, on the other hand, paid $43,500,000 in customs and excise taxes, a total that would have dropped to $30,333,333, if apportioned by population, and to $27,500.000, if levied by wealth. Needless to say, the tax bill of those subject to an unapportioned income tax would shrink to virtually nothing if the tax were apportioned, while those who had escaped the Civil War and 1894 taxes would be forced to pay. This inability to get a definitive interpretation of the direct tax clause confused the income tax debate for decades, giving opponents a formidable constitutional shield behind which to hide. The Pollock Decision even seriously divided the measure's advocates between those who wished to pass another statutory tax in order to confront the Court over the direct tax issue, and those who desired to enact a constitutional amendment that would specifically remove the income tax from that nebulous category.[12]

Its previously disastrous administrative record and confusion over charges of radicalism, sectionalism, its anti-democratic nature, and state rivalries not withstanding, the most serious obstacle faced by the income tax was that the threat of its enactment united in opposition the most economically powerful and politically influential segments of society. The nation's wealthy businessmen, who were the primary objects of a federal income tax, were by no means the monolith imagined by the Populists and Socialists. As Robert Wiebe and others have shown convincingly, big business was divided between urban and rural, by geographic section, and by the size of the enterprize involved. Above all, businessmen were differentiated by function -- financeers v. manufacturers, shippers v. carriers, importers v. exporters, merchants v. manufacturers and so on. Many of the reform issues of the Populist Progressive Era drove deep fissures into their ranks. Tariff reform set northeastern businessmen against southern and western ones, and importers against manufacturers. Banking and currency reform pitted big city eastern financeers against small town western ones. Railroad regulation often set shippers against carriers.[13] An income tax, however, was a levy against the income derived from any business activity, whether in the city or county, in whatever section of the nation, whether from big business or small, and no matter what the nature of a person's enterprise. If one's income put a person above the minimum, he or she was liable to taxation.

There was some tendency for importers and merchants to favor retention of the Civil War taxes as a possible argument for lower tariff rates, while manufacturers and bankers desired repeal of the levies. Nevertheless, even granting the obvious defects of the tax's administration and the declining need for revenue, Randolph Paul has argued, repeal still came primarily because the "pressure politics of banking and manufacturing interests won" by virtue of "a systematic propaganda and lobbying campaign."

Theodore Roosevelt's endorsement of a federal income tax in 1906 "caused something resembling consternation, even in intelligent quarters," in the view of tax expert Wayne Mac Veagh writing in the North American Review, because "capitalists exhibit a singular stupidity in resisting every attempt to impose upon them their proper share of public burdens." The one percent corporate excise tax of 1909 was vigorously denounced in business quarters. The Syracuse Chamber of Commerce called it "novel, unjust, inequitable, discriminating, inquisitional and unnecessary," while the Commercial and Financial Chronical stigmatized it as an income tax in disguise. Similar opposition was voiced by the National Association of Manufacturers, the Merchants Exchange of St. Louis, the Jacksonville Board of Trade, and various Chambers of Commerce. The American Economist, official organ of the American Protective Tariff Association, consistently attacked the income tax as a plot by importers and retailers to destroy the protective system. The periodical predicted that "an income tax, levied on all incomes, we believe, would prove so hateful and unendurable as to insure the defeat of any political party which should be responsible for it." If the tax were to be enacted, the Economist insisted, "there is great doubt as to its constitutionality, unless it applies to every person who either earns wages or clips coupons." John D. Rockefeller, Andrew Carnegie, J.P. Morgan, and other titans of industry and finance were outspoken in their denunciation of the income tax, with Carnegie insisting that he favored a fifty percent inheritance tax because an income tax would destroy initiative and create a "nation of liars."[14]

"When they faced a graduated income tax in 1913," Wiebe has argued convincingly, "businessmen everywhere judged it the most destructive legislation in the nation's history." Its enactment was opposed by the Commercial and Financial Chronicle, the Wall Street Journal, the Proceedings of the Iron and Steel Institute, Financial Age, the Proceedings of the N.A.M., and a myriad of business groups and individual businessmen. They insisted that it would promote government spying, put a premium on dishonesty, promote spurious notions of equality, array "ninety-seven percent of the people against three percent of the people." One prominent New York City banker, Herbert L. Griggs, wrote to Congressman Cordell Hull that he personally favored the tax, but that every single one of his colleagues opposed it. It would be hard to find a single issue that more tightly united the nation's most wealthy citizens. It is not difficult to see why businessmen reacted so negatively to the federal income tax. When it finally went into operation, people engaged in some aspect of business filed nearly eighty percent of the returns. Only 3.3 percent of those touched by the long arm of the Internal Revenue Service were in agriculture, but .5 percent were laborers, and only seventeen percent were in the professions, with physicians and lawyers accounting for well over half the latter. Most of that eighty percent were bankers, brokers, capitalists, manufacturers, merchants, or corporate officials. Businessmen, as a group, accounted for about eighty-five percent of the income reported, and almost ninety percent of the tax paid, with the six occupations listed above again accounting for approximately seventy and eighty percent in the respective categories.[15]

What made their opposition so significant was that the "three percent" who were candidly acknowledged as the sole beneficiaries of preventing a federal income tax wielded political influence far out of proportion to their numbers. It is true that even Gilded Age politicians were not simply the willing puppets of wealthy businessmen portrayed by Matthew Josephson in The Politicos or David Graham Phillips in The Treason of the Senate. Politicians were professionals whose success depended more upon the ability to get elected than upon earning a profit. The criterion for performance was "carrying a precinct," not "meeting a payroll." By definition, they had to be attuned to the moods and demands of several segments of society, and to avoid the appearance of favoring one, especially if that segment constituted only "three percent" of the population. Moreover, the business community itself was usually divided on important economic issues, often sending conflicting signals, thus allowing politicians considerable room to maneuver. Business influence was often diluted, too, by the need to hedge all bets and support both parties. With so much at stake, as Collis P. Huntington acknowledged, one "cannot afford to be too openly for the man that loses." The complexities and necessary compromises of politics and legislation also often proved beyond the ken of men who were used to running their own businesses in an authoritarian fashion. In short, businessmen often came to politicians, in David Rothman's words, as "supplicants not as patrons."[16]

For all that, though, the ability of the nation's wealthy to work their will on an issue on which they were solidly united was still formidable. Most of the qualifications to business influence on politics depended to a large extent upon divisions within the business community itself. If business spoke with substantially one voice on an issue, as it assuredly did on the income tax, it was clearly the loudest voice that politicians heard. Rothman, who has done the most highly effective revision of businessman-politician relations in the U.S. Senate, acknowledges, that the former still dominated political decisions at the onset of the twentieth century. "Politicians did hear several sides of an argument," he notes, "but many voices, belonging to the farmers, laborers, professional groups, minorities and consumers, were still absent from Washington." It was, in fact, the development of these others into effective pressure groups able to counteract the efforts of business that constituted much of the essence of progressive reform, making possible the enactment of such measures as the federal income tax. That was a long laborious process, however, and while it was taking place "the business groups rather than the farmers, or the laborers, or the consumers most diligently attempted to influence politics. Their efforts, more than any others, at once shaped and were affected by the place of party in government." The exact nature and extent of that influence on the adoption of the federal income tax varied from place to place, and will be considered in the appropriate place. The fact that such influence was more complex and sophisticated than the muckrakers alleged did not make it any less real or effective.[17]

To a large extent, all the obstacles faced by the federal income tax came together to defeat it in the Pollock Case. Having lost the Congressional battle to prevent the 1894 tax, its opponents turned to the last line of defense - the Supreme Court. The plaintiff's attorneys were all prominent corporation lawyers with a personal stake in invalidating the tax - William D. Guthrie, Benjamin H. Bristow, Clarence A. Seward, Joseph H. Choate, former U.S. Senator George Edmunds of Vermont, and Charles Southmayd. Choate, the chief attorney, was reportedly retained at a fee of $100,000, double that if he were able to win. The most distinguished constitutional lawyer of the day, Choate's social philosophy was best illustrated by his oft-quoted remark that J.P. Morgan was "the greatest power for good in America", and by his comment that former mentor Southmayd "had an ample income of his own which was affected and had a strong idea of the right of property being at the foundation of civilized government.[18]

The plaintiff's constitutional argument was based primarily upon the direct tax clause, despite the fact that five previous Supreme Court decisions had established contrary precedents. In the 1796 Hylton Case, a court containing two members of the Constitutional Convention had refused to declare a tax on carriages direct, reserving that designation exclusively for capitation and land taxes. Even Alexander Hamilton, arguing for the United States, asked rhetorically, "what is the distinction between direct and indirect taxes?" and answered that "it is a matter of regret that terms so uncertain and vague in so important a point are to be found in the Constitution." He concluded that "we shall seek in vain for any antecedent settled legal meaning to the respective terms - there is none." In 1868 the Court had declined to apply the provision to a tax on insurance company receipts. In 1874 it had taken a similar stand on inheritance taxes, and in 1889 on bank notes. In the Springer Case, in 1880, the Court, in a case brought by a group of lawyers, had specifically held that the Civil War income taxes were not direct, and need not be apportioned. Choate sought to circumvent these obstacles by arguing that since land taxes were direct so too were levies on the income derived from land. And, he continued, since income from land was inseparable from that derived from other sources, the entire section had to be invalidated.[19]

Not content with this shaky constitutional argument, Choate and his cohorts buttressed their case with charges that sectionalism and radicalism generated the income tax and that the direct tax clause had been intended by the framers to protect the wealthy eastern states "as against the vote of mere numbers." The Pollock Case was argued in the era of Populism, the Molly Maguires, the Homestead, Pullman and Cripple Creek strikes, and Coxey's Army. Many concerned, established Americans viewed these agitations as part of a conspiracy to overthrow the Republic and saw in the income tax a weapon by which this was to be accomplished. Others seized the opportunity to gain a substantial number of converts to the anti-income tax cause by portraying it as the opening shot of the revolution. Whatever his view, Choate engaged in a lengthy argumentum ad horrendum in which he stigmatized the tax as a western plot to despoil the East, as the first step in the total destruction of property rights, "and after that communism, anarchism, and then, the ever following despotism. Choate was, in the opinion of Alfred Kelly and Winfred Harbison, "dwelling upon the horrible results which would follow were the principles embodied in the legislation before the Court carried to a supposedly logical extreme, an extreme which in reality lay beyond all rational probability." Interestingly enough, just one year later, the Republican Party levied a 1/4 of 1 percent tax on the capital of the nation's largest banks and corporations to finance the presidential victory of William McKinley over income tax advocate William Jennings Bryan. It reportedly yielded $400,000 from the Chicago meat packers, a quarter of a million from both Standard Oil and the Morgan banks, and according to Sidney Ratner, "was paid for the most part without protest by men who had vilified the income tax as communistic."[20]

That Choate's peroration struck a responsive chord in the majority of the court is apparent from the language and tone of the final decision and from Justice Stephen Field's concurring opinion that "the present assault upon capital is but the beginning. It will be but the stepping stone to other, more sweeping and longer, until our political contests will become a war of the poor against the rich." Ironically, the government's most able attorney, James Carter, probably confirmed the fears of the Court's majority by candidly acknowledging that the income tax was a class tax, insisting that "this is a distinction which should always be looked to in the business of taxation." At this distance, his presentation seems a model of moderation and reason. To a Court made up of property conscious conservatives already sensitized by evidence of radical agitation, it probably sounded more like a clarion call to revolution. Faced with this prospect, Edward S. Corwin has charged that the Court's majority ignored nearly a century of precedent to the contrary, and sought "to convert the 'direct tax' clauses into positive protections of wealth."[21]

The two Pollock Decisions were masterpieces of legal obfuscation. In the first one, with Justice Howell Jackson absent, the Court, by a 6-2 vote, concurred in Chief Justice Melville Fuller's opinion that, as Pollock's attorneys had argued, the tax on income from land was a direct one, and hence, unconstitutional because it was not apportioned by population. This was accomplished by carefully separating that type of income from all others and by arguing that a tax on net income from rentals is a tax on rentals not a tax on land, a "double indirection" as Justice White argued. The justices were unanimous on only one point, one that would later play a major role in the debate over ratification of the Sixteenth Amendment - that Congress lacked the power to tax instrumentalities of the state. They were evenly divided on the questions of whether a levy on the income from personal property was direct, or whether any part of the tax, if indirect, lacked uniformity, and, most significantly, if the unconstitutionality of the section permitting a tax on the income from land invalidated the entire measure. When Justice Jackson returned a few weeks later, the Court proceeded to invalidate the entire income tax section by a 5-4 vote, ruling that there was no real difference between income from land and other types of earnings, thus ignoring the separate category it had so painstakingly created in the first decision. "The ladder having served its purpose," Corwin has concluded, "having put the Court in the second story - is kicked down." The switch constituted such a flagrant breach of the rudimentary rules of logic that Alfred Kelly and Winfred Harbison have termed it "a major solecism." The dissenting justices termed it "a cavalier reversal of precedent," and Corwin the "vulgar logical error of the 'undistributed middle'."[22]

Even more amazing was the later revelation that Justice Jackson had voted <u>for</u> the tax, meaning that another member of the Court had shifted position since the first decision. Many observers at the time suspected Justice George Shiras, but most legal historians have exonerated him. Some have argued persuasively that it was Justice David Brewer, a nephew of Field, who later defended the decision in several speeches. Corwin makes a case for Justice Horace Gray. Whoever the culprit, the <u>volte face</u> of one justice overturned one hundred years of precedents on the taxing power, delaying the enactment of a federal income tax for almost two decades. It was, according to Corwin, "the example par excellence of what judicial review should not be when it is combined with popular government."[23]

The dissenting opinion, written by Justice John Marshall Harlan, was one of the most impassioned ever delivered in the Supreme Court. Dismissing the majority opinion as one "which hardly rises to the dignity of an argument," Harlan assailed the decision as an overturning of precedent and a hamstringing of national authority. Opposition to the tax, Harlan charged, came from an influential minority that held large amounts of personal property, mostly in the form of investments. The conservative argument that the tax had to be apportioned among the states according to population was merely a subterfuge that would allow the states to continue to protect those vested interests. The inordinate influence of a favored few, Harlan concluded, had prevented the government from removing the burden of taxation from the great majority of the people. One of the other dissenters, Justice White, wrote the unanimous opinion of the Court upholding the 1913 federal income tax just two decades later. Incredibly, he contended that the Pollock Decision "did not in any degree involve holding that income taxes generally and necessarily come within the class of direct taxes on property, but on the contrary recognized the fact that taxation on income was in its nature an excise." A later Chief Justice, Charles Evans Hughes, called the Pollock decision "a self-inflicted wound," while the economist E.R.A. Seligman termed it "the Dred Scott Decision of government revenue."[24]

By 1895, then, the influence of the nation's most wealthy citizens, the fear of radicalism, sectional jealously, and the complexity of the constitutional questions involved had all combined to invalidate the first peacetime federal income tax. For many, the Pollock Decision seemed to end the matter once and for all. But despite the formidable obstacles against the enactment of federal income tax, a variety of forces were creating a broad based national consenus in its favor. In less than two decades, these forces led many disparate segments of society to concur in the belief that a federal income tax would provide at least a partial redress of their economic difficulties. High on the list of pro-income tax forces were the increased demands being made upon government at all levels for increased services by people from all walks of life. The massive dislocations brought about by industrialization and urbanization had led growing numbers of Americans to reject their allegiance to the doctrine of laissez-faire, and to turn to government for amelioration of their condition. Farmers pressed their demands for better education and for the creation of extension services. Westerners insisted upon public irrigation projects, land reclamation, and the conservation of natural resources. The proliferation of regulatory agencies, at all levels of government, greatly augmented the number of public employees, increasing operating costs. The nation's expansion into the Far East and Latin America required vastly increased expenditures for military and colonial affairs. It was in the exploding cities, though, where the pressures for increased revenue were greatest. Their unparalleled growth in the nineteenth century had engendered a seemingly insatiable demand for transporation, communication, recreation, housing, education, fire and police protection, sanitation, and welfare. Whether these needs were met by public agencies or by subsidies to private enterprise, the cost was staggering. This was all the more true because the fragmentation of urban government, combined with the stranglehold exerted over it by state legislatures, mandated the payment of graft to businessmen and politicians in order to get the job done. The urban middle class often responded to this situation by demands for retrenchment, for "honesty, efficiency and economy" in government, but their voices were also often among the loudest crying for more and better services. The urban middle class sometimes wanted it both ways - better services without increased cost - but when forced to choose, they frequently let their need for the former outweigh their distaste for the latter, especially if the tax burden could be shifted elsewhere.[25]

Urban politicians quickly found that the existing tax structure was inadequate to meet these increased costs. So too was the extralegal system of "contributions" by officeholders, interested businessmen, gamblers, saloon keepers, and brothel operators by which the urban political machine had traditionally financed its various activities. "With more applicants than places," as Oscar Handlin has observed, urban politicians often found that "each appointment made one friend and a half-dozen enemies." Increased democracy in the form of primaries, referenda, and the like also meant growing expenditures in the costs of administering elections. In the main, professional politicians enthusiastically responded to these demands by seeking to shift as many functions as possible onto the public treasury, meaning that new methods of taxation were necessary to fill the coffers. Most probably also realized that such changes could greatly enhance their own power and prestige, by increasing the dependence of other groups upon them.[26]

Under these pressures, governmental costs skyrocketed in the late nineteenth and early twentieth centuries. While public expenditures had been only three percent of national income in 1800, they were almost ten percent of a much larger total by 1900. Between 1890 and 1913 alone they almost doubled, rising from $13.72 per capita to $25.92. National welfare costs soared from $318,000,000 to $1,000,000,000 in the same period. The greatest increases were noticeable on the state and local level, but the growth of federal spending was still very significant. Per capita federal spending rose from $4.84 to $7.01 between 1889 and 1913, with total costs increasing almost 400 percent, while the population increased by eighty-five percent. Much of this rise was due to military and colonial obligations, but increased activity on the domestic scene also played a significant role. The depression of the 1890s brought demands for government aid to the unemployed; Populist Senator William Peffer of Kansas, among others, introduced a public works bill to employ four million men. The treasury surplus of 105 million dollars, in 1890, became a deficit of 70 million by 1894. According to Paul Studenski and Herman Krooss, authors of the standard work on the financial history of the U.S., Theodore Roosevelt was the first president "to engage in expenditures for the relief of individual citizens (except for veterans) on a significant scale," providing disaster relief to the Phillipines, to the victims of the San Francisco earthquake and of cyclones in the South and West. Woodrow Wilson followed up with relief to flood victims in the Midwest. The Country Life Commission was established in 1908, the Public Health Service was created in 1912, and pensions to veterans were also increased. Public works expenditures more than doubled between

1900 and 1914, while those on rivers and harbors more than tripled. Federal land reclamation, irrigation, and conservation programs added to the total, as did the burgeoning regulatory agencies and cabinet departments. Although still in their infancy, federal expenditures were clearly growing at such a pace as to require revenue sources that were at once more lucrative and more predictable than those currently in use.[27]

The existing tax structure, both state and federal, badly failed the tests of predictability and productivity. The states derived their income primarily from the general property tax, which was supposed to fall upon both real and personal property of all kinds. Its computation was usually in the hands of local assessors, leading to incredible fluctuations from district to district. Since assessors were generally elected, their continuation in office often depended upon their zeal in underevaluating property. Because they were usually underpaid, assessors often supplemented their incomes by accepting bribes from grateful owners of undervalued property. But even the most honest and conscientious tax assessor found it extremely difficult to discover the existence of such intangible property as stocks and bonds with the same ease with which he was able to discern land and buildings. A Kentucky Special Tax Commission reported a typical finding when it concluded that the "State of Kentucky received more revenue for the year 1912 from its dogs than it did from all the bonds, monies and stocks in the state." Tax assessments for New York City, with the greatest accumulations of intangible assets in the world, consistently estimated real property at about twice the value of personality. The Twelfth Assembly District of Manhattan alone, the home of Rockefeller, Vanderbilt, Russell Sage, Jay Gould, and other titans of finance, probably contained twice as much intangible property as the total valuation for all forms of property in the entire city of New York. In a candid letter to New York Governor Charles Evans Hughes, Andrew Carnegie acknowledged that "the law as you know being that I am required to pay what I am assest" (sic) and that the personal property tax "is evaded by the people of New York, each claiming his country place as his domicile." Economist G.P. Watkins, author of "Growth of Large Fortunes," estimated in 1907 that "the proportion of personality which is abstract approaches three-fourths," and that the tremendous increase of this "paper property" resulted from the "dominance of the differentiated capitalist and of abstract property over the personal and human factor in production." Evasion was so pervasive that even such tax reform groups as the Civic Federation of Chicago and the New York Reform Club consistently undervalued their real property. "Before the enactment of Prohibition," C.K. Yearley has concluded, "probably nothing in American life entailed more calculated or premeditated lying than the general property tax."[28]

The federal tax structure was based almost entirely upon custom duties derived from the tariff and excise taxes. The amount of revenue that they produced "fluctuated sharply with changes in business activity, resulting in heavy surpluses during prosperity and large deficits during depression." Assessing the federal revenue system in 1913, the House Ways and Means Committee charged that it "has been fluctuating, inflexible, unstable and oftentimes unproductive, thus exposing the Government to deficiencies or excesses with all their attendant embarrassments." The tariff, the chief source of federal revenue, had grown increasingly inadequate as its role in protecting industries came to overshadow its function as a producer of tax dollars. "Between the two", David M. Chalmers has noted, "when each is carried to its logical conclusion, there is conflict." The more protectionist the tariff became, the more discouraging it was to the importation of foreign-made products, a condition that severely limited its utility as a source of revenue. So uncertain was the tariff yield that, in 1897, it was "predicted with equal confidence that it would fail to secure the desired revenue, and that it would convert the deficit into a surplus." All calculations about possible revenue, in the opinion of tariff historian F.W. Taussig, rested "simply on guesswork." By the onset of the second decade of the century, the Ways and Means Committee spoke for many tax experts and government officials when it argued that "the great fiscal problem in government, therefore, is to secure a system of taxation adjustable enough to meet the Treasury's varying demands and to maintain an equilibrium between governmental receipts and expenditures." Significantly, the Committee report went on to propose a federal income tax as one that would best meet the "need of an elastic and productive system of revenue." These contentions corroborated the worst fears of the <u>American Economist</u> and of the protectionist <u>The Nation</u>, published by economic nationalist E.L. Godkin, which stigmatized the income tax as "rankest Bryanism" and the revenue argument as "the crassest sophism ever flaunted."[29] Ultimately the adoption of the income tax freed the tariff from its role as revenue raiser, and left it to survive or fail as protector of industry.

As important as these considerations of predictability and productivity were in the growing sentiment in favor of a federal income tax, they paled beside the demand for greater tax equity. There can be little doubt that the single most important reason for the eventual enactment of the tax was a growing conviction among people from nearly all walks of life that the existing tax system failed, almost entirely, to reach the great fortunes that had been amassed as a result of industrialization. Estimates concerning the distribution of wealth and income in this period vary somewhat in detail, but all point to heavy concentration at the upper levels. With the advent of the muckrakers, according to Randolph Paul, "the publication of lists of millionaires was becoming a new journalistic sport." Significantly, both the liberal Democratic New York World, published by Joseph Pulitzer, and the conservative Republican New York Tribune published lists of millionaires in the 1890s, complete with the sources of their income. These revelations spawned a spate of books by economists and social critics warning of the dangers inherent in the concentration of great fortunes, including those of G.K. Holmes, Charles B. Spahr, G.P. Watkins, Willford I. King, Robert Hunter, Thorstein Veblen, J.H. Underwood, Gustavus Meyers, F.H. Streightoff, and Thomas G. Shearman. Their works, in the judgment of Sidney Ratner "aided in building up the public opinion that became mobilized behind the passage of the Sixteenth Amendment." By 1910 the poorest sixty-five percent took in 14.2 percent, while the next eighteen percent received 26.8 percent. This meant that the richest four percent received nearly one-third of total income. The wealthiest two percent got 20.4; the top one percent nearly fifteen percent. Since only those who made in excess of $3,000 a year had to pay the income tax when it was finally enacted in 1913, the breakdown of the first returns by the Internal Revenue Service revealed an even more dramatic degree of concentration among the nation's most affluent three percent. The eighty-two percent with incomes of less than $10,000 received only 35.15 percent of the reported income. The .87 percent who reported incomes of over $100,000 received 23.87 percent of total income, while the fifteen percent who made between $10,000 and $100,000 per year took the remaining forty-one percent. Between 1895 and 1910, moreover, the share of the richest 1.6 percent families increased from 10.8 percent to nineteen percent, indicating a growing concentration. At the other end of the scale, social worker Robert Hunter claimed that one-seventh of the population lived in poverty.[30]

The breakdown of taxpayers by occupations also underscored the degree of income concentration in the United States in the early twentieth century. Only about nineteen percent of the country's lawyers earned sufficient incomes to be required to pay any tax at all, as did but eleven percent of engineers, twenty-one percent of bankers, eighteen percent of mine owners, ten percent of manufacturers, and about five percent of real estate operators and merchants. Only four percent of the nation's teachers, two percent of its saloonkeepers, and .24 percent of its farmers made it into this exclusive circle.[31]

This heavy degree of concentration of income in the upper brackets was due mostly to the income its members received from the intangible wealth created by the fantastic expansion of industry since the Civil War. While the most affluent five percent received only seventeen percent of total wages and salaries paid, they took in 78.77 percent of all the income from dividends, fifty-three percent of that from interest, and one-third of that from rent. The ninety-seven percent who failed to earn at least $3,000 a year made less than one percent of the income from dividends, interest, and rent. The nation's non-agricultural assets increased ninefold between 1860 and 1900, its intangible assets by thirteen times and its tangible assets by 7.5 times, while its agricultural assets increased by only 2.5 times. Between 1885 and 1913 the total income of life insurance companies increased by more than nine times, and that of electric light and power companies by almost four times. The net value of utilities nearly tripled and the total assets of banks more than doubled. In a little more than a decade after the Spanish American War, bank deposits nearly quadrupled, the value of corporate bonds and preferred and common stock almost tripled, and life insurance reserves jumped from 1.6 billion dollars to 41.1 billion. Total stock values increased from 38.5 dollars to 65.1 billion in the first twelve years of the century.[32]

It was this vast income, derived primarily from the ownership of the nation's financial and manufacturing assets, that the state and federal tax structures missed almost altogether prior to 1909. Faced with the complexitities of assessing the value of personal property, most states preferred to tax what was easily seen. The general property tax, for all practical purposes, became a real estate levy. This development threw the tax burden primarily upon farmers and the urban middle class of homeowners and shopkeepers. Real property carried eighty-eight percent of the general property tax burden in New York's twenty-four largest cities. Nationally, the figure has been estimated at eighty percent. In Manhattan only about six percent of the population were homeowners, while in most other cities the figure rarely exceeded one-fourth. The nation's wealthy naturally owned a great deal of real property, but such assets constituted a much smaller percentage of their total wealth than they did that of a homeowner or shopkeeper. The roughly three-fourths of the population who owned no real property ostensibly escaped taxation, but in most cases landlords simply shifted the burden onto them, as part of their rent. The propertyless were also negatively taxed because inadequate revenues meant that necessary social services could not be supported. In one fifteen year period in the late nineteenth century, the valuation of property in the nation's thirteen largest cities increased by 157 percent, taxation by 360 percent, and debt by 271 percent. In Chicago the figures were an incredible 720, 1,445, and 487 percent, respectively.[33]

The federal tax structure was, if anything, even less geared to reaching the bulk of business and professional income. Between the repeal of the Civil War income taxes and 1913, according to Studenski and Krooss, "the Federal tax system was to be heavily regressive resting solely on consumption." Customs duties constituted close to half of federal revenue, and virtually the entire cost of the tax was added on to the eventual price paid by the consumer. The excise taxes that accounted for the other half of federal intake were levied directly on the price of such commodities as tobacco and liquor. Not until the enactment of the 1909 corporate excise tax was there any federal tax which did not fall directly upon what economist E.R.A. Seligman referred to as "things men eat and wear." Even then returns constituted but slightly more than five percent of federal revenue.[34]

The nation's wealthiest citizens were naturally its biggest consumers, but there was a finite limit to their ability to consume. The ratio of their consumption to that of the lower and middle classes was considerably smaller than the ratio of their total worth. Conversely, there was also a minimum of consumption necessary to sustain health and decency, beyond which no human being could allow himself to fall in order to avoid taxation, particularly since necessities were often taxed at comparable rates as were luxuries. As early as the 1870 debate over the repeal of the Civil War income taxes, Senator John Sherman of Ohio insisted that the "consumption of the rich does not bear the same relation to the consumption of the poor that the income of one does to the income of the other." During the debate over the 1894 income tax, supporters were even more insistent that federal taxes had "been levied upon articles of common consumption and the proportion of a poor man's income spent for such articles is several times greater than the proportion the wealthy man spends." In 1901, city wage earners and clerical workers spent an estimated ninety-five percent of their income on items of common consumption, nearly all of which was touched by federal customs and excise taxes. It is certain that those with income many times greater did not expend anywhere near the same percentage on such items. In 1889 tax reformer Thomas G. Shearman calculated that federal taxes took but from three to ten percent of the savings of the rich, and anywhere from seventy-five to ninety percent that of the less affluent.[35]

By 1912, the inequity of the federal tax structure had become so widely felt that the Democratic platform identified it, and the tariff in particular, as "the principal cause of the unequal distribution of wealth, it is a system of taxation which makes the rich richer and the poor poorer; under its operations the American farmer and the laboring man are the chief sufferers, it raises the cost of the necessaries of life to them but does not protect their products or wages." Democratic Senator Ollie James of Kentucky denounced the existing system as one which "provides that Lazarus must divide his crumbs with the tax-gatherers, but that Dives shall not give of his riches." The following year the Democratically controlled House Ways and Means Committee echoed the same theme when it stated that federal revenue rested "solely on consumption. The amount each citizen contributes is governed, not by his ability to pay taxes but by his consumption of the articles taxed. It requires as many yards of cloth to clothe, as many ounces of food to sustain, the day laborer as the largest holder of invested wealth, yet each pay into the Federal treasury a like amount of taxes upon the food he eats, while the farmer at present pays a larger rate of tax upon his cheap suit of woolen clothing than the latter upon his costly suit." The committee concluded that "all taxes, National, State, and local, come alike off the American people."[36]

This inequity was severely exacerbated by the dramatic increase in the cost of living between 1897 and 1913. The three decades following the Civil War were characterized mostly by deflation, especially during the long severe depression of the 1870s and 1890s. The last years of the century, however, saw a sharp rise in prices. Estimates vary according to the methods of determination, but it is generally agreed that the increase was on the order of one-third between 1897 and 1913, an average of about 2.3 percent per year. Significantly, the cost of food and other necessities rose even more precipitately, with the price of commodities increasing 46.7 percent between 1897 and 1910. Farm products went up 93.2 percent, food 46.7, clothing 35.8, implements 48.2, drugs 23.9, and house furnishings 24.2 percent. The price of lard increased 184 percent, pork 122 percent, linseed oil 133 percent, bacon 70 percent, eggs 100 percent, flour 50 percent and butter 45 percent. The rise was so widely felt that the Senate Select Committee on Wages and Prices of Commodities, chaired by Standpat Republican Henry Cabot Lodge of Massachusetts, acknowledged that "retail prices in the United States in the spring of 1910 were for many articles at the highest point recorded for many years." By 1913, the House Ways and Means Committee stated that "probably the most striking economic change since 1897 has been the tremendous increase in the cost of living - a situation which has attracted the anxious attention of economists the world over."[37]

While income also rose appreciably during the same period, most people generally failed to maintain the pace. Union wages increased only fourteen percent in the decade from 1898 to 1907, while the cost of living rose by one-fourth, according to one calculation. Another estimates a twenty-two percent increase in the price level. According to Congressional staff economists, George F. Pearson and Frank A. Warren, the purchasing power of wages increased only about sixteen percent while prices rose 36.8 percent. The evidence was so overwhelming that the Lodge Select Committee found that "wages have not advanced as rapidly as have prices and practically all labor difficulties which have been the subject of mediation in the United States during the past two or three years have had as their basis the advanced cost of living." Noting that wages had fallen drastically during the panic of 1907, barely regaining their pre-depression levels by 1910, the committee concluded that they "are not on as high a level as are food prices" while "salaries had advanced but very little during the past ten years." The difficulties of small businessmen in holding down costs led to more business failures in 1913 than in any year since 1893. Farm income was in the throes of a steady decline that saw the farmer's share of national income drop fifty percent between 1909 and 1929. In 1913 farm income was only 74.88 percent that of non-farm income.[38]

All segments of the economy acknowledged the seriousness of the problem; it became the favorite topic of discussion of both politicians and the press. Even big business admitted the difficulty, generally blaming it upon government spending, unions, and farmers, and urging everyone to meet the problem by resorting to a more Spartan mode of living. "Americans as a rule eat too much" was a favorite business defense, while James J. Hill turned a neat phrase "the cost of high living" to dismiss the complaints of the discontented. The Lodge Select Committee was at great pains to contend that "the tariff seems to have been no national factor in causing the advance in prices during the past decade," blaming it on the desire to "keep up with the changing styles in clothing and shoes." Many other groups, however, blamed the protective tariff, and looked to the twin remedies of tariff reduction and a federal income tax.[39]

Although still the federal government's chief revenue raiser, the tariff was much more important to the nation's industries as a protection from foreign competition. Its benefits to industry were enormous; the maintenance of this high protective wall was the chief article of political faith for most businessmen. Keeping that faith, in turn, was the prime responsibility of the Regular Republicans in Congress, and one of the chief reasons for the national supremacy of the G.O.P. since the Civil War. Their leader, Nelson W. Aldrich of Rhode Island, Chairman of the Senate Finance Committee, father-in-law of John D. Rockefeller, Jr., and a traction millionaire in his own right, was primarily reputed for his skill in harmonizing the diverse interests of New England manufacturers, western mine owners and cattlemen, southern fruit growers, and lumbermen, and the steel, iron and coal producers of the Iron Rectangle. Western farmers and merchants were tied to the policy largely through the "home markets" argument -- that protected industries and the prosperity they produced would lead to greater demand for foodstuffs. Wage earners were carefully wooed by promises of a "full dinner pail", if they supported protection at the polls. Only the South, which had little to protect, and some importers seriously demurred but, except for a brief and uneven hiatus during the second Cleveland administration, tariff rates rose inexorably.[40]

By 1908, though, the protectionist consensus was showing unmistakable signs of disintegration. Farmers were discovering that selling in a free market and buying manufactured goods in a protected one had an adverse effect on their real income. Many had come to regard the duties on agricultural products as "dust in the farmer's eye", as Taussig has observed, "mere nominal imposts on articles produced as cheaply within the country as without, and not importable under any conditions." Congressional investigations showed that some of the nation's most protected industries, such as coal, iron, steel, and textiles, paid some of its lowest wages. The high wages argument was largely based on the level of money wages, not real wages. A high level of protection in industries with huge production costs often yielded little advantage in purchasing power. Even many businessmen began to voice objections that excessive protection fostered monopoly, a view which gave rise to the famous "Iowa Idea," devised by banker George Roberts, of denying protection to any industry with an intolerable degree of concentration of control. Many other business groups began to agree with a contention, long held by importers and exporters, that other nations retaliated against excessive protection by refusing to buy American-made goods. Demands for change was so widespread in the Midwest that they united farmers, millers, merchants, and grain traders, giving great impetus to the Insurgent movement within the Republican Party. Tariff revisionists of all sections and classes, Tom C. Terrill has concluded, "offered something for everybody" and "thus appealed to a wide coalition".[41]

Perhaps most important of all, a wide variety of Americans identified the protective tariff as the chief cause for the rising cost of living. In New York, such disparate political figures as Democratic state Senator Robert F. Wagner and the chairman of the state G.O.P. Timothy L. Woodruff agreed that the electorate's association of the rising cost of living with Republican insistence upon a high protective tariff was the single most important political issue of the day. "Rightly or wrongly" Studenski and Krooss have concluded, "the urban population blamed the tariff for the current rise in prices." Tariff reformers of both parties claimed to speak primarily in the interests of the consumer, insisting that the protective tariff caused high prices in two ways -- it added to the retail cost because the custom duties were added on and it fostered domestic monopoly by creating a virtual embargo on foreign made goods. In the words of the House Ways and Means Committee, the tariff led to "the practical reservation of the field of domestic production to the manufacturers in the more important lines." Under the circumstances, the report continued, "there is no relief for the consumer except to cry out for Government regulation." The chief concern of the Republican Insurgents in tariff reform, Kenneth Hechler has argued, was that the existing system "failed utterly in its comprehension of that vast, inarticulate group scattered throughout the country -- the consumers of finished products of these gigantic protected industries." By 1908, both major parties were pledging lower rates, although the Republicans, already experiencing tensions between their Regular and Insurgent wings, equivocated by promising "significant revision." According to Taussig, any "sensible person trained in economics would have to make his reservations concerning the connection between the tariff and inflation," because the price rise was world wide and because higher food prices, for example, were also due to such factors as temporary crop conditions and the disappearance of free land. Popular wisdom largely chose to ignore these qualifications and focus on the tariff as culprit.[42]

There were, of course, substantial areas of disagreement among the various critics of the existing tariff system. Most consumers were also producers of some sort, insisting upon continuing protection for their industry while blaming the high cost of living on others. While Southerners and most Democrats officially insisted upon scrapping the whole principle of protection in favor of a "tariff for revenue only," the Insurgents and most Northerners were committed to maintaining some reasonable degree of protection for most products. The Insurgents "desired a downward revision along protectionist lines." Typically, as Hechler has observed, they supported such changes as reducing the duty on red paint from 3-3/8 cent per gallon to 2-7/8, "thinking of the barns his Kansas constituents had to keep painted." Most often they stressed the need to deny protection to trusts and to equalize the difference between the cost of production at home and abroad. While seeking to add many items to the free list, they frequently sought to protect the raw materials provided in their own region.[43]

Such fundamental disagreements made tariff reform an incredibly complex and difficult process, but tariff reformers of all persuasions were generally agreed that remedying the inequities of the tariff mandated the need for an income tax. There was widespread support for the argument that the latter would be the ideal method for covering any possible revenue loss from reducing tariff duties. For decades, protectionists had defended high duties with the argument that reduction would mean huge federal deficits. The income tax provided tariff reformers with a logical answer to that objection, while many pro-income tax people felt that painting the levy as a revenue raiser made it seem both safe and necessary. Nowhere was the connection between tariff reform and the income tax more apparent than in the pages of the American Economist, which steadfastly maintained that "hostility to the Protective policy is the first root of the income tax growth," and that "with the greatly reduced Tariff duties which will surely come when the income tax shall have taken the place of Protective Tariff as a revenue producer the imports of competitive articles will reach a much larger sum, and the idle mills and factories and the hosts of unemployed working people will be much greater in number." There were occasionally those who argued that lowering tariff duties might actually increase imports, hence augmenting customs receipts. "Possibly, had the tariff duties been reduced, so as to remove the virtual embargo which they imposed on many articles of foreign commerce," tax reformer Arthur W. Machen, Jr. argued, "this prospective deficit might have been averted, but that remedy was regarded as even worse than an income tax." During the Congressional debates on the Payne-Aldrich tariff, exasperated Republican Senator Knute Nelson of Minnesota, after listening to the traditional argument that high duties were needed to raise revenue, snapped that "the Senator seems oblivious to the fact that the higher you raise the rates, the less the revenue." Such expressions were rare, however, probably because both sides were afraid to carry them out to a logical conclusion. For the protectionists to suggest that lowering duties might increase revenue would be to reveal the tariff solely as a public policy promoting private gain. For the reformers to admit the same possibility might be to run the risk of losing many timid supporters who could only be persuaded to swallow an income tax as a needed revenue raiser.[44]

Tariff reform tied in with the income tax in another sense. Both were fundamentally expressions of the burgeoning notion that the burden of federal taxation should be shifted from consumers, laborers, farmers, and small businessmen onto the financeers and capitalists who had been the major beneficiaries of industrial expansion. Both represented a shift from the old "pseudo-democratic" notion that each man's tax bill should be the same, regardless of means, to the new belief that "ability-to-pay" was the most just criterion for apportioning taxes. The notion was not really a new one, having been voiced by such pillars of classical economics as Adam Smith and John Stuart Mill, but that aspect of their theory had rarely been stressed by those who turned the philosophes into defenders of monopoly and privilege. Under the pressure of industrial dislocation, it was revived by many leading economists and echoed by other pro-income tax advocates. Some, such as Francis A. Walker of the American Economic Association, offered a twist known as the compensatory argument -- that the state had created inequality through its tax policies and had an obligation to redress the balance. Theodore Roosevelt voiced what has been called the benefit argument when he stated, in 1906, that "the man of great wealth owes a peculiar obligation to the state, because he derives special benefits from the mere existence of government." Most, however, agreed with E.R.A. Seligman that the dollars and cents value of such abstractions as benefit or compensation were almost impossible to calculate, and based their arguments on the faculty theory-that a person's obligation was best determined by the ability to pay.[45]

Tax expert Delos Kinsman attributed rising interest in income taxation to the notion "that individuals should contribute to the support of the government according to ability and that income is the most just measure of that ability," adding that "demand for justice appears to be the dominant force." Single tax advocate Henry George branched out to favor the income tax as "an attempt to tax men on what they have rather than on what they need," while the Chicago Times called for a "taxed income rather than a taxed breakfast table." Congressman Benton McMillin of Tennessee urged putting "more tax upon what men have, less on what they made", while Senator William Borah favored taxing wealth "that it might bear its just and fair proportion of the burdens of this government." After surveying public opinion on the income tax, Elmer Ellis concluded that a more just tax system was "the most common argument of those in favor of the tax." The 1906 American Federation of Labor Convention called for "a greater share of the burden of taxation upon those better able to bear it" in endorsing the income tax, while the 1908 Democratic platform favored the levy "to the end that wealth may bear its proportionate share of the burdens of the federal government." The Ways and Means Committee gave the justice in taxation argument top ranking in its pro-income tax report, while Yearley has pointed to the ability-to-pay concept as the central creed that animated the "revolution in taxation" that swept the nation in the early twentieth century.[46]

There were a few who urged the more radical notion of using the income tax to effect a redistribution of wealth. That notion was implicit, at least, in Walker's compensatory argument, and was voiced more explicitly by Richard Ely and others. Even so conservative a leader as President Benjamin Harrison once stated that tax reform was the best means to close the gap between rich and poor. Seligman occasionally used the argument that it was time "to interfere with the rights of private property in order to bring about a more equitable distribution of wealth." Tax expert Wayne MacVeagh urged income taxation and redistribution because "gigantic fortunes are in themselves, or in the methods of their acquisition, such serious obstacles to the contentment, the peace and the healthy growth of the community as to call for their abatement." The currency of the redistribution argument was also attested to by the warnings of such pro-income tax writers as K.K. Kennan, who chided that "it is not the proper function of an income tax to correct social inequities nor to take money from the rich for the benefit of those less fortunate. It is primarily and preeminently a fiscal measure which finds its justification in the extent to which it will adjust itself with reasonable fairness to the abilities of those who are called upon to pay it."[47] Kennan was echoed by economist Roy Blakey who argued that some Congressmen supported a high exemption and progressive rate for "Socialist reasons," that is "because they think it will tend to check swollen fortunes and to distribute parts of them for the benefit of the masses who vote but do not pay such taxes." It is possible to argue that the ability-to-pay principle itself is a form of redistribution, even that it was a less menacing way of getting across a more revolutionary concept. In any case, the degree of redistribution contemplated was not too sweeping; the highest rate levied under the 1913 tax was a flat one percent rate with a graduated additional tax of up to six percent on income over $500,000. There were those who wanted more, but they were a distinct minority, not nearly as influential as those who based their arguments primarily on the justice of an ability-to-pay system. After analyzing the debate over the income tax in 1913, John W. Hillje has concluded that only a few Congressmen openly advocated the levy as an instrument of redistribution and that "their major arguments were for justice in taxation and compelling wealth to bear its fair share of the tax burden." Outside of Congress, he has found, "the limited public debate on this subject came largely from critics of the policy."[48]

Pro-income tax sentiment was also aided immensely by the spirit of sectionalism rampant in the South and West. Sectionalism was, as previously noted, one of the arguments used by wealthy Easterners to mobilize lower and middle class sentiment against a federal income tax. In the long run, though, it proved to be of much greater significance as a cohesive force binding together nearly all the inhabitants of the South and West against the affluent of the Northeast. By the Progressive years the South and West alike had come to describe themselves as colonies of the Northeast. Their primary economic functions were that of suppliers of raw materials and consumers of finished products. The actual processing and manufacturing, the most lucrative aspects of any economic enterprise, were almost all done east of the Mississippi and north of the Potomac and Ohio. Sixty-two percent of southern workers and an even higher percentage of western ones were in the extractive industries, and both regions ranked pitifully low in value added by manufacturing, the most important indicator of wealth acquisition in an industrial society. With about one-fifth of the land and population, the South had but ten percent of the nation's income, while the eight major northeastern industrial states received over half the nation's income, with only thirteen percent of the land and about forty percent of the population. Income from dividends and rents in South Carolina was only $35 per capita, compared to $408 in New York, $169 in Pennsylvania, $252 in Illinois and $381 in Delaware. These and other statistics clearly indicate, according to Gerald B. Nash, that "there was much justice in the complaint of many westerners that they were in effect a colony of the industrial Northeast, which extracted most of the wealth to be had in the West, but offered little in return." In any case, they and their southern counterparts clearly felt so, and acted upon the assumption. In the Midwest, according to the historian of Minnesota progressivism, Carl Chrislock, one of the most powerful forces at work in the era "was a sense of regional injury, shared to some degree by all classes and clearly articulated during the Payne-Aldrich tariff debate."[49] Without a doubt, sectionalism and widespread antagonism against what was regarded as Northeastern colonialism was a major factor in the reform efforts of both the South and West during the Progressive Era. Its most important manifestations wre found in the search for "means other than the tariff to raise needed revenue," and in anti-trust and regulatory legislation. Logically the"leaders of the South and West advocated an income tax to equalize the federal revenue burden." The overwhelming support of the South and West for the federal income tax was demonstrated by the sponsorsnip of bills and by roll call votes. Probably the most consistent advocates of the tax in Congress were William Jennings Bryan of Nebraska and Cordell Hull of Tennessee. Bryan had drafted the income tax provision of 1894, defended it in a titanic debate with fellow Democrat Bourke Cochran of Tammany Hall, and insisted upon its inclusion in the Democratic platforms of 1896, 1900, and 1908. In 1904, he reluctantly agreed to the omission of the tax plank in exchange for a stronger anti-trust provision. Hull regularly introduced income tax measures in every Congressional session and ultimately gained renown as the "father of the income tax" in 1913.[50]

There can be no doubt, then, that the most long-standing and powerful sentiment in favor of a federal income tax existed in the western and southern regions of the United States, but it would be extremely misleading to overstate the case. As the contest over ratification of the Sixteenth Amendment was to show, there were influential people in both sections who opposed the tax and sought to block its adoption. Although generally unsuccessful in their efforts, they did help to prolong the struggle and to demonstrate that the contest over the adoption of the federal income tax was too complex to be subsumed under any purely sectional interpretation. More importantly, western and southern support for the tax, however powerful and consistent, would have been ultimately ineffectual without the development of comparable sentiment among a wide variety of people in the urban, industrial Northeast. Included in this diverse company were influential newspaper publishers, radical activists, prominent economists and respected tax experts, reform organizations, organized labor, and spokesmen for urban political organizations with sizeable ethnic working and middle class constituencies. Such widespread support effectively undermined the contention of the measure's opponents that the federal income tax was a plot hatched by southern and western radicals to despoil the Northeast.

By 1909 pro-income tax sentiment was so widespread in the Northeast that nearly all the region's Democrats in Congress joined in the attempt to enact the measure. The following year the platforms of nearly every state Democratic Party contained a plank in favor of ratification of the proposed income tax amendment. The region's Republican parties, on the other hand, largely chose to ignore the issue until it was forced upon them and then they generally constituted the political mechanism through which the opposition sought to exercise its way. Even so, such prominent northeastern Republicans as Theodore Roosevelt, William Howard Taft, and Elihu Root lent their qualified support to the pro-income tax movement by 1909, partly to placate the western Insurgents in their own party, partly to blunt the appeals of the Democrats, and partly out of a recognition of the spreading popularity of the measure among traditional Republicans.[51]

In a broader sense, sentiment for income taxation in the northeastern states was an integral part of what Clifton K. Yearley has identified as a "revolution in taxation." Energized by exploding expenditures and indebtedness, on the one hand, and by revelations of fiscal corruption, on the other, tax reformers sought to generate new sources of revenue and to administer their collection and disbursement through innovative procedures and structures. This revolution, according to Yearley, had four basic components: 1) the separation of sources of revenue of state and local fiscal authorities, 2) the extension and ramification of corporate taxation, 3) the structuring of fiscal laws and administration along scientific and non-political lines, and 4) the taxation of incomes and inheritances according to "progressive" principles. Underlying these reforms was a desire, largely held and articulated by intellectuals and professionals, to effectuate "a just distribution of communal burdens" through the "taxation of privilege." Even some businessmen, according to Yearley, were willing to pay somewhat higher taxes in exchange for an increase in predictability, uniformity, and equity. In this evolving scheme, a key ingredient was "the integration of progressive corporate and personal income taxation under the theory of faculty the better to distribute wealth, to ease middle class burdens, as well as to raise fresh revenues." Although the lower social orders and their elected representatives were not overly concerned about relieving middle class burdens, they shared the desire for greater equity and increased revenue. On the state level, this emerging consensus led to the adoption of income taxes in Wisconsin in 1911, and in New York, Massachusetts, and Missouri by 1919. In all cases the rationale for adoption included an urgent need for new and more productive sources of revenue, a desire to check the flight of intangible new wealth, the hope of equalizing burdens, the determination to reach property provided sanctuary by federal statutes, and the concern for more accurate methods of determining taxpayer capacity. During the ratification process, an occasional lawmaker or governor expressed opposition to federal income taxation on the grounds that it would impede state efforts and underscored the contention by attempting to substitute a state income tax. Such efforts were quickly squelched by the proponents of the federal amendment, who usually proved to be advocates of state income taxation as well.[52]

This emerging income tax consensus in the northeastern states involved the collaboration of many diverse social segments whose motivations were far from identical. Many of its advocates incorporated their preference for an income tax into a radical critique of American society. The Socialist Party consistently included the proposal among the immediate reforms in its platform, reasoning that its adoption would advance the realization of a cooperative commonwealth. Similarly, many of the followers of single tax advocate Henry George advocated income taxation as a temporary expedient. The inclusion of an income tax plank in the 1896 Democratic platform, as Harvy Wish has demonstrated, came partly at the behest of such urban Populists as Governor John Peter Altgeld of Illinois. In the first decade of the twentieth century, the income tax was also endorsed by many other political leaders associated with the cause of urban working and lower middle class voters, such as Mayors Edward F. Dunne and Carter Harrison,

Jr. of Chicago, Tom L. Johnson of Cleveland and New York State Senator Robert F. Wagner. Variously referred to as "social reformers", "radical Democratic reformers" "urban populists", or "urban liberals" these leaders viewed the income tax as consistent with a pro-labor, pro-consumer, pro-ethnic minorities orientation. As the struggle over ratification was to show, this was a view that was eventually adopted by most urban Democratic organizations in the region's major cities. They were pushed farther in that direction by the endorsement of the tax by the American Federation of Labor in 1906. This outlook was popularized by the mass circulation newspapers that catered to the tastes of the urban masses, such as Joseph Pulitzer's New York World and St. Louis' Post Dispatch and William Randolph Hearst's Chicago Times.[53]

As early as 1883 Pulizer advocated federal luxury, income, inheritance, and corporation taxes in order to further the "cause of the people rather than that of purse proud potentates." Hearst, who sought to portray himself as a champion of the urban masses in campaigns for mayor of New York City and U.S. president, advocated the income tax in his editorial pages and gave a stirring presentation in favor of ratification of the income tax amendment before the New York State Legislature in 1911. Although most other influential northeastern newspapers maintained a staunch opposition to the tax down to 1913, the highly respected Springfield Republican, founded by Samuel Bowles, joined the Hearst and Pulitzer papers in supporting the idea. During the debate over the 1894 income tax, a Republican editorial judged the arguments of the "so-called Populists and Communists" as "sound and feasible" and "simply overwhelming." In a typical analysis, Hearst's Magazine styled the Pollock Decision as a move by "the Criminally Privileged classes to make room for a higher tariff." So outspoken and influential was Hearst on behalf of the tax that the Democratic leadership of the New York State Senate invited him, along with Bryan, Seligman, Purdy, and others, to address that body on behalf of ratification of 1911. The flamboyant publisher vociferously flayed the intransigience of the states' wealthy and contended that ratification would lift "part of the undue weight of taxation from the burdened back of the poor."[54]

Simultaneously, the adoption of a federal income tax was advocated by a number of prominent academic economists and tax experts. Over the years, the tax was consistently supported by leaders of the American Economic Association, including Francis A. and Amasa Walker, Arthur L. Perry, Henry C. Adams, John Bates Clark, Richard Ely, John R. Commons, and Thorstein Veblen. Perhaps the most visible and dedicated advocate of the tax was Edwin R.A. Seligman, millionaire scion of a German Jewish merchant family and professor of economics at Columbia University. Seligman authored several books and articles on the subject, gave numerous speeches, and testified before several legislatures. Almost equally visible were Kossuth Kent Kennan, Delos R. Kinsman, wayne MacVeagh, Lawson Purdy, and Thomas S. Adams.[55]

Nearly all of these economists and tax experts were affiliated with the National Tax Association, the leading professional exponent of tax reform during the Progressive Era. Formed in 1907 the NTA was, according to Yearley, "distinctly Northern, urban, and solidly middle class", and "represented a convergence of such state and local organizations, inclusive of many of their leaders, personnel, and programs." The Association was "eminently reputable" and "manifested a ponderous sobriety coupled with a very positive sense of direction." It aimed to generate a thorough-going examination of the nation's tax structure with an eye toward restructuring it along more equitable, productive, and rational lines. The NTA's membership included industrialists, financeers, public officials and politicians, corporate lobbyists, writers, journalists, editors, "and a few inveterate full time reformers", but the core of its leadership was provided by political economists trained at such distinguished universities as Harvard, Yale, Princeton, the Massachusetts Institute of Technology, Columbia, Johns Hopkins, Oberlin, Cornell, and Michigan. Such credentials were too impressive for more established Americans to ignore or to dismiss lightly. By 1909, the notion of a federal income tax was so deradicalized that the president of Cornell University, J.G. Schurman, expressed his support at the prestigious St. Nicholas Society Dinner in New York City, provided that the tax be levied nationally and with fairness.[56]

Finally, the federal income tax was given a tremendous boost by two consecutive Republican presidents, even though their support proved to be highly qualified and tenuous. During a speech at the dedication of the new House Office Building, Theodore Roosevelt astounded his listeners by advocating the "adoption of some such scheme as that of a progressive tax on all fortunes beyond a certain amount." Even though he specifically proposed an inheritance tax, the reference to "fortunes swollen beyond all healthy limits" put the prestige of the presidency behind the notion of taxing accumulated wealth. In a December 3, 1906 message to Congress, the President reiterated his support for an inheritance tax and, "if possible, a graduated income tax" because the man of great wealth owes a peculiar obligation to the state because he derives special advantage from the mere existence of government." Qualifying his endorsement, Roosevelt acknowledged the difficulty in getting an income tax amendment to the Constitution ratified and opined that the power should only be exercised in time of emergency. Still, six months later, he insisted that "most great civilized countries have an inheritance tax and an income tax. In my judgment both should be part of our system of Federal taxation."[5]

In his private correspondence, however, Roosevelt betrayed a considerable degree of ambivalence concerning the merits of income taxation. On April 23, 1906 he informed Lyman Abbott, editor of The Outlook, that while he had always felt that the United States should have a graduated income tax, he felt that it would be very "difficult to frame such a tax that will be constitutional and effective and will not amount in large part to a tax on honesty." A few weeks later, in a letter to Wayne Mac Veagh, secretary of the National Tax Association, Roosevelt asked rhetorically if it had not been "fairly comic to think of the yells of fear and rage with which my proposition has been greeted?," and promised to take up the question of both a graduated income tax and a graduated inheritance tax the following year. Just three months later, in another letter to Abbott on August 6, he referred to the twin taxation proposals as "not something immediate, but as something for which the way must be prepared for future action." The Outlook, which listed Roosevelt on its masthead as contributing editor, consistently opposed the income tax, stressing that "property, not persons, should pay the taxes, and the taxes should be proportional, not to the ability of the person to pay, but to the value of the property." Two weeks later T.R. wrote to British historian

George Otto Trevelyan that "I shall hope later to get action taken along the lines of the graduated income tax and the graduated inheritance tax", but that for the present it was more important to prove that "we will not submit to the tyranny of the trade-unions any more than to the tyranny of the corporation." After leaving office without seriously pursuing enactment of either tax, Roosevelt corresponded with his close friend Senator Henry Cabot Lodge of Massachusetts during the income tax struggle of 1909. When President William Howard Taft substituted a corporation excise tax and a constitutional amendment for the income tax proposed by Democrats and Insurgent Republicans, Roosevelt informed Lodge on July 26 that "offhand, it would seem to me that a tax on the net receipts of corporations would be the best way out of this Income Tax business." On Septebmer 10, he wrote Lodge that "the Consitutional Amendment about the income tax is all right, but an income tax must always have in it elements of gross inequality and must always be to a certain extent a tax on honesty." He concluded that a graduated inheritance tax "would be far preferable to a national income tax." A year later, on September 12, 1910, he assured Lodge that if "we take the Inheritance Tax for the Nation, the Income Tax should remain with the States." Just after his defeat as Progressive Party presidential candidate in November of 1912, Roosevelt assured University of Chicago political scientist and reform alderman Charles E. Merriam that he agreed with him that both the "progressive income tax and progressive inheritance tax must be pushed forward." At the same time, however, he cautioned Merriam that the election had demonstrated a great need to strengthen the party's standing with farmers and small businessmen. Finally, on January 24, 1915 he applauded William

Emlen Roosevelt's assault on the income tax that had been enacted in 1913, insisting that "I have always made my fight for an inheritance tax," and confessing that he had only supported the income tax in 1912 because most prominent leaders of the Democratic, Progressive and Republican parties had done so. The former president insisted that "something on the line of those used in Germany and England, would do good. But....this income tax." There can be little doubt that Theodore Roosevelt gave the cause of the federal income tax an important boost in both 1906 and 1912, but it would seem that his personal attitude toward the measure was far from enthusiastic.[58]

Just a few months later, in Columbus, Ohio, Roosevelt's handpicked successor, William Howard Taft announced his support of a federal income tax in order to reduce the motivation for the accumulation of great fortunes and to help the federal government in time of great need. Stating that such a tax in ordinary times was inquisitional and provocative of perjury, Taft proposed to limit its utilization to times of national emergency. Noting that the Supreme Court had validated the 1894 tax, the Ohioan nevertheless expressed his belief that "it is not free from debate how the Supreme Court, with changed membership, would view a new income tax law." By the time that Taft accepted the Republican presidential nomination on June 28, 1908, the Democrats had already adopted a platform plank calling for a federal income tax amendment. In his acceptance speech, the Republican nominee deemed the amendment approach unnecessary, insisting "that an income tax, when the protective system of customs and the internal revenue tax shall not furnish enough income for government needs, can and should be devised, which, under the decisions of the Supreme Court, will conform to the Constitution."[59] Even with all the qualification, Taft's endorsement gave income tax supporters a major boost.

The 1908 presidential election, then, was contested by two candidates who were apparently favorably disposed toward federal income taxation in some form. William Jennings Bryan, the Democratic nominee, had been the nation's most visible and consistent champion of the tax since 1894. Most contemporary accounts concurred with The Outlook that the Democratic conclave had been "a Bryan convention, loyal to his policies and obedient to his will, because the party believes in him and wants his leadership." Bryan's biographer, Paola Colletta, has rendered a more qualified judgment, pronouncing the platform to be "largely Bryan's in conjunction with other party leaders," a combination of the Oklahoma Constitution, the Nebraska state platform, and American Federation of Labor proposals. It was designed, according to Colletta, to appeal to a "Western farmer - Eastern labor coalition." Although Bryan had been instrumental in the enactment of the 1894 tax, had savagely attacked the Supreme Court for the Pollock Decision in his 1896 race, and had often expressed his belief in the constitutionality of the tax, he apparently accepted the notion that a constitutional amendment was the most fruitful approach by 1908. On August 21, in a speech in Des Moines, Iowa, Bryan even argued that Taft was obligated to support an income tax amendment since it seemed improbable that Congress could design a tax which would be acceptable to the Court. With Taft also on record in favor of the immediate enactment of an income tax, it appeared that the measure's time had indeed arrived: But despite Taft's qualified endorsement of the tax, his party's platform completely ignored the widespread income tax agitation. Significantly, the majority

Republicans' Senate leader and Finance Committee chairman, Nelson W. Aldrich later proclaimed that there would be "no income tax, no inheritance tax, no stamp tax, no corporation tax."[60] The stage was set for one of the most titanic and historically significant legislative struggles of the entire Progressive Era.

CHAPTER II

AN AMENDMENT OF CURIOUS ORIGINS

The federal income tax amendment was proposed by the Sixty-first Congress in 1909 during one of the most contentious and significant special sessions in the history of the national Legislature. It was both a cause of and a product of the growing rift within the Republican Party that was to lead to the emergence of the Progressive Party and the triumph of the Democrats and Woodrow Wilson in 1912. The amendment itself was the result of a political compromise emerging out of a four way struggle among Congressional Democrats, Regular and Insurgent Republicans, and the Taft Administration, each of which was forced to alter its position on the income tax issue as the shifting sands of legislative politics reshaped the terrain. The Democrats, who promised to propose an income tax amendment during their 1908 campaign, spent most of the session arguing that such a course was unnecessary and then reluctantly accepted their own platform plank from the hands of the Republicans. The Insurgents joined the Democrats in pressing for the immediate inclusion of an income tax section in the revenue act of 1909 and acquiesced in the proposal of the amendment with even more reluctance than did their erstwhile allies, bitterly charging that the amendment was an Administration - Regular plot to delay or prevent the immediate income tax that they and the Democrats had the votes to enact. President Taft, reversing the stance of the Democrats, began by arguing that a constitutional amendment was unnecessary and ended by maneuvering Congress into proposing one. Finally, the Regular Republicans, who frankly admitted their unalterable opposition to income taxation in any form, were constrained to force its acceptance upon a largely unwilling Congress, proclaiming loudly all the while their hope that a sufficient number of state legislatures would rescue them by preventing ratification. Once the smoke of Congressional battle had cleared, the Regular Republicans, who functioned as the amendment's nominal sponsors, began to work avidly for its rejection, while the Democrats and Insurgents, who opposed its proposal as long as possible, labored mightily for ratification. Only President Taft and his closest advisors felt any real pride in their handiwork and followed a consistent course in pressing for ratification, but even they expressed serious reservations concerning the conditions under which Congress should exercise the power with which they were seeking to endow it. Seldom has a measure of such seminal importance issued from such curious origins or been enacted with so little real conviction or enthusiasm.

The Sixty-first Congress was solidly Republican -- 214-175 in the House of Representatives and 60-32 in the Senate. The dominant force in both houses were the Regular or Standpat Republicans, most of whom represented the urban, industrial Northeast. Because of that chambers' rules and the greater numbers involved, their control was especially effective in the House, even though the leadership there generally consisted of men of smaller calibre who shared the views and aspirations of their more powerful and glamourous Senatorial counterparts.

Most prominent among them were John Dalzell and Andrew Barchfeld of Pennsylvania, Frederick Gillette, Samuel McCall, and John Weeks of Massachusetts, Martin Madden and James Mann of Illinois, Martin Sulloway of New Hampshire, Hamilton Fish and George Southwick of New York, Nicholas

Longworth of Ohio, Ebeneezer Hill of Connecticut, William Calderhead of Kansas, Joseph Fordney of Michigan and James Tawney of Minnesota. Longworth, the son-in-law of Theodore Roosevelt, was the scion of a wealthy Cincinnati family and a millionaire. Dalzell was the chief attorney for the Pennsylvania Railroad, while Madden was prominent in the quarrying business as well as in banking and in the Illinois Manufacturers Association.[1]

The majority of the House Regular Republicans were less prominent or affluent, functioning rather as cogs in the well-oiled machinery operated by Sereno Payne of New York, Chairman of the Ways and Means Committee, and Joseph Cannon of Illinois, the bombastic Speaker of the House. Payne, from the upstate town of Auburn, was more flexible than Aldrich, but believed firmly in defending the rights of property. He was described by an opponent as "an honest devotee' of privilege." Cannon, the self-styled "Hayseed member from Illinois", was a profane speaker, hard drinker, and demon poker player, referred to by his colleagues as "foul-mouthed Joe." As head of the Rules Committee, Cannon was virtual dictator concerning committee appointments, approval of legislation, recognition of speakers, and most other parliamentary moves. He was, if anything, even more set against "class and social legislation" than his Senate counterparts, judging by his slogan "stand by the status," and by his oft-quoted statement that "America is a hell of a success." Had Cannon been present at the Creation, another Regular claimed, "he would have voted against the Lord for chaos."[2]

Party leadership in the Senate was wielded primarily by Nelson W. Aldrich and George Wetmore of Rhode Island, Frank Brandegee and Morgan Bulkeley of Connecticut, Eugene Hale of Maine, William P. Dillingham of Vermont,

Jacob Gallinger of New Hampshire, Henry Cabot Lodge and Winthrop Murray Crane of Massachusetts, Elihu Root and Chauncey Depew of New York, John Kean of New Jersey, Henry duPont and Harry Richardson of Delaware, Boies Penrose and George T. Oliver of Pennsylvania, Theodore Burton of Ohio, Shelby Cullom of Illinois, and Stephen Elkins and Nathan Scott of West Virginia. Nearly all of these Senators were millionaires in their own right and had close connections with the great industrial, financial, and commercial enterprises of their home states. Aldrich was president of the Rhode Island Street Car Company and, as John D. Rockefeller, Jr.'s father-in-law, had close connections with Standard Oil. Gallinger was chief lobbyist for the Boston and Maine Railroad, while Chauncey Depew was spokesman for the New York Central and numerous other railroads and banks. Root was corporation counsel to such financial giants as Jay Gould, Thomas Fortune Ryan, and E. H. Harriman, a situation that caused him to "canonize the statutes of the past," and to be "inured to the social evils of the day" according to Richard Leopold. Both duPont and Richardson were closely connected with former's family holdings, while Elkins and Scott owned a sizeable share of West Virginia's coal mining and railroad operations. Crane was president of a paper manufacturing company that sold much of its product to the federal government for making currency. The list could be extended, but it would only belabor the point that the eastern Senate leadership of the Republican Party generally had personal vested interests in maintaining the traditional policies of a high protective tariff and opposition to a federal income tax.[3]

Their western allies were generally men of similar economic standing and interests. Simon Guggenheim of Colorado was the wealthy president of the American Smelting and Refining Company, one of the nations largest. He candidly admitted to having secured election in 1907 by financing the campaigns of the majority of state legislators. Francis Warren of Wyoming was the nation's largest wool producer and, as chairman of the Military Affairs Committee and father-in-law of General John J. Pershing, had made his native state the best fortified in the United States. His colleague, Clarence Clark, was counsel for the state's largest coal mining operation. George Nixon of Nevada was a bank president and co-owner of the fabulously rich Topanah silver mine. Reed Smoot of Utah was the millionaire president of the Hotel Utah, the Home Fire Insurance Company, the Smoot Investment Corporation, and the Utah-Idaho Sugar Comapny. As one of the Twelve Apostles of the Mormon Church, he was also a conscientious defender of that body's considerable economic holdings. George Perkins of California was a millionaire merchant, miller, mine operator, and steam ship company owner, who had developed the first steam whaler and had substantial holdings in Alaska. Along with fellow western Republicans Thomas Carter of Montana, Wesley Jones of Washington, George Sutherland of Utah, Weldon Heyburn of Idaho, and Porter McCumber of North Dakota, they provided the support that the eastern leadership of the G.O.P. needed to maintain control of the Senate. In return, they received favorable treatment for the major economic interests of their native states.[4]

There was, therefore, much truth in the muckraker's charge that the Senate was a rich man's club. Its members were elected by legislatures acutely aware of the importance of the state's key industries. The salary was too low and the expenses too high to permit anyone to serve unless he had an independent source of income. The result was to produce Senators who were either professional politicians bent upon exacting tribute from business supporters or businessmen seeking a wider field in which to wield power and acquire status. The typical businessman Senator "was usually the leader in the state's most lucrative and important industry," who could probably have served his self-interest better by minding the store, but who had reached the point where manipulating people, power, and policy interested him more than the acquisition of a larger fortune. So pervasive was the influence of a senior Senator that he usually became the state's party leader, handpicking his junior colleague, "a close friend, obliging partisan, or potential heir." Although their self-interest, or that of their companies, was not their sole concern, many Senators turned political insights into private enrichment. Business responded with generous campaign contributions, tips on the stock market, the circulation of speeches, loans, and offers to purchase stock. If a Senator retired or was defeated, he could usually find lucrative employment as a lobbyist. The result was to create a close community of interest that virtually isolated the Regular Republican Senators from the growing popular clamor for tariff reduction, tax reform, and anti-trust legislation.[5]

The control of the G.O.P., and hence of the Senate itself, by the business-oriented Regulars had been skillfully accomplished by Aldrich and his associates by the mid-1890s. By various processes, the Rhode Islander and his cohorts had "institutionalized, once and for all, the perogatives of power." Membership on important committees became a function of a Senator's status with the Regular leadership. Questionable members rarely were appointed to any crucial bodies. Party discipline was increasingly exerted on legislation, from formulation through scheduling, committee hearings, and votes. The party caucus bound members to support or oppose specific pieces of legislation and excessive independence cost the dissenter his standing with the ruling clique. So complete was the Aldrich wing's control considered to be in some quarters that the Washington Post insisted that "it is an axiom in the Senate that when Nelson Aldrich permits a question to come to a vote he knows before the roll is called precisely what the outcome will be." So confident was Aldrich of success, even in the most acrimonious of debates on the Senate floor, that he rarely bothered to answer his critics, often retiring to his office for a nap until it was time to vote. As chairman of the Senate Finance Committee, he was regarded by many as a virtual dictator over the fate of revenue bills and was usually able, in the opinion of the New York Times, to "emasculate, prevent or postpone legislation which threatens to interfere with the profits of big business interests."[6]

But events were to prove that such claims were largely partisan and hyperbolic. A modern student of the Taft Administration, David Detzer, has pronounced Aldrich's domination of the Senate to be "awesome", but hastens to add that the Rhode Islander was much more a "judge" than a "dictator." Aldrich was, in Detzer's view, "neither absolutist nor corrupt, but a pragmatic and flexible defender of American industry." The leader of Rhode Island's G.O.P., General Charles R. Brayton, acknowledged his partner's limitation when he informed Aldrich that he had been approached by several businessmen "who think that you can write the Senate tariff bill just as you please." In reality, Aldrich's power rested largely upon his considerable skills as a broker who mediated among a wide variety of economic interests and upon his ability to coax campaign contributions from industries, railroads, and bankers in exchange for favorable legislation. Rather than a dictator, Aldrich was a primus inter pares who depended to a considerable degree upon the support and advice of his fellow Regular Republican Senators. But many of his most astute and powerful allies, such as Mark Hanna and Joseph Foraker of Ohio, William B. Allison of Iowa, John C. Spooner of Wisconsin, and Orville Platt of Connecticut were no longer present in 1909. "The new leaders who emerged to serve as Aldrich's lieutenants, Henry Cabot Lodge and Winthrop Murray Crane of Massachusetts and Eugene Hale of Maine," Stanley Solvick has argued, "lacked much of the political finesse that had characterized their predecessors." Even more importantly, the Rhode Islander found his authority increasingly challenged by a growing number of western and midwestern Insurgent Republicans who dissented from the party credo on a whole variety of economic issues including the tariff, taxation, and the trusts. So drastically did the Insurgents depart from the Regular Republican party line than an exasperated Cannon remarked, in the fall of 1909, that "if LaFollette, Cummins, and Fowler are Republicans, then I am not. If I am a Republican, then they are not." Such sentiments were widely shared by Cannon's colleagues despite the Insurgents' frequent insistence upon their Republicanism and Aldrich was forced to defend himself and his policies against their increasingly savage attacks. "Thus, if Aldrich, as the last of the old titans, reigned in solitary grandeur, his power was not so great as it seemed," Solvick has concluded. "He did not have the necessary assistance to maneuver his stalwarts to contend effectively with the rapidly forming insurgent columns". What was worse, Aldrich had few "moderate counselors who could induce him to follow a more circumspect

In the Senate the Insurgents included Robert LaFollette of Wisconsin, William Borah of Idaho, Joseph Bristow of Kansas, Albert Cummins and Jonathan Dolliver of Iowa, Moses Clapp of Minnesota and Albert Beveridge of Indiana. On some issues they were joined by Knute Nelson of Minnesota, Norris Brown and Elmer Burkett of Nebraska, Coe Crawford of South Dakota, Jonathan Bourne of Oregon, and Joseph Dixon of Montana. Their most prominent members in the House were George Norris of Nebraska, Victor Murdock of Kansas, Asle Gronna of North Dakota, Miles Poindexter of Washington, Gilbert Haugen of Iowa, and Andrew Volstead and Charles A. Lindbergh of Minnesota. The Insurgents were true sons of the Middle Border. For the most part they had been born out of the state they represented, raised on farms, educated in midwestern colleges, and practiced law in small towns. Though several had been in Washington for years, they retained much of their native mistrust of big cities, big money, and the East in general. They were inclined to see conspiracies of wealth and power behind the nation's economic problems. "It became almost a mental habit," Laurence Holt has argued, "to explain all problems in terms of conspiracies of private wealth." Although some Insurgents viewed themselves as the advocates of nationwide consumers, they remained primarily the representatives of a "section in revolt," reflecting the attitudes of farmers and small town merchants. Consequently, they generally eschewed those reform programs that accepted the realities of industrialization and urbanization. For the most part, they rejected the New Nationalism of Theodore Roosevelt in favor of trust-busting and looked with suspicion on advocates of public ownership and labor and welfare measures. Primarily, they sought to restore equality of opportunity by trust-busting, tax reform, and purification of the political systems. Many even leaned toward moral regeneration through prohibition and immigration restriction.[8]

The Insurgents were mostly men in their forties and fifties who had begun their political careers as Regulars and turned gradually to Insurgency, some because the party leadership had denied them advancement. They were "middle aged professionals who responded to the new political environment by transforming themselves from McKinley conservatives into progressive reformers," according to Holt. Despite their serious policy disagreements with Aldrich, Taft, and the Regulars, the Insurgents were Republican to the core, coming from one party states where reform elements had captured the G.O.P. to stave off Democratic gains. They reacted indignantly to any aspersions cast upon their Republicanism from any source. Dolliver once insisted that he and Iowa would remain Republican "until hell went Methodist," while Crawford and Nelson both castigated Aldrich's audacity in trying to define what it took to be a true Republican. When Aldrich tried to ostracize them and Senator Joseph W. Bailey of Texas offered them sanctuary on the Democratic side of the aisle, Norris Brown caustically replied that the Insurgents would not "consent either to be disinherited by the Senator from Rhode Island or adopted by the Senator from Texas." What they hoped to do was to commit the national G.O.P. to the same kind of policies they had espoused in their own states in order to keep the Democrats from riding the progressive tide to victory. Like LaFollette, they hoped they "could do nationally with the Republican party what we did with it in Wisconsin." So intense was their Republicanism that it held them back from a permanent alliance with the Democratic minority and generally prevented their answering the siren call of the Bull Moose in 1912. Even so, what they demanded in the way of policy changes, especially on the tariff and the income tax, was too radical a departure for the Regulars and the latter were willing to risk splitting the party rather than transform it into the reformist vehicle that the Insurgents desired.[9]

In a letter to a prominent Kansas Republican, Senator Joseph L. Bristow delineated what he considered to be the most salient ideological differences between Insurgents and Regulars. Their primary disagreement, Bristow argued, was that the Insurgents believed that "the people" could be trusted to govern themselves. Secondly, the Kansan contended, he and his fellow Insurgents regarded the federal judiciary, as currently constituted, as "a menace to the country's welfare" and favored an end to lifetime appointments and the utilization of judicial recall under reasonable restraints. Such proposals, Bristow claimed, were regarded by the Regulars as a "species of anarchy." The Insurgents also insisted that the federal government should have the power to "take charge" of corporations that violated statutes, to break up trusts or to "rigidly regulate those where monopoly seems a necessity", such as in transportation and communication. The Regulars, Bristow claimed, believed that "such action would be subversive of government and would destroy our civilization." Finally, he noted, the two Republican factions disagreed significantly over the degree of protection to industry that a tariff ought to foster. The Regulars, he explained, believed that there should be such a high degree of protection for American businesses as "to free them from the embarassment of competition from abroad" and that the resultant "prosperity of the rich helps the poor by filtering down to them." The Insurgents, Bristow insisted, favored a "scientific" tariff that would "protect legitimate industry and guarantee a high standard of wages." Disagreements over such specific issues, though,

Bristow concluded, were relatively minor compared to the basic quarrel between Regulars and Insurgents over the concept of democracy. "There would not be any difference between the two elements on the tariff, he confided, if it were not for this fundamental difference in the scope of popular government." Even allowing for his one-sided perspective, Bristow's analysis laid bare the philosophical and strategical differences that bisected the Republican Party during the stormy administration of William Howard Taft.[10]

The new president had given several indications of understanding and sympathizing with much of the Insurgents' perspective during 1908. Since Taft had never before run for elected office, it was difficult to get an accurate fix on his ideological orientation, but the circumstances of his nomination and the thrust of his campaign utterances gave the Insurgents cause for optimism. Taft was virtually the handpicked successor of Theodore Roosevelt, nominated over the objections and reservations of the Regular establishment, many of whom preferred Joseph B. Foraker or Philander C. Knox. Although the Insurgents had qualms concerning Roosevelt's progressive credentials, they nevertheless found the former president, and especially such advisors as Gifford Pinchot, James R. Garfield, and Charles G. Bonaparte, far superior to the Standpatters. Several of the Insurgents, including Beveridge, LaFollette, and Dolliver, had campaigned vigorously for Taft in 1908 in the belief that he would provide the leadership needed to reform the party. More importantly, Taft had clearly enunciated his commitment to a number of measures central to the Insurgents' program, such as tariff reduction, income taxation, federal supervision of corporations, railroad rate regulation, conservation, currency reform, anti-trust laws, the right of labor to organize, bargain collectively, and strike, and a postal savings banking system. More specifically, LaFollette had assured a Sheboygan, Wisconsin audience that Taft, along with Bryan and Roosevelt, recognized the "impending danger of concentrated wealth." Taft himself confided to a friend in 1907 that "Mr. Roosevelt's views were mine long before I knew Mr. Roosevelt at all." According to David Detzer, Taft "agreed with many of the Insurgents' assumptions but lacked their anger." Indeed, despite the traumatic conflicts that marred his administration and sundered his party, Taft compiled a more impressive reform record than Roosevelt had, including the proposal of the Sixteenth and Seventeenth Amendments, the corporation excise tax, the postal savings bank system, the Mann-Elkins railroad regulation act, worker safety laws in mines and on railroads, a Children's Bureau, an Employer Liability Act covering work done on government contracts, and an eight hour day for work on government projects. The Taft Administration also instituted many more successful anti-trust suits than did its "trust-busting" predecessor and, despite the condemnation that Taft received for his often inept, insensitive handling of the Payne-Aldrich Tariff, he was, as Alfred Dick Sander has insisted, "the only Republican who ever succeeded in getting even a slight lowering of the tariff." Indeed, anyone viewing the legislative achievements of the Taft Administration with no knowledge of the political machinations that produced them might easily conclude that Taft ranked ahead of Roosevelt and behind only Wilson in the pantheon of "progressive" presidents.[11] But, despite these real achievements, Taft was, to quote Coletta, "conservative by instinct, regular by training." By the time he assumed the presidency Taft had evolved from a firm believer in laissez-faire, privatism, and rugged individualism to a belief that changing socioeconomic conditions mandated greater intervention by the federal government. Taft was an intelligent conservative who recognized the need to change in order to preserve the fundamentals of society and he was flexible enough to alter his views when confronted with new information. In his inaugural address, he expressed the conviction that "the scope of modern government in what it can and ought to accomplish for its people has been widened far beyond the principles laid down by the old laissez-faire school of popular writers, and this widening has met popular approval." But, despite that, Sander has demonstrated, Taft "remained true to the conservative tradition and continued to abide by the Constitution, believe in the sanctity of private property, and a government of law rather than of men." Implicit in many of his positions was the conviction that an increased role for the federal government was a temporary expedient required to achieve a return to the untrammeled operation of natural laws. While Roosevelt and Wilson looked to a strong executive to lead a democratic nation to a Square Deal, New Nationalism, or New Freedom, Taft preferred to entrust the peoples' liberties and welfare to the judiciary. Although acknowledging that the courts were often slow, cumbersome, and expensive in their operation, Taft steadfastly maintained a belief in their integrity and objectivity. The courts were, in his view, the primary protection that society had against both trusts and labor unions. "The minute you weaken the power of your court to protect the rights of anyone," Taft insisted, "you put an instrument in the hands of the wealthy malefactor and of the greedy corporation that they can use a great deal easier than the workingman or the man not so fortunate in the world." Taft rejected out of hand the charges of Bryan, Roosevelt, and the Insurgents that the courts were bastions of special privilege unwisely protected from popular pressure. Bristow's comment to Pinchot that "of course, I haven't any faith in the courts" clearly encapsulated the difference. At bottom, Taft believed that the answer to the complex problems of an emerging modern, urban, industrial society was to "have it understood that the laws will be enforced no matter whom it hurts, and that the government is a pratical method of doing business, which can accomplish reforms and can put business on such a basis that we can all be proud of it." He condemned the anti-social behavior of the trusts and the wealthy, as much as anything else, because it provided ammunition for socialists, populists, and other radicals who attacked private property and the social order.[12]

Exacerbating Taft's philosophical differences with the Insurgents was the fact that he had become chief executive with no previous experience as a party or legislative leader. His entire career had been spent in the judiciary and in appointive offices where he was responsible only to the person who chose him. "In rising to the presidency through the appointive route," Donald F. Anderson has argued, "Taft acquired certain professional skills which, though appropriate for the confined world of a judge or administrator, became liabilities in a popularly elected leader. In the former posts, Taft had been insulated from the press and the public, and had never found it necessary to develop the political skills or antennae of the other directed politician." Even Taft's brother Horace acknowledged that "he was a very poor politician." In reply to a friend who had urged him to become more aggressive in mobilizing public opinion behind his program, Taft replied that "I cannot be more agressive than my nature makes me", adding that his judicial bent prevented him from emulating Roosevelt's tactics and style. "I realize", he added poignantly, "what you say of the strength that the president has by reason of those qualities which are the antithesis of the judicial, but so it is with me, and if the people don't like that kind of man then they have got to take another." Such a view prevented Taft from courting popular support and caused him to dismiss criticism as being ill-informed and malevolent in intent. He grew increasingly vexed by the attacks of the New York and Washington newspapers, eventually convincing himself that their attitude was motivated by his refusal to place newsprint on the tariff free list.[13]

As the Insurgents launched their increasingly savage attacks on the Regulars' policies and methods, therefore, Taft found himself gravitating toward the party establishment. Already disposed toward their economic and social philosophy and their insistence upon order and procedural regularity, the president was also influenced by intertwined desires to hold his party together and to enact his legislative program. Both of these considerations convinced him of the necessity of supporting the established leadership of the party, even if he did not always agree with their views on specific issues. Even though this alliance was, in Detzer's words "more a marriage of expedience than love," it was also inspired by Taft's preference for men who played the game by the rules and eschewed demagogic tactics. Taft was especially close to Elihu Root who had preceded him as Secretary of War and who had joined Taft in the Roosevelt cabinet on the Ohioan's recommendation. In their frequent correspondence, the two playfully referred to one another as "Athos" and "Porthos." Even though he personally detested Cannon, Taft regularly deferred to his judgment and refused to aid the Insurgents in their efforts to strip the Speaker of his power. Taft originally took great umbrage at Cannon's views and tactics, confiding to Root in November, 1908 that the Speaker's speech on tariff revision "was of a character that ought to disgust everybody who believes in honesty in politics and dealing with people squarely." Pressed by Roosevelt and others, however, Taft met with Cannon in December and considerably modified his opinion. By early March, Taft was asking friends, rhetorically, "how a man of sense...can expect me to do otherwise than support the regular organization in the House." Having already reached a working relationship with Cannon, Coletta has argued, Taft "found it much easier to agree with a refined if ruthless gentlemen like Aldrich, particularly since Aldrich had consistently championed his own views with respect to the Phillipines and was on his way to becoming an expert on currency and banking matters." Despite frequent disagreements over specific issues during the 1909 special session, Solvick has contended, the president "except in moments of picque, however, never really lost faith in Aldrich." "I have always found him fair," Taft observed of Aldrich to his wife during the heat of the tariff struggle, " I sincerely hope that he will continue to be." Thus there was much justification in Samuel and Marion Merrill's characterization of 1909 as the year of the "Taft-Aldrich-Cannon Triumvirate."[14]

By contrast, Taft soon came to have little but contempt and hostility for the Insurgents, regarding their criticisms of the Regulars as attacks on the president. As did Aldrich and Cannon, Taft blamed the Insurgents for the growing split in the party. He also regarded their tone and language and their frequent efforts to mobilize public opinion as little short of demagoguery. Taft styled Beveridge "a liar and an egotist and so self absorbed that he cannot be depended upon for anything." During the 1910 Washington primary, the president informed challenger John L. Wilson that he backed him against Miles Poindexter, "for a more blatant demagogue and Democrat never existed," and decried the "dirty methods that the gang who are doing the work for the Pinchot-Garfield crowd have adopted." To his brother Horace, he characterized Pinchot as "anxious to carry out a lot of reforms without respect for the law", and as "a good deal of a radical and a good deal of a crank," even though insisting that he was glad to have him in the government. In a letter to Judge Elbert Gary, Taft dismissed Moses Clapp as a "lightweight" and as "unstable, bitter, and extreme." To Root he stigmatized the rebels as the "LaFollette-Bryan wing of the Republican Party", and, on another occasion, he damned LaFollette, Cummins, and Dolliver as "blatant demagogues" and "yellow dogs." During the special session of 1909, Taft complained to his wife that, during a dinner at the home of Senator Francis Newlands of Nevada, the Insurgents present had confronted him on the issues of reclamation and irrigation in a manner that was "pretty stupid" and that "some of them were disposed to be rather forward."[15]

As the Taft Administration unfolded, the Insurgents grew correspondingly disillusioned with the president. Since they regarded tariff reduction and the income tax as litmus tests of Taft's "progressiveness", Solvick has argued, his conduct convinced the Insurgents that Taft was either an all-out Standpatter or a dupe of Aldrich and the Regulars. Thus Jonathon

Dolliver privately defined Taft as "a very large body entirely surrounded by men who know just what they want." Bristow was even more brutal in a letter to his brother in February, 1911, charging that Taft "seems wholly incapable of handling the job, and it will be a great relief to the country when his time is out. Anybody would be better than Taft, and I think even the standpatters are coming to that conclusion."[16]

With an almost certain knack for self-destruction, Taft "chastised those most likely to support his reforms," to quote Coletta. During his term of office, the Ohioan managed to alienate the Insurgents on a wide range of issues including postal savings banks, the Ballinger-Pinchot controvery, railroad regulation, Canadian reciprocity, the admission of Arizona and New Mexico to the Union, and the case of Dr. Harvey W. Wiley of the Pure Food and Drug Administration. Even most of the legislative achievements of his administration, as George Mowry has pointed out,"were passed by a Democratic-controlled House and a Democratic-progressive Republican coalition in the Senate, both ends of which were, to understate it, at extreme odds with Taft." Part of the difficulty lay in the fact that, as Anderson has observed, "the progressives were interested in immediate results", while "Taft was more concerned with the proper means of achieving those results." By May of 1910, Taft was so disgusted with the Insurgents that he complained to Roosevelt that the Insurgents "have furnished the press and the public alike enough ammunition to make a Democratic house" and that "whether they will bring in a Democratic administration in two years remains to be seen." Of all the issues that contributed to the fissure between the Insurgents, on the one hand, and Taft and the Regulars, on the other, none were more devastating in their impact than were the Payne-Aldrich Tariff and the income tax. That protracted struggle during the 1909 special session "cut the first gaping groove in Republican solidarity", Coletta has insisted, and "other issues followed naturally along the lines of this schism."[17]

The Democrats were even more fragmented, although their minority status enforced an artificial solidarity. Easily the largest single group were the southerners, whose devotion to the party of Jefferson Davis had a quasi-religious character, heightened by their association of Republicanism with the horrors of Civil War, Reconstruction, and black domination. Within that solidarity, however, southern Democrats varied immensely in their outlook on national economic questions. In the Senate, "One-gallus" Jeff Davis of Arkansas and "Pitchfork Ben" Tillman of South Carolina presented themselves as champions of the rednecks and neo-Populism. "Cotton Ed" Smith of South Carolina and Hernando Money of Mississippi represented the interests of the planters of the black belt. Thomas Martin of Virginia reportedly looked out mainly for the considerable investments of northern financier Thomas Fortune Ryan, while Joseph W. Bailey of Texas allegedly did the same for Standard Oil. The Louisiana Senators carefully guarded the fortunes of that state's sugar planters, while their Florida colleagues were properly solicitous of the holdings of Henry Flagler, a partner of John D. Rockefeller. A few, such as Charles Culberson of Texas, had reputations as moderate progressives. All, however, were forced by the political situation to damn northern business interests at every opportunity and to characterize the Republican Party as the tool of those interests, a circumstance that often caused them to support more radical economic measures on the national level than they would have permitted in their native states. Their counterparts in the House were generally even more prone to attack traditional Republican economic policies because they were popularly elected. Their numbers included Oscar W. Underwood of Alabama, Carter Glass of Virginia, Joseph Robinson of Arkansas, Morris Sheppard, Martin Dies, John Nance Garner, and Albert Burleson of Texas, Thomas Hardwick of Georgia, Ollie James of Kentucky, Arsene Pujo of Louisiana, Claude Kitchin of North Carolina, and Cordell Hull of Tennessee. In both houses, their numbers and general longevity of tenure gave the Southerners most of the leadership positions in the minority party.[18]

Western Democrats were much less numerous or influential in either house. The Senate had but five -- Charles Hughes of Colorado, William Stone of Missouri, Francis Newlands of Nevada, and Thomas Gore and Robert Owen of Oklahoma. The latter two represented the newest state and generally established themselves as economic progressives. Newlands was a millionaire, but developed into a powerful spokesman for land renovation, irrigation, and other federal projects for the region. Stone was commonly regarded as a pro-business Senator but, like the southerners of the party, was careful not to become too closely associated with anything smacking of eastern Republicanism. The only two western Democrats of any prominence in the House were Dorsey Schackelford and Champ Clark of Missouri, with the latter serving as minority leader. The western Democrats were something of a cross between Insurgent Republicans and southern Democrats, sharing the former's regional economic outlook and hoping to parlay sectional discontent into Democratic gains. This latter goal limited their degree of cooperation with the Insurgents, who were seeking to alter Republican policies significantly enough to keep the West for the G.O.P.[19]

The third, and increasingly important, component of the Democratic Congressional minority was its urban eastern wing. Although none of their number had yet reached the Senate, the House contingent included Adolph Sabath, James McDermott, and Thomas Gallagher of Chicago, John Keliher, Joseph O'Connell, and Andrew Peters of Boston, William Borland of Kansas City, Patrick Gill of St. Louis, William Hughes, Eugene Kinkhead, and James Hamill of north Jersey's urban complex, John Fitzgerald, Daniel Riordan, Henry Goldfogle, William Sulzer, Charles Fornes, Michael Conry, and Joseph Goulden of New York City, Michael Driscoll of Syracuse, Daniel Driscoll of Buffalo, and James M. Cox of Dayton, Ohio. Nearly all of these Congressmen were first or second generation Americans, mostly of Irish Catholic extraction, who represented heavily ethnic, working and lower middle class constituencies. They were generally the functionaries of tightly knit Democratic organizations, commonly known as "urban political machines" and run by "bosses". Traditionally, the boss and his followers had cooperated closely with the same business interests served by the predominantly old stock Republican politicians and the voting records of the two were hard to differentiate on economic issues.[20]

As the Progressive Era wore on, however, urban political machines were being forced, for their survival, to pay more attention to the needs of their constituents. Municipal reformers demonstrated conclusively that espousing economic change in the interests of lower and middle class ethnics earned the latter's political support. Bosses had to adjust or lose their following. Younger men within their own organizations, motivated by political ambition and a desire to better the socioeconomic status of their constitutents, pressed for new policy directions, harboring "vague ambitions that they might make a name for themselves by helping those who elected them," as Oscar Handlin observed. The more astute bosses responded by supporting reform legislation so long as it paid off in votes and offices. Although this shift in attitude was barely under way in 1909, its acceleration in the next few years was to have profound consequences for both the Progressive Era and the income tax. As eastern, urban, lower, and middle class voters grew increasingly discontented with the economic policies of the G.O.P., and as the Democratic machines became more open in their outlook, the fortunes of the latter party improved dramatically. Although aided immensely by the Republican split, the Democratic victory of 1912 was the culmination of a trend that had already ensconced that party's mayors, councilmen, governors, legislators, and Congressmen in the office in record numbers. In both the legislatures and in Congress, these urban, ethnic Democrats played a major role in the enactment of reform legislation and a particularly crucial one in the adoption of the federal income tax. In his study of Congressional support and opposition for progressive legislation between 1901 and 1913, Jerome V. Clubb discovered that "a significant number of Democrats representing Congressional districts in New York, New Jersey, and Masachusetts supported reform", and that "among the Democratic 'supporters' of reform were Senators representing Ohio, Maine, New York, and New Jersey." Clubb found that to be particularly noteworthy because "Republican Senators from these states had opposed reform with high consistency." Similarly, David Sarasohn in seeking the explanation for the "Democratic surge" of 1905-1912, has found much of the answer in the party's "forging a progressive majority."[21]

The pressure to reform the nation's revenue system in 1909 emanated form several interrelated causes. Perhaps foremost was a projected budget deficit for the next fiscal year that was estimated to reach $100,000,000. The major cause of this fiscal crisis was the fall-off in import duties that resulted from the depression following the financial panic of 1907. Added to this were the demands from a variety of business interests to readjust the rates set by the Dingley Tariff of 1897 in order to distrubute some of the burdens and profits that had resulted from the business reorganization of the ensuing decade. The dramatic growth in business mergers during that ten year period had decreased the rationale for protection in many industries and increased the need in others. The same condition caused westerners and midwesterners to call for a readjustment of duties to improve their position vis a vis eastern industry and financial houses. Many businesses seeking foreign markets were also calling for duty free raw materials in order to decrease their costs of production and improve their competitive position abroad. Many businessmen and economists were calling for more flexible duties that could be raised in order to retaliate against countries that discriminated against American products. Others called for a more "scientific" tariff in which the rates would be based upon a careful study of existing eocnomic conditions and the probable impact that duties might have on those conditions.[22] Running parallel to these considerations was the already mentioned concern that the Dingley tariff was primarily responsible for the substantial rise in the cost of living over the preceeding decade. This was an issue that, whatever its basis in reality, was fraught with dire political peril for the future of the Republican Party. The Insurgents generally identified themselves with that position and pushed for relief for consumers, as did most Democrats. But even many Regulars recognized the necessity of creating at least the appearance of downward revision in order to prevent the Democrats from exploiting the issue. Equally volatile was the growing identification of the protective system as the major cause of the growth of trusts, an issue that had the potential of uniting small business with labor, farmers, and consumers against the G.O.P.. Finally, there was the allied perception that the tariff was the nation's consumate "pork barrel", out of which all the "special interests" gorged themselves. In an era when political candidates were vying to outdo one another in denunciation of anything that smacked of favored treatment to any privileged group, it was political suicide to be perceived of as a defender of special pleading.[23]

With the exception of some Regulars, there was a general consensus that tariff revision, no matter how thorough-going, would not yield sufficient revenue to meet the nation's increasing needs. This was especially true since nearly everyone, except those same Regulars, assumed that the general thrust of any such revision would be "downward," thus resulting in a further decline in revenue. That naturally introduced the need for an additional tax of some sort to supplement the existing system of tariff duties and excise taxes. Although there was sentiment expressed for an inheritance tax, a levy on corporate profits, or a stamp tax, the overwhelming consensus was in favor of an income tax. Although its advocates differed over details and about whether or not a constitutional amendment was necessary, they all agreed that the conditions mandating tariff revision were made to order for inaugurating some form of income tax by whatever means were the most feasible. Since the Regulars were confident in their ability to revise the tariff so that it would yield sufficient revenue, they maintained that no additional taxes were necessary.[24]

The demand for tariff revision was so widespread and intense that the Republican Party platform in 1908 declared "unequivocally for a revision of the tariff by special session of Congress immediately following the inauguration of the next President." Indeed, the Ways and Means Committee, under the direction of its chairman Sereno Payne, began preparing a draft bill even before the November elections. The platform pledged to revise the tariff according to the "true principle of protection", namely that duties should "equal the difference between the cost of production at home and abroad, together with a reasonable profit to American industry." The document also called for the establishment of "maximum" and "minimum" rates, with the former to be levied against those countries that discriminated against American products and the latter to provide the "normal measure of protection." The party insisted that its primary aim was "not only to preserve, without excessive duties, that security against foreign competition to which American manufacturers, farmers, and producers are entitled, but also to maintain the high standard of living of the wage earners of this country, who are the direct beneficiaries of the protective system" Finally, in a statement clearly reflective of the nominee's views, the platform called for a "free exchange of products", except for sugar and tobacco, between the United States and the Phillipines.[25]

As is the case with all platform planks, the language was broad and vague enough to cover the differences among a variety of factions, in this case the Regulars, the Insurgents, and Taft. According to Aldrich's sympathetic biographer, the leader of the Regulars had four purposes in mind: 1) to effect a moderate readjustment of duties to redistribute the burdens and the profits that had been accumulated since 1897, 2) to placate the powerful eastern manufacturing interests without totally alienating the Insurgents, 3) to place most raw materials on the free list in order to decrease production costs, and 4) to do all of this without splitting the party and risking the passage of the monetary legislation that he was drafting. According to Solvick, the Regulars' attitude toward the tariff plank in the platform "was one of cynicism." None of the Regulars ever promised that revisions would be downward, and Aldrich matter-of factly pointed out that the term only implied change without specification as to direction. Stephen B. Elkins spoke for many Regulars when he said, "what folly to promise something in a platform to satisfy a minority - which if carried out will be a positive injury to the country." For over forty years, the protective tariff had been the keystone of the Republican economic program. Tariffs were ambitious attempts to harmonize the interests of producers from all sections of the country in the belief that such action would promote general prosperity. Farmers were to benefit from the escalating demand for food in a constantly expanding economy, while workers were to profit from consistently high wages and full employment.[26]

Not incidentally, this economic harmony was also designed to insure Republican hegemony. "The history of the tariff," E.E. Schattschneider has argued, "is the story of a dubious economic policy turned into a great political success," in which the Republicans constructed the tariff "as a means of attaching to itself a formidable array of interests dependent upon the protective system and intent upon continuing it." Since the late 1880s, Aldrich had orchestrated this economic symphony with consumate skill, taking reams of testimony from interested producers, trading off the potential conflicts, and presenting the carefully balanced packages to the Republican caucus for ratification. "The persons who appear as witnesses are almost invariably interested producers," Taussig discovered, "and the figures and statistics offered by them are of dubious value". Excluding the minority party, the Regular leadership generally ironed out the differences and bound their colleagues to vote for the finished product. On the floor, there was little or no debate permitted and almost no opportunity for alterations or amendments. In 1897, all but three of the Senate Republicans had pledged their support to the finished product even before the caucus began its deliberations.[27]

Although the "true principle" of equalizing the cost of production had what Taussig called the "engaging appearance of moderation," it also had the potential to virtually eliminate foreign competition. "Little acumen is needed," the Harvard economist contended,"to see that, carried out consistently, it means simple prohibition and stoppage of trade," adding that "a nation can produce almost anything if guaranteed cost of production plus a reasonable profit, even wine in Scotland and pineapples in Maine." Moreover, it was virtually impossible to determine comparable costs of production with any precision and the definition of a reasonable profit was clearly a highly subjective process. As events were soon to reveal, Aldrich and the Regulars were firmly determined to write the new tariff in the time-honored manner and to make only those concessions that appeared necessary to build their coalition and lead the process to fruition. Under no circumstances were they prepared to allow such extraneous issues as income or other taxes to distract them from the appointed task.[28]

Not surprisingly, the Insurgents had a strikingly different interpretation of the need for tariff revision. Although seeing themselves as "true and faithful and reasonable protectionists," they represented a region where nearly every economic group felt that the existing tariff system made it difficult to sell American farm products abroad, fostered domestic monopoly, and caused exhorbitant prices for manufactured goods. Although their desire for downward revision was partly caused by these considerations of self-interest and proceeded partly from a well-developed conspiracy theory, it also had its grander side. "The Insurgents," Kenneth Hechler has concluded, "were not fighting for greater consideration for any one group, but for a better balance in the entire protective system, an ending of excessive favors to specific classes, and a guarantee that prices of finished products would be within the reach of more people." They believed, as Bristow said, that Aldrich and the Regulars had "contorted" the protective system "into a synonym for graft and plunder." Aldrich dismissed their contentions as "sectional sniping" and asked "who are the consumers? Is there any class except a very limited one that consumes and does not produce? And why are they entitled to greater consideration?"[29]

Beyond their desire to aid western farmers and business interests and to relieve the burden on consumers, the Insurgents had a number of more specific objectives, some of them more political than economic. In general, they opposed placing raw materials on the free list. Although much of this opposition proceeded from a desire to protect western producers of raw materials, it also flowed from their broader concern for the welfare of consumers. As long as the tariff remained the main revenue producer, they argued, putting raw materials on the free list would simply shift that portion of the tax burden onto manufactured items, thus adding to the woes of consumers. Such reasoning reinforced their commitment to income taxation, since its adoption would permit both a free list status for raw materials and lower duties on manufactured items. For the present, the Insurgents favored placing wool and cotton on the free list in order to lower the cost of clothing. They also were strongly committed to the notion of a tariff commission that would gather sufficient data to make the tariff a vehicle for economic planning instead of a politicized pork barrel. For all their attacks on the Regulars, only eight Insurgents voted against Aldrich's rates more often than they voted for them in 1909 and only LaFollette, Clapp, Bristow, and Cummins were overwhelmingly opposed to the Rhode Islander's proposals. The remaining Insurgents voted with Aldrich anywhere from forty to sixty percent of the time.

Over and above these economic considerations, the Insurgents also saw in the tariff debate a vital political lever. LaFollette and Beveridge had obvious presidential aspirations which they hoped to foster by taking the leadership on tariff revision. Dolliver was reportedly angry with Aldrich for denying him the seat on the Finance Committee that he had been promised by his mentor, William B. Allison. Perhaps more importantly, LaFollette and some of his closest cohorts hoped to use tariff revision and tax reform as weapons with which to wrest control of the party machinery from the Regulars in order to transform the G.O.P. into a vehicle for reform.[30]

As usual, Taft occupied a position somewhere between the Regulars and the Insurgents on the issue of revenue reform. As an orthodox Republican, Taft was a firm believer in the protectionist principle but he insisted that the benefits of protection should be widely shared. He insisted that if the costs of production were to be equalized and the benefits resulting from increased productivity to be maintained, tariff rates should equal the actual difference between the costs of production at home and abroad. Since the costs of production in the U.S. had been steadily decreasing, Taft believed that the rates must be periodically revised in order to prevent a handful of businessmen from reaping an inordinate share from these technological advances. During his stint in the Roosevelt cabinet, Taft had pushed for tariff revision, but was consistently put off by his chief. Even though he was careful to preface his speech with the words "speaking for myself and no one else", Taft had created a furor by urging downward revision in Bath, Maine, nearly two years before he received the Republican presidential nomination. He repeated that notion so frequently during the 1908 campaign that Detzer and others have attributed the popularity of the idea primarily to Taft. In reality, Taft believed that while many rates should be lowered, others might have to be raised. Writing to the head of the United States Potters Association in August of 1908, for example, Taft assured him that "in reading the report of the American Manufacturer's Association, I became convinced that there were some industries that needed an increase in the tariff and the one which I felt was of chief importance was the pottery business." More specifically, Taft espoused placing raw materials on the free list and believed strongly in the concept of a tariff commission to provide the information necessary to permit periodic revision.[31]

Taft's outlook on the tariff forced him to look for other sources of additional revenue to make up for the projected decline in import duties. This, in turn, led him to advocate both inheritance and income taxes during the 1908 campaign. His ideas on the latter, as Solvick notes, were "complex and perhaps not completely consistent." Taft privately acknowledged that the Supreme Court, in the Pollock Case, had exhibited faulty reasoning in invalidating the 1894 income tax. He also believed that Congress should possess the authority to levy such a tax, even though he favored its use only in emergency situations, such as war. In ordinary times, Taft believed, the tax would lead to evasion and fraud which, in turn, would require the government to resort to heavy-handed methods of enforcement. On the issues of equity and redistribution, Taft remained largely silent, probably believing, as Solvick has suggested, that he was "so genuinely convinced of the impossibility of collecting the income tax effectively that he did not regard it as a useful instrument of social policy, good or bad."[32]

The Democratic minority had a long history of advocating a "tariff for revenue only." It was one of the few substantive issues that differentiated them clearly from the G.O.P. and one that fitted the party's anti-statist philosophy. It was this official line that prevented them from coalescing with the Insurgents on tariff revision. In actuality, however, the Democrats favored a "competitive tariff" that would allow domestic producers to compete on an equal basis with foreign business, as witness the Wilson-Gorman Tariff of 1894 and the Underwood-Simmons measure of

1913. Louisiana Democrats avidly sought protection for sugar, Texans for oil, Floridians for citrus fruits, and Georgians for cotton, silk, and lumber. Western Democrats shared the Insurgents' regional orientation and frequently voted with them on tariff issues. Eastern Democrats had supported a high level of protection historically, and their records were often indistinguishable from those of Regular Republicans on relevant rate schedules. In their 1908 platform, the Democrats declared for "immediate revision by reduction of import duties," and for placing articles in competition with trust-produced products in the free list. They also called for reduction of duties on the "necessaries of life," especially on those articles that competed with U.S. products "as are sold abroad more cheaply than at home." With a bow toward its historical tradition, the Democratic platform also pledged such gradual reduction on other schedules as was necessary to restore the entire tariff to "a revenue basis." Specifically, it singled out wood pulp, print paper, lumber, timber, and logs for inclusion on the free list.[33]

This demand for large-scale revision reflected the traditional anti-tariff orientation of southern Democrats, combined with the growing disillusionment of consumers and workers in the urban, industrial northeast with protectionist rationales. The representatives of the latter, especially, disagreed with both Regular and Insurgent Republicans largely over the magnitude of the duties and over which products deserved protection. In practice, as the Payne-Aldrich struggle was to reveal starkly, most Democrats were keenly interested in receiving their "share of the booty," as Claude E. Barfield has convincingly demonstrated. Even though only the two Louisiana Democrats ultimately voted for the Payne-Aldrich Tariff on the final passage in the Senate, David Sarasohn has shown that fourteen Democrats, mostly from the South, voted with Aldrich ten times or more in 1909, mostly on schedules that benefited their own constituents. Even had the Democrats remained faithful to their platform pledges, however, it is highly doubtful that that, in itself, would have produced a more equitable revenue system. "There is a question," as Taussig observed, "how far reductions or remissions will redound merely to the advantage of the manufacturer or middleman, how far to that of the ultimate consumer." Any relief for the latter would come "slowly and haltingly" at best and would depend upon the degree of competition among producers and middlemen and how evenly the reduction in the prices of materials affected those engaged in producing for the same market. Consequently, the Democrats balanced their concern for tariff revision with a demand for a federal income tax amendment on the grounds of both equity and the need for additional revenue.[34]

Although the Insurgents and the Democrats were at odds on many aspects of tariff revision, they were united in the belief that the projected budget deficit provided the ideal rationale for enacting an income tax. This was an argument that held out a real prospect of convincing many Regulars and conservative Democrats to back the new tax, even though the Insurgents and progressive Democrats believed that tax equity was a far more compelling reason. Although Insurgents and Democrats frequently disagreed on what specific functions the federal government should undertake, they agreed that the federal budget would continue to increase because, as Cummins contended, "governments are organized to care for the welfare of the people." They also concurred in the belief that the existing tax structure treated the bulk of their constituents unfairly while allowing the wealthy to evade their responsibilities. "I favor a system that will get them coming and going," Borah trumpeted, "for that is the only way you can get them at all." Despite their platform pledge to seek a constitutional amendment, the Democrats cooperated with the Insurgents from the outset in an effort to insert an income tax section in the revenue bill. So intent were they on their purpose that Insurgents and Democrats were able to compromise differences of opinion over rates, exemptions, and the principle of graduation and to achieve a degree of cooperation never possible on tariff legislation. Weighing all the arguments against the immediate enactment of an income tax, the Insurgents and most Democrats apparently concluded with Borah that there was really no good reason, "legal, moral, or economic," for not having an income tax "except the bias and stubborness of custom on the one hand, and the viciousness of greed on the other."[35]

The Regulars generally dismissed all these contentions out of hand, setting up a flurry of arguments against the income tax in any form. They charged that "it would lead to fraud and perjury unlimited," and that it would array class against class, paving the way for socialism. They opposed challenging the Supreme Court on the issue again because of what it might do to the "independence, dignity and sacredness of that great tribunal." They insisted that the pledge of the G.O.P. to pay the cost of government solely by recourse to tariff duties and excise taxes was "the most sacred ever made to the American people." They sought to split the Insurgent-Democrat coalition by stigmatizing the income tax as a Democratic measure, making opposition a test of partisan loyalty for the Insurgents. To the same end, the Regulars sought to exploit the known differences in tariff philosophy between the two groups of income tax advocates. While professing sympathy with the Insurgents' desire to use income tax revenue as a supplement to a revised tariff, Aldrich insisted that the Democrats' real intention was to raise so much revenue that the country would abandon the tariff system. Adoption of an income tax, Aldrich insisted, would necessitate "going back and revising every schedule in this bill," while Lodge charged that such a course "would amount to a large scale destruction of the protective system." All these arguments had little effect on the hard-core of the Insurgents, and were probably intended to hold in line those who were sympathetic to the income tax, but unwilling to risk party unity, the reputation of the Supreme Court, or the protective system.[36]

In his March 4, 1909 inaugural address, Taft renewed his commitment to revenue reform. He called for a special session of Congress to be convened on March 15 to revise the tariff in order to secure adequate revenue and to afford protection to labor, agriculture, and industry according to the "true principle" of equalization of the costs of production. This would involve the "reduction of rates in certain schedules and will require the advancement of few, if any." The prime purpose of the tariff, the new President insisted, was the raising of revenue and he argued that "due largely to the business depression that followed the financial panic of 1907 the revenue from customs and other sources has decreased to such an extend that the expenditures for the current fiscal year will exceed the receipts by $100,000,000. If it should prove impossible to raise adequate revenue by import duties, Taft stated, "new kinds of taxation must be adopted, and among these I recommend a graduated inheritance tax as correct in principle and as certain and easy of collection."[37]

Taft's endorsement of an inheritance tax as the most desirable revenue supplement was certainly surprising since he had endorsed an income tax during the campaign. Part of the explanation for his apparent volte-face lay in the tentative nature of his support for income taxation. As already noted, Taft viewed the tax primarily as a revenue raiser rather than as an instrument of social policy. Moreover, he viewed the income tax as an expedient to be resorted to primarily in wartime or fiscal emergency. As a fundamental conservative, Taft was, according to Solvick, "more interested in the establishment of a general authority than in the enactment of a specific impost." More importantly, Taft was genuinely concerned about the consequences that another income tax might have on the Supreme Court. Although he believed the Pollock Decision to be erroneous and expressed his conviction during the campaign that it was highly probable that an income tax could be constructed that would conform to the strictures set forth in that decision, he was reluctant to press the issue without a great deal of study. Regarding the judiciary as the most important branch of the government and as the bulwark of American liberties, Taft was frightened by the escalating criticism of Insurgents, Bryan Democrats, radicals, and even Theodore Roosevelt. On further reflection, Taft developed a "more mature opinion, that the almost certain challenge that would result from the immediate enactment of an income tax would harm the Court either way. If it should find such a tax unconstitutional again, the outcry by progressives and liberals might lead to demands for restructuring the Court in order to make it responsive to popular will, the death knell of the American system of government in Taft's view. If the Court should reverse the Pollock Decision, it would certainly look as if the judiciary simply responded to the shifting trends of popular opinion.[38]

Faced with this seeming conondrum, Taft instructed Attorney-General George W. Wickersham to examine the various Court decisions regarding income taxation and to draft a bill that would meet those requirements. Since Wickersham was unable to complete the task before Tafts' inauguration, the President decided to call for a graduated inheritance tax instead. When Wickersham had completed his investigation, he reported to Taft that there was no way that the Court would permit Congress to tax individual incomes without a constitutional amendment to do away with the apportionment requirement. Instead he suggested a tax on corporate earnings to be measured by their incomes, an approach similar to the revenue act that had helped finance the Spanish-American War and one that the Court had held to be constitutional in the case of Spreckels v. McClain. Wickersham's findings reinforced Taft's natural inclination to avoid a confrontation with the Supreme Court over an income tax and formed the basis for his eventual decision to support a corporate excise tax over a general income tax and to remove any doubts concerning the constitutionality of the latter by amending the Constitution.[39]

When the special session of the Sixty-first Congress convened on March 15, Taft sent them only a tersely worded message that provided virtually no direction and omitted any reference to downward revision or the need for additional taxes. He simply reiterated his views that the changing economic conditions of the past decade and the projected budget deficit mandated the need for swift action. Even so, action in the House was delayed for a day as a loose coalition of Insurgents and Democrats tried to curtail Cannon's power by transferring many of his prerogatives to a fifteen member Rules Committee. The attempt failed when twenty-three Democrats defected, amid charges that they had exchanged their votes for promises that the special interests of their respective districts would receive favorable tariff protection. Taft stood aloof from the fray and that position, coupled with his apparent lack of leadership on the revenue question, gave Insurgents and progressive Democrats cause for concern even before the special session began.[40]

On March 17, Payne reported the draft tariff bill of the Ways and Means Committee to the House. The measure provided for significant reductions on iron, steel, coal, and lumber and placed such raw materials as wood pulp, hides, petroleum, iron ore, and raw flax on the free list. But it also raised the duties on mercerized fabrics, women's gloves, hosiery, plate glass, and citrus fruits. Tea and cocoa were removed from the free list, while the rates on wood remained the same despite protests from consumers and manufacturers. Payne also reluctantly included the inheritance tax that Taft had asked for in his inaugural address. The President, through the medium of Nicholas Longworth, also attempted to get the committee to include the corporation tax that Wickersham had drafted, but Payne and Cannon were unwilling to concur. They contended that the Panic of 1907 had left many corporations in so precarious a position that such a levy might lead to a rash of business failures. The minority report, signed by the Democratic members, called for an income tax and Champ Clark tried unsuccessfully to have the bill recommitted in order to incorporate that provision. Payne and Cannon also defeated income tax proposals introduced on the House floor by Insurgent Frederick C. Stevens of Minneosota and Democrats Ollie James and Cordell Hull.[41]

On March 29, Hull made an eloquent speech in favor of the income tax, calling it "the fairest, the most equitable system of taxation that has yet been devised." Arguing that a constitutional amendment was impossible because a three percent minority could prevent ratification, Hull proposed to duplicate the 1894 tax section except for exempting the income from state and municipal bonds. He challenged Congress "to invoke every remedy at its command for the restoration of its lost taxing power and to secure a review of the Supreme Court of the questions erroneously decided." Hull concluded with a ringing plea to tax wealth instead of poverty, by reaching the incomes of "the Carnegies, the Vanderbilts, the Morgans, and the Rockefellers, with their aggregated billions of hoarded wealth." On April 9, the House approved the Payne bill 217-161 on a nearly strictly partisan vote, with the Insurgents feeling that the modest rate reductions and the inheritance tax were as much revenue reform as they were going to get. Taft pronounced the tariff a genuine effort at downward revision that met with his general approval, except for the increases on hosiery and gloves, and rejected LaFollete's plea to send a message to Congress calling the Payne bill a betrayal of the Republican platform. The Democrats scored it for increasing the burden on consumers and as worse than the Dingley Tariff in many instances.[42]

But if the Insurgents and Democrats thought the Payne bill had made a mockery of the pledge of downward revision, most manufacturers and Regulars believed it to be a blow at the protective system. "Publication of the Payne bill woke up all the producers of the country and a bigger army than Henry Watterson ever dreamed of moved immediately on Washington to insist on full protection and heroic reductions on the products of everyone else," Root confided to Whitelaw Reid, "while all the importers and their foreign representatives here are on the verge of insanity over the increases that are included in the bill." Bereft of the moderating counsel of Spooner, Allison, and other departed Regulars, Aldrich permitted every interested producer and every Senator to propose rate schedules. Even most of the Democratic Senators were allowed to propose schedules favorable to their constituents and to obtain their "share of the booty." Although Taft expressed some private misgivings about this course of events, his philosophy inclined him toward a hands off attitude, at least until the Senate completed its work. If the finished product were not to his liking, Taft felt that there would be ample opportunity to exert his influence on the Conference Committee and, as a last resort, he could always veto the measure or, at least, use that threat as a lever to force concession.[43]

Free of presidential involvement, Aldrich presided over a gigantic log-rolling contest that ended in the adoption of 847 amendments, one-half of them substantive and nearly all of them upward. Most damaging to Taft's wishes, the Finance Committee imposed rates on iron ore, coal, and hides and raised the rates on lumber, cotton, and hosiery. The committee's work, LaFollette charged, had been a combination of "addition, multiplication, and silence." What reductions there were were mostly on the raw materials of the West and Midwest, actions that encouraged Taft but incensed the Insurgents. So intent was Aldrich on raising certain rates that he upped the coal schedule even though the industry's lobbyists testified that no increase was necessary. The duty on split peas was raised "on the personal knowledge and evidence of a member of the House who knows all about the business." Many other rates were raised to placate Senators with a special interest in their protection and several amendments contained "jokers" - "obscure changes working to the advantage of particular individuals and concealed among the endless detail." Most of the rates were based upon data provided by interested producers with little or no independent investigation or verification.[44]

The main opposition on the Senate floor came from the Insurgents who divided the most important schedules among themselves and engaged in extensive research to question the data provided by producers. Thus armed, they challenged Aldrich and the Regulars in open debate and engaged in many protracted and acrimonious debates. Although their information was often more detailed and accurate, the Insurgents were rarely able to win any concessions because the log-rolling process molded the Regulars, and many Democrats, into a cohesive coalition. Aldrich was stunned at the savagery and the organization of the Insurgents. "Often Aldrich's only response was not to respond," journalist Mark Sullivan recorded, "to walk from the Senate floor, redfaced, for the first time in his life successfully defied." But, shaken though he was, the Rhode Islander generally held his troops in line with his consumate parliamentary skills and his sure instinct for the economic parochialism of his colleagues. The "great obstacle to securing reductions," Root reported to Reid, "arises from the fact most of the men who are earnestly advocating them are as earnestly insisting upon retaining or increasing the Dingley duties on the products in which their own states were interested." Rejecting even the semblance of concession in most cases, Aldrich, according to Holt, "preferred to stick to his original proposals unless defeat threatened on the floor of the Senate," and dismissed his Insurgent detractors as "Democrats in disguise."[45]

Even though Spooner, Roosevelt, and Taft were all on record in favor of the establishment of a non-political, "scientific" tariff board, Aldrich managed to frustrate Insurgent efforts to enact one. In the end, they had to settle for a badly watered down "tariff commission" that only provided data to Congress, rather than constructed a tariff. Ironically, the Insurgents believed that they were keeping faith with the Republican platform and that Taft supported their efforts, even to the degree of vetoing the bill if it failed to meet the standards of significant downward revision. For their part the Democrats generally refused to support the Insurgents, for several reasons. For one thing, they recognized that the Insurgents were almost as protectionist as the Regulars on many items and did not share the Democrat's sacred, if mostly rhetorical, devotion to a "tariff for revenue only." Secondly, most Democrats recognized that Aldrich's price for protection of their pet schedules was their acquiescence in the whole. Finally, the certain knowledge that the bill would pass the Senate ultimately allowed them to vote aginst the entire measure without endangering their favorite schedules. These Democratic Senators could have the luxury of voting against an inordinantly protective tariff for popular consumption while proving their own skill at protecting their states' special interests. When the Senate passed the Aldrich bill on July 8 by a 45-34 vote, ten Insurgents - Beveridge, Bristow, Burkett, Clapp, Crawford, Cummins, Dolliver, LaFollette, and Nelson -

voted against passage, joined by the entire Democratic contingent, except for the two from Louisiana who were expressing the gratitude of the sugar producers.[46]

While Aldrich was performing major surgery on the tariff, he deftly excised the inheritance tax, claiming that it would duplicate state levies, deprive the states of revenue, and subject heirs to double taxation. Believing in his ability to raise sufficient revenue <u>via</u> the tariff and philosophically opposed to the taxation of wealth, Aldrich steadfastly refused to countenance any attempts by Insurgents or Democrats to incorporate an income tax. On April 15, Joseph W. Bailey of Texas introduced his proposal for a three percent tax on incomes of over $5000, exempting only income from state and municipal bonds. His measure, drafted in consultation with Hull,.was also basically a reincarnation of the 1894 tax. Bailey was brilliant and enigmatic, a precise logician, and a spell-binding orator. In the tariff debates, he was an avid protector of Texas products and in 1906 he had been accused of being a defender of Standard Oil interests and an ally of Aldrich. But Bailey had also been a staunch advocate of income taxation since the 1890s and was anxious to disprove the charges of being a corporate tool and a closet Regular. Bailey defended his proposal on the grounds of tax equity and predicted that it would raise at least $60,000,000. Two days later, the Democratic caucus endorsed the Bailey bill as a party measure. On that same day, Borah and Cummins, representing the Insurgents, visited Taft to sound him out on the income tax issue. While supportive of the principle, the president informed them that his concern for the reputation of the Supreme Court forced him to conclude that an income tax was unwise unless preceeded by constitutional change. Not dissuaded, Borah and Cummins met with four other Insurgents at Cummins' home on April 19 and drafted their own income tax measure. Two days later, Cummins introduced a tax on individual incomes graduated from a low of two percent on incomes over $5000 to a high of six percent on those exceeding $100,000. Cummins defended the equity of the tax and the principle of graduation and explained that he opposed a direct tax on corporations because it discriminated against stockholders in favor of generally wealthier bondholders. Cummins' argument was so persuasive that twenty-one Republicans announced their support, meaning that a majority of the Senate had declared for some form of income tax.[47]

Pressed by both Insurgents and Democrats, Aldrich used all the parliamentary skill at his command to postpone a showdown over the income tax. His strategy was to delay consideration of the measure until the tariff had been adopted and sufficient revenue had been assured. Aldrich also hoped that the differences between the Insurgents and the Democrats over the tariff and over the details of the income tax measure would weaken their nascent coalition. Fearful of the latter possibility, Borah promoted a meeting between leaders of the two factions that resulted in what appeared to be an acceptable compromise. Cummins was empowered to draft a jointly sponsored measure that would levy a flat two or three percent tax on both corporate and indivdual incomes over $5000. Cummins agreed to a flat rate tax in order to prevent Aldrich from picking off those members of both parties who regarded graduation as a radical attack upon wealth and to taxing corporations as a concession to Democrats and to Taft. A few days later, Borah and Cummins went to the White House and informed a disturbed Taft that they had "secured the assent of nineteen Republicans in addition to all of the Democrats to the proposition to pass a regular income tax exactly in the teeth of the decision of the Supreme Court in order to bring it up before the Supreme Court." Unmoved, Taft announced that he favored an inheritance tax as the best means of raising the necessary revenue and, failing that, an excise tax on corporations. He contended that, of all the revenue supplements, the income tax was the least desirable because it would fly in the face of the Supreme Court, cause otherwise honest people to cheat, and force the government to resort to inquisitional methods in order to compel compliance. Aldrich took the occasion to express his determination that there would be no additional taxes of any kind because there was no need for them.[48]

As part of the Insurgent-Democrat compromise, Bailey retained the right to introduce his own measure independently of Cummins' action. As Aldrich's delaying tactics became more apparent, the Texas Democrat grew increasingly impatient, warning his colleagues that "if we postpone it until the Senator from Rhode Island is ready to vote, we will not carry it, for he will stay here until the dog days before he will allow us to come to a vote on this question, if he can help it, until he feels reasonably sure of defeating it." On May 27, Aldrich's dilatory tactics caused a temporary rift between the Insurgents and the impatient Bailey that almost wrecked the income tax coalition. The Texas Democrat moved to have his flat three percent tax measure brought to a vote because the Insurgents had settled on a two percent rate. When Aldrich asked for unanimous consent to postpone the vote until June 10 so that the tariff schedules would be set, Bailey objected on the grounds that his income tax would raise $89,000,000 and necessitate revising most of the rates. On further reflection, Bailey agreed to wait until June 10 if Aldrich would promise not to postpone beyond that date and not to refer the measure to committee, but both Aldrich and Cummins refused to concur. According to his biographer, Cummins felt that pro-income tax sentiment was on the rise while Bailey feared that it was declining. Sensing a possible rift, Bailey withdrew his objection, admitting that he didn't "want to see the Senator from Iowa and the Senator from Rhode Island get together." Cummins hastily assured Bailey that he "had no quarrel with the Senator from Texas," and only wanted "to preserve our strength for the income tax struggle." The Texan replied that the advantage was purely Aldrich's and that he would laugh at both of them if they allowed themselves to be outmaneuvered. When Bailey continued to press for an immediate vote, Cummins inquired if the Texas Democrat were questioning the honesty of the "progressives" and Bailey replied that he was skeptical only of the Insurgents' wisdom in following Aldrich. Finally, Borah intervened in this potentially disastrous situation to assure Bailey that he and Cummins and others intended to vote against postponment in order to prove their sincerity. True to their word, six Insurgents -- Cummins, Borah, LaFollette, Bristow, Clapp, and Dolliver -- joined the Democrats in a futile effort to avoid postponment. A seventh, Knute Nelson, insisted that he favored an income tax but feared that the tariff schedules were so high that the additional revenue might not be needed. Bailey's conduct appeared so inimical to the cause that New York Times reporter W. S. Manning accused the Texan of deliberately playing into Aldrich's hands in order to split the Democrat-Insurgent coalition and undermine the efforts of the "real friends of the income tax." Bailey was so incensed by the story that he physically accosted Manning in the Senate corridor and the reporter had to beat off his attacker with an umbrella. More calmly, Bailey denied the charge unequivocally and insisted that the accusation could only be true if Cummins had introduced his bill first and if Bailey had proposed a graduated tax. Despite this temporary rift in the income tax coaliton, the incident convinced most Democrats of the Insurgent's sincerity and strengthened their resolve to press for enactment of the measure.[49]

Even before this testing of Democrat-Insurgent solidarity, the Regular leadership recognized that the pro-income tax forces would carry the day without presidential intervention. Estimates of the voting strength of the income tax coalition ranged from a slight majority to a high of fifty-three, and Henry Cabot Lodge acknowledged to Roosevelt that "they had the votes." Even Aldrich's biographer, Nathaniel W. Stephenson, acknowledged that "there were disquieting rumors that the Senate Progressives were about to be reinforced by a considerable number of senators that Aldrich had hitherto counted upon" and that the Rhode Islander "appears to have been afraid that the situation might be breaking from his hand, that at the last moment the vote might be a surprise and a Democratic-Radical-Western coalition make a bargain among themselves and seize control of the Senate." Elihu Root, in an interview recorded in Current Literature, also acknowledged that "it became apparent that this movement (for the income tax) would receive the support of a majority in the Senate." Accordingly, on May 24, Aldrich, Lodge, and Winthrop Murray Crane went to Taft with a request for help. After listening to their recitation of the seriousness of the situation, Taft inquired if they were asking him for an alternative and Aldrich replied bluntly, "that is why we came to you." Taft then outlined his plan to substitute the corporation excise tax that Wickersham had drafted for the income tax and to propose a constitutional amendment that would permit an income tax to be levied when the need arose. Aldrich and his associates registered their opposition to both measures, but Taft was adamant. "Either you take the bill and the proposed submission of the constitutional amendment to the people, as I have suggested," Taft warned, "or else the alternative is the income tax law that the insurgent Republicans propose to pass in association with the Democrats." Realizing that he had no real choice, Aldrich was reduced to bargaining over the provisions of the corporation tax and to trying to convince the president to propose a two year limit on the levy. But, as Taft informed his brother Horace, he "objected to the limitation and said that I did not think that I could break up the nineteen Republicans if that limitation was in." Later Taft explained to Ohio Republican Congressman Albert Douglas that he opposed the two year limitation "because it was on the faith of its containing no limitation that I secured the defeat of the income tax." When Taft refused to budge, Aldrich went away but returned the next day to signify his compliance with the strategy. To Horace and others, Taft gleefully insisted that he had held all the "trump cards", was "elated over having out-maneuvered Aldrich," and that "the situation is not one of my yielding to Aldrich, but of Aldrich yielding to me."[50]

During the next three weeks, Aldrich labored mightily to prevent a showdown over the income tax, while he, Root, and Wickersham dickered over the detils of the proposed corporation tax. Meanwhile, Taft tried to pave the way through private meetings with moderate Senators whom he hoped to detach from the Insurgents. Taft and Aldrich met on June 9 to discuss the message that the President was going to send to Congress, and, two days later, Aldrich again won a battle to postpone both income tax bills until June 18. On June 15 Taft discussed his message with the cabinet and, according to Secretary of the Navy George von Lengerke Meyer, "it was unanimous opinion that it was the psychological moment to do so." The cabinet members agreed that such action would "defeat the income tax of the democrats who have made combine with Cummins of Iowa and a few others" and would "be the first step of Government Supervision of Corporations." Taft also informed the Cabinet that he was going to ask for a constitutional amendment on the income tax because "it would be most unfortunate for the prestige of the Court (Supreme) to have at this time to settle again the Constitutionality of the income tax."[51]

On June 16, Taft's message was read to both houses of Congress. In it he expressed his belief that the Pollock Decision "deprived the National Government of a power which, by reason of previous decisions of the court, it was generally supposed that the Government had." Taft stated that this was "undoubtedly a power the National Government ought to have" because "it might be indispensable to the nation's life in great crisis." Although acknowledging that he had not always believed an amendment to be necessary, the President contended that a "mature consideration has satisfied me that an amendment is the only proper course for its establishment to its full extent." Such a course, he insisted, was much wiser than "the one proposed of reenacting a law once judicially declared to be unconstitutional." For Congress to take that course on the assumption that the Court would reverse itself, he insisted, "will not strengthen the popular confidence in the stability of judicial construction of the Constitution." Moreover, Taft argued, passing an income tax law would not solve the fiscal crisis because many taxpayers would wait for a new court decision before paying the tax. Although acknowledging the difficulty of the ratification process, Taft insisted that he was "convinced that a great majority of the people of this country are in favor of vesting the National Government with power to levy an income tax, and that they will secure the adoption of the amendment in the States, if proposed to them."[52]

Continuing on, the President expressed his conviction that the Pollock Decision "left power in the federal government to levy an excise tax which accomplishes the same purpose as a corporation income tax, and is free from certain objections urged to the proposed income tax measure." Taft therefore recommended an "excise tax measured by two percent of the net incomes of such corproations," arguing that this would be a "tax upon the privilege of doing business as an artificial entity and of freedom from a general partnership liability enjoyed by those who own the stock." Estimating that such a tax would raise $25,000,000, the President contended that the decision in the case of Spreckels Sugar Refining Company v. McClain "seems clearly to establish the principle that such a tax as this is an excise tax upon privilege and not a direct tax upon property, and is within the federal power without apportionment according to population." Measuring such a tax by net income, he stated, was preferable to one proportioned on gross receipts "because it is a tax upon success and not failure" and one that "imposes a burden at the source of the income at the time when the corporation is well able to pay and when collection is easy." An additional advantage of the excise tax, Taft claimed, was that it provided for "federal supervision" over "the annual accounts and business transactions of all corporations." Such a function,he insisted, "made a very long step toward the supervisory control of corporations which may prevent a further abuse of power." In summary, Taft reiterated his recommendation for an income tax amendment and an excise tax on all corporations measured by two percent of their net incomes, "either as a substitute for, or in addition to, the inheritance tax."[53]

There can be little doubt that Taft sincerely believed that his compromise proposal was preferable to the immediate enactment of an income tax. In a letter to J. D. Brannan in late June, Taft insisted that "the income tax will certainly pass Congress unless the course that I have suggested is taken, and I think that the one I have recommended is much to be preferred." Perhaps most importantly, it would protect the Supreme Court, the institution that Taft regarded as the bulwark of the American way of life, from further criticism. In a meeting with his brothers Horace and Charles on July 1, Taft insisted that he preferred an income tax, "but the truth is that I am afraid of the discussion which will follow and the criticism that will ensue if there is another serious division in the Supreme Court on the subject of the income tax." Contending that nothing had ever so impaired the prestige of the Court more than had the Pollock decision, Taft expressed the conviction that "many of the most violent advocates of the income tax will be glad of the substitution in their hearts for the same reason." The amendment route, he concluded, "will admit an income tax without question, but I am afraid of it without such an amendment." By the same token, the President also believed that the corporation tax would cause no harm to the Court because Wickersham and he were in agreement that the principle of levying an excise tax on corporations for the privilege of doing business as a corporation and measuring the amount of tax by net income had already been upheld by the Court. Taft voiced the same concern about the potential damage to the Court in letters to Edward Colston on June 24, to Fredrick P. Fish on June 28, and to his sister Therese on the same day. In his Current Literature interview, Root stressed that the corporation tax was "as near as we can get to the principle of a general income tax without challenging the decision of the Supreme Court.[54]

Moreover, Taft and his two closest advisers, Wickersham and Root, appear to have been convinced that the corporation tax was a piece of constructive legislation rather than just a political expedient. In a personal letter to Rollo Ogden, editor of the New York Evening Post, Taft insisted that "I think a good many people who are attacking it now will be glad to use it as a means of preventing the income tax later on. I don't think that it will prove to be an objectionable tax." Besides believing in its constitutionality, Taft believed that the corporation excise tax would raise over $25,000,000 without forcing the federal government to construct elaborate and expensive collection machinery. Indeed, Taft asked for only $50,000 in operating expenses because the burden of figuring the tax was to be placed upon the corporations themselves. Taft also felt that the privilege of doing business as a corporation gave its beneficiaries many advantages for which they owed government some compensation.

Thus he told Frederick P. Fish that he was sorry that Fish did not feel that corporations owed government anything because corporations benefited substantially from limited liability and should pay for the privilege. Similarly, he assured General Felix Angus that the use of the corporate form had been greatly abused even in small businesses. Most importantly of all, Taft believed that the reporting requirements of the tax would force corporations to reveal much of their inner workings and provide the groundwork for federal licensing and regulation, a goal that he and Roosevelt strongly held in common. To his erstwhile mentor, the President expressed confidence that the tax "will furnish not only a valuable source of revenue but also a useful means of discovering and supervising the affairs of our corporations." He even insisted that the latter feature would help corporations by putting them on a "sound footing" and by instilling confidence in investors as to corporate integrity and efficiency. To his Secretary of State, Chicago businessman Franklin MacVeagh, a staunch opponent of the tax and especially of its disclosure provisions, the President insisted that "the publicity feature of the law is the only thing which makes the law of any special value, for it is not going to be a great revenue producing measure." When MacVeagh informed Taft early in 1910, that, as a businessman, he would resent the government prying into his affairs and would do all that he could to evade the law, Taft replied calmly that then MacVeagh "would be the one they would be hunting down."[55]

This belief in the intrinsic value of the corporation tax, and especially in its disclosure provisions, was also shared by Wickersham and Root who drafted the measure. The former insisted that the privilege of doing business as a corporation had a tangible value and that that value was the proper subject of taxation. He also confessed privately that he had little faith in the integrity of corporate managers and that the bill served the public interest while protecting corporations against unnecessary snooping. The reporting statement, Wickersham insisted to Judge Elbert Gary, required the disclosure of information "which any honest corporation management should be glad to put before its stockholders and the world at large at the close of each year." As did his leader, the Attorney General believed the corporation tax to be "such an improvement over the proposed income tax law that sober second thought will accept it as being a measure which has much to recommend it." He later called the tax "the most progressive piece of legislation on the statute books for many a long day." Root's defense of the measure on the Senate floor and in public pronouncements also smacked of sincerity, especially since he shared Taft's views that it and the proposed constitutional amendment were the only real alternatives to the enactment of an income tax law, that the latter would shake the Supreme Court to its foundations, and that Congress should be vested with the power to levy an income tax through the amendment process but should exercise that authority only during wartime or other emergency. When accused by the Insurgents of pressing the corporation tax solely as a device to defeat the income tax, Root replied: "Gentlemen may say that I am for the corporation tax to beat the income tax. I care not. I am for the corporation tax because I think it is better policy, better patriotism, higher wisdom than the general income tax at this time and under these circumstances." Longworth, Taft's liaison to the Ways and Means Committee, also insisted that "far from being a legislative trick, designed to meet a particular condition in the Senate, or designed to beat any particular measure, the corporation tax is a well-considered plan, designed to go upon the statute books on account of the merit it has in it." So strongly did Taft and Wickersham believe in the corporation excise tax that the latter urged the president not to forget to stress its enactment as one of the most progressive measures of his administration during his speaking tours and it seems certain that its inclusion in the Payne-Aldrich Tariff was one of the major reasons for Taft's ill-fated remark that it was the best tariff ever passed by the Republican Party. Finally, the President hoped that by getting the Regulars to accept the corporation tax and the income tax amendment, he could induce the Insurgents to support the tariff and prevent the party split that was seemingly inevitable if the Insurgents triumphed in the income tax fight.[56]

Nor can there be any doubt that Taft forced Aldrich and the Regulars to accept an alternative that they found only slightly less objectionable than they did an immediate income tax. Writing in 1930, Aldrich's biographer claimed that the Rhode Islander had been the one who suggested "a tax on the earnings of corporations to be inforced (sic) two years" and that "the President approved." The tax, he continued, "was paraded before the world as a great stroke of the President's, as convincing proof that he was wedded to the Progressive policies of Mr. Roosevelt." The New York Times concurred that this was "a compromise on which Senator Aldrich finally decided, and on which he has the full support of the President" and concluded that "the combination thrown around the struggling Insurgents is one Mr. Aldrich is believed to be capable of devising and one from which to-night the Insurgents see no outlet." But the bulk of the evidence suggests that Taft's version of the meeting is the correct one. Lodge, who was also present, wrote to Roosevelt that "in order to beat them (i.e. the Insurgents) we are determined to put in a tax on the net receipts of corporations which was recommended by Taft and which he has just urged in a special message." Wickersham informed Archibald Butt, Taft's military aide, that the President warned Aldrich and the Regulars that they would either accept the corporation tax and the income tax amendment or there would be no tariff. Butt was also told by Jonathon Bourne, an erstwhile Insurgent, that "instead of being duped by Aldrich and the other Senators, he (Taft) has chloroformed them." Unlike Root and Longworth, Aldrich made no attempt to defend the intrinsic merits of the corporation tax, admitting frankly, "I shall vote for a corporation tax as a means to defeat the income tax.---I am willing to accept a proposition of this kind for the purpose of avoiding what, to my mind, is a great evil." Interestingly enough, according to Butt, Taft interpreted Aldrich's admission as an attempt to throw the "odium" on him. Still, Butt concluded, Taft "seems determined to push the tax, and if others are weakening, he is not, at least." When fellow Regular Eugene Hale of Maine described the corporation tax as a "distressing and embarassing alternative for which there was no other." Aldrich responded that "if it had not been so I should never come to make the proposition which I did for a message and the submission of the amendment." Stephenson also acknowledged that Aldrich's "chief concern was to drive a wedge between Democrats and Republican Radicals."[57]

In presenting the report of the Conference Committee on the tariff on July 30, Payne admitted that "I have no use for an income tax, and what use I have for a corporation tax is the fact that you can sometimes get rid of an unconstitutional income tax appended to a bill." Although Aldrich, Payne, Cannon, Lodge and the Regular leadership eventually acquiesced in the Taft compromise and brought along most of their colleagues, there were several die-hard Standpatters in both houses who refused to vote for either the corporation tax or the income tax amendment. Five Regular Senators voted against the corporation tax and eleven, including Lodge, abstained on the adoption of the income tax amendment. In the House, fourteen Regulars voted against the income tax amendment while over forty more abstained. Since there was no separate vote on the corporation tax, there is no accurate way to gauge the magnitude of Regular opposition. On balance, then, Taft, Root, Wickersham and their closest allies gave every indication, both during the remainder of the special session and the ratification process, of believing in and working for the corporation tax and the income tax amendment. Aldrich and many of the Regulars, on the contrary, made no effort to conceal their disdain for both measures and widely advertised the fact that they had embraced them only under duress.[58]

The consternation of the Regulars, and Taft's sincerity, were also demonstrated by the storm of protest from corporate circles that greeted the corporation tax. Many of these reached the two authors during their deliberations and caused Root to manifest obvious picque at what he regarded as the unsophisticated viewpoint of corporate leaders who did not realize that Taft had saved them from a far worse fate. When several trust companies complained, Root wrote Wickersham that such protests were as instinctive as winking an eye when a bug gets in it. "I wonder," he commented wryly, "how they would like an income tax which would require them to make a separate return for each trust?" When Wickersham marveled at the numerous protests by corporate accountants concerning the complications involved, Root chided that "you seem to have failed to grasp a great truth, that business is done for the convenience of book keepers."[59]

Once the fact that a tax was being drafted became known, Taft and Aldrich were also bombarded with protests, suggestions for revisions, and pleas for exemptions. According to Stephenson, Aldrich was visited with an "avalanche of corporate objectors." On June 21, John D. Rockefeller, Jr. informed Aldrich, his father-in-law, that he and "father" would prefer a tax on dividends instead of one on net incomes. The latter, he insisted, would place all corporations under "inquiry, surveillance, and espionage," would involve government and business in "endless dispute and embarassment," and "would surely be a most unpopular measure with the business interests of the country." The vice-president of the New York, New Haven, and Hartford Railroad informed Aldrich that the disclosure provisions would "involve the extension to private corporations of the inquisitional process to which interstate commerce carriers are now subjected." Taft responded to a similar letter from the same correspondent by stating that "if they do not adopt my suggestions they will have to have an income tax, and an income tax will be inquisitional, not only with respect to corporations but with respect to individuals, and much more burdensome in every way." Aldrich was so exasperated by the protests and pleas that when Taft suggested to Payne that there would be amendments to the draft bill, the Finance Committee chairman stated flatly that "there will be no amendments."

Root, then laughingly made a mock introduction of Aldrich to Cannon, saying "Mr. Czar, meet Mr. Czar." Actually, Aldrich did accept one amendment on the Senate floor, a proposal by Moses Clapp that included holding companies under the law's provisions. The Clapp amendment was later excised in the Conference Committee, at the urging of Taft and Payne. The latter also claimed full credit for reducing the rate from two percent to one, a move justified by the argument that the tariff would raise enough additional revenue.[60]

The final bill, then, was a compromise between the administration and the Regulars. It provided for an excise tax of one percent on the privilege of doing business for every corporation, joint stock company or association, organized for profit and having a capital stock represented by shares, and on every insurance company. The tax was to be levied on the net income over $5000 received from all sources, except for dividends from other corporations subject to the tax. It exempted most non-profit organizations "no part of the net income of which accrues to the benefit of any private stockholder or individual." In calculating net income, corporations were allowed to deduct operating expenses, losses not covered by insurance, interest on bonded or other indebtedness, other taxes paid, and dividends from the stock of other corporations subject to the tax." Each corporation was required to file a return by March 1 of each year providing all of the above information as of the previous December 31, and were to be notified of the amount of tax due by June 1. Pehaps most galling to the corporations, and most gratifying to the administration, was the provision that these returns were to be filed with the Commissioner of Internal Revenue and would constitute public records open to inspection.

The bill also provided for a series of fines for filing late or fraudulent returns or for failing to file at all.[61]

Despite the fact that the amount of the tax was minimal, that it was the only viable alternative to an income tax, and that it was prepared by those generally sympathetic to business, the corporation excise tax of 1909 was attacked savagely by most business spokesmen. The New York Times stigmatized it as disreputable in its origins, false in its nature and its pretensions, dishonest in every line of its text and in the arguments by which it has been supported. It also called the tax "half muckrake and half money scoop." The New York Press charged that the country had "never known anything less worthy of serious consideration." The Philadelphia Public Ledger styled it "a trick, an evasion, a juggling with words, an income tax disguised as an excise tax on the privilege of doing business." The Hartford Times estimated that newspaper oppositon to the tax "is without precedent in the case of any administration scheme in many years."[62]

Businessmen all over the nation flooded Congress and the administration with protests and demands for repeal on a variety of grounds. They objected to the amount of the tax, to the filing deadlines because they did not coincide with corporate fiscal practices, and charged that the measure would raise so much revenue that downward tariff revision would be required. Many business men objected to having their records open to "cheap government inspections of the $1200 type." Many argued that the federal government had no right to levy a tax on the privilege of doing business as a corporation because that privilege was granted by state charters. But most of the protests came over the need for extensive record keeping for preparing the returns and over the disclosure provisions. Many businessmen professed to prefer a tax on the gross income of corporations because that would eliminate the need for elaborate documentation of deductions and for disclosing business practices and procedures. So intense and widespread were these objections that the law was amended in 1910 to make returns "open to inspection only upon the order of the President." As March 1, 1910 approached, there were dire predictions from business-oriented periodicals that thousands of corporations would refuse to comply, believing that the Court would soon declare the tax unconstitutional. But the Internal Revenue Service announced on March 4 that ninety percent of the nation's corporations had filed returns in the amount of nearly $30,000,000. But it also revealed that eighty-five percent of those filing had done so under protest and that there were sixteen lawsuits challenging the law. Most of these suits resulted from the Conference of Industrial and Commercial Organizations and Representatives of Corporations held in Chicago in January, 1910 under the sponsorship of the Illinois Manufacturers Association. The Conference was billed as "the first gun of a national movement which has in view the uniting of all" and its participants instituted law suits in every section of the country challenging the constitutionality of the law." However, the federal courts made no ruling on any of these cases in 1910 and by October 20, the Treasury Department announced that the tax had raised over $27,000,000 and was "collected with less annoyance and was paid apparently with less reluctance than any other internal revenue tax imposed."[63]

On March 13, 1911, the Supreme Court upheld the constitutionality of the corporation tax in a decision relating to eleven of the cases brought by the Chicago Conference under the general heading of <u>Flint</u>

v. Stone Tracy Company. These involved cases first argued in Vermont, New York, Massachusetts, Illinois, Minnesota, and Ohio and concerning corporations involved in real estate, insurance, public utilities, banking multigraphics, mining, and the taxi cab business. In a unanimous decision, the Court reversed its performance in the Pollock Decision by accepting the government's defense of the law seemingly without modification or question. One by one, it disposed of the thirty-two contentions of the plaintiffs ranging from the argument that the Senate had no right to initiate revenue bills to the assertion that the tax return constituted unreasonable search and seizure. On the main question, the Court ruled that the corporation tax was not a direct one, but "an excise upon the particular privilege of doing business in a corporate capacity," and, as such, could be measured by the entire income of the parties affected even though part of that income was derived from tax exempt property. The difference between the corporation tax and the 1894 income tax, the Court insisted, "is not merely nominal but rests upon substantial differences between the mere ownership of property and the actual doing of business in a certain way." The former had the "element of absolute and unavoidable demand" which required that a tax be levied because of mere ownership, while the latter mandated payment only if business were actually done in a certain manner. In short, the Court, in a semantical gem, "turned a tax on income into a tax on something else merely measured by income," as Sidney Ratner has argued. Yet, as Thomas Reed Powell put it, it was necessary to believe that it could be done "as the gentleman believed in baptism, because he had seen it done."

In the final analysis, as Ratner has argued persuasively, the Court "chose" to follow precedents and rationales that sustained the 1909 tax just as its predecessor has chosen to ignore such precedents and rationales in 1895. Given the popular pressure for an income tax, the Court seemingly found a moderate tax on corporate income proposed by a Republican president and passed by a Republican Congress much less threatening than the earlier judiciary has found the 1894 tax.[64]

Despite all the objections raised in Regular Republican and corporate circles, the strongest criticisms of Taft's compromise emanated from the Insurgents and the Democrats who generally regarded the corporation tax as "an income tax in disguise" that would be borne primarily by small stockholders and barely affect the nation's wealthiest citizens. By the same token, they regarded the income tax amendment as a scheme devised to postpone for several years, or to prevent altogether, the enactment of a genuine income tax. Believing that they had the votes to effect such a tax before Taft's intervention, and sharing none of his concern for the reputation of the Supreme Court, the Insurgents and Democrats openly branded the President's proposals as a plot hatched by him and Aldrich to scuttle the income tax. Fearing such reaction, Taft attempted to forestall it by calling in some of the more "tractible" Insurgents and convincing them of the wisdom of his plan. His success in winning over such marginal Insurgents as Jonathan Bourne, Norris Brown, Thomas Carter, and Charles Curtis, however, merely served to strengthen the resolve of the hard-core members and to convince the latter that Taft was in league with Aldrich. Taft later claimed that he had issued the compromise at the request of Bourne, Brown, and Curtis who were seeking a way to hold the party together. In LaFollette's view, Taft's message had given Republican moderates a "greased plank" that enabled them to pose as income tax supporters while preventing its enactment.[65]

When the President sought the support of Cummins and the hard-core Insurgents, he was flatly refused. Cummins insisted that Taft had encouraged them to pursue the income tax during that April meeting and promised that he would only resort to a corporation tax if the Insurgents failed. Taft complained to Horace that the "so-called progressives" were unable to "look beyond their noses" and that they do not seem to understand the only possible way of effecting the reforms to which we are pledged." Whenever he gave them "the opportunity to carry out these reforms, or to make real progress, as for instance in the proposition to amend the income tax and pass the corporation tax," he charged, "they turn and oppose that because they say that they will not accept anything that comes as a gift from Aldrich." If the Insurgents had "breadth of view and keeness of insight," the President insisted, "immediately upon receipt of my message they would have risen in their seats and said, this gives us all we have been claiming and seeking only by another method, and we now claim to lead the procession because the President and the reactionaries have come to our side." Taft also confided to Butt that the Insurgents "cannot afford to fight my propositions and yet, if the Finance Committee puts them in the bill, they will get none of the credit for them."[66]

Taft's opinion was echoed by former Republican Senator William E. Chandler in a letter to Root. "It is certainly not practical politics to seek through an income tax an issue with the Supreme Court when without a dangerous issue with the Supreme Court we could get a corporation tax, popularize the party, and by means of the constitutional amendment (a good issue before the people if resisted) put an end to all controversies about income taxes upon corporations and individuals," Chandler insisted. "Such short-sightedness as I have witnessed," he concluded, "amazes me." Although less directly critical of the Insurgents, Roosevelt also believed that they should have accepted Taft's proposals with better grace. He informed Lodge that he regarded "your success in putting in the corporation tax as most important; from the permanent and most important standpoint as establishing the principle of national supervision." In the short run, he continued, the administration and the Regulars had scored "a triumph which the West will appreciate, and which may take the sting out of some of the inevitable grumbling about the tariff, by diverting attention to what is really of far greater moment." As already noted, he also confided to Lodge that the Taft compromise "would seem to be the best way out of the Income Tax business."[67]

The Insurgents bitterly attacked the corporation tax on the floor of Congress, in the press, and in their private correspondence. They scoffed at the notion that the tax was an excise tax, agreeing with Arthur Machen that "if the tax is not a tax on income, it has all the appearance of such a tax. Its amount is to be calculated for all the world like the amount of an income tax." Even if one accepted the argument that it was an excise tax, they contended, it would fall heaviest upon small stockholders and miss altogether the wealthy bondholders who were to be the chief targets of an income tax. They also insisted that the tax could easily be passed on to consumers and stockholders, once again missing the very wealthy. At bottom, though, their major objection, and that of the Democrats, was that the corporation tax and the income tax amendment were not made in good faith, but represented a plot hatched deliberately by Taft and the Regulars to prevent the income tax that the Insurgent-Democra coalition had the votes to enact. Bristow complained to the editor of the Kansas City Star that "the President has joined with Aldrich to defeat us upon the only occasion where he was in any danger." Throughout the session, Bristow continued, Aldrich had been the Senator closest to the White House, and "his control of the Senate has never been in doubt, except as to the income tax amendment." The corporation tax, he charged, "relieves the biggest fortunes in the country from the burden" because nine-tenths of the tax would be paid by the consumers of corporate products making it "almost as much of a consumption tax as the tariff itself."[68]

Bristow reiterated the same charges to the editor of the Topeka Capitol, published by future U.S. Senator Arthur Capper. Bristow insisted that Taft had told Cummins and Borah that he would only resort to a corporation tax if the Insurgents were unable to enact an income tax and that Aldrich had accepted the corporation tax because "it was the only way he could beat the income tax - to get the President to help him." He also insisted that Taft had been personally responsible for the defection of several pro-income tax Republicans. To Kansas Insurgent Henry J. Allen, Bristow charged that "Taft took up the corporation tax idea with Aldrich and both of them used it as a means to defeat the income tax." To a constituent, the Kansas Senator explained that taxing corporate income would hurt small stockholders because the tax bore no relation to the income of the individual stockholder. On another occasion, he insisted that he opposed the corporation tax because it "taxes those who invest in corporations and not those who live off loaning money." Prophetically,

Bristow told another constituent that enacting a genuine income tax in 1909 "would meet with great popular approval, and it would hold that element in the party which will probably not be satisfied with the action of Congress respecting the tariff." The Insurgents also generally agreed that it was all but impossible to get a constitutional amendment through the necessary number of state legislatures.[69]

The only prominent Insurgent who dissented from the views held by Bristow was Albert Beveridge. Beveridge had opposed an income tax as unconstitutional and as one that would necessitate a national network of spies to collect. He regarded the Democrats' support of the income tax as "a purely political maneuver" and believed that his fellow Insurgents had been ensnared in a Democratic trap. Like Taft, he had concluded by 1909 that an inheritance tax was the better course. But he also opposed the corporation tax because it would burden only corporations and not partnerships. Should such a tax be levied, though, Beveridge favored taxing gross receipts in order to avoid the necessity of disclosure. His correspondence supports his contention that Indiana businessmen were adamantly opposed to the corporation tax, and Beveridge proposed to Taft a tax on tobacco as a substitute. He also believed that Taft could have defeated the income tax without such a maneuver, simply by taking a firm stand in opposition. For all that, though, Beveridge agreed to support the Taft proposals out of loyalty to the President who privately regarded him as "a liar and an egotist." Even Beveridge concurred with his fellow Insurgents in the belief that "it is rather easy to figure out how the Aldrich crowd could defeat such an amendment."[70]

For their part, the Democrats generally shared the attitude of the hard core Insurgents, although without the sense of being betrayed by Taft. Since they had always regarded Taft and Aldrich as being in league with one another, the President's actions only confirmed what they already believed. Beyond that, though, the minority party was bitterly frustrated and angry at having been outmaneuvered by the administration and the Regulars. The Washington Post reported that the Democrats were "madder than hornets". As a general rule, the Democrats regarded the corporation tax as an income tax in disguise, hastily contrived by Taft and Aldrich solely to defeat the income tax. They also saw it as a device that would give the illusion of taxing the wealthy while placing the actual burden on small stockholders and consumers. Since they were the minority party, they had no reservations against opposing it openly and unequivocally and they voted almost unanimously against substituting it for the income tax measure. But the income tax amendment proposal really put the Democrats on the horns of a dilemma. Since they advocated the idea in their platform, they could hardly afford to oppose its adoption. Some even tried to put the best possible face on it by claiming that Taft had been maneuvered into enacting a Democratic measure. Indeed, Senator Thomas P. Gore of Oklahoma quickly tried to respond to Taft's June 16 message by moving that the Finance Committee report an income tax amendment within two days, but the motion was summarily tabled. Hull, in his memoirs, asserted that the Democrats had only supported the enactment of an immediate income tax in order to get the Republicans to accept a constitutional amendment, and Bailey's biographer hailed its adoption as a great victory for the minority party. William Jennings Bryan also wrote LaFollette that "we have won a victory in getting the income tax amendment submitted." Despite their platform statement and later rationalizations, however, the Democrats had invested all of their efforts in cooperating with the Insurgents and they clearly shared all the latter's anger and frustration at being denied what they apparently had the necessary votes to achieve in 1909.[71]

The day after Taft's message, Norris Brown, one of the marginal Insurgents "pulled off" the income tax coalition through Taft's personal intervention, introduced a resolution calling for an income tax amendment. He had rejected a version drafted by Wickersham that would have empowered Congress to levy and collect taxes on the income of persons, associations, and corporations by providing that "such taxes shall not be deemed direct taxes within the meaning...of the Constitution." Brown's resolution stated that "Congress shall have the power to levy and collect direct taxes on incomes without apportionment among the several states according to population." As such, it accepted the Pollock Decision's reasoning that a tax on income derived from invested capital was direct and merely abolished the rule of apportionment in such cases. The belief that income is taxable regardless of its source, according to Ratner, would not have been supported by Brown's wording. Democratic Senator Anselm McLaurin of Mississippi tried to get Brown to propose instead that the phrases "direct taxes" and "other direct" be stricken from the Constitution, thus leaving only capitation taxes to be apportioned according to population. Brown rejected the suggestion and the measure was referred to the Finance Committee.[72]

During its deliberations, Aldrich accepted the notion of sometime Insurgent Knute Nelson that the word "direct" be stricken from Brown's resolution and that the words "from whatever source derived" be added after income. Nelson's object was to foreclose the possibility of any class of income being held exempt from taxation by the Court, but in so doing, he inadvertently laid the groundwork for the objection that the amendment would make possible the taxing of income from state and municipal bonds, the one action that the seriously divided Pollock Court had held unanimously to be unconstitutional. It was an error that income tax advocates would live to regret. Aldrich accepted Nelson's amendment, perhaps because he foresaw the possibility of the later controversy over the taxing of incomes from state and municipal bonds, perhaps because he did not really expect the amendment to be ratified anyway, and perhaps because he felt that it might improve the chances of Insurgent support for the tariff. What was to become the Sixteenth Amendment finally read: "The Congress shall have power to lay and collect taxes on incomes, from whatever source derived, without apportionment among the several states and without regard to any census or enumeration."[73]

Had Taft proposed the corporation tax and the income tax amendment _de novo_, instead of as devices designed to prevent the enactment of an immediate income tax, they almost certainly would have produced the same alignment as the latter had. But the circumstances of their introduction and the dictates of political expediency generated a curious realignment. Although the Regulars made no effort to conceal their disdain for both measures, the majority of their number became reluctant advocates. As Ratner correctly observed, "their hope was for a speedy repeal of the corporation tax and a defeat for the proposed constitutional amendment." Only a handful of Regulars permitted their distaste for income taxation in any form to justify defiance of the President and their party leadership, either by voting in the negative or by abstaining. The opposition to both measures, then, came from the Insurgents and the Democrats who were determined to hold out for enactment of an immediate income tax until all the possibilities had been exhausted. In the end, though, most of their number bowed to the political realities and voted for the corporation tax and the constitutional amendment as the nearest facsimilie possible.[74]

On June 28, Aldrich introduced the resolution for the income tax amendment in the Senate, hoping to get it adopted before debate on the Bailey-Cummins income tax bill, but the Democrats managed to table the proposal. The following day Bailey frustrated an attempt by Brown to consider the amendment resolution. Later that same day, Aldrich and Lodge cleverly contrived to have the corporation tax appended as an amendment to Bailey's income tax proposal, thus giving it precedence in consideration and virtually precluding any amendments to the measure. During the next three days, Cummins and Borah lead the assault against the Taft compromise and in favor of the income tax, stigmatizing the corporation tax as a "sugar coated drug." They denounced the corporation tax and the amendment as "instruments to defeat the income tax provision," and contended that the former would not reach the very wealthy because it taxed only corporations, not other forms of business organization, and only stockholders, rather than bondholders. They also charged that corporations could apportion the tax among their stockholders in order to protect the more affluent and could pass the burden on to consumers in the form of higher prices, as some Regular leaders frankly admitted that they had done in 1898. Borah closed his argument by urging the immediate enactment of an income tax, not as an assault upon wealth, but as an assault upon the vicious principle of exemption of wealth." He also insisted that the corporation tax was "born of fear" and that "nobody cares what becomes of it once it has served its purpose in shelving the income tax."[75]

The case in favor of the corporation tax was made primarily by Root, who stressed its innocuous nature and, ironically, faulted Cummins and Bailey for neglecting to provide for graduated rates and for discrimination between earned and unearned wealth in their tax measures, claiming that those omissions were harsh on the working classes. Cummins replied that the omission was only to avoid charges of radicalism that would defeat the measures. On July 2, the Senate voted 45-31 to substitute the corporation tax for the income tax proposals. The Democrats and six "bitter-end" Insurgents -- Borah, Bristow, Clapp, Cummins, Dolliver, and LaFollette-- were joined in opposition by Regular Morgan Bulkeley of Connecticut who was reportedly responding to the objections of the state's insurance companies. The corporation tax was then incorporated into the tariff bill by a vote of 59-11, with most Democrats deciding to opt for some form of tax on wealth. Three, Benjamin Shiveley of Indiana, Charles J. Hughes of Colorado, and George E. Chamberlain of Oregon refused to accept the corporation tax. The same six Insurgents plus Regulars Bulkeley and Weldon Heyburn of Idaho formed the bulk of the opposition, with the latter stating that he voted for the substitution to kill the income tax but that he believed the corporation tax to be a blow at the protective system. Bristow spoke for the Insurgents when he deemed the tax "a mere subtrefuge, and unjust and inequitable." On July 7, Bailey made a last ditch effort at enacting his income tax measure and failed, by a vote of 47-28. Five Insurgents, minus Dolliver, joined twenty-three Democrats in the vain attempt. That same day, Aldrich suddenly and inexplicably agreed to accept the Clapp Amendment to the corporation tax section permitting the taxation of holding companies, a proposal that he had previously denounced as double taxation. "The volteface," the New York Times reported, "came so quickly that Senators of all factions were dumbfounded." Rumors were rife that Aldrich planned to delete the corporation tax proposal in the Conference Committee and that he accepted the Clapp Amendment in order to make the tax even more unpalpable to his fellow Regulars. A few days before, Aldrich had rejected an amendment by Regular Stephen Elkins to lower the rate to one percent by stating that it didn't matter anyway because the tariff and government retrenchment would eliminate the deficit. President Taft adamantly opposed the amendment for the same reason and because he had little respect for Clapp. On July 8, the Senate voted for the Payne-Aldrich Tariff bill by a 45-34 count, with only one Democrat, Samuel McEnerny of Louisiana, voting with the Republican majority. Ten Insurgents -- Beveridge, Bristow, Brown, Burkett, Clapp, Crawford, Cummins, Dolliver, LaFollette, and Nelson -- joined the Democrats in opposition.[76]

Three days earlier, on July 5, the Senate adopted the proposal for an income tax amendment. The Insurgents and Democrats once again denounced the amendment method, with Bailey stating that he would vote for it "with reluctance, because I do not think it is necessary and I know the submission of it is fraught with extreme danger." Charging that "every expedient available to the organized wealth and greed of the country will be exercised to defeat it" and that the legislatures of the major industrial states were dominated by those "devotedly attached to the highest character of the protective tariff," the Democrats and Insurgents sought to have the amendment considered by popular conventions instead of state legislatures. Bailey's proposals to that effect lost on a 30-46 votes, with sixteen abstensions, on a vote that was nearly the mirror image of that on the substitution of the corporation tax for the income tax. Bailey also tried to append an amendment to the resolution giving Congress the specific power to graduate an income tax, but withdrew it when he saw that it would not pass. Failing in their last effort to guarantee that the amendment would benefit from the widespread popular support that they felt it enjoyed, the Democrats and Insurgents generally acquiesced in the inevitable as the resolution passed 77-0, with fifteen abstensions. Dolliver and five Southern Democrats were joined by Regulars Lodge, Brandegee, Bulkeley, Hale, Lorimer, Elkins, and Richardson, all long-time opponents of income taxation in any form. The remainder of the Regulars put their faith in Nelson Aldrich and in their state legislatures. As Jonathan Dolliver's biographer observed, the Insurgents and the Democrats generally voted for the resolution "because they believed in it as the fairest form of taxation, the Standpatters because it was a part of the "deal" Aldrich had agreed to and because they hoped to defeat ratification in the future."[77]

On July 9, the House received the tariff bill with its 847 amendments and the corporation tax substituted for its original inheritance tax. During the debate over whether to give complete power to the Conference Committee to resolve the differences between the two houses, Republican Charles E. Townsend of Michigan and Democrats Champ Clark, Charles A. Bartlett of Georgia, and John J. Fitzgerald of New York excoriated the corporation tax as an unacceptable substitute for an income tax and as a contrivance wholly designed to defeat the latter. Democratic leader Champ Clark challenged the authority of the Senate Finance Committee to substitute the corporation tax for the House approved inheritance tax since the Constitution prescribed that revenue measures had to originate in the lower chamber. Several Democrats expressed their determination to force the Conference Committee to consider an income tax section instead. At one point, Payne attempted to defend the "moderate" nature of the Aldrich amendments to the tariff bill by asserting that "there is nobody in the United States who knows as to some of these amendments whether they raise or lower the rates." Recognizing a straight line, Clark immediately queried if it would not "be doing a good thing to give ourselves the benefit of the doubt and vote against these amendments where you do not understand them?" The Regulars eventually beat back Democrat-Insurgent attempts to consider each of the amendments, including the corporation tax, as separate items, as well as a motion by George Norris for the House to concur in all downward revisions and to refuse to accept any increased rates unless adopted by House vote. In the end, the Regulars managed, on a 178-152 vote, to refer the bill to the Conference Committee without instruction, thus dooming any possible remaining chance for an immediate income tax.[78]

On July 12, the House considered the adoption of the resolution proposing the income tax amendment. Payne urged acceptance of the amendment as a necessity to produce revenue in an emergency, while Regulars Samuel McCall of Massachusetts and Ebeneezer Hill of Connecticut charged that the amendment could allow the small states to plunder the large ones and provide the revenue for the creation of a gigantic federal government. Clark and Hull urged adoption of the resolution, even though they insisted that it would have been far better to enact an income tax and directly challenge the Supreme Court. They also painted a dire picture of the hard struggle that would be necessary to secure the approval of the required number of state legislatures. Several Democrats and Insurgents expressed a preference for having the amendment considered by popular conventions, but they were unable to put the matter on the floor. In the end, most Democrats and Insurgents yielded to necessity and voted for the resolution, which passed 318-14, with fifty-five abstensions. The fourteen were all Regular Republicans from Maine, Pennsylvania, Massachusetts, Connecticut, New York, Michigan, and Kansas. The abstensions were almost evenly divided between other Regulars unwilling to carry their displeasure quite that far and Democrats who wanted to dramatize their belief that an amendment was not necessary.[79]

The Conference Committee labored for nearly three weeks, prodded by the intervention of the President and by rumors that he would veto any bill that did not meet his standards for significant revision. Taft preferred the House version of the bill because it provided for lowered duties on a number of raw materials. Eventually he settled for applying pressure on the lumber and glass schedules and, when Aldrich and Payne concurred, felt that he had won a great victory. During the committee deliberations, the President learned that the Regular leadership was being pressed by many businessmen and Congressmen to delete the corporation tax. Taft called Payne and Aldrich to the White House to protect the measure. Samuel McCall, a hard-core Regular who had led the opposition to the amendment resolution in the House, observed bitterly that Taft was "pushing it (corporation tax) with all his weight." Taft convinced them to delete the Clapp amendment because it made the tax even more offensive to many Regulars and, in exchange, agreed to lower the rate to one percent. Thus arranged, the corporation tax remained in the tariff bill that was reported out to the House on July 30. Taft considered a veto, which he felt would increase his popularity, but decided that the need for party unity mandated his acceptance. A veto would also destroy the few gains made and leave the Dingley rates in effect. The Times charged that the acceptance of the one percent rate proved that the tax was not a revenue raiser, but a regulatory measure.[80]

The bill in Ratner's opinion, "preserved the high rate structure and hostile attitude toward foreign trade embodied in the McKinley and Dingley Tariff Acts." Although it reduced rates in 584 cases involving about twenty percent of imports, it raised the duties in 300 instances and maintained a high level of protection for cotton, hosiery, zinc ore, silk, cotton, wool, and sugar. But Taft felt satisfied because it contained free hides and oil, and lowered duties on boots, iron ore, lumber, hosiery, inexpensive cottons, harnesses, shoes, and sole leather. He also was pleased with the corporation tax, the Tariff Board, the maximum and minimum rate provision, and Philippine reciprocity. By April 1, 1910 he ordered the minimum rates to be in effect for all countries. Taussig judged the tariff to be lacking any "considerable downward revision" but as "less aggresively protectionist than the previous Republican measures." The Merrills have concluded that "Congress made enough concessions to the President to allow him to claim a small measure of personal success, but he failed to achieve his goal of a bill that approximated the House bill in overall reduction of duties." Solvick, on the other hand, says that the President "embraced the Payne-Aldrich bill not reluctantly, but eagerly" and that it was "a law which conformed to his notions and which had received its final shape in large part because of his efforts." Taft himself wrote to his family that the "bill is really a very good bill," adding that it does not go far enough in certain respects, but it goes very far in others and a tariff bill no one can be entirely satisfied with." Bristow pronounced it "by all odds the most outrageous and indefensible tariff legislation in the history of the country."[81]

On July 31, the House received the Conference Committee report. Although Oscar Underwood attacked the corporation tax, Payne and Longworth defended it. The vote on the adoption of the report was 195-183, with the Regulars prevailing over the Democrats and thirteen Insurgents. Since the corporation tax was part of the package, that constituted House approval of the measure and its inclusion prevented any recalcitrant Regulars from voting in the negative on the corporation tax. During the Senate debate, the Insurgents and Democrats focused on the tariff schedules since the proposal of the amendment precluded any further action on an immediate income tax. Having failed to dislodge the corporation tax in the Conference Committee, the Regulars realized that they had no chance of winning a floor fight. The Senate approved the Payne-Aldrich Tariff on August 5 by a 47-31 vote, with the Regulars again besting the Democrat-Insurgent coalition.[82]

In the long run, it seems clear that Taft won the battle, but helped lay the groundwork for the eventual destruction of his presidency and his party. His actions helped produce a tariff that, whatever the merits of the question, strongly reinforced the growing public perception of the G.O.P. and the protective system as guardians of special privilege and as architects of a high cost of living. That image, exploited by Insurgents and Democrats, was largely responsible for the electoral disasters of 1910 and 1912. Taft also produced a corporation tax that conservatives and businessmen denounced as radical and inquisitional and that Insurgents and Democrats denounced as a farce and a plot. In 1912, the Democrats expropriated the idea and tried to extend it to individuals, a cruel, if apparently unintentional, *reductio ad absurdum*. In the process, Taft thoroughly alienated the Insurgents and saddled himself with a Standpat image that he was never able to shake and that undid him in 1912. Ironically, the only lasting achievement of the special session of 1909 was the income tax amendment, a measure that the Regulars accepted only under duress and that the Insurgents and Democrats generally regarded as an unwanted consolation prize.

Seldom has a measure of such monumental importance been acted with less conviction or enthusiasm. The Regulars, who had been maneuvered into serving as the amendment's unwilling sponsors, openly desired its defeat and entrusted that task to their allies in the various state legislatures. The Insurgents openly expressed their sense of frustration, while the Democrats tried, half-heartedly and unconvincingly, to rationalize the outcome as part of the design prescribed in their platform. Both sought to temper their disappointment with a resolution to work for ratification in their home states. Only Taft, his closest advisers, and a few moderate Republicans were satisfied that they had chosen the right course, and even most of them freely acknowledged that they would only resort to such an authority in time of emergency. What none of the participants could forsee in 1909 was that the divisions that had plagued the Congressional Republicans during that portentious special session would lead to the temporary disintegration of the anti-income tax forces in several key states.

CHAPTER III

THE CHRONOLOGY OF RATIFICATION

The ratification process of the income tax amendment consumed just over three years and seven months. Because the amendment was proposed after most state legislatures had completed their 1909 sessions and because most legislatures met only biennially, nearly a year and a half ensued before the majority of the states had an opportunity to consider the measure. However, this delay proved beneficial to the amendment's chances because the 1910 elections generally placed political elements sympathetic to the measure in command in most states, resulting in twenty-one ratifications in less than six months. The following year produced only four additional ratifications, as few legislatures were in session, but the 1912 elections further enhanced the strength of pro-income tax forces. Once the newly elected legislatures convened in January, 1913, it took less than one month to produce the necessary number of ratifications. Because there were just forty-six states in 1909, the amendment required favorable action by thirty-five of them. The admission of Arizona and New Mexico in 1912 raised the necessary number to thirty-six, but materially aided the cause of the amendment by adding two certain ratifications. In the end, the measure was approved by forty-two state legislatures and rejected by only six -- Virginia, Florida, Utah, Pennsylvania, Connecticut, and Rhode Island.[1]

Determination of the number of ratifications was confused and complicated by the problem of state legislatures reversing their original actions. There were a number of states that first rejected the measure one or more times and then ratified it in the same or a subsequent session.

New York, Vermont, Massachusetts, West Virginia, New Jersey, New Hampshire, Maine, and Arkansas all rejected the amendment at least once before granting approval. Maine actually rejected the amendment in the morning and then ratified it later the same day, for reasons to be considered later. Arkansas' original rejection caused such a reaction among pro-income tax Democrats in Washington that they unleashed a star-studded lobbying campaign that converted a sizeable number of the state's lawmakers. Governor George W. Donaghey, who had opposed the amendment in his annual message to the legislature, attempted to veto the ratification resolution, but the U.S. Secretary of State's office certified Arkansas' compliance. In the other states that moved from rejection to ratification, ensuing elections significantly altered the legislature's makeup and the political climate. In Kentucky, on the other hand, the legislature first ratified the amendment by an overwhelming margin in January, 1910. When Republican Governor Augustus O. Willson intervened, however, the state Senate reversed itself on a narrow 17-18 vote. Despite protests by the measure's opponents to the contrary, the Secretary of State certified Kentucky's agreement to the amendment. In the end, the various controversies firmly established two important points: (1) that state governors have no role to play in the ratification process other than submitting the amendment to the legislature and certifying the results, and (2) that a legislature could ratify an amendment no matter how many times it had rejected it, but that it could not rescind a ratification once given.[2]

Given the amendment's origins, most commentators were highly skeptical of the possibilities of ratification in 1909. A typical analysis was that of the Birmingham Age-Herald, a progressive Democratic organ. Noting that "deservedly popular" reputation of the income tax, the Age-Herald doubted that a majority of the people of twelve states could be found to oppose ratification and insisted that its defeat "cannot be accepted as a foregone conclusion." But the editors warned that there were powerful individuals within a number of states who could easily thwart the will of the majority, especially those who had substantial incomes and those who benefited most from a high protective tariff. Consequently, the Age-Herald concluded, political insiders in Washington were already counting the New England states, Pennsylvania, New York, Delaware, and New Jersey as sure defeats, and betting that at least two others would surface among the remainder of wealthy, industrial states. The reformist magazine World's Work, published by future Ambassador to Great Britain Walter Hines Pages, was equally pessimistic, counting New York, Pennsylvania, West Virginia, New Jersey, and the New England states as sure stumbling blocks. Tax expert and income tax advocate K.K. Kennan of Wisconsin warned that considerations outside of the desirability of the tax itself, such as states rights and eastern hostility to federal expenditures in the West, could defeat the amendment. He regarded New York, Rhode Island, Vermont, Connecticut, New Hampshire, New Jersey, Pennsylvania, and Delaware as sure negatives, with Virginia, Maine, Louisiana, and Ohio as "doubtful."[3]

The most detailed prediction of the amendment's doom was that of Professor James Woodburn of Cornell University writing in the Independent. The measure, according to Woodburn, bore a double burden because it would be difficult enough to get three-fourths of the states to agree to any amendment, but especially one that would be heavily under attack from the "moneyed interests." Three-fourths of the people, he argued, could easily favor this change in the taxation system and still be unable to effect ratification because state legislatures were not representative of their interest. Woodburn insisted, echoing the arguments of the income tax's Congressional proponents, that the amendment would stand a far better chance if it were being considered by popular conventions "as the astute managers of the U.S. Senate, who arranged for its submission, very well understood." As it was, he contended, the amendment would face powerful opposition in the eastern states "not by the masses of the people in these states -- but by a few rich individuals and corporate interests." The undemocratic nature of the legislative process forced Woodburn to fear for the life of the proposal because twenty state senators could defeat ratification in Rhode Island, eighteen in Connecticut, and only thirteen in New Hampshire. Closing on a pessimistic note, Woodburn flatly predicted the defeat of the amendment and admonished supporters of the income tax that their only real hope lay in electing representatives to Congress who would vote for a statutory income tax.[4]

But easily the most prescient analysis of the amendment's chances was that given by one of its staunchest opponents, the New York _Times_. Consistently stigmatizing the income tax as a plot of the poor against the rich and of the West and South against the East with a passion that sometimes bordered on fanaticism, the _Times_ filled its editorial pages with denunciations of the amendment for over three years. Yet, in an extended analysis on August 15, 1909, the paper candidly assessed the forces for and against ratification and rendered a cautious and balanced prediction. On the surface, the _Times_ began, the portents favored the amendment's proponents because there were more of them, because there was no time limit on ratificaion, and because a state could ratify eventually even if it had previously rejected the measure. But the paper predicted a long delay because "there is no organization among the income taxers, but among the opponents of such a tax, especially in certain of the Eastern States, there is not only a compact organization, in a business sense, but there is also a practical control of the dominant political organization of the State that is almost certain to prevent ratification." In the long run, the Times argued, organization always triumphs as it would be easier for party leaders to nominate anti-income tax candidates than it would be for pro-income tax people to gain control of the party machinery. "It is perfectly natural that the great fight over the proposed amendment would be in the East," the Times acknowledged, because the organizations of both parties in New England and the Middle Atlantic states were dominated by people who "detest the thought of an income tax."[5]

Admitting that there was no doubt that the amendment would be ratified by popular referendum because the poor outnumbered the rich, the Times frankly asserted that "the hope of the opponents of the amendment lies thus in the provision of the Congressional resolution submitting it to the action of the several Legislatures." Even more candidly, the paper flatly acknowledged that several northeastern states would defeat the measure because of the "powerful influence of strong manufacturing elements" and because of the "control over the political organizations which they exercise." Even in such southern states as Alabama, Florida, and Louisiana, the Times opined, there were "certain influences as work," namely eastern investment capital. It also deemed California as doubtful because of the influence of the Harriman interests and Wyoming because of the strength of the Republican organization. In summation, the Times foresaw two strong forces working in unison against ratification: the "interests" and the political organizations favorable to those interests, especially within the Republican Party. "Thus the situation as a whole is very complex," the paper concluded, "with the circumstances generally in favor of ratification of the amendment, but owing to the special vigor of the opposition, the prospects are somewhat on its side."[6]

Because few legislatures were still in session in late July of 1909, the amendment was considered by only three states. Alabama, the poorest state in the Union, quickly ratified on August 10, with a unanimous vote in both houses at the urging of reform Democratic Governor Braxton Bragg Comer. This quick action encouraged the amendment's proponents, but Alabama was a poor southern state controlled completely by Democrats and therefore expected to ratify. Their jubilation was short-lived because Georgia, a state with much the same economic and political makeup, refused to consider the measure until the next session of the legislature. The New York Times was overjoyed at Georgia's action, insisting that it seriously damaged the automatic assumption that all states controlled by Democrats would ratify. But the paper also reminded its readers that there was no time limit and that a state could ratify at any time, regardless of previous action. On August 12, the Connecticut Senate unanimously accepted the recommendation of its Committee on Federal Relations that the ratification question be postponed to the next session. This brief flurry of activity in 1909 heartened the amendment's opponents who claimed, publicly at least, that the measure had enjoyed one victory and suffered two defeats. The Times downplayed the significance of Alabama's ratification and applauded

Georgia for returning to "old time Democracy." Confidently, the New York paper predicted that other southern states might be expected to emulate Georgia because many of them were beginning to approach eastern states in terms of industrial development.[7]

1910 was a year of modest gains, bitter defeats, and significant controversies for the income tax amendment. Eight new states joined Alabama in the ratification column, beginning with South Carolina on February 19 and Kentucky on February 23. When Illinois, Mississippi, and Oklahoma followed suit in early March, the measure seemed to be gathering momentum. The victory in Illinois seemed especially propitious because the Prairie State was one of the most affluent and industrialized in the nation and was in the hands of a Republican governor and legislature. But, on March 10, the Virginia House of Delegates rejected the ratification resolution, making it clear that the amendment was not going to enjoy unanimous backing among the states of the Southern Democracy. Five days later, the Kentucky Senate, at the urging of Governor Willson, rescinded its ratification by the margin of a single vote. Even though the Blue Grass State was eventually recorded in the affirmative column, the abrupt about-face demonstrated that the opponents of tax were highly influential in the Upper South. Willson gained a strong national following among the tax's opponents, with the New York _Times_ featuring his full page analysis of the amendment and its potential consequences on February 26, 1911. The defeat of the measure in the Louisiana Senate proved that ratification was far from a certainty in all the states of the Deep South.

In the remainder of the states that acted in 1910, the results followed much more predictable lines. The amendment was ratified by Maryland on April 8, by Georgia on July 26, and by Texas on August 16. Although there was significant opposition recorded in the legislatures of the first two states, these three ratifications helped restore confidence in the belief that democratically-controlled lawmaking bodies, especially in the South, would generally be sympathetic. By the same token, the measure suffered fairly predictable defeats in Rhode Island and Massachusetts in late April and early May, reinforcing the notion that Republican New England would be the most difficult region in which to achieve success.[8]

But the most significant struggle of 1910, and the most disappointing defeat, occured in New York. As a subsequent chapter will demonstrate in detail, New York was regarded as the keystone state by both the advocates and the opponents of the income tax amendment. As both the wealthiest and the most populous state in the Union, New York was a microcosm of the struggle between the influential few and the disorganized many. The Empire State was also the home state of many of the principals in the ongoing national income tax debate, such as Joseph Choate, Charles Evans Hughes, and the New York Times, on the negative side, and E.R.A. Seligman, Lawson Purdy, and Elihu Root, on the affirmative side. Their activities for and against ratification in their home state influenced like-minded people elsewhere and the significance of the Empire State guaranteed the intervention of many non-New Yorkers of national stature, such as President Taft, Senator Borah, and William Jennings Bryan. But it was the opposition of New York Republican Governor Charles Evans Hughes, a highly respected reformer, that provided the opposition in New York with its margin of victory in 1910 and touched off a national debate on the question of whether the amendment would empower Congress to tax incomes from state and municipal bonds. Hughes' message opposing ratification on those grounds, on January 4, 1910, was seized upon by all opponents of the income tax, even though the New York Governor insisted that he would favor ratification if income from those sources were exempted. Governors in many other states applauded or disputed Hughes' interpretation, depending largely upon their own orientation toward income taxation, with the chief executives of Rhode Island, Connecticut, South Dakota, Massachusetts, Kentucky, and Arkansas siding with the New Yorker and the governors of New Jersey, Missouri, Washington, Oklahoma, and Florida disagreeing with his argument. Hughes' objection gained so much currency that the proponents of the amendment in Congress felt compelled to debate the issue there and to intervene in the New York ratification process, as a subsequent chapter will demonstrate. With the Democrats strongly behind ratification and the Republicans generally opposed, the debate over the amendment in the New York legislature dragged on for over five months in 1910. In the end, the Senate ratified the measure but a coalition of Democrats and urban Republicans in the Assembly failed on three different occasions to secure a constitutional majority.[9]

The defeat in New York was the low point for the pro-ratification forces. They had mounted a major effort in the most important state and had been bested by an even bigger effort on the part of the measure's opponents. In its first full year of opportunities, the amendment had been ratified by nine states, including Kentucky, and rejected by five states, exclusive of the Blue Grass State. Except for Illinois, all nine of the ratifications had occurred in southern or border states with predominantly Democratic legislatures. The bulk of the defeats had occurred in northeastern, urban, industrial states controlled by Republicans. The biggest shocks had clearly come in Virginia and Louisiana, states that much more clearly resembled those ratifying than they did those rejecting. The measure had also been postponed in New Jersey and Ohio, despite strong endorsements by their respective governors, Republican John Franklin Fort and Democrat Judson Harmon. More importantly for the future, however, were two interrelated conditions: (1) the amendment had yet to be considered by fully two-thirds of the states, including nearly all of the midwestern and western ones where it was expected to receive overwhelming support, and (2) that much would depend upon the outcome of the 1910 elections, especially since Regular Republicans were under heavy attack from both within and without the party in nearly every section of the country.[10]

In a post-election assessment, the New York Times found that in twelve states -- Ohio, Maine, Iowa, New Hampshire, Indiana, Wisconsin, Montana, Kansas, Idaho, Nevada, North Dakota, and Colorado -- the amendment had been endorsed by both parties. In eight other states, it had been endorsed by the Democrats -- Connecticut, Pennsylvania, Massachusetts, Rhode Island, Vermont, Minnesota, and Tennessee -- although the party was hopelessly without influence in the first six states. In California and Utah, the victorious Republican Party had officially favored ratification. Since all but four of the nation's legislatures would be in session in 1911, the year certainly promised to be a critical one for the fate of the amendment. Frightened by the number of endorsements and by the election returns, the Times called for "some firm check of reason and of leadership" to prevent ratification, particularly since

Charles Evans Hughes' appointment to the Supreme Court precluded any further involvement by him in the debate. Properly, or with exaggeration, the paper, credited Hughes' argument against the taxation of state and municipal bonds with the rejection or postponement of the amendment in Virginia, Massachusetts, Rhode Island, New Jersey, and Ohio, as well as New York.[11]

For the Times and other opponents of the income tax amendment, the 1910 elections were a virtual disaster. Nearly everywhere, the elections resulted in serious setbacks for those political organizations, chiefly the Regular Republicans, whose leaders, as the Times had earlier asserted, "detest the thought of an income tax." In the West and Midwest, Insurgent Republicans generally strengthened their hold on party machinery, on executive mansions, on states houses, and on Congressional delegations. In the Northeast, on the other hand, 1910 was a banner Democratic year, one that ranked with 1882, 1890, and 1892. In New York, Ohio, Indiana, and Maine, the Democrats captured control of the governorship of both houses of the legislature. In the latter state it was the first Democratic sweep since 1880. In New Jersey and Connecticut the governorship and one legislative house changed hands. Even where the Republicans retained control, as in Pennsylvania, New Hampshire, Vermont, and Rhode Island, it was by greatly reduced margins. In Rhode Island, the governor's plurality had been reduced from 12,000 in 1908 to 1200 in 1910. The New York Times headed its major election story "the Democratic Party carried the Union yesterday." In an editorial entitled "The Political Revolution", the paper proclaimed that "from Eastport to the Indiana border, broken only by a corner of New Hampshire and by Pennsylvania's Erie frontage, stretches a broad belt of Democratic territory."[12]

Although local conditions obviously played a role in several states, most analysts found the major cause of this political upheaval in the widespread desire of voters to "punish the Republican Party" in the belief, rational or irrational, that the high protective tariff was responsible for the escalating cost of living and for the construction of trusts. The Kansas City Star, published by progressive Republican William Rockhill Nelson and loyal to Theodore Roosevelt, roundly scored the Taft administration for the Payne-Aldrich Tariff and the consequent failure to bring consumers relief form the high cost of living. In Maine, according to The Nation, Republican congressmen who had voted for the Payne-Aldrich Tariff were "savagely heckled by the most direct and awkward questions," most of which related to taxing necessities at a higher rate than luxuries. Such an outlook was certainly conducive to the adoption of a federal income tax partially designed to undermine that very protective tariff system.[13]

Although 1911 opened with Vermont, one of the states where the Regular Republicans retained control, rejecting the amendment on January 17, the promise of the 1910 election was soon realized in a rash of ratifications. In the remaining two weeks of January, Ohio, Idaho, Oregon, Washington, Indiana, Montana, California, and Nevada all ratified, nearly all of them with little or no recorded opposition. February saw Nebraska, North Carolina, Colorado, North Dakota, Kansas, Michigan, and Iowa follow suit, again with almost no discernible opposition, making fifteen ratifications in a little over a month. The victory parade was interrupted in March when Utah and New Hampshire rejected the measure, but Missouri became the twenty-fifth state to ratify on March 18, 1911. The New Jersey Senate refused to concur with the favorable action of the Assembly on March 29, but Maine, after flirting with the idea of substituting a state income tax, ratified two days later. On April 7, Tennessee approved the measure and, on the 22nd, Arkansas reversed its earlier position and became the twenty-eighth state to concur. By May, the ratification trend apparently reached the end of its post-election momentum as Wisconsin's ratification was more than offset by defeats or postponements in West Virginia, Florida, Massachusetts, Rhode Island, Pennsylvania, and Connecticut. In all but the latter state, the Senate negated a highly favorable vote in the lower house. In all four northeastern states the contest pitted Democrats and urban Republicans against besieged Regular Republican organizations.[14]

But 1911 ended on a triumphal note for the advocates of the income tax, as New York reversed its 1910 action and ratified in July. The key was clearly Democratic control of the governorship and the legislature. The party platform strongly backed ratification and Governor John A. Dix and the Democratic leadership in both houses pulled out all the stops to achieve that goal. They engaged the services of such diverse Democrats as William Randolph Hearst and William Jennings Bryan and whipped recalcitrant members of their party into line through the use of the caucus. The struggle evoked nearly as much national attention as had that of the 1910 session, but the outcome was significantly different. On April 19, the Senate ratified on a largely partisan vote, but the contest in the Assembly consumed nearly three additional months. Finally, on July 12, New York became the thirtieth and most critical state to ratify the income tax amendment, prefiguring the trend that was to push it over the top in 1913.[15]

Ratification in New York capped a generally successful year for the amendment. Even though twelve states had either rejected or posponed the measure, twenty-one had signified their compliance. More importantly, the measure had made inroads into the supposedly impregnable industrial Northeast, securing ratification in Maine, Indiana, Ohio, and, most significantly, New York, states where the Democrats had captured control of both houses of the legislature and of the governorship. The pro-income tax World's Work concluded that the amendment "has not done so badly" and predicted its ultimate triumph in 1913. Reiterating its belief in the general popularity of a federal income tax, the magazine noted that in most of the states that had rejected the amendment, at least one house had already voted heavily in favor of ratification. The progressive Republican The Outlook reluctantly drew the same general conclusion, noting that there were only three states -- Rhode Island, Vermont, and Conecticut -- where both houses had rejected the amendment.[16]

The following year, 1912, was one of recess, so far as most legislatures were concerned, but it did produce a net gain for the advocates of ratification. Although Rhode Island, Massachusetts, and Virginia again refused assent, and New York Republicans attempted to undo ratification, four additional states joined the ranks of the measure's supporters. On February 3, South Dakota ratified the amendment unanimously, and, on April 6, Arizona, newly admitted to the Union, followed suit with equal enthusiasm. Minnesota certified its agreement on April 6 and, on June 28, Louisiana reversed its negative position of two years earlier. By July 1, 1912, the income tax amendment had received the favorable votes of thirty-four states and the prospects for ratification seemed bright, especially after the results of the 1912 elections.[17]

The 1912 elections completed the disintegration of the Regular Republican organizations that had begun in 1910. Aided greatly by the Republican-Progressive split and by the vagaries of the electoral college system, Woodrow Wilson forged what the New York Times called "the most tremendous victory ever cast in the political history of America." Although receiving less than forty-five percent of the popular vote, Wilson carried forty states with 435 electoral votes, about eighty-three percent of the total. President Taft, by contrast, garnered only about one-quarter of the popular vote, carrying Vermont and Utah with eight electoral votes, while Theodore Roosevelt captured nearly one-third of the popular vote and six states with eighty-eight electoral votes. The Socialist candidate, Eugene V. Debs, garnered nearly one million popular votes. In Congress, the Democrats enjoyed their most sweeping victory since 1892, winning a seventy three seat edge in the House and a six seat margin in the Senate. Such organization stalwarts as "Uncle Joe" Cannon, Ebeneezer Hill, John Dalzell, Nicholas Longworth, Samuel McCall, Charles Southwick, and William Calderhead were not returned to the House and Democratic majorities in several state legislatures doomed the Senatorial careers of several others. Such normally Republican states as Iowa, Connecticut, Indiana, Ohio, Massachusetts, Michigan, Nebraska, Illinois and Washington elected Democratic governors. In Massachusetts it was the first time that the Democrats had elected both state and national tickets since 1854. Wilson was the first Democratic presidential candidate to carry Rhode Island since 1852, even though the G.O.P. retained control of the state. In New York the voters soundly repudiated the Republicans at both the national and state levels, electing a Congressional delegation that was Democratic, a state Senate of the same persuasion 33-17-1, and an Assembly of that orientation 104-45-5. Even such "rock-ribbed Republican counties as Monroe and Onandaga", according to the Times, fell to the Democrats, but the latter's greatest support came in New York City, Buffalo, and other urban centers. More importantly, the Regular Republicans lost control of the state legislatures in New Jersey, Massachusetts, Delaware, Vermont, New Hampshire, Wyoming, West Virginia, and New Mexico, eight states that had either refused or postponed ratification. Only in drastically malapportioned Connecticut and Rhode Island did the Regular Republicans retain control of both legislative houses. In Pennsylvania they continued to dominate the Senate, even though Roosevelt and the progressive Washington Party carried most of the state's other offices. So complete was the Republican rout that the staunchly G.O.P. New York Sun headlined its election story "the End of Republican Rule", while the chairman of the most nascent Progressive Party, Senator Joseph M. Dixon of Montana, prematurely predicted that the Republicans had become a third party.[18]

Since the Democrats, Progressives, and Socialists were committed to ratification, it could be argued, however tangentially, that better than three-fourths of the nation's voters and a clear majority in at least forty-five states had clearly registered pro-income tax sentiments. Such prominent Democrats as Congressman Cordell Hull, Mayor John F. Fitzgerald of Boston, and Governor Edward F. Dunne of Illinois, among others, confidently linked the Democratic victory to ratification. Even many anti-income tax periodicals all but conceded ratification, while the Liberal British journal Living Age predicted that adoption of the income tax would provide "an engine which wil make the Government at Washington financially secure." Equipped with an income tax, the periodical reasoned, the Democrats "will be able to keep the tariff within strict bounds, and so relieve the consumer of certain irksome dues which have been largely buttressed by the contention that the revenue must be safeguarded." Along with most other observers, Living Age concluded that "the people of the United States have clearly condemned it [a high protective tariff] and marked it as the main cause of high prices and the mother of trusts." The nation's voters had rendered as clear a judgment as the vagaries of the American political process permit against the party that they associated with the high cost of living and with favoritism toward the organized and the affluent, conditions that a federal income tax was purportedly designed to counteract.[19]

Of the fourteen states that had not ratified, three were southern or border states that had already rejected the measure -- West Virginia, Virginia, and Florida. Three were western states -- New Mexico, Wyoming, and Utah. Of these, the first two had taken no position, since New Mexico had just been admitted and Wyoming had postponed consideration in 1911. Utah had defeated the amendment in the same year. In both the latter cases, the refusal to ratify could be attributed largely to the influence of Republican organizations headed by Standpat U.S. Senators, Francis Warren in Wyoming and Reed Smoot in Utah. The remaining eight states were all in the Northeast and all still under the partial or complete control of Regular Republican organizations that had survived the Democratic surge of 1910. Although Delaware and Pennsylvania had merely postponed consideration in 1911, the others -- Vermont, New Hampshire, Rhode Island, Connecticut, Massachusetts, and New Jersey, had already rejected the amendment at least once. Together with New York, these eight states constituted the geographical, economic, and political core of the expected resistance to ratification. The defection of New York, the Democratic resurgence of 1910, and the growing split between Progressives and Regulars had severely strained the ability of the Republican organizations in these states to fend off ratification, but they were determined to do so for as long as they could. Those who "detest the thought of an income tax" were not expected to yield, unless they had lost control of their respective state governments in the 1912 elections. Proponents of the amendment were reasonably sure of securing the necessary number of states from among the western or southern states but advocates of the federal income tax within those northeastern states were determined to record their legislatures in favor of ratification. While the income tax amendment was not a crucial issue in the momentous 1912 elections, the results did give the measure the impetus it needed in all but six states.[20]

With the possible exceptions of Virginia and Florida, the eventual fate of the amendment in the remaining fourteen states was largely a function of the election results. In those state where the Regular Republican organizations, aided significantly by legislative malapportionment, were able to maintain control of at least one lawmaking house, the amendment did not succeed, namely Utah, Connecticut, Rhode Island, and Pennsylvania. In New Jersey and Massachusetts, where the Democrats gained control of the governorship and both legislative houses, ratification quickly ensued.

In West Virginia, Delaware, New Hampshire, New Mexico, and Wyoming, the elections produced majority Democrat-Progressive coalitions that were able to force ratification on temporarily disabled Republican organizations. In Vermont, the Regular Republicans included ratification among the concessions tht they made to the insurgents in their own party in order to retain control of the governorship. In Florida and Virginia, where politics was strictly a contest among Democratic factions, the outcome of the elections failed to generate any fresh support for ratification. The Florida house unanimously approved the ratification resolution on May 21, repeating its action of 1911. The Senate once again killed the measure in comittee, however.[21]

The sweeping Democratic victory of November 5, 1912 caused even the New York Times to concede that the amendment would be ratified before Woodrow Wilson's presidential inauguration on March 4, 1913. Because the Democrats also gained a commanding lead in both houses of Congress, most observers also predicted that the federal government would not wait for an emergency, but move immediately to utilize its newly acquired authority. In a speech to the annual conference of the National Housing Association on December 5, 1912, Democratic Mayor John F. Fitzgerald of Boston promised the delegates that the early passages of a federal income tax by Congress would provide greatly increased funds to facilitate the enactment of a variety of social welfare programs. Other income tax proponents, such a Democratic Congressman Cordell Hull and Insurgent Republican Senator Norris Brown were already unveiling their own income tax proposals before the necessary number of states had ratified. Those who had advocated ratification with the qualification that Congress should only resort to the tax in times of emergency, such as President Taft and Senator Root, were already beginning to raise objections.[22]

Despite all the portents of certain and rapid ratification, the measure's opponents refused to give in easily. Even though the Pennsylvania house had already approved ratification, the Senate accepted the recommendation of the Comittee on Judiciary Special that the resolution "do not pass" on January 28, 1913. But, on January 31, West Virginia reversed its 1911 action, favoring the amendment by unanimous vote in both houses. Since only one more state was necessary, Delaware, Wyoming, New Mexico, and New Jersey engaged in a vigorous four cornered contest to become the determining state. At 10:55 a.m. on February 3, Delaware became the thirty-sixth state to ratify, edging Wyoming and New Mexico for the honor by a few hours. The following day, the New Jersey Senate, on a nearly perfectly partisan 12-9 vote, made the Garden State the thirty-ninth to concur. But even the existence of a fait accompli did not end the battle between the proponents and opponents of the federal income tax in a number of states. The principle involved was too strongly held for either side to acquiesce, whatever the eventual outcome. The measure's advocates wanted to share in the victory and its antagonists were equally desirous of permanently recording their state's refusal. Although there was evidence of a "bandwagon effect" in Wyoming and Delaware, everywhere else the established lines of conflict remained hard and fast. When the Vermont Senate concurred in ratification on February 18, eleven regular Republicans refused to join their thirteen affirming colleagues. In the New Hampshire Senate the following day the vote was 20-2. In Massachusetts the majority Democrats forced the measure through both houses on February 27 and March 4 without a recorded vote. In Florida, the Senate accepted the negative report of the Committee on Federal Relations on May 27. In Rhode Island and Connecticut, the still commanding Republican organizations of General Charles R. Brayton and J. Henry Roraback refused to give in to the minority Democrats on the issue. All told, forty-two of the nation's forty-eight states eventually gave their assent to the Sixteenth Amendment.[23]

In order to understand the forces and patterns at work during the ratification contest and to comprehend the reasons for the amendment's ultimate victory, it is necessary to consider the comparative experience of the measure in the nation's three major regions - the West, the South, and the Northeast. It is to that task that we must turn in the next four chapters.

CHAPTER IV

TRIUMPH IN THE WEST

The region west of the Mississippi River was friendly territory, so far as the federal income tax amendment was concerned. The initial enactment of the tax during the Civil War had been largely in response to the demands of westerners. It was primarily through western efforts that the tax was retained after Appomattox. During the next twenty years western representatives had bombarded Congress with petitions and proposals for the reenactment of a federal income tax, only to have them quickly strangled. Western votes coalesced with southern ones to add the abortive income tax section to the Wilson-Gorman Tariff in 1894, and the most dramatic appeal for the tax had come from the conventions of the western-dominated Populist Party at Omaha in 1892 and St. Louis in 1896. Western congressmen also generally pushed for immediate enactment of the income tax in 1909, only to see their efforts frustrated again by the influential eastern wing of the Republican Party. The latter all but conceded favorable action on the amendment in the West while its advocates realized they would need the votes of every single western state to offset likely defeats in the eastern half of the nation. In the end, the amendment swept every western state but Utah. The region supplied exactly half the votes necessary to effect ratification.[1]

The trans-Mississippi West, with its fertile plains, mountain ranges, great deserts, and Pacific Coastal region was hardly a section in any geographic sense. The economic interests of its farmers, miners, fishermen, cattlemen, sheepherders, and lumbermen were far from identical and, at times, were competitive. Yet most westerners, whatever their location or occupation, shared a similar economic condition and professed a common regional outlook that united them in support of a federal income tax. With 20.3 percent of the population and 21.1 percent of the nation's income, the West had by far the most even distribution of income in the nation. The great bulk of that income was received by people whose intake had derived only 6.5 percent of their total revenue from the inhabitants of western states. Missouri and California residents provided nearly three-fourths of that amount.[2]

The West contained only twelve people with incomes in excess of one million dollars per year, and six of those were in Oklahoma. By contrast, New York alone had 119, Pennsylvania 19, Illinois 14, and several other eastern states had six or more. The region contained only 666 people with incomes over $100,000 a year; over two-thirds of those resided in California, Oklahoma, Missouri, Minnesota and Colorado. New York alone had 2,234 such people, Pennsylvania 760, Massachusetts 570, Illinois 500, and Ohio 351.

Thirteen western states had no one with an income over one million dollars, and three had none over $100,000. Except for California and Washington, no western state equalled the national average of people with incomes over $10,000 per year. Only about one-half of one percent of westerners received over $10,000 a year. In North Dakota and New Mexico that figure was only two-tenths of one percent. The Mountain States, according to Maurice Leven and Willford I. King, authors of the most thorough study of income distribution by states, "seem to present the least concentration of income in the highest income classes." Only .4 percent of their inhabitants exceeded the $10,000 figure and they received only 4.3 percent of the area's income, in contrast to the national figures of .7 percent and 9.9 percent, respectively. The Plains States also fell well below the national averages in this regard, while the Pacific Coast had .9 percent of its residents over $10,000 a year but taking in only 8.8 percent of its income.[3]

The same general pattern prevailed for incomes over $5,000. Nationally 1.9 percent of income receivers were over that mark and they took in 14.8 of the national income. The Plains States exactly duplicated the national average for people with such incomes, but they accounted for only 12.3 percent of the region's intake. The Mountain States were again the most evenly distributed in the nation, with the 1.7 percent over $5,000 taking in only nine percent of the area's income. The Pacific Coast States were almost a full percentage point over the national average in number of people over $5,000, but right at the national figure for percent of income received. In the Middle Atlantic States an almost identical percentage of people with incomes over $5,000 took in over one-fifth of the region's total. In short, even with the prosperous Pacific Coast states included, the West as a whole had the most evenly distrubuted income in the nation and a correspondingly low number of people with any great stake in preventing ratification.[4]

The largest occupational groups in the western states were far below any liability for income taxation. Less than two percent of the nation's farmers had incomes in excess of $2,000 and estimates for farm laborers ranged from a "rather absurd" low of $102 to a high of $651. Farm income was also very difficult to calculate accurately, and much easier to conceal than the land, buildings, and machinery that bore the burden of the property tax. Miners, fishermen, lumberjacks, cowboys, and sheepherders rarely received money income much greater than that of farm workers. Significantly, residents of the West received only about twenty percent of the nation's income from dividends and interest, one of the prime targets of income tax advocates. Mountain States' citizens realized only about two percent of income from dividends and interest. New Yorkers alone exceeded the share of the entire West, while the residents of northeastern states took in about sixty percent of the national total.[5]

This regional disparity in the nation's income contributed to a growing feeling among nearly all westerners that their section was an economic colony of the industrial and financial Northeast. The region had been settled largely by easterners and developed by their capital and technology. "Extractive natural resources industries" -- farming, lumber, fishing, mining, cattle and sheet -- "were the very foundation of the economy," according to Gerald Nash. The processing of these products was done almost entirely east of the Mississippi, except for a few sugar beet refineries in Utah, some flour mills in Minnesota, and a handful of meat packing plants. The railroads on which the goods were shipped were largely controlled by eastern financers. Shipping costs often shrunk profit margins drastically. With few exceptions, western states ranked in the bottom half of the nation in value added by manufacturing, the best index of who benefits most in the industrial process. The West added but 14.6 percent to the value of the nation's products and only a handful of the region's states exceeded one percent. Efforts to develop its own manufacturing centers faced severe handicaps because of the lack of skill and capital, the relatively small local market, and the tremendous transportation costs to populous eastern outlets. As a result, westerners were primarily producers of raw materials and consumers of finished products, colonists whose "mother country" was east of the Mississippi. "The West," according to Nash "became prey to the more highly industrial East, which had the capital, the markets, and the skills to utilize many of the region's natural riches."[6]

This western feeling of colonialism was more than just economic and embraced the region's entire outlook. The West looked to the East as its source of settlers. It copied the customs, fads, and styles of the older section, and felt unable to develop any distinctive culture. Nor were western Congressmen a sufficiently powerful independednt force to combat exploitation or secure federal help. Even such westerners as Reed Smoot, Thomas Carter, or Francis Warren, who had achieved substantial political power and status, were but "junior partners in the national establishment," that was dominated by northeastern Republicans. "This heavy dependence of the West on the East," Nash has demonstrated, "also cultivated a state of mind among many westerners, a psychological outlook that had many of the earmarks of a love-hate relationship." Painfully aware of their dependency, yet resenting it bitterly, and struggling for greater independence in all aspects of life, westerners "exhibited typical characteristics of colonials." This anti-colonial feeling broke down many of the internal class and ethnic barriers, directing western anger outward at the Northeast. Much of the ferment of the Populist-Progressive years in the West was animated by a desire to rid the region of anything that smacked of eastern domination and to establish economic, political and cultural independence. "For more than a decade and a half,"

Carl Chrislock has observed of Minnesota, "this combination of idealistic discontent and regional frustration contained-but did not overcome-the tensions which stood between grain traders and farmers, employers and workers, main street and the open countryside and, less visibly, between native Americans and recent immigrants."[7]

Although westerners disliked many aspects of the cosmopolitan, polyglot East, they were most concerned about the influence of the special economic interests that exploited their resources. Everywhere during the Populist-Progressive years, westerners railed against "the company," whether it was a railroad such as the Southern Pacific or the Great Northern, a mining company such as the Anaconda, or the Stock Growers Association. Even the San Francisco Chamber of Commerce expressed official concern that the Southern Pacific, with its outside control, was stifling the economic development of California. The Non-Partisan League earned the support of wheat farmers in the Dakotas and Minnesota by branding local grain brokers, merchants, bankers and stock buyers as agents of eastern "Big Biz." Insurgents in Congress blamed the West's economic woes variously on the "trusts," the "money power," the "invisible government," and the "interests." Whatever the sobriquet, western spokesmen agreed that eastern industrialists and financiers were the chief cause of the region's unhappy condition and that the West should be a major beneficiary of remedial efforts. It is significant that while westerners had sought a federal income tax since the Civil War, almost no western state had enacted its own income tax, despite the growing popularity of such measures. The target was clearly eastern wealth, not that of the relatively few prosperous residents of their own region. With their Texas counterparts, most westerners were "disturbed at foreign concerns" whose non-resident owners limited opportunity for indigenous enterprises. What westerners were after, as Colorado agriculture professor and political reformer Edwin F. Ladd put it, was "the two percent of the people with their sixty-five percent of the wealth of the country."[8] This anti-special interest emphasis was the most potent force in western politics from the 1890s on. It provided much of the rhetoric and symbolism for Populist and Progressive successes. Although the reformist impulse in the West was varigated, the discontented focused primarily upon the problems of corporate domination and special interests. There was no universal agreement on who "the interests" or "the people" were in any given situation, but it was generally agreed that anyone connected with eastern business was on the side of the exploiters. Prior to the Populist revolt, most western states were controlled by tightly-knit political organizations run by allies of the dominant economic interests. Most often, these organizations were Republican and run by the state's senior U.S. Senator and his closest allies. The relative success of the Populists, however, made western politicians leery of being connected too closely with the forces of eastern finance. A few, such as Francis Warren in Wyoming, were able to accommodate the Populists and still remain cogs in the Aldrich organization, but "his good fortune was unique," as David Rothman has noted. Most western politicians saw that the key to personal political success lay in projecting the image of being against "the company," and they reacted accordingly. Albert Cummins in Iowa, Walter Stubbs in Kansas, Coe Crawford in South Dakota, Edward Costigan in Colorado, George Sheldon in Nebraska, and Hiram Johnson in California used the anti-special interest issue to wrest leadership of their party organizations from the Old Guard. On the Pacific Coast, the anti-interest forces generally captured Republican Party organizations after a bitter struggle, turning them into vehicles for Insurgency. In the Mountain states, it was more common for such groups to work through the Democrats and to unseat the G.O.P. by the second decade of the century. "By 1908 Progressive Republicans and a few progressive Democrats controlled the Midwest," Blaine Nye has concluded, "and, with occasional setbacks, kept control until 1914."[9]

John Johnson, the progressive Democratic governor of Minnesota, a former Populist, and a Swedish immigrant, probably best expressed the political mood of the West in a 1906 speech to a group of midwestern businessmen:

> New York, with its vice, and New England with its virtue to balance the ledger, today control the economic policy of the nation. The time has come to transfer the seat of the empire across the Adirondacks, to Illinois, to Indiana, Michigan, Ohio, Kentucky, Iowa, Minnesota, Wisconsin, Kansas, Nebraska, Missouri and the Dakotas. The best brain and surest brawn of the nation is found here and it should be organized into one mighty moral material and patriotic force to overthrow paternalism and plunder and regenerate politics and the Republic.[10]

William Borah voiced a similar sentiment on the floor of the U.S. Senate, when he proposed to save the nation from the clutches of the urban, industrial colossus by "the supply of brain and brawn and muscle and manhood and citizenship" from "the great rural precincts of the country." It was clearly this rescue of the nation from Eastern mammon by the virtuous West that most westerners saw as the meaning of progressivism and it was this conviction that led them to support such remedial measures as tariff revision, anti-trust legislation, the Federal Reserve Act, and tax reform. In this context, overwhelming western support for a federal income tax was a foregone conclusion.[11]

Western sympathy for the measure was fortified considerably because it was the one region in the nation that openly sought federal aid for its development. The only feasible way to develop western resources without becoming more beholden to eastern finance was to tap the federal treasury. Washington was the only source capable of meeting the West's financial needs for developmental capital, as Samuel P. Hays and Nash have shown. Such a course was difficult for a frontier society that loudly proclaimed the virtues of self-help and rugged individualism, but westerners, like most people driven by necessity, were able to resolve the contradiction to their own satisfaction.

"Despite loud protestations of individualism," Nash has noted, "government had a crucial role to play in the further development of the country." In 1894 Joseph Carey of Wyoming authored a law that granted western states public lands to sell in order to finance irrigation projects. In 1902 Francis Newlands of Nevada fathered a federal irrigation law that created a Reclamation Fund from the proceeds of public lands to provide developmental capital, and in 1911 the Bureau of Reclamation was established. Cattlemen succeeded, in 1901, in having the Division of Animal Husbandry created in the Department of Agriculture. The increasingly important tourist industry was given a tremendous boost by the creation of national parks and monuments. Their establishment also kept outsiders from further depleting the region's timber and mineral resources. Western spokesmen, such as Kansas editor William Allen White, frequently asserted that the most pressing need was for federal expenditures to finance "internal improvements under expert direction," while working also for increased spending on education and conservation. From then until the present day, most western states have received considerably more federal money than they have paid in the form of taxes, the reverse of the situation in the eastern states. Indeed, eastern opponents of the federal income tax amendment frequently countered the argument of increased revenue needs by charging that the money would be spent in the West. Clearly the West, more than any other region, had expectations of immediate increases in federal expenditures. Its spokesmen urged the income tax openly as a device to raise the necessary revenue.[12]

The West's relatively even distribution of income, then, coupled with a widespread reaction against colonialism and special interests, along with anticipation of burgeoning federal expenditures, led to overwhelming support for the ratification of the Sixteenth Amendment. The measure found its greatest favor in the underdeveloped Mountain States, but the Pacific Coast and the Great Plains were close behind. Based upon the evidence of roll call votes, the region's urban representatives were as supportive as those from small town and rural areas. The issue united professionals, businessmen, organized labor, miners, farmers, ranchers, fishermen and lumbermen. What opposition there was in the state legislatures was scattered, formed no discernible geographic, economic, or partisan pattern and generally has to be charged to the personal views of particular lawmakers. If any organized opposition to ratification existed west of the Mississippi, it almost never surfaced and enjoyed real political effectiveness only in Utah, and, to a much lesser extent, in Kansas and Wyoming.

So all pervasive was support for the Sixteenth Amendment in the West that six states--Nebraska, South Dakota, Idaho, Montana, Nevada, and Arizona--ratified it by unanimous votes in both houses of the legislature. In terms of income, these states were among the least concentrated of any in the nation, having only thirty-five residents with incomes in excess of $100,000. Less than .4 percent of their inhabitants made as much as $10,000. Not quite two percent earned $5,000. Nevada had the lowest number of eligible taxpayers in the nation, only 364, while Idaho, South Dakota and Arizona had less than a thousand. Each of the six states had originally been dominated economically and politically by outside business interests. Nevada was "an agency of the Southern Pacific and the plaything of San Francisco nabobs" to quote Gilman Ostrander. Montana was ruled by a coalition of stockowners, businessmen, and professional interests, headed by the Northern Pacific Railroad, the First National Bank of New York, Standard Oil, and Anaconda Copper. Arizona was controlled by the Santa Fe and Southern Pacific Railroads, and various mining companies. Each had mounted a successful revolt against this domination, led by such nationally prominent politicians as Coe Crawford of South Dakota,

William Borah of Idaho, Thomas Walsh and Burton K. Wheeler in Montana, Key Pittman and Francis Newlands in Nevada, and George Sheldon Norris in Nebraska, many of whom played a leading role in the 1909 congressional income tax struggle. Their success had left their constituents highly sensitized to questions of economic privilege, all but guaranteeing easy ratification of the Sixteenth Amendment.[13]

The other states in the mountains and on the Great Plains were only slightly less unanimous in their support of the amendment. The ease with which ratification was achieved in New Mexico was somewhat surprising, given its close historic connection with Pennsylvania financial interests and the forces of U.S. Senator Boies Penrose. New Mexico had very few residents who would be personally affected by a federal income tax. Only 813 residents filed returns in 1913, about one percent of the state's income receivers. New Mexico's territorial economy and politics had been dominated, however, by such out-of-state interests as the Pennsylvania Development Company, the Phelps-Dodge Corporation, and the Santa Fe and Southern Pacific Railroads. Conservative Republican U.S. Senators Albert B. Fall and Thomas B. Catron, allies of Penrose, had exercised political hegemony, turning the legislature into "a pit in which the Republican Old Guard conducted its concert of attitudes and interests," according to Jack E. Holmes. Reaction against these conditions crystallized around young Bronson Cutting, a brilliant and affluent New Yorker who had come to the Southwest for his health. Although nominally a Republican, Cutting founded the Progressive-Republican League and the Progressive Party of New Mexico, constructing a bipartisan coalition of laborers, farmers, Mexican-Americans, and professionals that eventually seized political power, mostly on the issue of outside interests. The last gasp of the Old Guard came in the 1911 Constitutional Convention, but Cutting's Democratic- Progressive coalition carried the state the following year on a platform that included support for the income tax amendment. The state's first legislature quickly ratified the measure, with but one dissenting vote in the upper house.[14]

The admission of New Mexico and Arizona to the Union in 1912 added two sure votes for ratification, reducing the number of eastern or southern states necessary for success. There is, however, no evidence that the fate of the income tax amendment played any role in influencing Congressional votes on admission. The enabling legislation was the result of a bipartisan trade off--Democratic Arizona for Republican New Mexico. Beyond that, the major concern was the "radical" constitution drafted by Arizona, containing such innovations as the recall of judges, written by a convention dominated by an anti-mining and railroad slate, and endorsed by the state's labor unions. Its chairman was George Hunt, a wealthy pro-labor reformer who had traveled to California and Oregon to study the workings of direct legislation. The recall provision particularly disturbed President Taft who considered vetoing the enabling legislation, but thought better of it. Hunt was elected the state's first governor in 1912, despite a huge campaign chest raised by the mine and railroad owners for his opponents. The unanimous ratificaiton of the amendment came amidst the passage of several regulatory measures.[15]

Iowa, the home state of Insurgents Cummins and Dolliver, had a higher percentage of potential income tax payers, but was also dominated by an anti-special interest mood. In the last two decades of the nineteenth century, Iowa politics had been dominated by U.S. Senator William B. Allison, director of the Union Pacific Railroad and powerful ally of Nelson Aldrich. In 1900, Cummins, an attorney for the Farmer's Protective Association who had first gained fame by representing various farm organizations against the "barbed wire trust," was elected governor. Cummins had earlier been denied nomination by the Allison Regulars, but built his own constituency on the issues of business regulation, political reform, and tariff revision, popularizing the "Iowa Idea" that no trust should receive protection. Despite the significant opposition of railroads and other corporations, Cummins eventually enacted most of his programs, going on to join the Insurgents in the U.S. Senate. In this atmosphere, the Sixteenth Amendment was ratified unanimously in the lower house of the Iowa General Assembly, but ran into some opposition in the Senate. Henry Adams, a West Union lawyer, moved to postpone consideration, failing by only five votes. Those who favored postponement were lawyers, physicians, bankers, or stock dealers, men who might have had a personal stake in preventing ratification but, who shared no significant geographic or partisan characteristics. Once Adams ploy failed, only three Senators--two small town bankers and a manufacturer of carriages and automobiles--voted in the negative.[16]

In North Dakota, ratification came as consequence of a widespread revolt against the state's railroads, the milling and financial houses of Minneapolis-St. Paul, and the Republican political organization headed by Alexander McKenzie, counsel for the Northern Pacific and U.S. Senator Porter McCumber. For nearly a decade and a half, this revolt united wheat farmers, professionals, and small businessmen against the forces of "Big Biz" and produced a flurry of political and economic legislation.

General antagonism against an outside foe temporarily overcame the cultural differences over prohibition between the native Americans and Scandinavians in the eastern part of the state and the Germans and Russians in the western part. Before the formation of the Non-Partisan League in 1915, sectionalism also contained the differerences between the moderate expectations of the middle class and the much more radical demands of wheat farmers. Eventually the latter, under the leadership of Arthur Townley, William Lemke, and William Langer, went beyond regulation and taxation of business to government ownership, alienating the property-conscious middle class. After failing to capture the Republican Party machinery, dissident elements united behind the gubernatorial candidacy of Democrat "Honest John" Burke, an Irish-American lawyer, in 1906. During his three terms, Burke held together his volatile coalition and produced laws regulating railroads, lobbyists, and corrupt practices. The 1911 legislature, which finally enacted most of Burke's programs, also ratified the Sixteenth Amendment, with but one dissenting vote in each house.[17]

Ratification came with equal ease in Oklahoma, despite the presence of six income receivers with a total intake of almost 30 million dollars. Even with those individuals, and the forty-nine with incomes over $100,000, the state still maintained the typical western pattern of income distribution, having only .4 percent over $10,000 and 1.5 percent over $5,000. This situation had led Oklahomans to incorporate a state income tax in their constitution, one that exempted all of those who made less than $3,500, a clear indication of the attitude of the vast majority of Oklahomans. The state voted heavily for the pro-income tax William Jennings Bryan in 1908, had a strong residual Populist movement led by the colorful

"Alfalfa Bill" Murray, and was to give the highest portion of its popular presidential vote of any state in the nation to Socialist Eugene Debs in 1912. In addition, as Keith L. Bryant has demonstrated, "the voices of social workers, unionists and the lower classes were heard and transmitted into humanitarian reforms." In this atmosphere, the overwhelmingly Democratic legislature ratified the amendment, with only one negative vote cast in the lower house in 1910.[18]

Ratification was scarcely less difficult in Minnesota, even though it was more affluent than the average western state. Minnesota was the "most completely in the grasp of organized business" of any state in the region prior to 1900, with its politics largely dictated by the railroads, the grain millers, and the Chamber of Commerce, as Carl Chrislock has demonstrated. The reaction against this situation began with the non-urban middle class, but quickly spread to the urban counterparts and to organized labor. Their program of tax reform, insurance and banking codes, and business and utilities regulation soon gained the support of grain farmers, iron miners, and Twin Cities Socialists. As they did in North Dakota, the latter groups eventually made more radical demands for state ownership of railroads, mills, and grain elevators, and for labor and welfare legislation, forming the Non-Partisan League, a forerunner of the Farmer-Labor Party that was to dominate the state during the New Deal years.[19]

This break occurred in 1914, though, and the income tax amendment came before the Minnesota legislature at the height of cooperation among the diverse elements of the anti-big business coalition. In 1904 many of these groups had united behind Governor John Johnson whose three terms as governor featured the enactment of regulatory and tax legislation.

Minnesota had begun taxing the earnings of railroads as early as 1901, but Johnson worked for a "wide-open" tax amendment that created a permanent tax commission and an inheritance tax in 1906. These actions demonstrated the willingness of most Minnesotans to tax accumulated wealth, even though a state income tax was not seriously advocated until the 1930s. Johnson's successor, Adolph Eberhardt, was generally accounted a conservative, but was flexible enough to adjust to the demands of the times. The special session of the legislature in 1912, which ratified the Sixteenth and Seventeenth Amendments, was "in many ways . . . the most memorable in the history of the state," and brought about sweeping political changes, according to Chrislock. The unanimous vote on ratification in the lower house bespoke the unanimity of pro-income tax opinion throughout the state with only five Republicans from the Twin Cities area casting their votes against it in the Senate.[20]

So pervasive was pro-income tax feeling in Missouri that it even cut across the traditional political division between the two metropolises of St. Louis and Kansas City and the rest of the state. These forces continually clashed over legislative apportionment and prohibition, while Joseph W. Folk rode to power on the anti-urban feeling generated by his prosecution of St. Louis Political boss Colonel Ed Butler and by his drives against saloons, gambling, and prostitution. The two cities contained the bulk of the professioals and businesmen who would be liable to pay a federal income tax but these were a handful compared to the metropolises' middle and working classes, whose incomes were scarcely larger than those of rural and small town Missourians. Only 244 farmers and 267 laborers in the entire state had taxable incomes, a fact that helped overcome the usual antipathy between old-stock ruralites and heavily new-stock urban workers. The amendment was also considered by the legislature in the anti-privilege atmosphere created by Folk and his successor, former trustbusting attorney-general Herbert Hadley. Hadley proposed a variety of corporation tax levies on liquor and tobacco, and a higher license fee for automobiles. The amendment passed the Senate unanimously and received only eight adverse votes in the House. The latter were scattered throughout the state and came from both parties. None were from Kansas City and only one from St. Louis.[21]

The success of the amendment in Colorado was due to the cooperation of two distinct anti-special interest groups. With its neighbors, Colorado had been dominated by what Progressive Party leader Edward B. Costigan termed "politico-business corporations," chiefly the Mine Owners and Operators Association, the Colorado Fuel and Iron Company, the Great Western Sugar Company, and the American Smelting and Refining Company. The latter was controlled by the Guggenheim brothers and, as late as 1907, their influence was still sufficient to secure Simon's election to the U.S. Senate. The resultant uproar galvanized the urban middle class and the truck, dairy, and fruit farmers into a reform group led by Costigan, who was working to wrest control of the G.O.P. from Guggenheim and his cohorts. A second group, led by Judge Ben Lindsay and Governor John Shafroth, gained control of the Democratic Party, backed mostly by the labor vote in Denver and Pueblo. Both attacked the mining and grazing interests, demanded regulatory and labor-welfare laws, sponsored direct legislation and called for an end to corporate influence in state government. Both also endorsed the ratification of the income tax amendment.

The resolution was introduced by Harvey Garman, a pro-labor Democrat from Denver, and received bipartisan support from all sections of the state. The vote in the House was unanimous. In the Senate one Denver Democrat joined two rural Republicans in opposition, on the grounds that a federal income tax would take money out of the state "where it belongs."[22]

In spite of their greater affluence, the three Pacific Coast states offered scant resistance to ratification. California was the only western state to approach the northeastern states in the number of potential taxpayers, with a figure close to five percent, but the Golden State was also dominated by an intense political reaction against outside economic interests. For almost fifty years, the legislature had been under the powerful influence of the railroads dominated by the Big Four of Collis P. Huntington, Leland Stanford, Mark Hopkins and Charles Crocker. The real leader of the state was alleged to be railroad lobbyist William F. Herrin, who looked out for the interest of the Big Four and condescendingly dispensed favors to other corporations. "We have to let these little skates get their's," Herrin confided to Lincoln Steffens, "We have to sit by and see them run riot and take risks that risk our interests too." So complete was Herrin's control that the mayor of Oakland once charged that "you couldn't pass the Lord's Prayer in this legislature without money." The working class vote in San Francisco was organized by Abe Reuf, an entrepreneur of French-Jewish extraction who controlled the city's rackets and vice, while cooperating with Herrin at Sacramento. Revelations of Reuf's activities, largely through the efforts of prosecutor Hiram Johnson, touched off a sweeping investigation of statewide corruption, giving rise to a predominantly middle class reform movement called the

Lincoln Roosevelt League.[23] At the same time, two Bay Area labor groups--th Building Trades Council and the San Francisco Labor Council--began to mobilize working class support for labor and welfare measures, causing Reuf to found the Union Labor Party and press for many similar programs. After Reuf's conviction, the U.L.P. elected Patrick Henry McCarthy, and Irish born carpenter, to the mayor's office and continued to sponsor remedial legislation for the working class. In 1910 Johnson, backed mostly by Southern California and the Lincoln-Roosevelt League, was elected governor, after a campaign in which both candidates outdid themselves in promising to end business influence in politics. Johnson won by virtue of his pledge to "kick the Southern Pacific out of politics." Despite the predominantly middle class nature of his original support and programs, Johnson gradually shifted his emphasis to labor and welfare measures and his political following changed accordingly. By 1916, according to Michael Paul Rogin and John L. Shover, "the greater the number of foreign-born and first generation immigrants in an assembly district the higher the vote for Johnson," with his major support coming from the San Francisco political machine, from Catholics, Irish, and other ethnic groups, and from organized labor.[24]

The native middle class Lincoln-Roosevelt League disagreed with the new stock, working class, San Francisco complex over cultural issues and over how far labor and welfare legislation ought to go, but they did find many areas of cooperation in tax reforms, regulatory laws, and political innovations. Both the League and the U.L.P. were in favor of ratification of the Sixteenth Amendment and their agreement was clearly indicated by the vote in the legislature. Johnson, still in the early phases of his development as a social reformer, was reportedly "luke-warm" toward the income tax, but Congressman William Kent, a co-founder of the League, endorsed it as a device that would "tend toward a leveling of property-holding which is a desirable thing in a democracy." The vote in the lower house was unanimous, while the only reluctance evidenced in the Senate was thirteen abstensions out of a possible thirty-nine votes. Three of the abstensions were San Francisco Union Laborites but the other five, including former Reuf lieutenant Thomas Finn, voted in favor. The remainder were cast by Senators from districts scattered throughout the state.[25]

The opposition to ratification in Oregon was numerically larger, but of no more real consequence. Oregon politics, according to muckraker Burton J. Hendrick, had been controlled by the "more powerful moneyed interests," by "briefless lawyers, farmless farmers, barroom loafers, Fourth of July orators and political thugs." In the 1890s William S. U'Ren religious mystic, single taxer and prohibitionist, organized the Peoples Power League and ran for governor on an antibusiness Populist platform. Although denied election and the enactment of his single-tax panacea, U'Ren popularized the "Oregon System" of direct democracy that was copied by numerous other states during the Progressive Era. Building upon that base, Oregon reformers enacted several regulatory laws. The reaction against "privilege" was so irresistible that Jonathan Bourne, a wealthy railroad attorney, rode the tide into the U.S. Senate in 1906 where he joined the Insurgents in their quest for a federal income tax. Although the "reformed" Republican Party was the major vehicle in the drive against economic privilege, the Oregon System encouraged Republican legislatures and reform-minded Democratic governors. "The decisive battles of Oregon politics," John M. Swarthout and Kenneth R. Gervais have observed, "were fought out almost entirely apart from party labels and without the intervention of party machinery as well."[26] Enthusiasm for the income tax amendment in Oregon was so widespread that ratification in the lower house "consumed less than one-tenth of the time used in selecting an assistant sergeant-at-arms", according to the Portland Oregonian. The vote was 45-8 and the opposition was an unlikely combination of such recognized good government reformers as Allen H. Eaton and such acknowledged "corporation men" as T.J. Mahoney of rural Morrow County. Eaton, a University of Oregon professor and author of a book that popularized the Oregon System, had broken with U'Ren, opposed Bourne's election to the Senate, and led the fight against their candidate for speaker. The opposition was geographically dispersed and the two Democrats joined the Republican majority in support. The result in the Senate was an even more decisive 25-2. The resolution was sponsored by John Miller, a Linn County rural Democrat. He was joined in his advocacy by two Irish-Americans from Portland, floor leader Daniel Kelleher and George Sinnott. Miller urged ratification to "take away from Payne and Aldrich their chief argument for passing such an inequitous tariff bill," while the Republicans stressed the fairness of taxing on the basis of the ability to pay. The opposition consisted of W.W. Calkins, a Eugene Republican described by Smith and Edward as a "courageous and outspoken standpatter," and Thomas Nottingham, a wealthy Portland businessman and opponent of U'Ren and Bourne. Calkins based his opposition on states rights, although he admitted that he was not a states rights man normally, while Nottingham pleaded for immunity from taxation for the rich because they "pour out money like water in time of war." He was answered by another Irish-American Republican from Portland, Thomas Oliver, who said he did not "believe in exempting the rich because they had the ability to make money and the dishonesty to avoid taxation."[27]

Easy ratification in Washington proceeded from the widespread reaction against perceived exploitation by railroad, lumber, and other business interests. This feeling united such middle class organizations as the Direct Primary League and Direct Legislation League with the Grange and the Federation of Labor. It first expressed itself through the Populist Party and later sustained the capture of the Republican organization, by the followers of Miles Poindexter, through the device of the open primary. Building on that base, Washington quickly enacted an array of political and economic reforms. The 1911 legislature which ratified the Sixteenth Amendment is generally regarded to have been the best in the state's history. Even though Republican Governor Marion E. Hay was a former businessman who was to endorse Taft for reelection in 1912, he largely concurred with the legislature's enactment of initiative, referendum, and recall, an eight hour day for women workers, workmen's compensation, pure food and drug laws, and the ratification of the income tax amendment. The lower house voted 80-1 in favor of ratification and the Senate 32-5. Two of the dissenting votes came from rural Clark and Chelon counties, two from Seattle, and one from Tacoma. The remaining small town Senators joined with three Seattle, seven Tacoma, and five Spokane lawmakers to effect ratification. Support was heavily bipartisan and the measure evoked almost no overt dissent.[28]

Except for Utah, then, the only hint of organized and effective opposition to ratification in the West came in Kansas and Wyoming. Neither state differed from its neighbors significantly in income distribution. Wyoming had no income receivers over $100,000 and Kansas had but twenty-three. Only .6 percent made over $10,000 in Wyoming and only .3 percent in Kansas. Their respective percentages of those earning $5,000 or more were 2.2 and 1.5. Wyoming residents filed only 673 income tax returns in 1915 and Kansas dwellers, although much more numerous, filed but 429.[29]

What made ratification somewhat uncertain in Kansas was the relative success of the state's corporations in resisting the anti-monopoly forces led by Arthur Capper, Walter Stubbs, Joseph Bristow, Victor Murdock, and William Allen White. In 1905 the latter gained their first victory with the regulation of Standard Oil, but the major corporations retaliated by preventing Stubbs from gaining the G.O.P. gubernatorial nomination the following year. When Stubbs unsuccessfully urged other regulatory and tax measures in his first term as governor in 1909-10, the railroads, Standard Oil, Bell Telephone, International Harvester, and other large corporations mounted a massive campaign to prevent his reelection. Stubbs won, however, and the 1911 session of the legislature, at his direction, enacted a Public Utilities Commission, workmen's compensation, blue sky laws, state tax reform, and the ratification of the Sixteenth Amendment. William Allen White's Emporia Gazette joined Stubbs, Murdock, and Bristow in endorsing ratification. The regular Republicans, aided by a handful of Democrats, continued to oppose Stubbs' programs and to fight confirmation of his appointments. On February 15, 1911, the Governor's personal secretary, David Leahy, charged that "pork barrel politics" and "crookedness" were rampant in the legislature. Though his charges were largely unsubstantiated, they did help cause the legislature to become more receptive to Stubbs' program.[30]

The hardcore of the group was a dozen or so Republican senators from throughout the state who sought to bottle major regulatory and tax laws in committee. They were led by J.L. Brady of Lawrence, chairman of the Railroad Committee, F.L. Travis of Iola, chairman of the Committee on Assessments and Taxation and on Insurance, and the majority of the members of the Committee on Corporations. By virtue of their control of strategic committees, the regulars killed bills to regulate telephone corporations, to extend the powers of the railroad commission, to outlaw rate discrimination, to appoint an insurance superintendent, to regulate and tax various types of insurance companies, to impose an inheritance tax, and to form a tax commission. Typically their leaders insisted that the "less legislation we have the better off we are" and that they were "not anxious for legislative experiments." One of their number introduced an income tax brief drafted by the chief attorney for the Missouri Pacific Railroad while three spoke against ratification on the floor, despite the endorsement given the measure by the Stubbs-controlled party convention. All but two of the anti-administration Republicans voted against ratification and they made up twelve of the fourteen negative votes. The twenty-five pro-income tax votes were cast by the chamber's five Democrats and nearly all the Stubbs' Republicans. As the Topeka Daily Capitol, published by future Governor and Senator Arthur Capper put it, "most of the progressive Republicans voted for it, as did two or three of the anti-administration crowd and the five Democratic senators. The bulk of the standpatters and one or two of the progressives voted against it."[31]

What made the opposition more formidable in Wyoming was the continued influence of the Republican organization headed by U.S. Senators Francis Warren and Clarence Clark. Both were close supporters of Aldrich with a personal stake in preventing ratification. Their organization remained reasonably effective even in the face of an Insurgent-Democrat challenge. Warren was reputedly the richest man in the state, president of the American Protective Tariff League and the National Wool Growers Association, and a major beneficiary of the wool schedule he helped to draft. As father-in-law of General John J. Pershing and chairman of the Senate Military Affairs Committee, Warren located over two million dollars worth of military installations and public buildings in Wyoming between 1902 and 1912. He was, according to Lewis L. Gould, a "pork barrel artist" and a man "possessed of an unerring sense for the location of power and moved by an ability to benefit self and state." By general acknowledgement, Warren built the most successful political organization in the West through judicious milking of the federal treasury. Warren cooperated with the Union Pacific Railroad, which a Cheyenne paper charged in 1906 had ruled Wyoming since statehood, through the medium of the Republican Party. His colleague Clark was a Union Pacific attorney, whose brother was vice-president of the Union Pacific Coal Company, which the Senator aided by drafting high coal schedules. The Warren-Clark organization survived Populism and held its own against the onset of Progressive Era Insurgency.[32]

In 1910 those who were dissatisfied with its activities united behind the Democratic gubernatorial candidacy of Joseph M. Carey, former Republican Senator and author of the land conservation act. Carey was elected on the anti-special interests platform that the 1911 legislature refused to honor, while it postponed consideration of the Sixteenth Amendment. Carey was reelected in 1912, fashioning a slim Insurgent-Democratic majority in the lower house. In 1913, the ratification resolution was introduced by John R. Kendrick, a Sheridan rancher whom Warren had defeated for reelection in the previous session. Since Wyoming was in competition for the honor of being the thirty-sixth and decisive state to ratify, only three regular Republican Senators and seven Representatives were willing to vote against the amendment.[33]

Wyoming's belated assent to ratification left Utah as the only western state to reject the income tax amendment. On the basis of income distribution, there was little to separate Utah from her neighbors. Only eight people made over $100,000, but .3 percent over $10,000, and a mere 1.3 percent over $5,000. Only 1259 income tax returns were to be filed there in 1915. What made this limited concentration of wealth influential, however, was the fact that it was geographically centered in the north central basin around the Great Salt Lake and Utah Lake, an area that contained the urban centers of Salt Lake City, Logan, Ogden, and Provo. The rest of the state was rural, isolated, and poor. The prosperous, populous north central region had been settled by the Mormons who quickly made the desert flower. The church itself directed the area's economic development, building considerable interests in agriculture, sugar refining, telegraph and telephone services, hotels, and insurance companies. Although the value of the church's holdings were difficult to determine, and were probably exaggerated by outsiders, they were substantial. The elders skillfully used political action to protect their investments. "The charge here," a U.S. Senator concluded after a 1903 investigation, "in its widest scope, is that the Mormon church controls the politics and industries of Utah." A 1922 study by Ephraim Edward Erickson found that church leadership had a tendency "to take sides with the capitalistic class and with large corporations against the working class."[34]

The state's lenient incorporation laws also induced many non-Mormon enterprises to locate in Utah, including the Union Pacific, Central Pacific, Oregon Short Line, and Salt Lake Railroads, the Pacific Fruit Express Company, and the Union Pacific Equipment Association. After the 1903 Congressional investigation, the church divested itself of some of its holdings, selling the Utah Sugar Company to Henry Havemeyer and its telegraph interests to Western Union, among other transactions. Gentile miners, such as Irish Catholic millionaire Thomas Kearns, "the Silver King," feuded openly with the church but strove equally hard to defend their own positions through politics.[35]

Prior to 1903, the state had been predominantly Democratic, although its representatives in Washington regularly supported Republican tariffs to gain protection for beet sugar, wool, and minerals. In 1903 the Republican Party gained ascendancy through the efforts of Reed Smoot, one of the twelve Apostles of the L.D.S. Church. Smoot courted the endorsement of church president Joseph F. Smith for the United States Senate and secured election. His success also led to the defeat of Kearn's bid for reelection the following year. Since the Irishman had been endorsed by the previous president, Lorenzo Snow, the volte face caused Kearns to turn violently against the church. Kearns purchased the Salt Lake Tribune, turned the editorship over to Frank J. Cannon, a former United

States Senator and apostate Mormon, and used its pages to castigate church influence in Utah affairs. The two also helped to found the American Party, a Gentile faction that engaged in a power struggle with the Smoot forces, although often sharing their views on substantive issues.[36]

When Smoot arrived in Washington, the Senate Democrats launched an investigation against him on the grounds that he practiced polygamy. The attendant charges against the political and economic activities of the Church were sufficient to ensure temporary Mormon loyalty to Republicanism. For the next decade, according to Smoots' biographer Milton Merill, "God, the church, the Republican Party and Reed Smoot were all on the same side." In the Senate, Smoot joined the Aldrich circle, defended the protective tariff, and attacked the income tax. At home he sought to dominate state politics through his "federal bunch," an amalgam of pro-business Gentiles and Mormons. The American Party continued to contest the Smoot forces, both in the state and in Salt Lake City, until they reunited. This pro-business orientation made Utah "both conservative and respectable" and "staunchly orthodox in relation to her neighbors," according to R. J. Snow. Utah was the only state west of the Mississippi to reject either the Sixteenth or Seventeenth Amendments, to vote for William Howard Taft in 1912, and to fail to enact many of the hallmark reforms of the Progressive Era.[37]

The income tax amendment was endorsed by the Republican state convention and by the Salt Lake *Tribune*. However, Governor William Spry, a charter member of the federal bunch and Smoot's hand-picked candidate, declared against ratification in his message to the legislature. Despite this opposition, Carl Badger, Smoot's former secretary and an erstwhile leader of the American Party forces, introduced the ratification resolution that passed the Senate 12-2. The only two negative votes were cast by Republicans from Brigham City and Nephi, both in the prosperous north central basin. The remaining Senators from that area joined with the chamber's two Democrats and Republicans from the rest of the state to effect ratification. The federal bunch-dominated Committee on Federal Relations, however, followed Spry's lead and recommended rejection of the amendment. The body's two Democrats filed a minority report in favor of ratification. The committee chairman, Theodore Holman of Brigham, and two of its other prominent members, James Anderson of Morgan and C. C. Crapo of Sandy, were from the Salt Lake City area and were allies of Smoot. Holman's rejection resolution passed by a 31-10 margin with only three Republicans and the body's seven Democrats, all from outside of the basin, willing to go against the governor and the committee. The entire Salt Lake City, Ogden, Provo, and Logan delegations provided the bulk of the votes in favor of the resolution and against ratification. The Salt Lake Tribune, opponent of the federal bunch, charged its defeat to the Republican Party, "faithless to its pledge to the people."[38]

With the exception of Utah, though, the western states fulfilled the fondest expectations of income tax advocates. The happy confluence of the region's economic conditions and its favorable political climate produced the easiest series of victories that the amendment enjoyed. The area's very small degree of concentrated income guaranteed widespread support. Its self-conscious feeling of colonialism gave the income tax the flavor of a crusade against eastern exploitation, creating an environment in which it was fatal for politicians to appear to be defending special economic interests. Only the followers of Reed Smoot and Francis Warren dared to defy popular opinion on the income tax, and even the latter had to give in eventually. The desire of westerners to use the income tax to raise sufficient revenue for tariff reduction also contributed to the amendment's popularity, as did the belief that federal funds were the only feasible source of the capital necessary to develop the region's resources without further aggrandizement of eastern financiers. These assumptions and attitudes united farmers, miners, merchants, fishermen, lumberjacks, ranchers, professionals, and small businessmen from the Mountain States, the Great Plains, the Pacific Coast and from both major parties in favor of a tax that might help to redress the balance. Together their efforts gave the Sixteenth Amendment much of the powerful impetus it needed to receive eventual adoption.

CHAPTER V

UNEXPECTED TROUBLE IN THE SOUTH

By most surface indications, the South should have been as receptive to the Sixteenth Amendment as the West was. The region's self-conscious sectionalism, its historical position in favor of tariff reduction, and its devotion to the Democratic Party were all widely regarded as pro-income tax conditions. Above all, the region's general economic situation was the worst in the nation. The federal tax collector's hand would touch few southerners. Many southern states had also levied income taxes during the Civil War and continued them for decades afterward, while the region's representative's in Congress consistently supported the federal income tax from the 1860s through 1909. Yet, for all that, the Sixteenth Amendment experienced highly effective opposition in all but a handful of southern legislatures, with two states refusing ratification and three others granting it only on the second try.

Pro-ratification predictions rested strongly upon the South's economic condition. With over 31 percent of the nation's population, the region had barely 22 percent of its income. Texas, the wealthiest state in the South, ranked eighth in the nation in total income while Florida placed thirty-eighth and the other states fell somewhere in between. Southern states generally received a slightly higher portion of national income than western ones did, because of their larger population, but their position was far worse than it was apportioned on a per capita basis. While national income stood at $1165 per person in 1910, it was only $509 in the South. The bottom twelve states in per capita income were all southern, with Alabama ranking last at only $321. This unenviable position was substantially the same for both farm and non-farm income, although agricultural workers were worse off in absolute terms. The region's heavy reliance upon sharecroppers and tenant farmers and its huge pool of agricultural labor combined to keep farm income below $300 per capita in every southern state, save Texas. The average income of the gainfully employed was less than 75 percent the national figure, with wages lagging anywhere from 12-40 percent behind U. S. norms. The profits of the textile and other industries resulted largely from low wages. Nor did the South fare any better in terms of unearned income. With nearly one-third of the nation's population, the region received only about eleven percent of the returns from dividends and interest and had only about ten percent of bank deposits.[1]

More pertinent to the fate of the income tax amendment, the southern states generally had a relatively low level of concentration in the upper income brackets. Only five southerners had incomes in excess of a million dollars. Only 214 made over $100,000, about three percent of the nation's totals in those brackets. Slightly over .3 percent of the South's income receivers took in over $10,000. They accounted for but six percent of the region's income. The 1.1 percent who exceeded $5000 a year accounted for about eleven percent of total income. This meant that the South had even fewer potential taxpayers, proportionately, than the Mountain and Plains states did, although these individuals took in somewhat more of their states' income. These statistics plainly bore out the judgment of the chairman of the Mississippi House Judiciary Committee that "we are not particularly concerned in this matter, as there are only a small number of people in Mississippi who have incomes worth taxing."[2]

Like the West, the South was heavily infused with the spirit of anticolonialism. Southerners called their perceived oppressors "the North" rather than "the East," but they clearly saw themselves as being exploited by the same financial and industrial giants. Sixty-two percent of the southern work force was engaged in extractive industries in 1910, principally agriculture, forestry, fishing, mining, and animal husbandry. The region's major products -- wool, beef, lumber, copper, sugar cane, turpentine, resin, cottonseed oil, and cotton products -- were at most "semi-processed" in the South before being sent North for finishing. The textile mills that constituted the region's largest industry generally produced only yarn or coarse unfinished cloth for northern manufacturers. The steel and iron mills in Alabama and Tennessee were subsidiaries of the Pittsburgh giants and their output and pricing structure were regulated by such devices as "Pittsburgh plus" and "Birmingham differential." Southern mills were forced to sell their steel at higher prices than those in Pittsburgh and Gary, even though the Federal Trade Commission found that they could produce it at three-fourths the cost. "Basing point pricing in steel," the Federal Trade Commission concluded, "has contributed to the South's poverty by curbing the expansion and utilization of its steelmaking facility and by retarding the growth of steel consuming industries." Northern-controlled railroad lines insured the South's colonial status by charging lower rates for raw materials going north than they did for finished products. The Pennsylvania Railroad raised its rates on southern iron products at the request of the Keystone State's ironmongers. Northern business interests dominated large sections of southern states. Milton Smith, president of the Louisville and Nashville

Railroad, owned 500,000 acres of land in central Alabama and invested $30,000,000 there in a period of two decades. The Missouri Pacific possessed a million acres in Arkansas, while the North American Land and Timber Company, a British corporation, held vast tracts in Louisiana. Henry Flagler, a Standard Oil partner, built the Florida East Coast Railway and developed the "Flagler System" of hotels, newspapers, real estate, utility and transit companies, while New York financeers Thomas Fortune Ryan and August Belmont had sizeable interests in Virginia and Kentucky. With few exceptions, "the new businessmen, agents and retainers of northern industry returned their profits to stockholders who lived outside the West or South."[3]

For many years, the South was so hungry for capital that it almost invited such exploitation. State legislatures tempted northern investment with easy credit, low taxes, liberal exemptions, generous subsidies, cheap labor, and the absence of regulatory or labor legislation. After the repeal of the Southern Homestead act in 1876, several states in the region leased or sold sizeable chunks of land to companies that extracted their lumber, coal and iron. In Florida, Alabama, Mississippi, Louisiana, and Arkansas such lands accounted for about one-third of their territory. Florida was so generous that it conveyed 22,000,000 acres to private promoters even though it had but 15,000,000 to dispense. Despite the persistence of the belief that anything that attracted northern capital was good, large numbers of Southerners were questioning the wisdom of being so beholden to outside forces by the Progressive Era. Anti-colonialism was a major theme of the Populists and their agrarian descendants continued to rail against "foreign" control in the new century. Increasingly, they were joined by more urban and sophisticated segments of southern society. Many businessmen called for stemming the flow of profits, while professionals and humanitarians, such as Edgar Gardner Murphy and Alexander McKelway, decried the exploitation of the region's children by northern owned industries. Responding to these pressures, southern Congressmen articulated the anti-colonial theme, supporting numerous measures designed to correct sectional imbalance, such as railroad regulation, anti-trust and regulatory legislation, decentralized banking, and tariff reduction. By the same token, they pressed for a federal income tax as a weapon "to correct sectional inequalities."[4]

During the ratification debates, southern legislators regularly used the anti-colonial argument in support of the Sixteenth Amendment, with one Alabama lawmaker insisting that New Yorkers would pay a thousand dollars for every one paid by an Alabaman. A University of Arkansas economist prepared a detailed analysis to show that the eastern states would shoulder the tax burden, while William Shelton, a prominent Georgia academic, writing in the Journal of Political Economy, noted that most southerners favored ratification "because none of us here have four-thousand dollar incomes, and somebody else will have to pay the tax." For many southerners the income tax was seen as a levy upon the northern industrialists who exploited them, and that fact would have recommended its acceptance all by itself.[5]

In addition to its unfavorable economic position and selfconscious colonialism, the South was expected to favor ratification for two other reasons -- a belief in a tariff for revenue only and a devotion to the Democratic Party. Ever since the days of John C. Calhoun, the South had refused to join the national consensus in favor of tariff protection. In 1831 its dissent had precipitated the nation's most serious sectional crisis prior to the slavery controversy. Despite the growth of industry, most southerners still remained committed to the concept of a tariff for revenue only, partly because they still had relatively little to protect, and partly because the doctrine had become a clear means of differentiation from the hated G.O.P. In 1894 southern Democrats had supported a federal income tax primarily because its additional revenue would allegedly allow for a major reduction of tariff rates, a supposition that still held sway in 1909. With the possibility of Democratic control of Congress becoming more likely, and the Insurgent revolt on the tariff in full swing, southern spokesmen who urged favorable action on the Sixteenth Amendment to pave the way for tariff reduction were expected to strike a favorable chord in the hearts of most of their compatriots.[6]

There were some dissenters who were skeptical of the possibility of Democratic resurgence and meaningful rate reduction. A few others argued that lowering the rates would produce more revenue and obviate the need for an income tax. Still others, such as the representatives of the Louisiana sugar interests and some iron, steel, and textile spokesmen, had a stake in the maintenance of the protective system, even though it would have been foolhardy to attack the income tax openly on that ground. Despite these occasional dissents, few observers in 1909 doubted that the South's historic antipathy to the protective tariff was a sizeable plus in its attitude toward the income tax amendment.[7]

Perhaps even more crucial was the income tax's identification as a Democratic measure. The party had led the fight for its retention in the 1870s, enacted it in the 1890s, and consistently endorsed it ever since. Its 1908 platform had called for a constitutional amendment and its 1912 one was to demand ratification. To most southerners that was tantamount to calling it a southern measure. The Democracy was the party of the Lost Cause, of Redemption, and of white supremacy. The identification of region and party was almost total, and to fail in a test of loyalty to the Democracy was to betray the South. Such prominent Democratic spokesmen as Champ Clark, Joseph Bailey, Ollie James, and Cordell Hull urged ratification upon southern legislators in just those terms, a compelling argument in a region where it was said that one could be elected to office for life if one stayed out of jail and voted Democratic. Opponents of the income tax in the South laid themselves open to the serious charge of being "Republicans in disguise," so few were expected to attack it openly. Some enemies of the measure tried to turn the tables by objecting to giving such power to a national government controlled by Republicans but the 1910 elections signaled a Democratic trend nationally, undercutting such arguments. In a few border states, such as Kentucky and West Virginia, a viable two party system prevented income tax advocates from urging ratification on grounds of party loyalty alone, but in the rest of the South it was expected to be a powerful condition in support of the amendment.[8]

With the South's position on ratification supposedly guaranteed by its economic condition, its historic position on the issue, its sectional pride, its party affiliation, and its desire for tariff revision, few could foresee anything but success for the amendment there in 1909. But as compelling as these considerations were, they masked some very important barriers to ratification. Despite the fact that a federal income tax would touch relatively few Southerners, those who would be adversely affected were in positions to wield influence far out of proportion to their numbers. The remnants of the once powerful planter class were still a major force in the Black Belt counties. Those indigenous southern families that had profited by the development of southern industry -- the Reynolds and Dukes of North Carolina in tobacco, the Candlers of Atlanta in soft drinks, Vick's Chemicals in Charleston, Cannon towels and Maxwell House Coffee in Nashville, and Belk chain stores in Charlotte, plus numerous others in oil, textiles, and insurance were also politically significant. Despite the significant control of southern industry by northern capitalists, the latter were generally careful to leave the actual operation of their subsidiaries in the hands of "regional overseers," native Southerners from respected families who lent an air of legitimacy and tradition to the enterprise involved. They were joined by what Jasper Shannon has termed the "banker - merchant - farmer - lawyer - doctor class" of the county seats, the complex that usually controlled court house politics and produced a large portion of state legislators. Only in the South did people engaged in agriculture make up any significant segment of potential income taxpayers, constituting over ten percent in Texas, Mississippi and Arkansas, and around five percent in Georgia, the Carolinas, Florida, Kentucky, and Tennessee. Merchants also constituted a greater share of the total than elsewhere in the nation, ranging generally between five and fifteen percent in most states. Shannon's "class" dominated the economic life of the sharecroppers, tenants, dirt farmers, and mill hands and, as he argued, "the ethics of the market place lurk in its inner conscience." Together the planters, the regional overseers, the indigenous capitalists, and the county court house elites, Leonard Reissman has concluded, sat atop "a pyramidal stratification structure, with a small white elite at the 'Apex', a small urban middle class, and a gigantic base of urban workers, white peasants, and almost all the blacks."[9]

There were also potential opponents of ratification who did not even reside in the South but who wielded a considerable amount of influence in some states. The northern capitalists who controlled so much of southern industry had an opportunity to defeat the amendment in their "colonial dependencies." Thomas F. Ryan was the major financial backer of U. S. Senator Thomas S. Martin, the acknowledged head of the Democratic Party in Virginia. In Congress, Martin and his lieutenant, Congressman Hal Flood, voted more like New York Republicans than Virginia Democrats. Both had opposed the income tax in 1909. Through their organization, headed by Speaker of the House Richard E. Byrd and Governor Claude Swanson, Martin and Flood were also able to protect Ryan's considerable interests in the Old Dominion. Similarly, Henry Flagler's holdings were so extensive that many Florida politicians bent over backwards to give him favorable treatment, particularly in draining much of the land that he developed for real estate. By the same token, the Louisville and Nashville Railroad was headquartered in the former city but controlled by the J. P. Morgan Company and August Belmont. The railroad, through its president Milton Smith, exercised tremendous leverage on the actions of both political parties in Kentucky, successfully fighting off many taxation and regulatory measures. Many even held the Louisville and Nashville responsible for the 1899 assassination of Governor William Goebel, a farmer-labor supported Democrat and advocate of taxing and regulating railroads. In any case, the convicted assassins were pardoned by Republican Governor Augustus Willson and it was he who led the fight against the amendment in 1910. As noted in Chapter III, the New York Times also frankly acknowledged that "the powerful influence of strong manufacturing elements" and the political organizations that they controlled would be used against ratification in several southern states, especially Louisiana, Alabama, and Florida. Such evidence is certainly not conclusive, but it does suggest that the probability of northern industrialists and financeers working through their regional overseers and political allies in certain southern states to block ratification was a widely held belief.[10]

Since Redemption, the South's economic elites had ruled through a group of politicians popularly known as "Bourbons." The latter were planters, former Confederate leaders, and nouveau riche businessmen, united in a desire to industrialize the South and aggrandize themselves. Although the northern press often proclaimed the Bourbons as the reincarnation of ante-bellum aristrocracy, "Redemption was not a return of an old system nor the restoration of an old ruling class," C. Vann Woodward has observed, but rather a new phase of the revolution begun in 1865." For the most part, the Redeemers engaged in "the Great Barbecue" -- gathering up the natural resources of the South for sale to the highest bidder. They governed by a formula of low taxes, little or no regulation of business, and a minimum of public expenditures for social needs. As original leaders died out, younger ones arose to perpetuate control. Bourbon composition and style varied from state to state but its political orientation was similar. The Martin - Flood - Byrd organization in Virginia was a northern style political machine with a huge patronage army, substituting the county courthouse for the ward clubroom. The Choctaw Ring in New Orleans was an alliance of sugar planters, oil and timber barons, and New Orleans corporations. The Bipartisan Combine in Kentucky was allied with the state's railroads, mines, racetracks, and liquor interests, supported by the Louisville Courier-Journal of "Marse Henry" Watterson. Its counterpart in West Virginia ruled in the interests of mine owners and railroads, under the leadership of U. S. Senators Stephen Elkins, Henry Davis, Nathan Scott, Clarence Watson and William Chilton, the first three Republicans and the last two Democrats. In Georgia the pro-corporation faction united mill towns and Atlanta-based banks and railroads, with the editorial support of the Atlanta Constitution, chief spokesman for the "New South" philosophy. In Florida the "corporation faction" consisted of those who hoped to gain by having the state drain swampland and give it to private enterprise. Although most Bourbons were nominally Democrats, many affected the name "Conservatives" and "abhored Bryanism, with its promise of business regulation, social reform, and political democracy," according to Dewey Grantham. Some even flirted with Aldrich-style Republicanism on the national level, with the Constitution and the Charleston News and Courier endorsing Taft in 1908, but they generally clung to the Democratic label in state politics. Despite the challenge of the Populists and more urban-based reform groups during the Progressive Era, Bourbons still exercised considerable political power in most southern states.[11]

The difficulties of ratification were exacerbated by two salient characteristics of southern politics. First was the disfranchisement of the South's most economically deprived residents, both black and white.

Through the use of the poll tax, the literacy test, the white primary, the grandfather clause, and similar devices, nearly all the region's blacks had been deprived of the ballot by 1910. In South Carolina and Mississippi, this meant disfranchising better than half the eligible voters, in Florida, Louisiana and Alabama about 40 percent, and in Georgia, Virginia, and North Carolina about one-third. The impact was less in the border states, but still exceeded ten percent everywhere except West Virginia. In Louisiana there were 136,334 eligible black voters in 1896; a decade later there were but 1342. Blacks had been a majority in twenty-six parishes in the former year, and were that nowhere by the latter. Even though poor whites had been among the loudest in clamoring for black disfranchisement, many of the devices used, particularly the poll tax and literacy test, affected large numbers of them also. In Louisiana the qualified number of white voters declined from 164,088 to 125,437 in the same eight year period, while in Mississippi the 1890 voter requirements left only about two-thirds of the white males eligible. Many more who were not legally proscribed simply refrained out of apathy, ignorance, or frustration. Some Bourbon politicians and landlords paid the poll tax for white sharecroppers and tenant farmers, voting them _en masse_, while others, as in Virginia, sought to keep the electorate as small as possible. This severe constriction of the right to vote significantly enhanced Bourbon influence, removing from political participation vast numbers of southerners with something to gain and nothing to lose by the ratification of the federal income tax amendment. "By 1900 the white farmer and the Negro had been effectively disfranchised," C. Vann Woodward has noted, "and the Bourbons were in control."[12]

The amendment also suffered because southern politics were those of faction rather than party. The requirements of one party rule prevented the Democrats from playing any of the roles that parties must play to make government function. Despite its obvious flaws, as William Nisbet Chambers has argued, "some sort of party system has proved necessary to the operation of modern democratic politics." Parties in competition with one another present alternative policies to the electorate, contain the forces of pluralism, provide an area for accommodation and compromise, shape public opinion, coordinate the actions of various branches of government, and act as a responsible opposition. Bereft of those benefits, southern politics quickly degenerated into a multisided struggle among interest groups, often producing a dozen or more candidates for office in a statewide primary. Even the most discerning voter was usually unable to see much difference among them. In Florida, factionalism reached the point of being "every man for himself." Such a situation according to Key, tended "to thwart popular participation or influence over policy," made "the realities of the legislative process virtually invisible, or nearly incomprehensible, to the voters", rendering "it extremely difficult for voters to hold representatives responsible for their acts." Southern politics resembled the colonial model where, Chambers has explained, "blocs, alliances or cabals formed and dissolved almost independently of themselves; and thus, voters were baffled by frequent discontinuities from election to election or by the smudging of choice on issues in a given election."[13]

The main beneficiaries of factionalism were those segments of society that were well organized, articulate, and affluent. They were "able to 'work' the system more advantageously than plain men or less favored groups." This tendency has been cogently summarized by Allan P. Sindler:

> A politics that lacks coherence, i.e. that is insufficiently structured to give voters a meaningful choice or to impose responsibility to the voters both when campaigning and when in office, tends to impede the formation of aggressive popular majorities and to play into the hands of the adherents of the status quo. Consequently the principal beneficiaries of southern one-partyism have been those groups and interests which are cohesive, alert, informed, well-organized, well-financed and capable of effective action, and which have a tangible material stake in governmental policies to impel them to political activity. The adverse effects of the one-party structure on state politics, in short, have been borne most heavily by the disadvantaged elements of the population, by have not persons who score low on the characteristics just cited. It is well to remember . . . that economic conservatives have a considerable stake in maintaining politics at a low level of clarity and coherence.

The implications of factionalism for ratification of the income tax amendment are obvious. Its intended beneficiaries were largely those "plain men or less favored groups" who had such difficulty comprehending or influencing the actions of the state legislature. Its targets were "cohesive, alert, informed, well-organized, well-financed and capable of effective action." Only immense, wide-spread, and unmistakable public sentiment for ratification could overcome the latter's advantage.[14]

In addition to the disabilities of disfranchisement and factionalism, the amendment was also vulnerable to appeals based upon cherished southern beliefs. How many of these arguments were made out of sincere concern for the region's unique history and culture, and how many were proferred by self-interested parties seeking to obfuscate the economic issues involved, is impossible to determine. The arguments were so pervasive and effective, though, as to credit at least some of their exponents with a deeply held conviction that no innovation emanating from Washington could be of benefit to the South, no matter what the appearances. Most frequently, the amendment faced the objection that it would violate the cherished doctrine of states rights by augmenting federal power and by allowing its tax collectors to ravage the South. An Arkansas Senator typically objected to having his business pried into by a "snippy little deputy U.S. marshal."[15] Several southern lawmakers coupled this theme with the contention of New York Republican Governor Charles Evans Hughes that the amendment would permit the taxing of state and federal bonds, discouraging such investments. The speaker of the Florida House, even though he favored ratification, moved to have the resultant revenues returned to the states of their origin. The states rights argument was raised in some form in almost every southern legislature and was the most frequently voiced reason for voting against the amendment. Some opponents added that they would vote for ratification if the Democrats controlled Congress, but were loath to give the Republicans such power. Proponents of the measure often charged that such appeals were blinds for special interests, as did the Birmingham Age Herald when it stated that opponents of ratification were using the states rights argument "for all it is worth," but in reality were mere "lobbyists." Most advocates of ratification, though, acknowledged the sincerity of the concern and sought to prove that a federal income tax would not seriously impair state sovereignty.[16]

Closely tied to the states rights issue were appeals to the "Lost Cause," highly influential with a generation that had learned the horrors of Civil War and Reconstruction at their parent's knee. Some legislators were Confederate veterans who objected to the amendment as a plot by the Grand Army of the Republic to gain additional benefits for Union veterans. Most opponents of the amendment, though, simply styled it a northern plot to complete the destruction begun by the Civil War and Reconstruction, linking it with the infamous 13th, 14th and 15th amendments. Ratification advocates in Alabama successfully countered these contentions by presenting the amendment as an opportunity to get even for the earlier ones, but the Lost Cause appeal lent itself much more readily to preservation of the status quo. Not until Huey Long, as T. Harry Williams has argued, did the South produce a political leader who could lay aside "appeals to the gold-misted past" and address himself directly to the socioeconomic problems of his people.[17]

Appeals to the Old South were often linked with those to the New by opponents of social change. It was traditional, as Paul Gaston has observed, for southern legislatures to select one Senator from its "traditional agricultural interests", and the other from the "New Departure business interests." The prophets of this new dispensation held that the only hope for the South to recover from the ravages of war and Reconstruction was to industrialize. This widespread faith in business progress was the cement that held the Bourbon alliance together, and often moderated the demands of reformers. The New Departure judged all legislative proposals primarily by whether they would attract or discourage investment capital, causing many southerners to shrink from the taxation, regulation, labor, and welfare measures that normally characterized the Progressive years. "The New South myth, fully articulated," Gaston has concluded, "offered a harmonizing and reassuring world view to conserve the essential features of the status quo."[18] Although the regions's economic elites clearly benefited most from its implications, the New South idea was not limited just to them. "Conscious manipulation," Gaston insists, "cannot fully acount for its vitality and effectiveness."[19]

Finally, many southerners were skeptical of a federal income tax because the region had a tradition of low taxes and minimal public expenditures. Prior to the Civil War, most southern states had almost no public education or social welfare programs. During Reconstruction there were serious attempts to remedy these deficiencies with sharp increases in expenditures, mostly paid for by taxes on the well-to-do. This juxtaposition identified such measures with rule by blacks, carpetbaggers, and scalawags and, conversely, associated low taxes and expenditures with southern rights, white supremacy, and one-party rule. Since many Southerners did not even look to their state governments for such measures, they were more reluctant than were westerners to turn to the federal government. A growing number of southerners were petitioning for government aid by 1910, mostly to shore up the region's sagging agricultural base. The Farmers Alliance and the Populists had pressed for commodity-secured loans in the 1890s and their efforts were to bear partial fruit during the Wilson Administration with the Rural Credits, Federal Farm Land Bank, and Warehouse Acts. In 1917 southern demands led to a Mississippi River flood control measure. Even so, the South's economic elites were more prone to look to private investment than to federal expenditures or developmental capital.[20]

Despite these formidable political and emotional obstacles, pro-ratification forces did develop highly effective coalitions in most southern states. The most consistent support for ratification generally came from the representatives of agricultural regions, areas that had been most favorable to Populism and income taxation in the 1890s. Populist-like spokesmen remained prominent during the Progressive years and "the cause of "the common man" did not disappear easily from southern politics. In Alabama, party supporters fragmented into various factions, "varying from fascism to socialism," as Sheldon Hackney has demonstrated. In Louisiana a genuine rural socialist movement developed, while, in several other states, farmers functioned through the National Farmers Union and similar organizations. Most, though, drifted back into the Democratic Party and sought to reorient it toward Populist-type measures, fighting "the battle of the poor white farmer against the planters and industrists, to quote Thomas D. Clark and Albert D. Kirwan.[21]

Their cause was articulated primarily by a new breed of spokesmen who often combined the most virulent form of race-baiting with a Populist economic program. Chief among these were James K. Vardaman and Theodore Bilbo in Mississippi, Jeff Davis in Arkansas, Tom Watson in Georgia, and "Pitchfork Ben" Tillman and Cole Blease in South Carolina. The sincerity and effectiveness of these "demagogues" varied greatly but they kept up a steady barrage of demands for measures to serve the white farmer. The support of their followers was instrumental in securing ratification in most southern states. Vardaman, Bilbo, and their "redneck" supporters were solidly united behind ratification in Mississippi, while the "White Chief" went on to the U.S. Senate to lead the fight for a "radical" income tax law in 1913. Agrarian support in Georgia was nearly unanimous, united behind Watson, former Populist Senator John Johnson, and Charles Barrett, president of the National Farmers Union. Barrett strongly endorsed ratification on the grounds of equity, tariff reduction, and the need to stem the rising cost of living, insisting that the only one who would benefit by the amendment's rejection would be "the man of great wealth who will, under its provisions, be called upon to meet governmental burdens he has these many years evaded." Almost everywhere else in the South the representatives of farm districts were virtually unanimous in their support, constituting the most consistent segment of the pro-income tax coalition.[22]

But the amendment also received backing from more urban representatives. Hoke Smith, Governor, Senator, and publisher of the Atlanta _Journal_, lent his support and the Atlanta delegation and Smith legislative faction voted for the measure. Braxton Bragg Comer, prominent businessman and reform governor, carried the representatives of urban Alabama along with him. All the representatives from Charleston in the South Carolina lower house and half of those from New Orleans voted for ratification. Representatives from Memphis, Nashville, Louisville, Houston, and other large cities of the South were nearly unanimous in their support. On the other hand, the smaller industrial and mill towns, such as Greenville, Macon, Savannah, Augusta, Albany, Athens, Columbus, Danville, Norfolk, Alexandria, Staunton, Charlottsville, and Roanoke, were often less enthusiastic. These were generally "company towns" dominated by a few mills, factories, or railroads that exerted considerable political influence. The larger cities were more diverse and had a substantial middle class and even a nascent labor movement for lawmakers to cultivate. The income tax amendment cut across urban-rural lines, appealing to the representatives of farmers, workers, and the urban middle class in almost equal measure.[23]

Similarly, support for the amendment in most southern states spanned regional differences. It was equally supported by lawmakers from the East Texas cotton regions, from the Panhandle, from west Texas, and from the cities of the central plain. In Tennessee and Kentucky, ratification sentiment pulled together lawmakers from the Mississippi counties, the middle piedmont, and the mountainous eastern regions, even though the latter regions were usually Republican strongholds in Democratic states. In Alabama the amendment received the votes of Huntsville, Birmingham, Montgomery, and Mobile and the regions around them. In the South Carolina House it was endorsed by tidewater and piedmont representatives in equal degree. In Mississippi the measure was supported heavily by both the Vardaman-Bilbo "pineywoods" agrarian faction and the planter aristocracy of the Delta that bitterly opposed the "White Chief." In Georgia it was backed almost unanimously by both the neo-populist followers of Tom

Watson and the more urban forces of Hoke Smith. Despite the very real difficulties that the amendment encountered in several southern states, it is indicative of its widespread popularity that there were almost no legislative districts that did not cast at least some votes in one legislative chamber in favor of ratification.[24]

By the same token, there was only one southern state where the amendment did not receive at least 80 percent of the votes cast in the lower house. It passed the Alabama house unanimously, received but one negative vote in North Carolina and Texas, acquired over 90 percent in Arkansas, Louisiana, Tennessee, South Carolina and West Virginia, and over 80 percent in Florida, Kentucky and Georgia. In Mississippi fifty-one lawmakers abstained on the grounds of states rights, but the official vote was 85-0. Such percentages compare favorably with those in the western states, attesting to the widespread popularity of the amendment among nearly every class and in every geographical section of the South. Even reservations on grounds of states rights, or other southern traditions, were most frequently expressed by abstentions, demonstrating the unwillingness of the lawmakers involved to declare openly against ratification even for the most hallowed of reasons. Only the Virginia House failed to cast an overwhelming majority of its ballots in favor of the amendment, defeating it by a 54-38 vote. Even then, though, the Senate reversed the usual pattern by voting to ratify by a solid 19-5 majority, maintaining the general pattern of having at least one house ratify by a substantial majority.[25]

With the exception of Virginia, and five other states where it encountered no appreciable opposition in either house, the amendment ran into difficulty in the Senate. After receiving 80 percent of the votes cast in the Georgia House, it received a bare 56 percent in the upper chamber. After getting 94 percent in the South Carolina House, the amendment managed only 66 percent in the Senate. In five other states -- Kentucky, Arkansas, West Virginia, Louisiana and Florida -- the amendment was rejected by the Senate after garnering anywhere from 88 to 96 percent of the house vote. The South's upper chambers were much more insulated from popular pressure than were the lower houses and were more capable of being controlled by cliques or factions. Their memberships were much smaller and easier to contact on an individual basis. Senators also served for longer terms and did not have to face the electorate every other year. Generally, Senators tended to come from a higher socioeconomic class and were much more likely to be potential taxpayers than were representatives. By the same token, the position of state Senators in the planter-business class guaranteed their greater sensitivity to issues that might affect that complex adversely. The southern state Senator often viewed himself as the guardian of tradition who must prevent the more popularly elected house from following the whims of public opinion. In most instances, the negative vote of a state Senator was in direct contrast to the position taken by his district's representatives in the lower house. In South Carolina nine of the eleven opposition Senators came from districts whose representatives had voted unanimously for ratification, while the other two voted contrary to a majority of their counterparts in the lower house. The Senator from Little Rock led the opposition to ratification in the Arkansas Senate, despite the fact that three of the city's four representatives had voted yes. Virginia's unique reversal of the roles of the two houses was largely due to the personal intervention of Speaker Richard

Byrd, Hal Flood's son-in-law and the legislative leader of the Martin-Flood organization.[26]

There were five southern states where no important opposition surfaced even in the Senate -- Alabama, Texas, North Carolina, Tennessee, and Mississippi. In the main, these were states where both houses and the governor's mansion were firmly in the grip of anti-special interest forces that stressed programs for the regulation and taxation of business, as well as for increased expenditures on education and other social services. Alabama, probably the poorest state in the nation, was the only one to ratify the amendment in 1909. It did so at the urging of Governor Braxton B. Comer, a prosperous business man who contended that "it is a very good way to keep the country away from greater deficits." The income tax issue united the four groups that Sheldon Hackney has identified as the major political factions in the state -- planters, agrarians, bosses, and progressives. No one arose to challenge the claim that New Yorkers would pay $1,000 for every one contributed by an Alabaman. The brief debate centered around the tax's possible impact on salaries and wages and both houses ratified unanimously. Texas was probably the wealthiest state in the region, but its political orientation has been tilted leftward by the assaults of the Alliance and the Populists. In an effort to undercut agrarian radicalism Texas Governors from James S. Hogg in the 1890s through James E. Ferguson in the late 1910s had adopted Populist rhetoric and advocated moderate economic reforms, while fostering white supremacy and placating the prohibitionists. The mixture was so successful that Texas earned a reputation as a place where "foreign" investors and corporations did not receive equitable treatment. The state's fame was enhanced by its production of such nationally prominent Democratic politicians as Joseph W. Bailey, Charles Culberson, David M. Houston, Thomas W. Gregory, Morris Sheppard, and Col. E.M. House. Significantly, Bailey, one of the foremost advocates of the income tax in Washington, was generally regarded as a conservative with ties to Standard Oil in his home state. In this volatile atmosphere, anything that smacked of a defense of eastern industrialists and financeers would have been tantamount to political suicide. Accordingly, the income tax amendment received but one negative vote in each house.[27]

The same vote brought ratification in North Carolina, a state whose politics had also been dominated from about 1900 on by reform governors Charles Aycock, Robert Glenn, and William W. Kitchin. In Tennessee, where the vote on ratification was 80-3 and 20-4 in the respective houses, the amendment was so popular that it cut across both partisan and regional differences, uniting the Republicans of the mountainous east with the Democrats of the middle and western sections of the state. Its success was assured by the triumph of an insurgent group of Democrats led by U.S. Senator Luke Lea. In 1908 they broke with the regular Governor Malcolm Patterson over his alleged reluctance to press strongly enough against the state's corporations. Two years later the rebels captured the party machinery along with the governorship and both houses of the legislature. Tennessee was also the home of Congressman Benton McMillin, co-sponsor of the 1894 income tax, and of Cordell Hull, who was to be manager of the 1913 income tax measure.[28]

There was somewhat more reluctance to endorse the amendment in Mississippi, but it was expressed primarily in abstentions and turned, overtly at least, on the issue of states rights. The Jackson Daily News found absolutely no opposition to the amendment in the legislature, primarily because there were so few people in the state who would be affected. The most vocal support came from the followers of James K. Vardaman, a Populist-type reformer who appealed to "the piney woods and tenant farmers" with his program of radical economic legislation and white supremacy. His proteges, Theodore Bilbo and Frank Burkitt, were the leading voices for ratification in the Senate and House, respectively. Their major political opponents were the Delta planters, led by U.S. Senators John Sharp Williams and Leroy Percy, the latter "the apostle of culture and the corporation," as Bilbo's biographer styled him, a wealthy planter and counsel for several railroads, banks, telegraph, telephone and express companies and oil refineries. Percy defeated Vardaman for the Senate in 1910 amid charges of bribery. Several Percy legislators in both houses made states rights speeches during the income tax debate and abstained on the final vote, including Van Buren Boddie, the faction's floor leader. Many other Percy lawmakers, though, joined the Vardaman forces in voting for ratification because the benefits that would accrue to most of the state's citizens were apparent.[29]

Everywhere else in the South, except for Virginia, the pattern of easy victory in the lower house and strong opposition in the Senate prevailed. In South Carolina and Georgia the dissenters were numerically significant, but not powerful enough to prevent ratification. Although the South Carolina house ratified 100-3, the Charleston News and Courier harshly castigated the amendment. When Senator Joseph W. Bailey spoke before the legislature in favor of ratification, the News and Courier denounced his "craftily worded speech," styling it a "subtle attempt to awaken class feeling." The state's leading progressive newspaper, the Columbia State, edited by reformer William E. Gonzales, however, strongly urged ratification on the grounds of equity and sectional advantage. The News and Courier's arguments were echoed in the Senate by several prominent Carolinians with personal economic stakes in denying ratification. The most outspoken critic was Huger Sinkler, scion of an old line family and attorney for the Vicks Chemical Corporation, who argued that the tax would do nothing to correct sectional inequalities or aid the South but would go instead to pay pensions to Yankee soldiers. He was joined by Wiley Hamrick, a physician, planter, and banker from Cherokee County, and Daniel T. McKeithan of Darlington described by the Senate Biographical Directory as, "a man of large affairs and a leader in the business and financial world about him," with holdings in cotton, lumber and banking. The majority of the eleven dissenters were from tidewater counties and all represented districts whose representatives in the lower house had almost unanimously voted in favor of ratification. The pro-amendment forces, led by future lieutenant-governor W. C. Mauldin of Greenville, were able to muster double that amount of votes.[30]

The senatorial opponents of ratification in Georgia were able to command a higher percentage of votes, but still fell short of defeating it. The amendment was openly endorsed by two of the state's most important Democratic factions and caused a split in the ranks of the third. The first, led by Tom Watson, was a continuation of the Populist movement that he had led in the 1890s. Watson's newspaper strongly urged ratification as did his ally Charles Barrett, president of the National Farmers Union.

The ratification resolution was introduced by another former Populist, John Johnson, and endorsed by such Watsonite lawmakers as Joe Hill Hall. The second faction was led by Hoke Smith. His support was much more urban than Watson's, but their mutual interest in railroad and other regulatory legislation caused the two to combine on Smith's election as Governor in 1906. Smith remained silent on the amendment but he was later to play a leading role in the enactment of the 1913 income tax. The Journal endorsed ratification and a leading Smith lawmaker, Representative James. J. Slade, wrote a long letter to the paper expressing the former governor's support. Slade attributed the opposition to the state's third faction, that of Governor Joseph M. Brown. The latter was a former traffic manager for the Western and Atlantic Railroad, whom Smith had fired from his position on the regulatory commission for alleged favoritism to the rail lines. When Watson and Smith had fallen out over the issue of legislative apportionment, Brown had secured the former Populist's endorsement, unseating Smith in 1908. As chief executive, Brown proved sympathetic to the railroad, corporate, and liquor interests and opposed legislation hostile to outside investment in the state, causing Watson to roundly denounce him by 1910. This fluid factionalism made the fate of the income tax uncertain, leading the Birmingham Age-Herald to comment that "politics in Georgia is too peculiar to admit of immediate ratification in that state, even if the burden of support would in that way be thrown upon the North and East." As if to prove that contention, the Georgia Senate voted to postpone the amendment until the following year when it was introduced late in the 1909 session. The amendment's advocates contended that three lobbyists for out-of-state multimillionaires were responsible for the postponement, while its opponents questioned the wisdom of lodging such power in the federal government.[31]

In 1910 Brown submitted the amendment to the legislature without recommendation and the most outspoken opponents of ratification were such administration followers as Joseph Ellis, J. Rudolph Anderson, and Joseph Davis. On the other hand, the usually pro-Brown Atlanta Constitution, published by Clark Howell, successor to Henry Grady as a proponent of the New South, endorsed the measure. In the House the pro-amendment forces were led by Smith and Watson men, the opposition by Ellis. The final vote was 129-32, divided generally along those factional lines. Several of those who cast "nay" votes inserted explanations in the House Journal justifying their action on the grounds of states rights, while protesting their belief in the essential justice of taxing the rich. In the Senate, President John Slayton, usually a member of the Brown faction, further emphasized the division in those ranks by speaking in favor of the amendment "for the good of the nation," even though he expressed serious reservations. Several of the amendment's advocates charged that the opposition was being organized and financed by "paid lobbyists" for state and outside interests. The opposition Senators came mainly from the state's smaller commercial and industrial cities, chiefly Macon, Savannah, Augusta, Albany, Athens, and Columbus, and were led by railroad attorney W. B. Burwell, who had earlier commanded the fight against Smith's railroad commission. Burwell and his allies disparaged the notion that only the rich would pay or that the revenue was needed, argued that the tax would injure the state's railroads and industries, and insisted that the amendment would greatly augment federal power. The combination of rural and Atlanta votes, delivered primarily by Watson and Smith leaders, was just enough to save the amendment from defeat on a close 23-18 vote. 32

In four other states -- Kentucky, Arkansas, Louisiana, and West Virginia -- the forces of opposition in the Senate were strong enough to defeat the measure on one occasion, but were eventually overcome. In Kentucky the amendment's difficulties were largely due to the influence of a group of pro-busines Senators known as the Bi-Partisan Combine and to Republican Governor Augustus Willson, a Harvard educated attorney who represented the American Tobacco Company. With the Democrats often split into two or more factions along geographic or other lines, the Republicans, whose strength was largely in the mountainous eastern region of the state, were often able to elect a governor and to make common cause with the Bourbon Democrats. The latter, financed heavily by the Louisville and Nashville Railroad and American Book Company and endorsed by the Louisville Courier-Journal, were usually able to play off the western Democratic farmers against Republican miners and hill people. In the 1890s, though, many western farmers bolted to the Populists, achieving some success before the Bourbons lined up the eastern Republican vote against Bryan in 1896 and elected a G.O.P. Governor. This Bi-Partisan Combine was united by a common belief in the New South philosophy and governed largely in the interest of the race track, coal, railroad, and liquor businesses. In 1899, former Populists united with urban laborers to secure the nomination of William Goebel, whose ethnic background also appealed to the heavily German-American vote of the Louisville and Covington areas. After a bitter election in which the railroads and corporations reputedly spent a great deal of money, Goebel lost, but charges of vote buying and fraud caused the Democratic legislature to reverse the results. As Goebel was about to take office, he was fatally wounded by a shot fired from the window of the Executive Office Building occupied by a Republican. His death a short time later restored the Bourbons to power in the person of Democratic Lieutenant Governor J.C.W. Beckham. The Goebel affair, as Thomas D. Clark has demonstrated, "forced Kentucky into a long period of partisan factional war which prevented passage of much needed progressive legislation." This outcome meant that "the Bourbons were the victors in their first clash with a coalition of western Kentucky farmers and the labor immigrant vote of northern Kentucky," according to political scientist John H. Fenton. In 1907, the Bipartisan Combine secured the election of Willson who pardoned the two men convicted of Goebel's assassination. Willson took the side of the tobacco companies against the state's farmers and introduced only two pieces of reform legislation, a uniform system of accounting and a corrupt practices act.[33]

The general popularity of the income tax amendment throughout Kentucky was clearly reflected in its endorsement by both party caucuses and its ratification by both houses of the legislature on votes of 69-7 and 22-9. The dissenting votes were geographically scattered and about equally divided between the two parties, with the representatives of all three sections of the state voting heavily in favor. On February 28, though, Willson sent a strongly worded message to the legislature, insisting that the resolution had been improperly worded. He further denounced the amendment as an inordinate grant of power to the federal government, calling for the substitution of a state income tax. In a New York Times feature article, Willson called the amendment the "most serious encroachment on states rights since the organization of our government." He repeated his preference for a state income tax and charged that the people, and not the millionaires, will pay. Democratic Senator Ollie James sought to hold his party in line by calling Willson's action an illegal veto and declaring that "the owners of the mighty fortunes of the country may endorse the course of Governor Willson in this matter, but the plain citizens of Kentucky will indignantly resent it." When the legislature reconsidered the amendment, the House ratified it again by an even bigger margin with only two Republicans and one Democrat dissenting. The Senate, however, completely reversed itself, defeating the measure 18-17 with the deciding vote cast by President William Cox, like Willson a Maysville Republican. Fifteen Democrats and Two Republicans voted for ratification while ten Republican joined eight Bourbon Democrats in opposition, an illustration of the workings of the Bi-Partisan Combine. During the two months that elapsed between Senate votes, Willson and other opponents of ratification had managed to convince eleven Senators to change their votes, despite their caucus pledges and the magnitude of the House vote. Ironically, their lobbying efforts were all in vain because the U.S. Secretary of State ruled that both houses had legally ratified the measure in January and certified Kentucky's agreement.[34]

Gubernatorial opposition, based upon a states rights appeal, also played a major role in the measure's temporary defeat in Arkansas. Democratic Governor George Washington Donaghey was a wealthy railroad contractor whose two administrations were notable primarily for his efforts to institute a businesslike, efficient, orderly administration and moderate regulation of business, in contrast to the Populism of his predecessor Jeff Davis, hero of the one-gallus farmers. Donaghey, who soon became one of the earliest southern supporters of Woodrow Wilson, also pressed for tax reform within Arkansas, and he objected to the amendment because it would take needed revenue out of the state. Donaghey accordingly recommended the substitution of a state income tax. This theme was reiterated by several Senators who conjured up visions of the federal government using the revenue to finance new civil rights campaigns and interfering with the conduct of southern business. These same Senators also denigrated the notion that the wealthy in the Northeast would shoulder the biggest burden. One of their number insisted that a federal income tax would take eight dollars out for every one brought in. The amendment's proponents stressed the equity of the tax and argued that it would have little impact on the South. One favorable Senator warned his colleagues that New York had gone Democratic after the Republicans had refused to ratify and that Arkansas voters would retaliate against anyone who opposed the amendment. The powerful states rights appeal by Governor Donaghey and his supporters failed to prevent easy passage by the house, 54-2, but it did allow or cause forty-four Assemblymen to abstain. In the Senate, Donaghey's message was so influential that only three Senators were willing to support ratification.[35]

To counteract Donaghey's influence and the states rights arguments, the amendment's supporters called upon several nationally prominent Democrats, including William Jennings Bryan, Champ Clark, and both Arkansas Senators. Twelve other southern Democratic Senators sent a telegram urging ratification, insisting that the amendment would not destroy state sovereignty. Several Senators acknowledged the importance of this intervention in explaining their vote change, stating that they had been convinced that the Northeast would pay the tax and that the South would benefit. Donaghey and his strongest supporters in the Senate remained unmoved, with a Little Rock member charging that Bryan was really a Populist who had radicalized the party. The prestige of the nationally prominent Democrats proved to be more influential than that of Donaghey though, as almost half those who had abstained on the first House vote switched to the affirmative side and the amendment carried 73-2. In the Senate the outside intervention was so persuasive that only six members were willing to go on record against ratification on the second vote. Still unwilling to concede defeat, Donaghey attempted to veto the resolution. Congressman Joseph Robinson of Arkansas, a Jeff Davis Democrat whom Donaghey had defeated in the 1910 gubernatorial election, introduced a resolution in the U.S. House of Representatives to overrule the Governor's action, but the Republicans buried it in committee. Once again, though, the Secretary of State ruled that governors had no role to play in the amendment process, adding Arkansas to the list of those acting favorably.[36]

In Louisiana and West Virginia the vagaries of electoral politics caused the Senate to reverse itself in the ensuing session of the legislature. From Redemption to Huey Long, Louisiana politics were generally controlled by the Choctaw Ring, a union of New Orleans businessmen with oil, lumber, and manufacturing interests in Shreveport, Alexandria, Baton Rouge, Monroe, and Delta sugar planters. These groups often shared ethnic and religious as well as economic ties, for the Delta region was largely a Catholic, cosmopolitan enclave in a white Anglo-Saxon, Protestant state. The latter inhabited the uplands and the southeastern and southwestern parishes, where populism, socialism, and, later on, Longism, flourished. At the state capital the Ring and its planter allies regularly opposed business regulation, taxation, labor measures, and, specifically, the income tax amendment. But the anti-machine New Orleans Times-Picayune, organ of the business progressivism epitomized by John Parker, also editorialized against ratification, charging that the income tax would force a lowering of the tariff that would let in foreign goods and put people out of work. Several sugar planters joined the opposition, out of fear that the sugar schedule might be lowered, with several Assumption Parish planters and merchants also protesting the measure's alleged violation of state sovereignty. The organization governor recommended against ratification in his message to the legislature. Despite the Ring's opposition, though, the amendment enjoyed widespread and effective popular support outside the Delta and with segments of the New Orleans population. One senator from St. Landry Parish readily volunteered that he voted for the amendment, even though personally opposed, "because I believe my constituents are almost unanimously in favor." House Speaker Henry Garland Dupre expressed similar sentiments and that chamber responded with a favorable 78-31 vote in 1910. The amendment received almost unanimous support outside the Delta and even garnered half the votes of the New Orleans delegation. The dissenters were mostly from the sugar parishes, New Orleans, and Baton Rouge and were planters, physicians, lawyers, merchants, real estate agents, stock brokers, and lumber manufacturers. State senator T.J. Gleason, a New Orleans corporation lawyer, moved to have the amendment submitted to a referendum, a tactic designed to remove the lawmakers from the cross pressures being exerted upon them by public opinion and special interests. The motion carried 26-11, with Delta region Senators leading the support. The House refused to concur, and the session ended without further action.[37]

The 1911 election was one of two losses suffered by the Ring between the time of the Populists and the advent of Huey Long. The defeat was largely a reaction to revelations of corruption and corporate influence. The income tax was not widely discussed. The capture of the governorship and the legislature by anti-Ring forces, though, removed much of the organized opposition to ratification, creating a climate in favor of the passage of legislation directed at special privilege. This led to an even more decisive 101-6 victory for the amendment in the House, with only four planters of French extraction and two New Orleans corporation attorneys opposing. The Senate was less affected by the election than the lower house and the opponents of ratification sought to substitute a state income tax. The attempt received only thirteen votes, including six New Orleans attorneys, a Natchitoches banker, an Acadian merchant, three sugar planters, and two manufacturers. Failing this, only eight of the thirteen were willing to go against the demonstrated popularity of the measure and it passed 30-8.[38]

In West Virginia the ultimate success of the amendment was due to the pressures exerted, in both political parties, against control by railroad and coal mining interests. The Republicans had dominated the state since the Civil War, led first by U.S. Senator Henry B. Davis, a millionaire coal miner, and later by his son-in-law and business partner Stephen B. Elkins. Elkins, "the businessman in Congress," was a vital cog in the Aldrich organization, upholding the coal schedule and chairing the Interstate Commerce Committee. In 1909, he and Davis' successor, Nathan B. Scott, had faithfully followed Aldrich's lead on both the tariff and the income tax. The state's Democrats had an almost identical economic orientation and were led by Clarence Watson and William Chilton, businesmen-politicians popularly known as the "gold-dust twins." By 1910, though, the legislature's favoritism to industry and its refusal to pass legislation beneficial to the mill workers in the northeast Panhandle and the farmers and miners in southern West Virginia caused widespread dissatisfaction among the electorate. Discontent over the rising cost of living was also expressed in every section of the state. Capitalizing on this feeling by promising reform, the Democrats grabbed a forty vote edge in the House and a 15-15 tie in the Senate. Fortunately for the Republicans, Elkins had been astute enough to see the trend developing and salvaged the governorship by nominating William E. Glasscock, a man not closely identified with the organization and open to reform proposals. A bipartisan compromise in the Senate gave the presidency to Henry Hatfield, a McDowell County physician interested in health and safety legislation, while Glasscock received the support of both parties for several pieces of social and regulatory legislation.[39]

Both party platforms pledged ratification of the income tax amendment. Governor Glasscock recommended it in 1911 stating that "I think we ought to be willing to trust Congress in this matter and I see no reason for any particular anxiety upon the part of the average citizen, but I can see reasons why men of vast wealth might desire to avoid any taxes of this kind by the government of the United States." The lower house responded with a 70-2 affirmative vote. The two negative votes were cast by one member from each party, while ten of the fourteen who abstained were Democrats, including four of the five Charleston representatives. The Senate, more immune to the results of the 1910 election, rejected the measure on a 13-17 vote, with the Republicans splitting 8-7 in favor and the Democrats 10-5 against. The debate consumed an entire legislative day with the opposition led by the most prominent leaders of both parties. Despite his generally progressive outlook and the fact that he was "not one to oppose taxation," Hatfield and other prominent Republicans objected to tinkering with the direct tax clause and to the possible taxing of state and municipal bonds. Ex-Governor William MacCorkle and floor leader R. F. Kidd spoke for the Democrats, basing their objections largely on states rights and insisting that they were not bound to follow the platform all the time. As in Kentucky, a bipartisan, pro-business Senate coalition acted contrary to both party platforms and a heavy affirmative vote in the House.[40]

As the 1912 elections approached, Glasscock responded to mounting reform pressure by joining a group of governors calling upon Theodore Roosevelt to secure the Republican nomination. This was a course that Elkins had also been urging before his death in 1911. When this failed and Roosevelt formed the Progressive Party, Glasscock and Hatfield, the former's designated heir to the governorship, worked desperately to prevent a split in party ranks that would give the state to the Democrats. Ultimately, they agreed to support Roosevelt for president if the Progressive Party would not run a statewide ticket to cut into the normal Republican vote. To complete the deal, Hatfield pledged himself to the Progressive platform, including ratification of the Sixteenth Amendment. The strategy paid off as Roosevelt carried the state while Hatfield and the entire G.O.P. ticket were also elected. Hatfield took office "at a time when the mood of the public was committed to reform" and when "public opinion had been agitated to a point where it accepted innovation," to quote Carolyn Karr. With the Democrats responding to the same pressures, Hatfield "was able to crystallize in the state a half-century of progressive agitation and to channel the full force of this agitation into constructive legislation." Running the Republican caucus personally, the Governor forced through a blue sky law, a public service commission, workmen's compensation, woman suffrage, the direct election of senators, mine safety codes, an eight hour day for women, and proposals for taxing corporations. At his direction, both houses of the legislature also ratified the income tax amendment unanimously in 1913.[41]

Only in Florida was the Senate able to disregard an overwhelmingly affirmative vote in the lower house more than once. This was partly due to a widespread concern for keeping state revenue in Florida, a view shared by many of the amendment's supporters, and to the "every man for himself" character of Florida politics, as V. O. Key put it, both extremes of attitudes that were common to every southern state. The state's politics were generally characterized by a split between the "corporation" or "Anti" and "anti-corporation" or "Straighthout" factions, a bifurcation that arose out of a dispute over the millions of acres of public land that had been granted to such railroad tycoons as Henry Flagler as an incentive to build. Both factions wanted to drain the swampy land as a new inducement to outside settlement and investment, but their disagreement lay "in the advantage that they were willing to give the private wealth they wished to attract," as Kathryn Trimmer Abbey has observed. The anti-corporation faction, headed by Governors William S. Jennings, Napoleon Bonaparte Broward, and Park Trammell, wanted the state to reclaim the land from the railroads first, a position supported by organized labor and former Populists. The corporation faction, headed by Governor Albert Gilchrist and U.S. Senators Duncan U. Fletcher and James P. Taliaferro and popularly "identified with eastern finance capital and reactionary politics", according to Abbey, wished the state to drain the land as a service to its present owners. According to Edward W. Akin, "most of the politically powerful personages along Florida's east coast were beholden to Flagler." He also controlled several newspapers, including the Florida Times-Union which staunchly opposed ratification of the income tax amendment. The income tax issue cut across these lines, with several corporation faction members publicly urging ratification while several anti-corporation people expressed public concern over states rights. Indeed Governor Gilchrist publicly disputed the contention of New York Governor Charles Evans Hughes that Congress would use the power to tax state and municipal bonds, arguing that Congressmen represented those very governmental and political entities and would hardly vote to impair their operations.[42]

In 1911 the House ratified 52-4, on a motion by Speaker T. A. Jennings, the leader of the anti-corporation forces. Half the negative votes were cast by corporation men, but several others voted for ratification with Gilchrist and Fletcher appealing for ratification. One anti-corporation legislator explained his negative vote by insisting that he favored an income tax, "but oppose its exaction and collection by the federal government," while Jennings introduced a follow-up resolution to have Washington return the revenue to the states. The Senate debated the issue for over a month, with the amendment's proponents using the argument of tax equity and tariff revision while its opponents stressed states rights and styled the measure a Republican plot. When a supporter insisted that "no Democrat elected in a Democratic primary would have the timerity to arise and oppose this resolution," George Dayton of Dade City replied that the income tax was "a Populist hybrid grafted upon Jeffersonian doctrine." J. E. Calkins, Governor Broward's railroad commissioner, sought to mediate between the factions by proposing to submit the measure to a referendum, but failed on a narrow 14-15 vote, with most of the amendment's supporters voting in the negative. Senator Dayton, an outspoken opponent of ratification and a member of the corporation faction, then questioned the Senate's competence to consider the matter since the state constitution forbade it from ratifying a federal amendment that had been proposed after the membership was elected. The chair appointed a committee, headed by Dayton, to consider the question and it reported back in the negative, thus killing the amendment in the 1911 session.[43]

The 1912 election saw the triumph of the anti-corporation faction, with Trammell elected governor, but the Senate again maneuvered to defeat the amendment. The lower house voted for ratification unanimously, although it did so two months after the necessary three-fourths of the states had acted. The Senate turned the measure over to the Committee on Constitutional Amendments, consisting of three members of the corporation faction who had opposed ratification in 1911. The Committee finally recommended against ratification and the Senate accepted its report. Thus, two Senate committees in two different sessions negated the popular sentiment expressed in the lower house, allegedly out of concern for states rights and on something other than a clear-cut factional split.[44]

The defeat of the amendment in Virginia was attributable to the strength of the Martin-Flood-Byrd organization and the intensity of states rights feeling in the state. That it took place in the lower house was due to the personal influence of Speaker Byrd at a time when some other organization leaders were inclined to permit ratification as a concession to reform demands. In 1893 a "party-business entente" had secured the election of Martin, a Chesapeake and Ohio Railroad attorney and the son of an obscure storekeeper, for the U.S. Senate over Fitzhugh Lee, the ultimate triumph of "realism over romanticism." Martin, "the Bismarck of modern Virginia politics," developed one of the most effective political machines in the nation, a classic alliance of courthouse and counting house. His "officeholding coterie" consisted of eight to ten thousand state and local officials, each controlling at least five votes and all beholden to Martin, Flood, Byrd, or their ally Claude Swanson. The governor was usually a one-term functionary while the organization controlled the legislature by installing its followers as floor leaders and committee chairmen. So effective was its control that Byrd won the speaker's chair without a dissenting vote in 1910. He and his lieutenants "managed the frantic sessions with skill and ease." Martin and Flood voted regularly with Aldrich and Payne in Washington, while Byrd and Swanson pursued similar policies in Richmond, primarily at the behest of Ryan and Belmont. The major threat to organization rule came from such independents as Andrew Jackson Montague, Westmorland Davis, Carter Glass, St. George

Tucker, and W. A. Jones, who pressed for a more open political system and the taxation and regulation of business. Generally, the Martin organization was able to crush or co-opt such opposition. Montague was elected governor in 1901, but the organization-controlled legislature scuttled his program. In 1911, Martin and Swanson won Senatorial races from Glass and Jones, forcing the latter to become more cooperative. The challenge of the independents was serious enough, though, to force the organization to take more progressive stands on certain issues and machine leaders occasionally disagreed over how far they had to go. As governor from 1905 to 1911, Swanson proposed less drastic versions of several economic and political measures, despite the reluctance of Martin to concur. The possible presidential candidacy of Woodrow Wilson caused a division in the ranks, since Martin opposed the former Virginian as a "radical" while Byrd, a former law school classmate of Wilson's, announced for him despite reservations about his record as governor of New Jersey.[45]

The Martin organization's attitude toward the income tax was one of longstanding antipathy. Martin had voted against the 1894 tax, while the Richmond Times-Dispatch, the machine's leading organ, had enthusiastically applauded the Pollock Decision. In 1909 Martin had followed Aldrich's lead on the income tax issue, opposing both the Bailey and Cummins bills, while reluctantly agreeing to the proposed amendment. Although Swanson continued his policy of placating the independent faction by recommending ratification, Byrd decisively established himself as the opposition leader. Senator Don Halsey of Lynchburg, the "independent's" floor leader, invited Senator Bailey to speak in favor of ratification, and the Texan responded with a powerful plea based upon party loyalty, tax equity, and revenue needs, while insisting that the amendment did not violate state sovereignty. The Times Dispatch conceded the fairness of the tax but raised strong states rights objections. The paper noted that no one had spoken for or against the measure at committee hearings, that the Joint Committee on the Judiciary had unanimously recommended ratification, and, sadly, that Virginia would probably be among the first states to ratify. "So far as the committee was concerned," the paper added sarcastically, "the presence of Senator Bailey was not needed." The following day, though, Byrd stepped down from the speaker's chair to level a strongly-worded blast at the amendment. Although conceding its essential justice, he nevertheless conjured up a horrifying picture of the results of the amendment's adoption:

> A hand from Washington will be stretched out and placed upon every man's business; the eye of the federal inspector will be in every man's counting house. ...The law will of necessity have inquisitorial features, it will provide penalties, it will create complicated machinery. Under it men will be hailed into courts distant from their homes. Heavy fines imposed by distant and unfamiliar tribunals will constantly menace the taxpayer. An army of federal inspectors, spies and detectives will descend upon the state. ...Who of us who have had knowledge of the doings of the federal officials in the Internal Revenue Service can be blind to what will follow? I do not hesitate to say that the adoption of this

> amendment will be such a surrender to imperialism that has not been seen since the Northern states in their blindness forced the fourteenth and fifteenth amendments upon the entire sisterhood of the Commonwealth.

Such dire consequences, Byrd continued, could hardly be justified by a mere attempt to create a fair system of taxation. "God forbid," he warned, "that this commonwealth should give up her birthright for the mess of pottage offered by the Senator from Texas."[46]

This same theme was repeated by organization representatives in both houses during the final debate, with Byrd again leading the dissenters. Some of the measure's opponents were so carried away with Lost Cause allusions that even the Times-Dispatch dismissed most of their appeals as "mere fustian." The paper insisted, though, that Byrd had delineated the central issue of states rights versus federal power so persuasively that the amendment's proponents were unable to refute him. The pro-amendment forces were so exasperated by the tenor of the debate that one sought to remind his opponents that "the United States is not a foreign land." The House responded by defeating the amendment 37-54. Opposition was strongest from the representatives of many of the state's industrial and commercial cities, but it was so widespread as to leave the Martin machine and Byrd's personal influence as the major organizing principles. The opposition in the Senate was outnumbered so it sought to prevent a vote by refusing to constitute a quorum, until Halsey had the sergeant-at-arms arrest enough members. Even then, one organization Senator unsuccessfully moved to adjourn before the measure finally passed 19-5. The Times-Dispatch praised the House of Delegates as the "conservator of common sense," assuring its readers that "not everything that is written in the Democratic platform is Democratic." Considering everything, there seems little reason to quarrel with the judgment of the Petersburg Index-Appeal that "to the lion Richard E. Byrd, more than to any other man, the people are indebted for their escape from a blunder that would have been worse than a crime." Two years later, the proponents of the amendment reintroduced the ratification resolution which failed on an even larger 20-54 vote.[47]

The defeat of the amendment in Florida and Virginia was a serious blow to the amendment's proponents at a time when its ultimate fate was still very much in doubt. Coupled with the very real difficulties that the measure encountered in Kentucky, Arkansas, Louisiana, West Virginia, Georgia, and South Carolina, these setbacks graphically demonstrated that most observers had underestimated the depth and effectivenss of southern oppositon. Locating the sources of that opposition precisely is a difficult task. It was not partisan since outside of a few border states the amendment's opponents belonged to the same party as its supporters. There were certainly very few southerners with a personal economic stake in preventing ratification and it is clear that not everyone who did necessarily opposed the amendment. In a few cases, it is possible to center the opposition in a certain geographic region, such as the Louisiana bayou or the smaller industrial and commercial cities of Virginia or Georgia. Occasionally, the evidence points to a politcal organization usually identified with fostering special economic interests such as the Choctaw Ring in Louisiana, the Martin-Flood-Byrd machine in Virginia, or the Bipartisan Combine in Kentucky, but their operations were usually conducted behind the scenes and their spokesmen were not always united against ratification in public. In the main, the opposition followed no clear-cut geographical, partisan, or class lines and only two rough patterns emerge with any consistency.

The first pattern is that of the opposition to the amendment seeking to scuttle it in the Senate after being unable to mount any effective campaign against the measure anywhere else. Party platforms and legislative caucuses consistently pledged ratification. Virtually no one testified against the amendment in committee hearings and those bodies almost always recommended favorable action. Where serious opposition surfaced in one house, it did so after the other had ratified by overwhelming margins of over eighty percent. Those Senators who voted "nay" generally did so in stark contrast to the stand taken by the Assemblymen from the same district. In Kentucky, Arkansas, and Virginia, at least, those who voted against ratification followed the lead of politicians associated with the defense of the state's business interests, such as Governors Willson and Donaghey and Speaker Byrd. In Louisiana and West Virginia, where intervening elections demonstrated the desire of the electorate for more forward-looking policies, the respective Senates lost little time in reversing themselves at the next session. Only in Virginia, where the amendment was openly opposed by the Martin organization and its influential speaker, did the measure fail to carry the more populous house of the legislature by an overwhelming margin. Such a pattern suggests strongly that opposition to ratification came from a small, but politically influential group that was able to function effectively only in a body whose smaller numbers and relative insulation from public opinion allowed it the occasional luxury of defying the wishes of the electorate. Their ability to do so was enhanced immensely by the disfranchisement of the most economically deprived segments of the population and by the politics of faction. Party stands on issues represented, at best, only what several diverse segments agreed upon. There was no effective way to prevent those who dissented from going their own way. Thus many Arkansas Democrats could stigmatize the pro-income tax appeals of nationally prominent members of their party as the work of a radical fringe, while the Richmond Times-Dispatch could chide South Carolina for ratifying the amendment out of a sense of "party regularity."[48]

The other pattern that emerged was the unwillingness of the amendment's opponents to attack the idea of the income tax itself, either in newspaper editorials or legislative debates. A few expressed doubts that the measure would throw the burden of taxation on the nation's wealthy or that the extra revenue was needed, but most of the amendment's opponents conceded the fairness of the tax and its economic benefit to the South. Instead they argued that the amendment, however desirable in theory, would augment federal authority and violate the hallowed doctrine of states rights. Many coupled their arguments with emotional appeals to the Lost Cause, conjuring visions of a new invasion of the South by an array of federal tax collectors, while others pleaded for a state income tax or warned of the threat to the ability of the state to sell its bonds. It is tempting to see such concerns as red herrings being dragged across the scene by self-interested parties. State income tax proposals usually appeared out of nowhere backed by lawmakers with no previous record of advocacy, while legislators in several states did not hesitate to borrow their arguments on the taxation of state bonds from such northern, Republican, "capitalist" newspapers as the New York Sun. Even so, the frequency and passion of states rights arguments against the amendment makes it necessary to concede the sincerity of many who made them. Most southern legislators in 1910 had personal or family memories of the Civil War and Reconstruction Era and looked to state sovereignty as the only guarantee of white supremacy and the survival of the region's unique culture. To risk that in support of a tax to be collected by a federal government that posed the greatest threat to those values seemed to many southern lawmakers too high a price to pay. Such reservations clearly served the needs of those who sought to prevent the taxing of their own incomes, but that does not mean that they were not real concerns for many other legislators. It seems fair to conclude that many southern legislators felt themselves on the horns of a double dilemna -- popular support and the undeniable justice of the income tax argued for its ratificaton, but behind the-scenes pressures and concerns over states rights pulled the other way. Many sought to avoid the dilemna by abstaining, but the vast majority made the hard choice and it is not surprising that a significant number in several states came down on the negative side.

For all its difficulties, though, the amendment was ultimately ratified in eleven of the thirteen southern states. The establishment of a federal income tax simply had too many potential benefits at little or no cost to the great majority of southerners. The amendment provided an opportunity to shift the burden of federal taxation on to people who mostly lived outside the region and whose incomes seemingly came largely from exploiting southern resources. Ratification also provided the possible leverage to topple the hated protective tariff, emancipating southern producers and consumers. The votes in the lower house of almost every southern legislature demonstrate that these considerations generally outweighed fear of federal power or the influence of a few wealthy citizens. These expectations united the representatives of farmers and mill hands with the urban middle class, bridged the gap between city and countryside, and transcended the division between tidewater and piedmont. In this case, at least, the instinct of the average white Southerner for his own self-interest proved strong enough to overcome those who sought to appeal to his fears.

CHAPTER VI

TOPPLING THE KEYSTONE: THE AMENDMENT IN NEW YORK

The key to the fate of the proposed Sixteenth Amendment lay in the northeastern industrial states. The various commentators on the chances of the amendment differed somewhat in their assessment of individual states, but friends and foes alike were agreed that the greatest opposition to ratification would come from the populous states of the industrial Northeast. The Census Bureau divided the area into three districts -- New England, Middle Atlantic and East North Central. Its statistics and those of the Internal Revenue Service spoke volumes about the regional concentration of wealth in the nation. The Middle Atlantic and East North Central regions were ranked first and second in the amount of wealth per state. New England appeared well down in that category but led the nation in the value of all products manufactured. Northeastern states also ranked well up in per capita income, despite their generally large populations, with only Vermont and New Hampshire placing in the lower half of states in that category. Collectively, residents of the three regions received almost sixty per cent of the nation's income. When the federal tax eventually went into effect, the inhabitants of five northeastern states--New York, Pennsylvania, Ohio, Massachusetts and Illinois--paid nearly seventy per cent of the bill.[1]

Even more significant than the amount of income in the northeastern states was its degree of concentration in the upper brackets. The most thorough study of national income distribution found that "the greatest disparity is in the Eastern States, particularly those with large cities." The "Iron Rectangle" contained 189 of the 206 people in the nation with incomes in excess of a million dollars a year. New York, Pennsylvania, and Illinois had 152 of these. The Northeast was also the home of about eighty-five percent of those who made over $100,000, with New York, Pennsylvania, Massachusetts, Ohio and Illinois accounting for about three-fourths of the national total. The region was significantly above the national figures for those earning more than $10,000 a year and the percentage of the state's incomes they received, with the Middle Atlantic division leading the nation with percentages of 1.1 and 15.2, respectively. In that census area, the 2.7 percent with incomes over $5,000 took over twenty percent of their state's total. In New England the figures were 2.2 and 15 percent and in the East North Central region 2 and 13.2 per cent, with Ohio and Illinois accounting for much of its standing. Even within the northeastern region, wealth and income were concentrated in a rough quadrangle encompassing the southern New England states, the Great Lakes area of Illinois, Michigan, and Ohio, and the Middle Atlantic States. Significantly, individuals from these three census divisions accounted for over sixty percent of the nation's income from interest and almost seventy percent of that from dividends. Despite this massive concentration of personal property, state tax burdens typically fell much more heavily upon the owners of real property, a testimony to the political influence of those who owned the region's industrial and financial resources. Real property was, on the average, valued at from three to five times more than personal, with Delaware and Pennsylvania approaching an incredible 20-1 ratio.[2]

For defense against taxation of this considerable wealth, its holders looked primarily to the powerful Republican organizations that had dominated their states' politics for several decades. These organizations were essentially alliances of urban business leaders and rural and small town legislators, unions of "business interests and rural Yankees" who came together for "cultural-religious, as well as political and perhaps at times economic self-protection," as political scientist Elmer E. Cornwell, Jr. has observed. Both groups shared a mutual fear of the potential power of the city, particularly of the hordes of immigrant-stock people who inhabited it. Businessmen identified urban dwellers as the major source of demands for regulation, taxation, costly welfare schemes, and the recognition of organized labor, looking to small town lawmakers for protection. The latter were under little pressure from their own constituents for such measures, and as farmers, small town laywers, merchants, and bankers, they were committed to notions of laissez-faire, rugged individualism and small government. Party leaders, such as Thomas Platt in New York, General Charles R. Brayton in Rhode Island, J. Henry Roraback in Connecticut, Boies Penrose in Pennsylvania, or Joseph Foraker and Mark Hanna in Ohio were also careful to endow their small town allies with important sinecures and generous patronage plums. As with General Brayton, they did so "because these were the 'old Codgers' the General trusted," as David Patton later observed, adding that "he did not have much use for city slickers who were likely to be Democrats anyhow."[3]

Their rural and small town constituents supported this alliance with their votes because it helped them maintain political and cultural hegemony over the city and its polyglot populace. The overwhelming majority were descendants of the British Protestants who originally settled the state and set its cultural tone. When the waves of European immigrants came, they brought with them customs and practices that were antithetical in such areas as Sunday observance and the use of alcoholic beverages. The old stock people responded by seeking to legislate conformity to prevailing cultural values through such devices as prohibition, Sunday blue laws, immigration restriction, mandatory use of English, and forced attendance in public schools. Although many business leaders and professional politicians in the G.O.P. had reservations about such measures, they generally accepted them as the price necessary to maintain rural and small town allegiance on economic matters.[4]

This Republican alliance of board room and village was facilitated by two political mechanisms--legislative malapportionment and denial of home rule to the city. The former was accomplished by simple refusal to reapportion despite major population shifts, by representing towns or counties with little regard for population, or by fixed limits on the representation allotted to a major city. In Connecticut, apportionment by towns in the lower house meant that villages of 300 or 400 people had the same representation as New Haven, Hartford, and Bridgeport, each of which had well over 100,000 residents, allowing an estimated twelve percent of the population to elect a majority. In the Rhode Island Senate the same situation limited Providence, with forty percent of the state's population, to one of the body's thirty-nine seats, placing control in the hands of 7.4 percent of the population. Upstate lawmakers in New York and downstate lawmakers in Illinois both limited their respective metropolises to a fixed percentage of seats, well below their share of the population. The method and the degree varied from state to state, but legislative malapportionment was, everywhere in the Northeast, a highly effective mechansim for perpetuating minority rule and for fending off popular measures.[5]

Malapportionment was even more significant because it was coupled with the inordinate control exercised over cities by state legislatures. Most cities were, by virtue of their charters, unable to alter their form of government, change their tax base or rate, regulate utilities, or update the terms of service contracts without permission from the legislature. Many city officials were appointed and removed by the legislature. Uncooperative mayors could often be brought to heel by surrounding them with hostile subordinates. Between 1867 and 1870, the New York Legislature passed more urban laws than did the English Parliament between 1835 and 1885. Chicago, as late as the World's Fair of 1893, was unable to grant concessions for checking hats or selling popcorn on the new municipal pier without a special act of the state legislature. In the days before the Seventeenth Amendment, the vice-like grip of these Republican organizations over northeastern state legislatures guaranteed the selection of the Standpat leadership of the U.S. Senate. Some bosses, such as Platt, Penrose, Foraker and Hanna, secured their own election, while others, such as Brayton or Roraback, relied upon such allies as Aldrich, Brandegee, and Bulkeley to handle things in Washington while they ran the state. Whatever the arrangement, the Standpat Republicans in Congress were primarily the representatives of the alliance of "business interests and rural Yankees" that produced them, and their national policies were carbon copies of those the organization pursued on the state level. Even though they had been forced to acquiesce in the proposal of the federal income tax amendment, the Standpatters were still confident that the organizations that produced them would remain in sufficient control of the legislatures of the northeastern states to deny ratification.[6]

The major flaw in this strategy was that it was set in motion at the precise moment when Regular Republican organizations were losing control of the situation in most northeastern states. Besieged by demands for change from a variety of elements within the party, and seriously challenged by rejuvenated Democrats for the first time since 1986, Regulars in most northeastern states were either swept from power or forced to alter long-standing policies. Between 1910 and 1915, the state legislatures of most northeastern states were dominated by politicians of both parties whose primary constituency was other than the traditional business-small town alliance. There is little evidence that the income tax issue played a major role in the revolt against eastern Republicanism but, as developments in individual states indicated, many voters were reacting at least partially to an association of the rising cost of living with a high protective tariff, a situation that the income tax was supposedly designed to correct.[7]

A major factor in this changeover was the altered attitude of the urban middle class of small business men, managers, professionals, and intellectuals. Mostly native born Protestants of British ancestry, they shared their rural cousins' fear of the ethnic working class and had habitually stuck with the G.O.P. as the party of respectability and prosperity. Jolted by the revelations of the muckrakers and the evidence of their senses into a realization of the problems of urban, industrial life, and aroused by the arrogance and corruption of the business-politician alliance, they sought to purge the party and alter its policies. Acting from a variety of ideological, socioeconomic, and ethnocultural motives, the native, urban, middle class dominated such reform groups as the National Tax Association, National Consumers League, the National Municipal League, the American Association for Labor Legislation, the National Child Labor Committee, and the Civic Federation. Through these organizations, they lobbied for a myriad of socioeconomic, political, and cultural measures and exerted pressure upon political leaders, especially within the Republican Party. It was primarily these native middle class Americans who were shortly to back Theodore Roosevelt against William Howard Taft at the 1912 Republican convention and to form the nucleus for the Progressive Party. Within their own states, their actions either resulted in a Progressive-Democratic coalition with significant policy alterations or, more commonly, in a split which led to Democratic victories.[8]

Simultaneously, business-small town Republican alliances were challenged by a much different internal group--professional urban politicians with foreign-stock, working-class constituencies. These were men whose political careers depended upon their ability to keep a significant portion of the urban new stock within a party dominated by "business interests and rural Yankees." "The party that eliminated the hyphen," as Chicago Republican Fred "Poor Swede" Lundin succinctly put it, "would eliminate itself from politics." Consequently, such astute urban Republicans as Lundin, William Lorimer, the "Blond Boss" of Chicago's West Side, Hazen Pingree in Detroit, the Vare brothers in Philadelphia, the Ullman brothers in New Haven, and William Flinn and Christopher Lyman Magee in Pittsburgh wooed the New Immigrant vote. They fought for the inclusion of ethnic candidates on party slates and for their acceptance in the party hierarchy. They sought to turn the party away from its insistence upon legislated morality through prohibition and Sunday blue laws. Although often closely tied with business interests themselves, these urban leaders also recognized the need to establish better relations with organized labor and to accept some socioeconomic measures that benefited their constituents. Business-small town alliances fiercely resisted these efforts, but the success of Lorimer, Pingree, the Vares, and their counterparts eventually forced some policy changes. Where their advice was not heeded, the immigrant stock lower and middle orders moved steadily into the Democratic camp, greatly weakening the party's ability to retain control of state politics. Unlike middle-class Insurgents, the representatives of the urban, ethnic masses generally stuck with Taft in 1912, thus further fragmenting the party.[9]

This Republican disintegration in most northeastern states paved the way for Democratic success. Beginning in Ohio in 1908, the Democrats captured governors' mansions and state houses in Illinois, New Jersey, New York, Massachusetts, Connecticut, Indiana, Maine, and New Hampshire during the next six years. The party's portion of Congressional seats in the Northeast increased by 74.6 percent in 1910 and by 54.6 percent in 1912, enabling the Democrats to capture both national chambers. "The center of the upsurge," Samuel Hays has noted, "lay in a belt of states from New York and New Jersey on the east to Illinois on the west." This resurgence placed the party in a position to make or break the federal income tax amendment, and led to its eventual victory.[10]

The causes of this Democratic revival have long perplexed historians. For most, to quote Hays, "the roots of the Democratic revival remain an enigma." This perplexity stems largely from the fact that this same Democratic Party was largely dominated by urban political machines, led by such reputed "bossess" as Roger Sullivan in Chicago, Thomas J. Spellacy in Hartford, Charles F. Murphy in New York, Robert "Little Bob" Davis in Jersey City, James "Big Jim" Smith in Newark, Thomas Taggart in Indianapolis, and John F. Fitzgerald, Martin Lomansney, and James M. Curley in Boston. Fundamentally non-ideological professionals whose major goal was to remain in power, these Democratic leaders had only to be convinced of the vote-gathering potential of certain reform issues, and to contemplate the consequences of ignoring them. "Progressive issues were becoming so popular," Ransom E. Noble has observed of New Jersey, "that politicians of both parties ignored them only at their peril." The success of middle class reformers in wooing normal Democratic machine votes made a strong impression. Many bosses were talked into experimenting with reform ideas by social workers and reformers finding that it paid off in votes. Younger men with broader vision, such as Al Smith, Robert F. Wagner, Jeremiah Mahoney, James Foley, and Edward Flynn in New York convinced party leaders that embracing reform paid off in increased spoils for distribution. Some came to this realization through political experience, some by education, others by contact with social workers and other professionals. All proceeded from an environment where they had experienced the evils of urban, industrial life firsthand and sensed the possibilities of legislative redress for those in similar circumstances. "Give the people everything they want," Murphy told his lieutenants at Albany, while Baltimore boss John J. "Sunny" Mahon insisted that "a politician is not acting for his own interests or those of his party when he flies in the face of the people."[11]

Whatever their motives, Democratic politicians rode the reformist tide to victory in many northeastern states, controlling the machinery of government during the high point of the Progressive Era. In Ohio reform activities fueled the administrations of Judson Harmon and James M. Cox, backed primarily by the Cleveland Democratic delegation. In New York, the Democratic legislatures of 1911 and 1913, under the leadership of Tammany sponsored governors John Dix, William Sulzer, and Martin Glynn "compiled a record that has never been surpassed in the history of the New York state legislature," according to the standard history of the state. In New Jersey, Woodrow Wilson relied heavily upon north Jersey Democrats for his reform program, while in Illinois the high point of reform came under Irish Democrat Edward F. Dunne of Chicago. In Connecticut and Rhode Island, urban Democrats fell short of capturing the legislature, mostly because of malapportionment, but they did pressure the Republicans into accepting many compromise reform measures. With local variations, the Democrats, as the primary representatives of the urban, ethnic populace, emerged as the dominant political force in the key northeastern states between 1910 and 1915, becoming largely responsible for whatever reform record was achieved there. "Largely as a result of the Democratic victories of 1910," David Sarasohn has argued in his study of the party's resurgence, "Democratic governors brought progressive state legislation to most of the two-party states of the country, including New York, Massachusetts, Ohio, and Illinois." Within a period of eight years, he has concluded "the Democratic party had shaped itself into a progressive majority party."[12]

The middle class progressives, urban Republicans, and machine Democrats, although all in revolt against the business-small town alliances, clearly had different motives and goals. They often disagreed sharply over specific pieces of legislation, and never formed a stable alliance. Yet they did find many areas of cooperation, particularly where the corporation and its owners provided a common symbol of discontent. An income tax amendment that burdened only the richest three percent of the population was certainly an issue around which a wide variety of social groups could rally. Whereas southerners and westerners saw the federal income tax largely as a device to tax "foreign" wealth, the eastern lower and middle classes viewed it as a tax that fell only upon a small portion of their state's population, one whose actions had earned little claim upon their allegiance or sympathy. The efforts of the "three percent" to make their fellow citizens view the income tax as a case of "outsiders" trying to despoil the state's wealth failed to convince most of the "ninety-seven percent" that they would be injured in any way by its adoption.

The amendment also benefited from the growing internal effort in the northeastern states after 1890 to shift much of the burden of taxation on to incomes and corporations. State income taxes were adopted in Wisconsin in 1911, in Massachusetts in 1917, and New York in 1919. Some federal income tax opponents tried to argue that ratification would prevent the state from taxing incomes, but their impact was blunted by the fact that such spokesmen had generally opposed state taxation also. The struggle over ratification in the northeastern states was difficult, and the issues were often obscured by extraneous matters, but in the end the amendment carried the day in all but three of the region's legislatures. It did so because people of diverse ethnoreligious, socioeconomic, and geographical backgrounds overcame their other differences and cooperated in enacting a tax system based upon the ability to pay. Together they launched a veritable political revolution that made a temporary shambles out of long entrenched Regular Republican organizations.[13]

Nowhere was the process more evident, and the results more significant, than in New York. The Empire State was clearly the keystone of the anti-income tax defense, a fact attested to by the number of nationally prominent opponents who interjected themselves into the fray. Realizing the impact of achieving ratification by the wealthiest state in the Union, the amendment's supporters also rushed to its defense. The conflict over ratification in New York made headlines in several other states and the arguments used by opponents of the measure there were reiterated by like-minded people throughout the nation. One of the arguments generated so much controversy that it even reverberated back to the halls of Congress. "The action of the great state of New York," The Outlook claimed in a typical assessment, "carries with it far more influence than any other state possibly could," adding that Empire State residents would probably pay more federal income tax than would those of the poorest one-third of the remaining states combined. Similarly, the prestigious Review of Reviews averred in early 1910 that "other states, it was known, were waiting on the action of New York."[14] A detailed study of the fate of the amendment in the Empire State is indispensable to an understanding of how and why the measure fared much better in the industrial Northeast than even its most enthusiastic advocates dared hope.

No matter which economic category one chose, New York emerged as the unquestioned leader. It had the highest per capita income of any state, almost $300 above the national average. It ranked first in the amount of total wealth, led in the value of its products, with 16.3 percent of the national total, and contributed 17.7 percent of the value added to American products by manufacturing. New York residents received 14.4 percent of national income, nearly double that of any other state. When the federal income tax actually went into effect, they filed twenty-one percent of all returns, reported almost thirty percent of affected incomes, and paid forty-four percent of all the revenue collected. The state's residents acquired 20.5 percent of national income from interest and almost the same portion of that from dividends.[15]

But as wealthy as New Yorkers seemingly were, a small portion of their number clearly received the major share. Five of the state's citizens made over five million dollars per year, dividing up $61,636,523 between them. One hundred nineteen New Yorkers had incomes in excess of one million dollars, with a combined total of 282 million dollars. The 2,234 residents who took in $100,000 or more constituted better than one-third of the national total. The 1.5 percent of the population who made in excess of $10,000 received nearly one-fifth of the state's total income, while the 3.5 percent who made over $5,000 took in nearly one-fourth. "This would seem to indicate that, although the per capita income of the entire population in the state of New York is comparatively high," a National Bureau of Economic Research study concluded, "the per capita income of the majority falling within the lower income classes may not make as favorable a showing."[16]

For protection of their considerable holdings, New York's most affluent citizens looked primarily to the formidable Republican organization constructed by U.S. Senator Thomas C. Platt. Early in his political career, Platt had found that business leaders, "although they were constantly seeking government favors, were too loath to come under government control," according to political scientist Harold F. Gosnell, and that "party funds were available to those who were regarded 'safe' by the big business interests." David Rothman has argued that "four-fifths of the legislature at Albany would have no wish except to record his wants. And for many years, he dominated the most powerful organization in New York's history." This connection between the Republican Party and the corporation was to become common knowledge in 1914 when Theodore Roosevelt, a former Platt protege, accused the latter's successor, William Barnes, of nefarious dealings. Barnes sued for libel, Roosevelt won the suit and, during the course of the trial, many of the machine's operations were unveiled. But in 1910 the general public was still largely in the dark. "In the two decades preceeding the 1929 boom and crash," political journalist Warren Moscow has argued, "the Republican Party in the state was run by a group of men who believed sincerely that was good for the big business was good for the people of the state."[17]

To insure the loyalty of the upstate voters, the Platt organization also worked to protect the political and cultural hegemony of the state's old stock citizens from encroachment by the hordes of immigrants who were swarming into the larger cities. By 1910 the descendants of the state's original settlers felt themselves a besieged minority, since 29.9 percent of the population were immigrants and another thirty-three percent were second generation Americans. Significantly, though, two-thirds of the state's rural population was listed by the Census Bureau as native - born of native parents contrasted with only 27.2 percent of the urban population, clearly indicating that the recent immigrant was a highly urban creature. Only 12.8 percent of the population of metropolitan

New York City was of native stock and the city had about one-half the population of the state. There were heavy immigrant stock populations in Buffalo, Rochester, and Albany, but upstate was generally native territory. The hostility between the city and the rest of the state had heavy ethnoreligious overtones. "It is little wonder," Gosnell observed in his book on the Platt machine, "that the inhabitants of the upstate regions, with their Protestant faith, their native parentage, and their local traditions running back a hundred years or more looked with condescension upon the polyglot population of the great city."[18]

The Republicans upheld the supremacy of the native culture by sponsoring such measures as prohibition and Sunday blue laws and insured old-stock political advantage in the face of declining numbers by opposing devices designed to augment the urban vote, such as initiative, referendum, and the direct election of Senators. In 1894, they had effectively blunted the impact of the New York City vote by limiting the metropolis to a fixed percentage of the members of the upper house, no matter how sizeable her population, making the Senate, in Al Smith's words, "constitutionally Republican." In return, upstaters allowed their representatives to endorse economic policies primarily designed to aid the interests which, ironically enough, were mostly located in New York City. It was this harmony of interests that accounted for what Gosnell termed "the blind allegiance of the great mass of upstate farmers and shopkeepers to the Republican tradition." It was to this marriage that the state's more affluent citizens looked to stave off the ratification of the federal income tax amendment.[19]

There were more progressive forces in the Republican Party, primarily led by Governor Charles Evans Hughes. An old-stock, Protestant, upper-class advocate of good government and social responsibility, Hughes clashed with the party leadership, and earned a reputation as a crusading reformer, by investigating the insurance trust. As governor he sponsored measures, such as the direct primary, that the Platt organization clearly did not favor. Hughes had a sizeable following in the legislature and great personal prestige. His endorsement of the measure might have swung a large number of Republicans votes in favor of ratification.[20]

The outcome, however, depended largely on the attitude of the Tammany-controlled Democrats, a prospect that did not hearten the amendment's proponents. Tammany had traditionally cooperated with the business interests of the state almost as readily as had the Platt Republicans. Many Democrats were members of the notorious "Black Horse Cavalry" that regularly scuttled reform measures, and Tammanyite Bourke Cochran had been one of the most outspoken Congressional opponents of the 1894 income tax law. But things changed for Tammany Hall in the ensuing years. The Irish and a few "New Immigrants" became state legislators themselves. Richard Croker was replaced by Charles F. Murphy who, although no ideological liberal, was astute enough to realize that Tammany's major source of strength lay in the mass vote of the polyglot working class, and that this could be courted by endorsing measures designed to benefit that group. His highly pragmatic attitude toward reform was illustrated by Murphy's response to social worker and future Secretary of Labor, Frances Perkins. When she petitioned Murphy for Tammany support of some factory legislation, Murphy reminded Miss Perkins that he had earlier, at her urging, given his endorsement to a fifty-four hour week bill that he had first opposed. "It is my observation," he admitted, "that that bill made us many votes.

I will tell the boys to give all the help they can to this new bill."[21]

By 1910 Murphy was ready to trust Al Smith, Robert Wagner, and their associates with positions of leadership in the legislature and to allow them to prove their contention that reform was also good politics. Tammany men, such as William Sulzer, supported the income tax in Congress in 1909 and the Democrats were on the brink of emerging as the party of progress. In short, as a prominent good government leader Robert S. Binkerd later reminisced, "Tammany was in a state of flux so that the reformer was no longer in excusive possession of reform, if you know what I mean. That was a very subtle change which I have never seen referred to very much."[22]

The hope that ratification of the amendment could easily be achieved by a coalition of progressive Republicans and refurbished Democrats was severely jolted by Governor Hughes' message to the legislature on January 5, 1910. Hughes began by acknowledging that the federal government ought to possess "the power to levy and collect an income tax without apportionment among the states according to population" in order "to equip it with the means of meeting national exigiencies." But, he warned, that power should not be granted "in such terms as to subject to Federal taxation the income derived from bonds issued by the State itself, or those issued by municipal governments organized under the State's authority." In a statement that was soon widely quoted, Hughes charged that "to place the borrowing capacity of the state and of its governmental agencies at the mercy of the Federal taxing power would be an impairment of the essential rights of the State which, as its officers, we are bound to defend." Since this was a constitutional amendment rather than a "mere statue," the Governor warned the legislators, it constituted "in effect a grant to the Federal government of the power which it defines." The offending words "from whatever source derived," Hughes contended, were so comprehensive that, "if taken in their natural sense, would include not only incomes from ordinary real or personal property, but also incomes derived from state and municipal securities."[23] Reiterating that he did not object to conferring the power to tax incomes upon the federal government, Hughes insisted that he only objected to the all-inclusive nature of that grant. If Congress should tax the income from state and municipal bonds, he asserted, the market for them would be severely depleted. "To permit such securities to be the subject of Federal taxation," Hughes insisted, "is to place such limitations upon the borrowing power of the State as to make the performance of the functions of local government a matter of Federal grace." Surveying several Supreme Court decisions, Hughes concluded that even the divided justices in the Pollock Case "were unanimous in their conclusion that no Federal Tax could be laid upon the income from municipal bonds." Consequently, Hughes argued, the words "from whatever source derived" could only have been introduced into the proposed amendment "as if it were the intention to make it impossible for the claim to be urged that the income from any property, even though it consist of the bonds of the State or of a municipality organized by it, will be removed from the reach of the taxing power of the Federal Government." The present immunity of State and municipal bonds from federal taxation, he quoted from the case of The Collector v. Day in 1870, rested not upon any Constitutional prohibition, but only "upon necessary implication, and is upheld by the great law of self-preservation," namely that neither the states nor the federal government would tax one another out of fear of retaliation. Questioning whether such tenuous guarantees would survive the adoption of this explicit and comprehensive amendment," Hughes cautioned the legislators that "we cannot suppose that Congress will not seek to tax incomes derived from securities issued by the State and its municipalities," especially since the federal legislature had "repeatedly endeavored to lay such taxes and its efforts have been defeated only by the implied constitutional restriction which this amendment threatens to destroy." That being the case, he concluded, "I therefore deem it my duty, as Governor of the State, to recommend that this proposed amendment should not be ratified."[24]

Newspaper reactions to Hughes message followed the already established lines of opposition and support for the amendment itself. Those papers that had consistently denounced the income tax all through 1909, such as the New York Times, the New York Tribune, and the Albany Evening Journal, carefully ignored the fact that Hughes had been at great pains to endorse the idea of a federal income tax and added the Governor's objection to the taxation of state and municipal bonds to the list that they had. Reform Republican Herbert Hadley of Missouri, on the other hand, dismissed Hughes' objection as too "narrow or technical" to be taken seriously. Democrats Charles N. Haskell of Oklahoma and Albert Gilchrist of Florida disputed Hughes contention, with the latter insisting that Congressmen would not vote to impair or destroy the states that they represented. Robert S. Vessey of South Dakota replied, engimatically, that he would agree with Hughes if he were right and favor ratification if the New York Governor were wrong. Progressive Democrat John Burke of North Dakota expressed doubts that Congress would use such power, but still was reluctant to take the risk.[25]

Hughes' personal correspondence indicates that all of the responses that he received were highly favorable to his position. Nicholas Murray Butler, president of Columbia University and outspoken foe of the income tax, wrote to congratulate Hughes and revealed that Butler had "presented the view of the matter which you hold to both Senator Root and Attorney-General Wickersham some months ago, and the arguments on which that view rests seem to be fatal to the amendment as now proposed." Events were soon to show that Root and Wickersham had not concurred wth either Butler or Hughes. In a reply to Butler on January 9, Hughes asserted that "it is absolute folly to ratify an amendment to the Constitution, trusting either the Supreme Court to disregard its express words, or to Congress not to exercise its power." J. Warren Greene, a Brooklyn businessman, informed the New York governor that his criticism was too limited because the amendment would convey the right for the federal government to tax all state and municipal income. Other laudatory responses came from Detroit attorney John Miner and from W. John Bigelow, a prominent New York city author. On February 3, 1910, Fredrick D. Colson, law librarian of the New York State Library, wrote to inform the governor that Professor Raleigh C. Minor of the University of Virginia had written an article on the income tax amendment for the Virginia Law Register. In the article, according to Colson, Minor contended that the phrase "from whatever source derived" was specifically designed to make income "a single indivisible entity to be taxed on its entirety or not all." He went on to say that Minor argued that the real purpose of the amendment was to permit Congress to tax state and municipal bonds and to overrule the Supreme Court's unanimous ruling to the contrary in the Pollock decision. "If there were nothing else to condemn the proposed amendment," Colson quoted Minor, "this should suffice."[26]

But Hughes' objection also called forth a number of public rebuttals, mostly from prominent members of his own party. As Sidney Ratner has observed, these took two different tacks. One denied that the amendment would confer on Congress any power that it did not already possess and that the conventions that had prevented federal taxation of state and municipal instrumentalities would continue to operate. The other approach conceded the possible correctness of Hughes' contention, but disputed the notion that the income from state and municipal bonds should be treated any differently than was income from other sources. The first to reply was New Jersey Governor John Franklin Fort, who took issue with his New York counterpart in his own message urging ratification upon the Garden State legislature. Insisting that an income tax would reach all property, real and personal, and that Congress should have "the unquestioned power to tax incomes," Fort questioned the twin contentions that a tax on their income would decrease the value of such securities in the market and that by levying such a tax Congress might diminish the power of the states. Even if a one per cent tax were levied on four per cent state or municipal bonds worth $1000, Fort argued, the resultant tax would be forty cents per annum. "If the patriotism of our citizens and the interest of our financial institutions, who take and hold state and municipal securties, is at so low an ebb as to cause such a tax to affect the value of state or municipal securities," Fort insisted, "we are, indeed, in our unfortunate condition in the Republic." Turning to the claim that Congress might injure the states by taxing the income from their bonds, Fort offered two arguments: 1) that Congress consists of representatives of the states whose citizens would surely punish them severely for such irresponsible action and 2) that no Congress would be elected that would levy any tax designed to destroy the power or integrity of the state. "If this be not true," the New Jersey governor suggested, "the relation of our States to the Republic is surely of much less importance than many of us have hitherto supposed." Recalling that even the sharply divided Supreme Court in the Pollock Case was unanimous in its condemnation of federal taxation of states and municipalities, Fort urged the legislators to place their trust in the courts. "The inability to impose an income tax, if the necessities of the Government required it," Fort concuded ominously, "would amount to a calamity."[27]

Next to respond was U.S. Senator Elihu Root, one of the Empire State's leading Republicans, who had voted for the proposal of the amendment and helped design the corporation tax despite a long record of opposition to income taxation. In a letter to State Senator Frederick Davenport, a Hughes Republican, Root hastened to assure the lawmakers that the sole purpose of the amendment was to remove the necessity of apportioning the income tax among the several states according to population, a tactic made necessary because the Supreme Court had ruled it a direct tax in the Pollock decision. It did not "in any degree whatever" enlarge "the taxing power of the federal government," Root denied explicitly that ratification would have any effect upon "the well settled rule which restrains the national government from taxing state securities." The amendment, he contended, contained "but a single idea" that was "obviously introduced to make the exemption from the rule of apportionment comprehensive and applicable to all taxes on income." Root concluded by admonishing the legislators that "it would be cause for regret if the amendment were rejected by the legislature of New York." Davenport, an avid supporter of ratification despite Hughes reservations, read the letter on the Senate floor.[28]

Root's intervention naturally raised the issue of President Taft's position on the ratification controversy in the Empire State. The anti-amendment Times insisted that "Mr. Root always speaks with the weight of the Administration behind him." On the other hand, Taft responded to a request for intervention in the dispute between Hughes and Root made by the leader of anti-amendment forces in the state Senate, Republican Josiah Newcomb, by pleading that "I wish I could help out in New York, but I really know so little about it and feel such a hesitancy about interferring, even in my own State and still more in other States, that I don't know what to say." Enigmatically, Taft assured Newcomb that "I am with you in your desires as you state them, but I don't know how to help out in my position." Yet, just about six weeks later, Taft reportedly sent a series of telegrams to several prominent legislators urging ratification. The situation was complicated significantly because Taft was privately negotiating with Hughes concerning the latter's impending appointment to the U.S. Supreme Court, a position which Hughes resigned from the governorship to accept in late April of 1910. Moreover Root and Hughes were in disagreement over the strength of their party in the upcoming elections. On March 25, 1910, the Senator wrote the governor that "our party management in the state was pursuing a course which will result in inevitable and disastrous defeat next fall." Much of Root's concern lay in the unfavorable publicity surrounding the impeachment trial of Republican Senator Jotham P. Allds, but much also lay in the public's increasing dissatisfaction with G.O.P economic policies. If the party refused to impeach Allds and if it did not "do something to relieve thousands," Root warned party chairman Timothy L. Woodruff, it "will be condemned and the sentence will be executed upon the whole Republican Party at the polls." Despite Taft's reluctance to become personally involved, however, Attorney-General Wickersham wrote to the Republican leadership of both houses of the New York legislature on April 26 that the administration had an "earnest desire" for ratification and that "New York with its vast wealth ought not to take a position which to the country at large would seem to be based upon purely selfish considerations." Thus it would seem that Taft, torn between his own views on the amendment and those of the man he hoped to appoint to the Supreme Court, refrained from serious involvement in the ratification controversy but permitted his two closest advisors to campaign actively for the amendment.[29]

Another answer to Governor Hughes came from Senator William Borah of Idaho, a long time advocate of the federal income tax in any form. Having failed to receive a reply from the conservative Judiciary Committee as to whether the amendment would have the effect feared by Hughes, Borah stated his own view that it was ridiculous to think the amendment was meant to confer any new power, because the power was already there. "The amendment," he contended, "does not deal nor does it purport to deal with the question of power. It is intended to deal, and does deal, alone with the manner of exercising and using that power." The sole purpose of the measure, Borah added, was to abolish the rule of apportionment in taxing incomes.[30]

Senator Norris Brown of Nebraska, who had introduced the amendment in Congress, used even stronger language. The key phrase "from whatever source derived," he argued, added or subtracted nothing from the power of the government to tax incomes, since this was an unquestioned right for a century before the Pollock decision, one that was necessary for survival in wartime and for the general welfare in peacetime. Furthermore, Brown could see no reason to hesitate even if Hughes' interpretation were correct since, if Congress were that untrustworthy, it would find other means to destroy the federal system.[31]

But the most detailed rebuttal to the Hughes argument came not from Congress, but from the noted economist Edwin R. A. Seligman, in a book on the income tax that appeared at the height of the controversy. As a perennial advocate of the income tax, Seligman foresaw none of the dangers to the federal system that the Governor did and held Hughes to be wrong on three counts. Seligman argued that Hughes' interpretation of the legal force of the amendment was faulty, that the economic facts of life would prevent an income tax from damaging state and municipal bonds, and that even if Hughes were right the government should still be granted the power. The whole effect of the amendment, as he saw it, was to do away with the artificial and meaningless distinction between direct and indirect taxes, thus allowing the tax to be levied without apportionment. The federal government had never taxed the income from state and local securities, Seligman continued, and there was no reason to believe it would use this as an excuse to do so. Even if it should, the tax fell equally on all securities and was not discriminatory. "Central authority," the Columbia professor concluded, "should not be opposed in those cases where self-government means retrogression rather than progress." Seligman had pressed for a state income tax for several years, but temporarily dropped the idea to push for ratification because the debate was so "heated and close."[32]

Finally, Cordell Hull, being freer to criticize Hughes than were any of the governor's fellow Republicans, let loose the harshest verbal blast of all at his "officious intemperance." Accusing Hughes of placing himself between the plutocracy and the people, the Tennessee Congressman questioned Hughes' authority to even comment on ratification. The governor, Hull argued, had no constitutional role to play in the amendment process and had no right to veto what the legislature did. After reiterating all the arguments that others had cited to counteract Hughes' contention, Hull concluded by castigating Hughes for splitting hairs over this particular grant of federal power when he readily accepted more sweeping ones. "He swallows the camel," Hull chided, "but strains at the gnat."[33]

Despite the disagreement of such noted experts, however, Hughes' objection to the adoption of the amendment received much currency in several states. The governor of Connecticut, Frank B. Weeks, based his opposition to the measure upon it and the legislative Committee on Federal Relations in Massachusetts cited the argument as the reason for its unfavorable report. Lawmakers in Louisiana, South Carolina, and Utah cited it in their speeches. Governor Augustus Willson of Kentucky, as previously noted, lavishly praised Hughes' interpretation of the amendment in the

New York Times on February 26, 1911. In the extensive article, Willson called the amendment the "most serious encroachment on States Rights since the organization of our government," declared that ratification would empower Congress to destroy states and municipalities, and insisted that Congress would use the power if it were so granted. Governors who favored ratification, such as Democrat Judson Harmon of Ohio and Republican Fort of New Jersey, found it necessary to dispute the view in messages urging ratification. Fort was particularly critical of Hughes' reasoning, opining that "if our patriotism is so low that the possibility of a one percent tax will affect the value and sale of bonds, then we are in a sorry state."[34]

While it is difficult to assess the influence that the Hughes argument had in other states, or even in New York, it is certain that it did nothing to help the cause of the amendment. It is also difficult to judge either the merits of the Governor's objection or the depth of his conviction. In 1916, while Hughes was an associate justice of the U.S. Supreme Court, he assented to the unanimous decision in the case of Brushaber v. Union Pacific. This decision upheld the constitutionality of the 1913 income tax law that was based directly on the power conferred by the Sixteenth Amendment. The decision, written by Chief Justice Edward White, took the opposite position from Hughes' earlier stand by stating that the amendment "does not purport to confer power to levy taxes in a generic sense -- an authority already possessed and never questioned [emphasis mine] -- or to limit and distinguish between one kind of income tax and another, but that the whole purpose of the amendment was to relieve all income taxes, when imposed, from apportionment." In effect, as Hughes' biographer Merlo J. Pusey matter-of-factly admits, this decision was a reiteration of Root's refutation of Hughes' contention. Pusey insists that Hughes' interpretation "was clearly permissible" but that when the Court accepted the Root view, Hughes assented and considered the matter to be closed. Dexter Perkins, in his brief interpretive study, suggests that Hughes "took the conservative point view" on the amendment and admits that he "perhaps overstated the matter" in his message. Perkins also contends, curiously, that "the Courts so construed it as virtually to accept Hughes point of view." Actually the Brushaber decision represented a victory of sorts for Hughes since it implied that the Court would not permit Congress to tax the income from state and municipal bonds, even with the Sixteenth Amendment. In the long run, as Sidney Ratner and others have pointed out, this exemption has provided a tax-exempt haven for the wealthy, helping to blunt the intended impact of progressive taxation. In any event, Hughes' latter acceptance of the contention that he had rejected in 1910 raises serious questions concerning the wisdom of his action.[35]

For whatever Hughes' motives, there can be little doubt that many who opposed the whole idea of federal income taxation eagerly seized upon his argument, conveniently ignoring the Governor's endorsement of the notion. The World immediately grasped the significance of Hughes' intervention when it charged that "Governor Hughes has furnished the opponents of the income tax amendment the one thing they have been seeking -- a plausible argument from a highly respected source."[36] Although opposition to the amendment unquestionably came from individuals and corporations primarily desirous of preventing an income tax in any form, they were now able to camouflage their antipathy as patriotic concern for New York and the federal system. One of the first to testify against ratification was Congressman Charles Southwick, a Standpat Republican whose aversion to taxing wealth was so great that he could not even bring himself to support the 1909 compromise. Southwick stigmatized the income tax as "socialistic" and "populistic," and found it "without warrant or reasonable excuse, sectional and therefore unfair, of the nature of an attack upon the wealth of New York State, a penalty upon industry and thrift."[37]

Similarly, in a letter to the legislature in 1911, Stuyvesant Fish, prominent banker, railroad executive, and scion of one of the state's oldest and wealthiest families, condemned the proposal as a device by which partisan leaders might seek to destroy the industry of the state. The problem, Fish insisted, was for each state to keep what it had, and to husband its own resources. Justice David Brewer, who had sat on the Court in the Pollock case, likewise urged rejection, while John D. Rockefeller argued that the people had no share in the income of honest men. The vast Standard Oil interests were also represented by the company's chief attorney, John Milburn, who testified against the resolution to ratify and helped edit a pamphlet, The Proposed Sixteenth Article of Amendment to the Constitution of the United States, that the firm distributed to all lawmakers. The New York Tribune found the measure to be "class taxation," charging that people who made less than $5,000 outside New York City lived better than those who made from $6,000 to $10,000 in the city. Austen Fox, an attorney for the bankers association, testified that the amendment was a western plot to make the East pay for internal improvements, while Francis Lynde Stetson, an attorney for J. P. Morgan and former law partner of Grover Cleveland, filed a memorandum with the Judiciary Committee urging rejection. Finally, George F. Edmunds, former Senator from Vermont and another of the attorneys in the Pollock Case, wrote to the legislature on February 14 extolling the requirement that direct taxes be apportioned according to population as "this great and strong bulwark of the safety of each State against the oppression of any State or number of states."[38]

But the most elaborate brief against the amendment came in the above-mentioned pamphlet from an old foe, Joseph Choate, who had been one of Pollock's attorneys in 1895. Aided by five other corporation attorneys, including Milburn, Fox, William Guthrie, and Victor Moravetz, Choate attempted to stave off income taxation again by a combination of sectional appeal and _argumentum ad horrendum_. If the amendment were adopted, the six argued with unconscious irony, ten or twelve states would pay. Soon even the billion dollar budget would pale, as the western states clamored for hundreds of millions more to be spent on irrigation, national highways, canals, and "other innumerable fads and schemes." But the most frightening thing of all, Choate and his cohorts concluded, was that its fate would depend on "the wishes and interests of the electorate, upon party politicians seeking for a cry and competing for the votes of the very poor and very ignorant men."[39]

Throughout the 1910 session, the amendment was subjected to a barrage of fire from the states' business and financial leaders and from the spokesmen for Regular Republicanism. The Syracuse Chamber of Commerce added its voice to those already mentioned, while the bankers and financiers of the state almost unanimously opposed ratification.[40] Their appeal to state loyalty and the federal system barely obscured the fact that the tax was to be paid by individuals and opponents corporations, rather than by states. The fact that most of the amendments' opponents favored a tax apportioned by population rather than individual income was a strong indication that such a tax would not really reach the state's wealthiest citizens. Many lawmakers reiterated the objections of the state's most influential citizens. The Albany Evening Journal, long an organ of the Republican organization, reported that much of the opposition to the amendment was based upon an alleged statement made in the Alabama legislature that New York would pay a thousand dollars for every one paid by Alabama. Although unverified, the story had its effect. Senator Ralph Thomas, a professor at Colgate University, upped the ante to a million to one and changed the state to Arkansas but the moral was obviously the same. The Republican majority leader in the Assembly, Edwin Merritt, protested against delivering New York, bound hand and foot, to her sister states.[41]

But not all Republicans responded either to the Hughes argument or to the influence of the state's wealthy citizens. Lawson Purdy, secretary of the New York Tax Reform Association and a Hughes supporter, wrote an article urging ratification in the Journal of Accountancy, citing the economic and political justice of the measure. Like its national counterpart, the state association was primarily concerned with shifting the tax burden from middle class holders of real property onto corporations and personal property. In 1906 its arguments had been instrumental in influencing the state tax commission to propose a habitation tax as "the nearest approach to the income tax which seemed feasible at the time." A number of those in the Senate and Assembly who had backed the Governor on other reform issues took exception to this interpretation of the amendment. In the Senate, the progressive Republicans split almost down the middle, when one of Hughes' most consistent supporters, Frederick Davenport, introduced a motion for ratification. In a magazine article, Davenport, who was to author the state income tax in 1919, defended the conservative nature of the tax, characterizing it as "financially and economically innocuous and desirable." To his Republican colleagues he urged ratification, lest defeat of the measure give the Democrats ammunition for the fall elections.[42] There were also Republicans favorable to the amendment in the lower house, mostly the representatives of New York City's working class districts. One of their number, Andrew Murray of the Bronx, introduced the resolution to ratify while several others spoke in favor of it.[43]

But the Senate opposition to Davenport's resolution was led by Newcomb, a Hughes Republican and New York City corporation lawyer. To his way of thinking, the income tax was "a dangerous and unwarranted attack on wealth similar to the greenback craze." As a reformer of the Mugwump variety, Newcomb saw the solution to most problems in placing good honest men in office. "When the control of our legislative bodies has finally been wrested from the hands of the special interests," he declared in a classic condemnation of social and economic reform, "when the departments of the governments, national and state, have been schooled in equal justice to all, there will be no need for enactments aimed at wealth."[44]

From the outset, it was the Democrats who took the lead in sponsoring the measure, led by their younger members. Wagner was especially vocal on behalf of the measure in the Senate, urging the efficacy of the measure to those who, like himself, represented predominantly working-class constituencies. "Unlike our high Republican tariff," he contended, "this is a tax on plenty instead of necessity. It will lighten the burdens of the poor."[45] Since the Democrats were outnumbered by a sizeable margin, they had to seek Republican help, from such Hughes men as Davenport and such city representatives as Murray. With the Democrats formally committed to ratification in their caucus, Wagner and Smith tried to stress the Republican origins of the measure whenever possible. They were also careful to allow Murray and Davenport to introduce the resolutions for passage. Wagner sought to confound the opponents of the amendment by introducing a resolution to have Elihu Root address the legislature. Ironically, the Senate was treated to the spectacle of having the Republican majority arguing strenuously to prevent one of the most prominent Republicans in the state from speaking to the legislature. Hughes Republican Harvey Hinman even sarcastically inquired if Wagner were Root's mouthpiece, to which the Democrat replied that he did not care who got the credit, so long as the amendment was ratified. Another Tammanyite Senator, Thomas F. Grady, announced that the Democrats would hire a hall to hear Root if the Republicans refused to allowed him access to the Senate chambers. In the end, the Republicans managed to table the motion by a 21-18 vote, with all but five of them opposing Root's appearance. The Senator eventually had to address the legislature through a letter read by Davenport, in which he not only disparaged Hughes' constitutional objections, but also took serious issue with the selfish interests of the state's wealthy. Of course, New York would pay the lion's share, he countered, but, after all, its citizens had the money. Striking at the heart of opposition to the tax, Root urged New Yorkers "to share the burdens of the national government in the same proportion as we share its benefits." When the letter was read to the lower house, Democratic Assembly leader Daniel F. Frisbie jibed the Republicans by stating that it was a distinct pleasure to listen to "such as sound argument from the junior U.S. Senator of Democratic doctrine." Privately, though, Root assured Choate that opposition to the amendment was unnecessary, since the tax would only be used in an emergency, and that he favored standing pat against the westerners who were in "a craze for radical change.[46]

Root's argument was echoed by Senator Borah in a speech delivered before the city's most prominent business men at the New York Economics Club, in which he urged them to support ratification, and repeated Root's contention that "New York has all the money." Borah's remarks were delivered in a debate before 700 members of the Club, one of the city's most prestigious, that pitted the Idaho Senator and Lawson Purdy against Fox and Guthrie, with Stetson presiding. The others generally reiterated what they had already stated in writing.[47]

On March 29, the Assembly Judiciary Committee began hearings on the Murray ratification resolution. Murray began the deliberations by characterizing Hughes' constitutional construction as being "of an imaginary character." The opposition largely took refuge behind the Governor's message and behind the document produced by Choate, Guthrie, and their colleagues, men whom the Times described as the "leading lawyers of New York." Murray and Democratic leader Frisbie pressed for a vote in mid-April, but the Republican leadership continued the hearings in order to allow the opposition all the time possible in which to attack the measure. Finally, on April 20, Murray's resolution was brought to a vote and failed of the necessary majority, even though it received seventy-four affirmative votes and but sixty-six negative ones. Forty-eight of the fifty Democrats present favored ratification, justifying the *Times* observation that the party's representatives were "practically committed to the Federal Income Tax." The Republicans divided 64-26 against the resolution. Fourteen of the affirmative Republicans were representatives of metropolitan New York, with Brooklyn's Republican delegation dividing eight to three in favor of the amendment. The three Brooklynites who opposed ratification were men of old stock antecedants whose respective occupations were iron contractor, patent broker, and real estate agent. The other New York City Republicans who refused their assent were primarily corporation attorneys who shared socioeconomic status with the amendment's upstate Republican opponents who were predominantly bankers, attorneys, produce dealers, or fruit growers.[48]

During the debate, the frustrated Murray angrily charged that lobbyists for Standard Oil, led by the company's chief counsel J.I.C. Clarke, were orchestrating the opposition to ratification. Murray insisted that Standard Oil had paid for the pamphlet written by Choate and his colleagues and had distributed it to each member of the legislature. Clarke vehemently denied the charge and even asked for a copy of the brief. Murray continued to make the allegation, contending that Standard Oil's opposition was the best possible argument in favor of ratification. When a Republican Assemblyman moved to change the wording of his resolution by dropping the phrase "from whatever source derived" in order to meet the Governor's objection, Murray called the motion on "insult to the Congress of the United States" and "assinine, boyish, trivial, and dodging." Challenging his opponents, the New York city Republican Assemblyman urged them to "be men and meet this issue squarely. Let us stand up and be counted and not seek to beat this measure by indirection." Assembly Speaker James Wadsworth, future U.S. Senator and a key figure in the Regular Republican organization, departed from the normal procedure in having his own name inserted in the roll call so that he could be recorded in the negative. A few days later Wadsworth revealed that he had received a letter from Wickersham urging his support for ratification and that he had replied that he concurred with Hughes and regarded his interpretation of the amendment to be "absolutely correct." Throughout the entire debate, the Times sustained a steady editorial barrage against the amendment, claiming to favor the idea of a federal income tax but concurring with the Hughes interpretation and arguing that it was foolish to even vote on the measure since it was, in all likelihood, unconstitutional. Finally, on May 3, the Assembly again defeated the Murray Resolution on an almost identical vote. Two Republican Assemblyman had changed positions since the first time, with the one who moved from positive to negative citing the Hughes interpretation as his rationale. Two additional Democrats deserted the party platform on the second vote, but their ranks generally held firm.[49]

Meanwhile the amendment fared somewhat better in the Senate. The Senate Judiciary Committee began hearings on the Davenport ratification resolution in mid-April and received powerful positive testimony from Seligman and Pusey. The amendment's cause was also aided by a detailed letter to the committee from John Hampden Daugherty, prominent New York attorney, official of the Civil Service Reform League, and author of several books and articles on government. Daugherty was the son of an Irish-American Democratic alderman who had later become a judge. In his brief, Daugherty presented a brilliant point-by-point dissection of both the Hughes interpretation and the Choate-Guthrie brief. Seligman and Daugherty were so effective that the Times published lengthy refutations of their statements. Choate and Guthrie declined to testify before the committee, preferring to stand on their written statement. The bipartisan pro-ratification forces in the upper house were led by Davenport and Harvey Hinman for the Republicans, and Grady and Wagner for the Democrats, while the almost entirely Republican opposition was led by Newcomb. The latter introduced amendments to delete the phrase "from whatever source derived" and to substitute a state income tax. On motions by Wagner, both amendments were defeated on a nearly three to one vote by a curious coalition of pro and anti-income tax Senators, with the latter opposing any form of income levy. Inasmuch as Davenport, who was later to be the author of the state's income tax, joined Wagner in defeating the two motions, it seems safe to conclude that the sources of support and opposition to income taxation at both levels of government were basically identical. Hinman, a Hughes Republican from Binghampton, made the most impassioned and revealing speech in favor of ratification, declaring that "if people knew how dearly the present tax system makes them pay they would get up on their hind legs and kick the roof the capitol." Describing the orginators of the amendment as men of wisdom, integrity, and justice, Hinman also warned his fellow Republicans of the possible political consequences of rejecting the amendment. "If you want to create a political issue you can do it right now," he prophesied ominously. "As for me," Hinman added, "I shall take to the cyclone cellar when the storm hits this Fall." On May 17, the Senate approved the amendment by a narrow 26-20 margin, with only one Democrat, Howard Bayne of suburban Richmond County, joining nineteen Republicans in opposition. Thirteen G.O.P. senators, led by Davenport and Hinman, voted with thirteen Democrats to effect ratification in the upper chamber.[50]

Encouraged by the Senate action, Murray attempted to discharge the Davenport Resolution from the Assembly Rules Committee wherever it had reposed for nearly three months. For one heady momend he appeared to have succeeded on May 25, when an upstate Republican Assemblyman switched his vote from affirmative to negative after the roll call vote. Since Wadsworth and the Assembly Republican organization were openly opposed to the discharge resolution it seems likely that the Assemblyman, like so many other Republicans, were caught between constituent preferences for ratification and organization pressure. Consequently, he voted for the measure for popular consumption and switched when the organization needed his vote to prevent ratification. Only four Democrats, all from upstate New York, voted with the Republican majority to keep the Davenport Resolution bottled in committee, while thirty Republicans opted to bring the measure to the floor. Thus, for the third and final time, the New York Assembly defeated attempts to ratify the income tax amendment during the 1910 session.[51]

The anatomy of the amendment's defeat was reasonably clear to most observers. At bottom it failed due to the influence of the state's most affluent individuals and corporations acting through the medium of the Regular Republican organization and aided by a number of "reform" Republicans following the lead of Governor Hughes. Sidney Ratner cogently attributed defeat to "the pressure of the moneyed classes upon the legislature, reinforced by the prestige of Hughes, Choate and other opponents of the amendment." The New York World, a Democrat - oriented, pro-income tax paper, charged the setback to a "combination of Hughes reform leaders and 'straight goods' Republicans," singling out the roles of state G.O.P. chairman Timothy Woodruff and Rochester political boss Congressman George Aldridge. The World also blamed "the corporation combine popularly supposed to be headed by Standard Oil interests." Austen Fox, in a letter congratulating Hughes on his Supreme Court appointment, acknowledged that "we owe to you, too, the defeat of the proposed amendment," a judgment echoed by Pusey, Hughes biographer, in 1951. In a November 16, 1910 editorial, the Times, with some exaggeration, credited Hughes not only with the rejection of the amendment in New York and Virginia, but also with its postponement in New Jersey, Massachusetts, Rhode Island, and Ohio. In a May 31 letter to the Times, a correspondent signing himself only "E.D." insisted that Taft had dealt a "sad blow to the income tax amendment by placing Hughes in a position where he would probably be able to exercise the right of judicial review on any statute based upon the amendment. Perhaps, he added, that was only the "lesser of two evils" because it removed Hughes from a position to prevent ratification in 1911. The reform Republican Chicago Tribune struck at the heart of the matter by contending that the amendment was rejected because "the concentrated wealth of New York State would contribute more under a tax that was not apportioned according to population." Republican Assemblyman Seymour Lowman of Elmira, who had voted against the amendment on all three occasions, claimed, with unconscious irony, that the measure failed because a majority of the legislators were unwilling to let the South and the West tax New York's wealth. Of the ninety-five percent of New Yorkers who would escape income taxation and who might benefit by a shift away from property, excise, and import duties, the Elmira Republican Assemblymen said nothing. As predicted, the Platt-Barnes Republican organization, with unexpected aid from the leader of the reform elements within the party, had wielded sufficient power to defeat a measure that the state's most affluent individuals and corporations openly and vehemently condemned.[52]

But within six months after the defeat of the income tax amendment, the regular Republican organization received a decisive repudiation at the hands of the electorate. Whereas Hughes had enjoyed a plurality of 69,462 votes over his Democratic opponent Lewis Stuyvesant Chanler in 1908, Democrat John Dix bested reform Republican Henry Stimson by 64,074 votes and carried New York City by over 105,000. Dix, a businessman and banker from Glen Falls, was the chairman of the state Democratic Committee and a director of the reformist Democratic League. Modest, soft-spoken, and courteous, Dix proved an effective link between the Tammany dominated organization and independent Democrats. He also proved to be an outspoken and forthright champion of reformist legislation in general, and of the income tax in particular. Moreover, the makeup of the legislature was nearly reversed, with the Democrats enjoying a twenty-three vote edge in the Assembly and a 30-21 advantage in the Senate. The party's greatest gains came in the state's major metropolitan centers and so complete was their victory in New York City that only one Republican, William M. Calder of Brooklyn, was elected to the United States House of Representatives. As in most other states of the Iron Rectangle, the triumph was the party's first real taste of power since the debacle of 1896. The split that was to sever the national G.O.P. in 1912 occurred in New York in 1910. At the party's Saratoga convention, Theodore Roosevelt had bested the Regular Republican organization of Barnes, Aldridge, and Woodruff by being elected temporary chairman, writing a New Nationalism plank into the platform, and nominating Stimson, a long time friend of T.R. and a legal associate of Root. But the Barnes organization wrote the rest of the platform that endorsed Taft and the Payne-Aldrich Tariff with lavish praise, as many of their number already demonstrated a preference for maintaining ideological purity and control of the party machinery rather than winning with progressive candidates and enhancing Roosevelt's power. The Democrats, by contrast, evidenced unprecedented harmony at their Rochester conclave. "Never before," claimed the hostile Times, "has Tammany Hall been in such unquestioned control of a State Convention. Never before has any Tammany boss been enthroned as a State leader in the unlimited way in which Murphy is recognized today. The Convention is in the hollow of his hand." At Murphy's behest the convention nominated Dix, roundly denounced both the New Nationalism and the Payne-Aldrich Tariff, and endorsed economy in government, an income tax, the direct election of U.S. Senators, state-wide direct primaries, and conservation. "Both platform and candidate," Elting E. Morison has observed, "satisfied the liberal as well as the machine Democrats and appealed to many independents." The result was a veritable Democratic landslide, one that fully justified Harold Gosnell's judgment that "a political cycle closed in the state of New York."[53]

The role played by the income tax in this political revolution was far from critical. The New York G.O.P. suffered from two closely related perceptions on the part of the electorate. The first was its image as a boss-ridden, corrupt, machine-run party, an image which the Democrats and the Hughes Republicans had done much to implant in the public consciousness. That perception was epitomized in the Senate's investigation of majority leader Jotham P. Allds for accepting a bribe from the American Bridge Company in exchange for lucrative franchises. The resultant scandal compromised the entire Platt-Barnes organization and sparked divergent efforts by Taft, Root, Hughes, and Roosevelt to reform the party machinery. The resultant divisions were clearly revealed in a letter from Taft to Root on September 24 in which the President actually suggested that a Republican defeat might benefit the party in 1912 if it would "eliminate if possible from New York the dead lot that we would have to carry with Woodruff and Barnes and the rest of them as the chief representatives and the controlling representatives of New York Republicanism." The second negative perception was that of the party as protector of economic privilege and designer of an oppressive rise in the cost of living, an impression reenforced by the G.O.P.'s self-destructive paean to the Payne-Aldrich Tariff. Tariff expert F. W. Taussig ascribed the Republican defeat in New York and elsewhere to the "popular verdict -- against the stubborn maintenance of a rigid protective policy" and to "the industrial conditions of the moment." Since the G.O.P. had erroneously identified the protective system as the guarantor of prosperity, Taussig concluded, the voters logically surmised that the same tariff policy was "responsible for the rise in the cost of living." Democratic candidates pressed that theme hard, as witness Congressman Francis B. Harrison of New York City's charge that "today the Republicans are riding the backs of ninety million American citizens. Their ringleader is the great apostle of privilege, Nelson W. Aldrich." Even Woodruff, the Republican state chairman, frankly attributed the party's disaster to "great economic unrest." Since the income tax was presented as a partial cure for that very situation - as a device to equalize the tax burden, to shift the onus from consumer to producer and financier, and to provide sufficient revenue to allow for the reduction of the despised Payne-Aldrich Tariff it is difficult to see how anyone could have interpreted the results as anything but a ringing mandate for ratification. Not that the amendment emerged as a critical issue during the campaign. The Democrats strongly endorsed ratification and blamed the defeat squarely on the G.O.P. as defender of privilege and author of inflation, but their references to the question were relatively few and the Republicans largely ignored the matter. Many Republicans who had voted against ratification were victims of the deluge, but so were such supporters as Davenport, while the leader of the Senate opposition, Josiah Newcomb, was reelected. An occasional pro-ratification lawmaker in another state warned that refusal to ratify had cost the G.O.P. New York, but there is little way of determining the accuracy of such observations. There was, as we shall see, some testimony on the part of legislators during the income tax debate in the 1911 session that the amendment had played a role in individual campaigns and elections. On the whole, though, the 1910 election was a rejection of the Republican Party as corrupt political machine, protector of special interests, and oppressor of the middle and working classes and the income tax amendment was significant primarily as a component of that perception.[54]

In any case, the electoral upheaval temporarily removed the legislature from the control of the Republicans who had generally opposed the amendment in 1910 and placed it in the hands of the Tammany - dominated Democrats who had given it their overwhelming support. Everyone concurred in the judgment that Tammany, under the leadership of Charles Francis Murphy, was in absolute control of matters. "The Democrats commanded a majority in each chamber," James MacGregor Burns has observed," and Tammany commanded a majority of the Democrats." State Senator, burgeoning boss of the Bronx, and future architect of New Deal landslides, Edward Flynn later reminisced that "nothing could have been done at Albany unless Charles F. Murphy permitted or encouraged it.". And yet, as the standard history of the state matter-of-factly concludes, the Democratically controlled legislatures of 1911 and 1913 "compiled a record that has never been surpassed in the history of the New York legislature." The election returns had proven beyond a doubt what such younger organization men as Smith, Wagner, Flynn, Jimmy Walker, Jeremiah Mahoney, James Foley, and Daniel Cohalan had been insisting - that running respectable candidates and espousing progressive issues paid off in electoral victories, patronage, and power. Thus convinced, Murphy instructed his lieutenants to "give the people what they want," and he underscored his conviction by elevating Smith and Wagner to the top leadership posts in their respective houses. The result was an unprecedented outpouring of progressive legislation, including utility regulation, factory codes, tenement laws, a direct primary, the ratification of the Seventeenth Amendment, and workmens compensation. More specifically, according to Yearley, "every fiscal measure passed by the New York legislature in the banner year of 1911 had been proposed to Albany by the National Tax Association, most recently through the medium of the State Conferences on Taxation, many of whose members were disciples of N.T.A." While Yearley stresses that these proposals were largely developed by middle class intellectuals and experts and endorsed by various business and professional organizations, it is perfectly obvious, given the conditions already described, that none of these reforms could have been translated into law without the party discipline and the votes of the Tammany - dominated Democrats. By the same token, the debates and votes over the amendment in 1911 clearly revealed that the issue was, if anything, an even more partisan one than it had been in 1910, with the Democrats assuming full responsibility for ratification and whipping potential dissidents into line.[55]

In his inaugural address on January 4, 1911, Governor Dix strongly endorsed ratification of the income tax amendment in order "to give to the legislative branch of our National Government the power to impose a tax used by all other civilized countries, and which falls most evenly upon the people in proportion to their ability to share in the necessary expenses of government." The Democratic caucus quickly made ratification a party measure, but events soon demonstrated that many adherents of the new majority party had strong reservations concerning a federal income tax. One challenge came from a small but influential group of old-line, anti-Tammany Democrats, led by Francis Lynde Stetson and including Austen Fox, Herbert Satterlee, J.P. Morgan's son-in-law, Charles Peabody, the president of the Mutual Life Insurance Company, and George F. Baker, president of the First National Bank. They apparently sensed a possibility to prevent ratification in the fight being waged against the selection of Murphy's candidate for the U.S. Senate, William F. "Blue-Eyed Billy" Sheehan, by a handful of young, independent Democrats led by Senator Franklin D. Roosevelt of Hyde Park and Assemblyman Edmund R. Terry of Brooklyn. Stetson and his colleagues reportedly offered to provide Republican support for a non-Tammany Democrat if Roosevelt's and Terry's followers would help kill some "undesirable" legislation, chiefly the resolution for the ratification of the income tax amendment. Murphy got wind of the proposed deal and used it to discredit the erstwhile rebels while securing the election of Tammanyite Judge James O'Gorman. Terry, however, continued to lead the fight against ratification and remained the sole Democrat to vote against the amendment in the lower house.[56]

On April 6, the apparent Democratic consensus on the income tax was challenged by a second threat, that of New York City Mayor William J. Gaynor. Although elected with Tammany support, Gaynor was an independent and clashed frequently with the organization during his term of office. The Mayor's primary concern was that any potential statute based upon the amendment would likely make banks responsible for collecting taxes at the source of payment of interest and dividends, thus creating a flood of paper work, and that taxing such income would discourage the purchase of bank securities. Even the <u>Times</u> admitted that "it is understood that the mayor wrote the letter on the urgent request of several of his friends." In an heated exchange of letters and newspaper interviews, the Democratic governor and the Democratic mayor debated the justice and wisdom of the federal income tax. In the end, Dix stressed that Congress would not do anything to damage either the state's or the nation's financial institutions, and that, even if such a tax were levied, it would be too small to affect the purchase of securities. Echoing Governor Fort of New Jersey, Dix argued prophetically that to admit any exemptions would be to invite an avalanche of special pleaders and that true patriots would proudly pay such a tax. The Times strongly endorsed Mayor Gaynor's position, contending that the federal government did not need the revenue, that Congress could not be trusted, and that the tax was "an attempt by spenders to tax possessors" and a "disfranchisement of those who are the best judges of how money should be raised and spent to advantage."[57]

On April 19 the ratification resolution, introduced by Wagner, passed the Senate on an almost strictly partisan 35-16 vote. The opposition was led Republicans Ralph M. Thomas, Newcomb, and Edgar Brackett of Saratoga, a frequent critic of the regular G.O.P. organization. Thomas reiterated the arsenal of opposition arguments - that it would damage the sale of state and municipal bonds, that the power should be limited to wartime or other emergencies, and that the wording was "dangerous, dubious, equivocal, and ambiguous." He concluded by quoting the "grand slogan" of Arkansas, "for every dollar spent by Arkansas, New York will spend a million." Senator Brackett reversed his position from 1912, contending that Congress could adopt such a tax in short order in the event of an emergency. The pro-ratification forces were led by Wagner and Grady and the latter replied to Republican concerns over the federal system by contending that "the tax dodger has become the representative States Rights man." When Brackett moved to send the resolution back to the Judiciary Committee, the Democrats beat back the effort on a strictly partisan 30-21 division, a clear indication that many Republicans, caught between the amendement's demonstrated popularity and their party's orientation, would have preferred not to go on record either way. Just prior to the vote, Howard Bayne of Richmond, the only Democrat to vote against ratification in 1910, gave some indication that the amendment had been a significant issue in the fall elections, at least in his district. Although he still personally disapproved, Bayne confessed, he intended to vote for ratification because his previous refusal to do so "met with the extreme disapproval of my constituents and I deem it my duty to reflect their views." One Hughes Republican, James Emerson, future author of the state's corporation tax law, also switched his position to a favorable one with no official explanation. The final vote was 35-16 with only one of the thirty Democrats, Frank Loomis of Buffalo, voting in the negative. Six Republicans, five of whom had supported ratification in 1910 plus Emerson, split from their fifteen colleagues.[58]

But the Senate victory was not quickly emulated in the Assembly. The Judiciary Committee hearings, which commenced on May 10, attracted a multitude of what the Times called "men of prominence and influence from many sections of the state" who "appeared to register an impressive protest against the proposal tax." These included Stuyvesant Fish, Austen Fox, and "a number of other bank Presidents from different parts of the State." Dix continued to push the Assembly to ratify but suddenly became involved in a controversy with the chairman of the Judiciary Committee, Aaron J. Levy of New York City. Levy announced his intention of reporting out an amended resolution reworded to exempt state and municipal bonds.

He and several other Democrats, following the lead of Fox and the Times, also raised the highly questionable argument that the Democrats at Rochester had pledged only to support "an income tax amendment, not "the" amendment. On May 16, in a letter to Speaker Daniel J. Frisbie, Dix demanded a vote on "the" amendment, terming the Times - Fox-Levy rationale "trickery," a "juggle of words," and "perfidy and dishonor." Insisting that no other country exempted the income from state and municipal bonds and that it would be "grotesque" to do so, the governor insisted that it would create two classes of taxpayers -- one exempt and the other liable. Echoing Governor Fort, Dix charged that municipal bond investment was almost risk-free and that the tax on $3000 worth of bonds would only amount to $2.40 a year. Rhetorically, he asked if such objections could possibly be made in good faith "or are they part of a plan to continue a system of federal taxation which practically puts the entire burden upon commodities citizens buy and consume, rather than upon the wealth they possess and the income they enjoy." If New York is wealthy, Dix argued, it was largely because other states paid it "tribute," both directly and indirectly, noting that over one half the tariff duties were collected in the port of New York. Nothing, the governor alleged, could be more "illogical" or "absurd" than to imagine that Congressmen elected by states and municipalities would vote to impair or destroy their own constituencies. Ending on a defiant note, Dix challenged his fellow Democrats to cease their "fanciful and improbable" discussions and enact the only tax possible that "will bear upon the wealth of our people evenly and cannot be shifted to the producer and consumer."[59]

Pulling out all the stops, the Senate Democratic leadership, headed by Wagner and future Governor Martin Glynn, sponsored the already mentioned speech by William Randolph Hearst on May 17. That same day Speaker Frisbie and Assembly Majority Leader Smith pledged that their fellow Democrats would vote solidly for ratification. Frisbie argued that ratification would do much to allay the impression that New York exploits the rest of the nation and warned that the voters would be perfectly justified in repudiating the Democratic Party if it failed to live up to its platform pledge. "Political considerations, therefore, urge its endorsement," Frisbie concluded, "as well as sound business and economic reasons." On May 20, Seligman and Purdy returned to testify before the Assembly Judiciary Committee. The Columbia political economist sarcastically remarked that he would flunk any student who did not demonstrate more knowledge than did Governor Hughes. Insisting that he was a "good Republican," Seligman charged that the Republican Party had been "snowed under" in the 1910 elections, exactly as he had predicted they would if they refused ratification. At worst, he argued, an income tax would decrease the value of state and municipal bonds by only one per cent. Elaborating on one of Dix's themes, Seligman contended that seventy-eight per cent of the nation's import levies were collected at the Port of New York in 1910 while New Yorkers paid but one-fifth of the tax. "It taps the entire country," he charged, "and everything centers here."[60]

When Asemblyman Terry interrupted to ask if Seligman had read more than one authority on the subject, Seligman's supporters responded that the Columbia professor was the authority. When Levy asked how much tax John D. Rockefeller paid, Seligman replied that the oil millionaire didn't smoke and drank little, so that he paid few taxes. Purdy, J. Hampden Daugherty, and attorney J. Holden Weeks also strongly urged ratification. Daugherty turned the tables on Terry by asking if the Brooklyn Democrat did not, at least partially, owe his election to the Democrat's Rochester platform. Terry replied caustically that he didn't "believe one in a hundred of my constituents read the platform." When William Jennings Bryan testified on May 23, Terry again interrupted to insist that the Democrats had only promised "an amendment" Bryan asked sarcastically if a party could possibly ask the voters for support on a platform "not specific enough to be understood as to what it endorses." Sensing his advantage, the Great Commoner opined that he believed that "a man who accepts election on a platform and then violates it can learn morals from those in the penitentiary for accepting money under false pretenses."[61]

The Judiciary Committee hearings dragged on for three more weeks as Levy refused to discharge the Wagner resolution. Meanwhile the Times was filled with editorials and letters clarifying, refuting, defending, and attacking the testimony of the various witnesses. Seligman was the particular center of controversy, especially since his attack on the now Justice Hughes disturbed so many people that the Columbia political economist attempted to clarify his position. Saying that he had no desire to impugn Hughes and that reporters had left out part of his statement, Seligman insisted that what he "was attempting to attack was the reasoning not of Governor Hughes, but of those who shelter themselves under his great reputation." On June 1 the Times reported that a majority of the members of the Judiciary Committee opposed the amendment as worded because it "would jeopordize the value of State and municipal securities in the market," although the paper added that one committee member had been convinced by Governor Dix's letter that the amount of the tax "is not iniquitous." Three days later Levy announced that the Committee would probably not report out the resolution favorably because the majority of the members had the "courage of their convictions," and contended that once people understood the nature of their objection they would realize that the committee had acted wisely and "for the real and best interest of the states." Dix replied sternly that "either the Assembly will vote on the resolution providing for the ratification of the income tax to the Federal Constitution or the Legislature will be summoned for an extraordinary session." The Democratic leaders of both houses expressed their hearty concurrence with Dix's ultimatium. On June 6, Andrew Murray threatened to introduce a discharge petition if the committee would not report out the resolution, only to have Al Smith accuse him of playing to the gallery. Both Smith and Speaker Frisbie assured the Assembly that they would force a discharge by whatever measures were necessary. On June 8, the Times fired its last salvo against the income tax by charging that the "modern rationale of taxation is to worry taxpayers and to stop the making of money." The paper also defended the intervention of Hughes and Governor Donaghey of Arkansas in the amendment process, while accusing Dix of "dragooning the Legislature in true Rough Rider style." Since the Times regarded Theodore Roosevelt as the most dangerous villain in politics, the comparison was obviously intended to be the ultimate insult.[62]

The log jam was finally broken on June 13 when Levy emerged from a stormy three hour Democratic caucus with the incredible news that ratification had become a party measure and that he personally had introduced the resolution to that effect. Only Terry refused to concur, while former Lt. Governor Lewis Stuyvesant Chanler, Hughes opponent in the 1908 gubernatorial election, revealed that he had voted "no" in the caucus but would vote "yes" on the Assembly floor. Finally, on July 13, the Assembly passed the Wagner ratification resolution on a nearly completely partisan vote of 91-42. Terry was the only Democrat to vote no, while Chanler and James Oliver of New York City announced that they were following party discipline even though personally opposed. The eighty-three Democrats in favor were joined by nine Republicans, including Murray, six of whom were from New York City districts. One of the latter, Artemas Ward, Jr., switched his vote from the 1910 session. Thirty-two of the forty-one Republicans present voted against ratification. The most prominent spokesman in favor of the amendment was Democratic floor leader Al Smith who assured his fellow Assemblyman that he didn't "think Congress will ever unjustly tax us," and averred that the nation would be better off without any millionaries who threatened to leave the country rather than pay their fair share of taxes. The Times refused to take defeat gracefully, stigmatizing the measure, in contradictory fashion, as both a "Republican income tax," and "Bryanism," warning that it was "not a wise play for the government to break faith with the buyers of its bonds," and decrying the "betrayal of New York into the hands of the income taxers." The Times, most Republican legislators, and the opposition of many of its wealthiest and most influential citizens notwithstanding, New York became the thirty-first and most important state to ratify the income tax amendment on July 13, 1911.[63]

But the amendment's New York opponents were not quite finished. In one of the most incredible electoral reversals in history the Republicans regained overwhelming control of the Assembly in the 1911 elections, winning ninety-nine of the chamber's 150 seats. Despite the legislature's outstanding record, the Republicans, the Times, and other anti-Tammany Democrats had persuaded large number of voters to repudiate "Murphy's puppet candidates" and that "the legislature must be redeemed from the control that has disgraced it." The party's heaviest losses came in metropolitan New York where it was successfully challenged by a Fusion ticket that elected John Puroy Mitchel as mayor and gained control of the Board of Aldermen. The Times designated all regular Democratic candidates as "Tammany" and hailed the victory as a "rebuke to Tammany Leader Charles Francis Murphy and his lieutenants in the Boroughs of Brooklyn and Queens." The Republicans gained sixteen Assembly seats over 1911 in Kings and New York counties. The new majority party's leaders began to predict the reversal of the 1911 ratification almost from the beginning of the 1912 session. The Times was skeptical at first, arguing that "political considerations will prevent any action this year to repair what many conservative lawmakers regard as grave blunder" because to do so would mean a "black eye for Taft's reelection chances. Nevertheless such prominent Republicans legislators as Edgar Brackett, Ralph Thomas, Edwin Merritt, and Harvey Hinman urged that the legislature rescind its earlier action, despite the statement of majority floor leader Frank L. Young that certification by the U.S. Secretary of State had rendered such action impossible. On January 31, Hinman, with the "full approval" of William Barnes, introduced a resolution to rescind ratification on the grounds that 1) the tax would unconstitutionally permit taxation of state and municipal bonds, 2) the uniformity requirement had been violated, 3) the tax should be limited to war and other emergencies, and 4) there was no current emergency to justify its use. Since Hinman had been one the amendment's staunchest supporters in the two previous sessions, his about-face seems highly curious and can be attributed partly to the fact that Democrats in Washington were already beginning to indicate that they did not regard the tax only as an emergency measure. The Times immediately endorsed the effort and predicted that the "sober judgment of the people of New York" would concur. Hinman contended that if New York could reverse itself in 1911 it could do so again in 1912. On March 7, the Assembly Judiciary Committee favorably reported out the Hinman resolution. "Owing to the large Republican majority in the Asembly," the Times correctly predicted, "it is certain that the resolution, which has the backing of the organization, will pass the House." The paper listed the Senate as doubtful it best. The debate lasted five hours and covered most of the same ground that had been plowed in 1910 and 1911. Held in line by Al Smith, the Assembly Democrats continued their near unanimous support of the amendment, joined by eleven New York City Republicans, the single Socialist member, a Fusion representative, and two Independence League (Hearst) Democrats. Eighty-eight of the ninety-nine Republicans in the lower house voted to repeal despite the opinion of their floor leader that it was a useless gesture. The Times hailed the action, noting that the 1911 ratification was not reflective of the political mood in March of 1912. Since the Democrats retained a slim margin in the Senate, however, they were able to prevent the rescinding resolution from reaching the floor.[64]

This desperate and almost irrational effort by the Republicans to rescind ratification serves primarily to underscore the depth and intensity of the opposition to the income tax amendment on the part of most of the states' affluent citizens and the Platt-Barnes Republican organization. The amendment had clearly achieved ratification only because the electoral upheaval of 1910 had temporarily broken the stranglehold that the organization had held on state politics for nearly two decades. That political upheaval had resulted, in large measure, from voter dissatisfaction with traditional Republican economic policies epitomized in the Payne-Aldrich Tariff, policies that the income tax was supposed to help correct. To a great extent, the Regular Republican organization had self-destructed, as responsible conservatives, such as Root and Wickersham, reformers, such as Hughes and Davenport, and urban, working-class spokesmen, such as Murray and his colleagues, had attacked the party's corruption, its small-town Protestant orientation, and its blatant alliance with the state's business and financial interests. Except for Hughes, these had all given their backing to ratification and even he had endorsed the principle of an income tax. The main beneficiaries of that disintegration had been the Tammany - dominated Democrats whose leadership was astute enough to respond to the mood of times and to the counsel of younger, better educated, more socially aware politicians within their own ranks. After making an outstanding mark in 1911, they recovered from the debacle of the fall election to sweep back into power in 1912 and to compile an even more outstanding record on progressive legislation. They did so in a year when Charles Francis Murphy was so in command of events that he could cause the impeachment of his own hand-picked governor William Sulzer. After another brief setback from 1915 to 1918, the party went on, under the leadership of Governor Al Smith, Franklin D. Roosevelt, and Herbert

Lehman, to make New York the most progressive state in the Union. Wagner, Roosevelt, and others also later carried the programs that they had developed in New York to Washington.[65]

In the final analysis, New York ratified the income tax amendment through the medium of a coalition of disaffected Republicans and Democrats responsive to the needs of urban-industrial life and to the political potential inherent in meeting those needs. To a great extent, the chances of the amendment in the other states of the Iron Rectangle depended upon the creation of similar coalitions to overcome the advantage long held by similarly based and similarly oriented Republican organizations. The victory in New York was an enormous psychological and material boost, but the battle was far from over.

CHAPTER VII

BREAKING THE IRON RECTANGLE: THE NORTHEASTERN STATES

The other state legislatures of the industrial Northeast divided into three fairly distinct categories, with respect to their attitude toward the federal income tax amendment. Seven of them--Wisconsin, Illinois, Michigan, Indiana, Ohio, Maine and Maryland--ratified the measure on the first attempt in 1910 or 1911. Five others--New Jersey, Delaware, Massachusetts, Vermont and New Hampshire--first defeated or postponed the measure, only to take favorable action following the critical election of 1912. In the end, there were only three northeastern states--Rhode Island, Pennsylvania and Connecticut--that fulfilled the predictions of defeat so generally made in 1909.

The seven early successes came in states that were on the geographic periphery of the Iron Rectangle--the Old Northwest, Maine, and Maryland. These were primarily agricultural states with, at most, one or two urban, industrial enclaves. The hard core of the opposition came from southern New England and the Middle Atlantic States--the most highly urbanized and industrialized region in the nation. With the exception of Illinois and Maryland, the seven early ratifications came in states whose degree of income concentration in the higher brackets was substantially below the national average. Wisconsin had only .4 percent over $10,000 a year and 1.3 over $5,000; these individuals took in only 4.7 and 8.8 percent of total income. Indiana and Maine were scarcely more concentrated, while Ohio and MIchigan, even with Detroit, Cleveland and Cincinnati, were still below national averages. Those states most resistant to the Sixteenth Amendment were all significantly above the national averages in income concentration, with Delaware, Massachusetts, Rhode Island, Connecticut, New Jersey and Pennsylvania ranking only behind New York. Yet Maryland and Illnois, which ratified in 1910, were just as concentrated, while Vermont and New Hampshire, which held out until 1913, were even less concentrated than Wisconsin and Indiana, indicating that political factors were at least as important as economic ones in determining the fate of the amendment.[1]

The major variable in the rate of ratification was the degree and speed of the disintegration that affected the once- powerful Republican organizations in the northeastern states. Even in the most highly concentrated of states, less than five percent of the income receivers stood to be adversely affected by enactment of a federal income tax. Of those, the overwhelming majority were engaged in some form of business activity--capitalists, brokers, bankers, corporation officials, superintendents, merchants, manufacturers and accountants. Taxpayers in these occupations constituted fifty-five percent of the total in Wisconsin and Michigan, and seventy-eight percent in Maryland, with most of the other northeastern states showing figures between two-thirds and three-fourths. Beyond these, only physicians, lawyers, and engineers would be affected to any substantial degree. The only way that such a small minority could have prevailed against the income tax amendment was through the continued dominance of the legislature by business-small town Republican alliances. Only the latter had the party discipline, parliamentary skills, and the propaganda mechanism necessary to stave off a measure so obviously in the interest of the mass of voters. It was their misfortune, and the amendment's salvation, that it was considered in one of the few periods between the Civil War and the New Deal when these regular Republicans were not in firm control of the legislative process in most northeastern states. The split that rent the national G.O.P. during the Taft administration was felt with equal or greater intensity on the state level. In several states, as in New York, the defeat of the regular Republican organization came in 1910. In most others it awaited the disastrous Taft-Roosevelt split of 1912.[2]

As in New York, there is little evidence that the income tax amendment played a primary role in this electoral upheaval. The Democrats and the Progressives made ratification a platform plank in 1912, but the Republicans generally gave it no mention. Some legislators, as in New York, acknowledged that strong sentiment for ratification existed among their constituents and influenced their votes. Democratic governor Edward F. Dunne of Illinois stated, in his inaugural address, that voters in 1912 had "overwhelmingly reiterated" their support for the amendment, but such explicit expressions were rate. The revolt of 1910-1914 was a reaction against the traditional policies of business-small town Republican alliances, political and cultural as well as economic. The party's increasing committment to prohibition, for example, was a major cause of Democratic resurgence in several states. Mostly, though, Democratic success flowed from a widespread belief that Regular Republicans had betrayed the interests of the lower and middle classes for the benefit of wealthy individuals and corporations. This notion was heightened by the rising cost of living, and focused on the protective tariff as both a cause and a symbol of discontent. The G.O.P., as Taussig observed, "had reasoned _post hoc ergo propter_ when they ascribed all prosperity to their protective tariff, so the Democrats now reasoned with at least equal speciousness when they ascribed not only depression but the high cost of living to that same tariff." Voters also blamed the tariff for fostering monopoly and oligopoly, another contention requiring several qualifications, but "also an effective campaign argument." The notion of a federal income tax also squared generally with the "revolution in taxation" described by Yearley in which most states moved from property taxes to levies on income and inheritance and sought to rationalize the collection of revenue and the disbursement of expenditures. This movement produced state income taxes in Wisconsin, New York, Massachusetts, and Missouri by 1919. In a few cases, state income taxes were introduced in opposition to the federal income tax amendment, on the grounds of keeping revenue in the state. In the main, though, the patterns of support and opposition for both forms of income taxation were substantially the same. The Democrats and Progressives identified themselves with this general movement, while the G.O.P. was usually perceived of as the defender of wealth and privilege, an image exacerbated by its stand on the income tax.[3]

In most states, this electoral upheaval gave the Democrats rare and temporary control of the legislature. In others, it created a situation where Democrats, Progressives, and dissident Republicans could cooperate in enacting legislation traditionally opposed by the dominant organization. In some states, it left the Republicans in apparent control, but sufficiently shaken to make legislative concessions in order to placate restive voters. Either of these three outcomes was more conducive to ratification of the Sixteenth Amendment than anyone could have imagined in 1909. Only three Regular Republican organizations in the Northeast survived the onslaught of 1910-1912--the Penrose machine in Pennsylvania, the Brayton-Aldrich combine in Rhode Island, and the Roraback complex in Connecticut. By malapportionment, patronage, manipulation of legislative rules, dispensation of economic favors, and other devices, Penrose, Brayton, Roraback and their successors were able to perpetuate their organizations' control of their respective legislatures until 1935 in Rhode Island and Pennsylvania and until 1937 in Connecticut. Their continued strength during the electoral upheaval of 1910-1912 insured the defeat of the Sixteenth Amendment in those three states.[4]

The early ratifications came in states that generally had low levels of income concentration and that overturned their regular Republican organizations before the Great Schism of 1912. Wisconsin's, Maine's and Indiana's incomes were actually less concentrated, on the average, than those of the southern states and about the same as those of the mountain states. The drive against Regular Republicanism in the Badger State had begun as early as the depression of 1893, when the demand for government services, combined with revelations of tax evasion and "corporate arrogance," united "workers and businessmen, foreign born and native born, Populists and Republicans, drinkers and abstainers, Catholics and Protestants" in a coalition for economic and political change. Although their efforts encompassed many facets of public policy, tax reform was "the most popular and powerful of the states' reform movements," according to David P. Thelen. Middle class organizations, such as the Civic Federation, and the Municipal League joined with the state Federation of Labor and urban politicians to press for reform. All were in substantial agreement, as Thelen demonstrates, that "the tax question has really nothing to do with their assessment or distribution, but with their apportionment of the burdens." Their efforts produced crack-downs on property tax delinquency, more equitable taxation of intangible property, a state tax commission, an inheritance tax, and increased taxation of utilities and other corporations. They culminated, in 1911, in the enactment of the most successful state income tax system the nation had yet witnessed. The same session of the legislature ratified the Sixteenth Amendment unanimously. Indiana followed suit, with but one dissenting vote in the Senate.[5]

Maine experienced a similar revolt against Regular Republicanism in the first decade of the century. The G.O.P. had ruled the state since the Civil War, catering to the timber, water, textile and shoe manufacturing interests while guaranteeing the cultural and political hegemony of Yankee farmers and shopkeepers over Irish and French-Canadian laborers. The Democrats were virtually moribund, forced to rely for support mainly upon the Catholic working class. The economic squeeze of the era, though, swung many Yankees temporarily to the Democratic side. In 1910 Maine's voters returned a Democratic legislature for the only time between 1879 and 1932. In a last ditch effort to stave off defeat, the Republican convention endorsed some popular economic measures, joining the Democrats in calling for ratification. During the 1910 campaign the victorious Democratic gubernatorial candidate Fredrick M. Plaisted, son of the last Democratic governor, charged the G.O.P. with three serious defects - extravegance in state spending, failure to enforce prohibition legislation, and refusal of the national party to support progressive measures and to reform the national party organization. "An increased number of voters in the state elections," Elizabeth Ring has concluded, "were voting the

Democratic ticket to reprove Republican leadership." Plaisted made great inroads by equating the state G.O.P. with "Cannonism", while the Democratic Bangor Daily News proclaimed that "a Republican vote this year is a vote for high prices, for Sturgis deputies (prohibition enforcers), and for trust inequity." The Republican Congressmen who had voted for the Payne-Aldrich Tariff, as already noted, were subjected to constant harassment during the campaign. The victorious Democrats made an impressive record in the 1911 legislative session, enacting corrupt practices legislation, strengthening the direct primary law, equalizing the state tax burden, reducing the public debt of nearly one million dollars, and ratifying the Sixteenth and Seventeenth Amendments. But the issues of prohibition enforcement and retrenchment sharply divided their ranks. The party's legislators were divided between those who wished to enforce the former in order to make prohibition seem intolerable and those who wanted to repeal it. More important to the fate of the income tax amendment was the fact that Maine's financial woes led many Democrats to question the wisdom of granting the federal government the authority to tap tax revenues that might better be retained within the state. Eventually a Democratic legislative faction attempted to substitute a state income tax for the ratification resolution and, on May 28, the Assembly voted 82-58 to advance that proposition to a second reading. During the debate, nearly every speaker acknowledged the desirability of some form of income tax to "relieve the burden of the common people," but they divided between those who felt that the state's need for revenue justified abandonment of their platform pledge to ratify and those who argued that such promises had to be honored. Two days later, both houses voted to substitute a graduated state income tax that exempted all those with incomes under $2,000. Governor Plaisted, however, threatened to veto the measure unless the exemption was raised to $5,000, thereby increasing its popularity while reducing its potential revenue yield. Faced with that prospect, both houses reversed their earlier actions in an extraordinary evening session, with only five Democratic Senators holding out for the state income tax proposal.[6]

Ohio and Michigan also ranked below national averages in income concentration, despite seven individuals in the former and two in the latter with incomes over $1,000,000. More than 500 people in the two states made over $100,000 a year. These affluent individuals accounted for nearly thirty percent of total taxable income in Ohio and almost one-fourth in Michigan. Excluding them, the two states were much more midwestern than eastern in their income distribution. For years the Buckeye State had been governed by the Republican Party, headed by Senators Mark Hanna and Joseph B. Foraker, the former a prominent Cleveland industrialist and the latter a successful Cincinnati corporation lawyer. These two men had built a political organization "that extended its sway into almost every courthouse and city hall in Ohio," as Hoyt L. Warner has shown. They convinced the state's business leaders that the G.O.P. was "created in their own image," while defending the rural populace against the alien masses of Cleveland, Cincinnati and Toledo. In the small towns, Brand Whitlock reminisced of his boyhood, "one became in Urbana and in Ohio, for many years, a Republican just as an Eskimo dons fur clothes." Yankee farmers generally "remained 'true blue' to the Republican Party." Although Hanna and Foraker often fought over spoils and patronage, they usually managed to unite at election time.[7]

The revolt against "Ohio unreformed" began in the major cities before the turn of the century, led by such outstanding mayors as Samuel "Golden Rule" Jones and Whitlock in Toledo and Tom L. Johnson in Cleveland. Although the first two were political independents, Johnson was a former Democratic congressman who forged that party into an instrument for change. In his five terms as mayor, Johnson regulated the street railway system, reorganized city government, revamped the tax structure, and fought for municipal ownership of utilities. In the process, he constructed a powerful organization based largely upon the foreign stock, working class vote that constituted the bulk of Cleveland's electorate. In short, Johnson became a "reform boss" and "transformed the loyal Democracy of Cleveland and Cuyahoga County into a party in his own image, dedicated to social reform." As did most urban reformers, Johnson and his counterparts soon turned to state politics and bid to capture the Democratic Party. Although he never fully gained control of the state organization, Johnson did contribute a great deal to its reorientation as the party of reform.[8]

The Democrats made significant electoral gains in the first decade of the twentieth century, aided considerably by the death of Hanna and revelations of corruption within the Republican Party, especially those involving Cincinnati Boss George B. Cox, a Foraker lieutenant. In 1908, despite the fact that Taft, a native son of Ohio, carried the state, Democrat Judson Harmon became governor. Two years later he was reelected by over 100,000 votes. Harmon was succeeded by James M. Cox in 1913 and, except for a two year interim, the Democrats controlled the state for over a decade. Although Harmon and Cox were personally rather conservative, their administrations produced such a vast outpouring of reform legislation as to give Ohio a fairly high rank among the nation's progressive states. Included in the Democrat's achievements were increased taxing power for cities in 1911, a state tax commission in 1913, and an inheritance tax in 1919. They also took the lead in pressing for ratification of the federal income tax amendment in 1911.[9]

The Democrats promised ratification in their 1910 platform, and party leaders in the legislature quickly assumed sponsorship of the measure. Standpat Republican opposition was severely undercut by Taft, who lobbied for ratification in a number of letters to prominent legislators. On January 8, 1910, for example, the President wrote to G.W. Mooney, speaker of the Ohio General Assembly, that "I sincerely hope that your General Assembly will deem it wise to approve the income tax amendment, for I think that would be a help to us." Taft also solicited the lobbying efforts of Arthur L. "Jake" Vorys, his Ohio campaign manager and of the state's Congressmen. In a letter to Congressman Albert Douglas, for instance, he stated that "I am very glad that you wrote to Ervin urging the passage of the income tax amendment by the Ohio Legislature," adding that "I have already written to Vorys on the subject and have a letter from him saying he will do what he can to help out." The Democrats put the Republicans on the spot, as they had in New York, when they introduced a resolution to have President Taft address the legislature in person, but the effort died in committee. The effect of Taft's intervention is difficult to assess, but it certainly did the amendment no harm and served to reinforce some of his credibility on the income tax question. His insistence that he would only use it in the event of a national emergency was probably reassuring to troubled Republicans. In the end, only one Republican in the Senate and three in the lower house voted against ratification, with even the Cincinnati delegation adding its support. Democratic control of the legislature was clearly the key factor, however, as the Cleveland Plain Dealer was quick to point out.[10]

In Michigan, on the other hand, it was the growth of a reform faction within the Republican Party that contributed to ratification of the amendment in 1911. For many years, the G.O.P. had been controlled by an organization popularly known as the "McMillan Alliance," after its creator U.S. Senator James H. McMillan. A millionaire traction magnate from Detroit, McMillan welded the Republican Party into an effective protector of the state's industries, while assuring the continuation of his basically rural support through patronage and a favorable attitude toward prohibition. Until his death in 1902, McMillan allegedly ran the state from Washington, giving orders by telephone to his son William. The most severe challenge to the Alliance came in 1889 with the election of Hazen Pingree as mayor of Detroit. Elected as a typical middle class, good government reformer, Pingree soon shifted his emphasis in favor of thorough going social and economic reform in the interest of the city's foreign-stock working-class. Among his most popular efforts were taxation and regulation of McMillan's streetcar combine.[11]

After four terms as mayor, Pingree ran for governor and sought to extend his program statewide. Bitter opposition from the McMillan-dominated legislature hampered his effectiveness, but his career alerted reformers and conservatives alike to the possibilities inherent in his program. Pingree died unexpectedly in 1901 but the divisions within the party remained. Although the rebels were seldom able to elect their own governor, they did manage to force the Alliance to a more liberal posture. Three term governor Fred M. Warner was elected as a McMillan man in 1904, but was gradually forced to embrace the role of reformer and repudiate the machine. His legislative achievements, Stephen and Vera Sarasohn have observed, were "in essence the development of the policies of Pingree and other anti-McMillan Republicans" centering on the taxation and regulation of corporations. In desperation, the McMillan Alliance backed Chase Osborne against Warner in 1910, only to have him turn out to be even more sympathetic to change than was his predecessor.[12] It was during the twilight of Warner's last term in 1910 that he submitted the amendment to the legislature. Although he made no recommendation, the lower house voted 92-1 in favor while the Senate total was an equally impressive 23-1.[13]

Early ratification in Illinois was more remarkable, given the state's high level of income concentration. The 2.9 percent of income receivers who took in over $5,000 garnered 16.3 of its income. The .9 percent over $10,000 got 10.1 percent of the total. Fourteen of its residents received over $1,000,000 a year while another 500 or so took in $100,000 or better. Most of these affluent individuals were Chicago industrialists or financeers, so that the amendment benefited from the traditional antipathy of the downstate area toward the Windy City. The amendment's biggest asset, however, was the factionalism present in both political parties, preventing the development of a statewide Republican organization. There were, first of all, the followers of U.S. Senator William Lorimer, the "Blond Boss" of Chicago's west side and his ally, Fred "Poor Swede" Lundin.

Next were the "federal bunch," headed by such national office holders as Speaker Joe Cannon and Charles Dawes. Then there were the Chicago "reform" elements, headed by the publishers of the city's major newspapers-the Medills, Pattersons and McCormicks of the Tribune, Victor Lawson of the News, and Herman Kohlsaat of the Inter-Ocean. In the early 1900s, Governor Charles Deneen broke away from the Lorimer faction and began building his own organization. Sensing early the growing reform sentiment in the state, Deneen sought to make himself its leader by endorsing many progressive measures, but still experienced great difficulty in retaining the support of the more active insurgents in his own party. Led by Harold Ickes, Frank Funk, and Raymond Robins, the latter eventually formed the nucleus of the Progressive Party in Illinois. Superimposed upon this chaotic situation was the intense rivalry between Chicago and the downstate counties that seriously damaged attempts at party unity.[14]

The Democrats were even more bothered by the sectional split than were the Republicans. Cook County's heavily foreign stock population was anthema to the old stock people downstate. Since the Democratic Party was heavily dependent upon the Irish, Czechs, Poles, Italians, Slavs, and other ethnic groups in Chicago, it experienced great difficulties in recruiting followers downstate. The bitter struggles among Roger C. Sullivan, the reputed boss of Cook County, former Mayor Carter Harrison, Jr., and former mayor and future Governor Edward F. Dunne seriously hampered the effectiveness of the minority party, preventing it from taking fullest advantage of the Republican divisions. Although Chicago Democratic politics had an unsavory reputation, often richly deserved, each of the factions was not adverse to progressive legislation. Dunne had been elected as a reform mayor, fighting the traction companies, and his gubernatorial administration coincided with the height of the Progressive Era in Illinois. Harrison looked the other way at vice and political corruption, but was very sympathetic to economic and social reform. Even Sullivan often "threw his strength without reserve for strictly progressive measures," according to Harold Zink. The Democrats, under Dunne's leadership, were particularly interested in the creation of a state tax commission and in removing the constitutional prohibition against graduated taxation.[15]

The existence of so many elements in both parties bidding for control by appealing to the growing reform sentiment led to a remarkably easy victory for the income tax amendment in 1910. Governor Deneen publicly endorsed the measure, although adding that it "is disputed a question whether or not such a tax should be imposed by the nation in ordinary times." The Chicago Tribune not only favored ratification but challenged the other industrial states to follow suit, lest they be considered selfish and unpatriotic. The bipartisan nature of support for the amendment was underlined by its introduction in the Senate by Republican Charles Hurburgh of Galesburg and in the House by Democrat Martin Dillon of Galena. The vote in the upper chamber was 41-0, with twelve of the thirteen Democrats and twenty-nine of the thirty-eight Republicans voting for ratification. Although nine of the ten who were either absent or abstained were Republicans, there was no definite pattern. Their number included Frank Funk of Bloomington who was to be the Progressive Party's gubernatorial candidate in 1912.[16]

In the lower house the tally was 83-8, with sixty-two members either absent or abstaining. Of the eight nay votes, two were cast by Democrats from outside Cook County and six by Republicans, including Speaker Edward Shurtleff of Marengo. Frank McNichols, the Republican floor leader from Chicago, was not recorded. On the Democratic side, such prominent leaders as Anton Cermak and John H. McLaughlin, Sullivan's chief lieutenant, were also absent or abstained, but another prominent Sullivanite, Robert E. Wilson, was recorded in favor. All in all, the income tax amendment was sufficiently popular with people from most social segments and all sections of the state that only a few representatives were willing to go on record gainst it. Many others, caught between the pressure of the state's economic interests and the desires of their less affluent constitutents, refrained from voting.[17]

Maryland, which ratified in 1910, presents a somewhat different case. The Free State was habitually Democratic, largely because of its former status as a slave state and its substantial Afro-American population. Since attempts at Black disfranchisement failed twice, the survival of white supremacy dictated stringent loyalty to the Democratic Party, as it did further South. Otherwise, the statewide machine of Senator Arthur Pue Gorman and his Baltimore lieutenant, Isaac Raisin, was a carbon copy of its Republican counterparts, a union of Baltimore businessmen and eastern shore rustics. As such, it was subject to the same internal stresses as the Republican organization in Michigan. A viable reform movement began in Baltimore, a loose coalition of intellectuals, labor leaders, social gospellers, social workers, genteel socialites, and professionals. In the opinion of Raymond S. Sweeney, the most thorough student of Maryland in the Progressive Era, the reformist impulse was a "bewildering variegated evolution" characterized by "strong diversity" and constituting not a movement but rather an "organism without any central nervous system." It flourished primarily in the most urban counties where Socialists, Catholics, the foreign born, Blacks, and wage earners were most numerous and was closely connected to organized labor. The death of Gorman and Raisin opened the way for more flexible political leaders who recognized the necessity of adjusting to the demand for reform. In Baltimore the substitution of the "open, generous, approachable and democratic" John J. "Sunny" Mahon for the "autocratic, withdrawn and conservative" Raisin produced a notable shift in the machine's orientation, as James L. Crooks has observed. Mahon freely supported a wide range of reforms, pledging to send a delegation to Annapolis so good "that not even a mugwump can find fault with it." Austin Lane Crothers, elected governor as the organization candidate in 1908, did an about-face endorsing the direct primary, a corrupt practices act, utility regulation, an employers liability law, and many other reform measures. "A. L. Crothers underwent his surprise metamorphosis, from a presumably pliant party wheelhorse to an agressive champion of reform," Sweeney argues, just in time for he, Mahon, and Baltimore County Democratic Chairman J.F.C. Talbott to capture the 1909 party convention and force through a reform platform that included ratification of the income tax amendment. The Republicans, pressed by former U.S. Attorney-General Charles Bonaparte, also endorsed ratification.[18]

While endorsing the principle of income taxation, however, Crothers recommended the rejection of the amendment. He opposed lodging the power in the hands of the federal government and felt that adoption would encourage Congress to keep tariff rates high. Depsite his objections, the heavily Democratic lower house ratified the measure by an overwhelming 83-1 vote on March 21. In the Senate, though, the forces of President Arthur Pue Gorman, Jr., his father's heir as head of the statewide organization, moved to defeat the measure. The Committee on Federal Relations, which contained a majority of Gorman supporters, recommended rejection of the measure, with the Republican member and Baltimore Democrat Peter Campbell filing a minority report. The Senate overturned the recommendation of the committee on a close 15-11 vote, with the Gorman forces forming a solid bloc against ratification. Several days later the amendment passed the upper house by a 16-9 vote, with Gorman and his followers still in opposition. Eleven other Democrats, including Governor Crothers' brother Omar, joined the Chamber's five Republicans to secure passage.[19]

The federal income tax amendment, then, made significant inroads into the industrial northeast even before the crucial election of 1912. There were several other states, though that were only able to effect ratification after the Republican split. Prior to 1912 the regular G.O.P still retained sufficient vitality to defeat or postpone the measure. Three of those states, New Jersey, Massachusetts and Delaware, were heavily industrialized, with income concentrations well above the national average. The 2.4 percent of their income receivers who took in over $5,000 averaged close to one-fifth of their state's incomes. The one percent over $10,000 netted over fourteen percent. In New Jersey the Republicans were able to exercise considerable influence, even after the election of Woodrow Wilson as governor in 1910, because the apportionment system in the Senate gave each county one representative, regardless of population. This enabled the New Jersey G.O.P. to control the upper house by retaining the loyalty of the old stock populace from the rural and small town counties in the southern part of the state. Their motto, expressed by G.O.P. boss David Baird of Camden, was "never trust anyone who lives north of the Shrewsbury River." Baird's lieutenants, Colonel Sam Dickinson in Jersey City and Major Carl Lentz in Newark, kept the party competitive there until the height of the Progressive Era. Then the "New Idea" Republicans, led by George Record and Mark Fagan, arose to seek reform from within.[20]

Democratic strength in New Jersey was centered in the six northern counties--Essex, Hudson, Passaic, Union, Bergen, and Middlesex. They were all highly urban and industrialized, containing two-thirds of the state's population and three-fourths of its foreign stock citizens. The party was actually a loose confederation of powerful city machines, such as those of former U.S. Senator James "Big Jim" Smith in Newark and Robert "Little Bob" Davis in Jersey City. Until the Progressive Era, the party was as protective of wealth and privilege as were the Republicans. Smith had been one of the most outspoken opponents of the 1894 income tax. Pressure for reform arose from two sources within the party. One was the established middle class of professionals and intellectuals, represented by Wilson and James Kearney, editor of the Trenton Times. The other came from within the big city machines. Just as Smith and Wagner convinced Boss Murphy in New York that reform was good politics, such younger machine politicians as Joe Tumulty and Charles Egan in Jersey City persuaded Davis to allow them to support a growing number of progressive measures. Their efforts led to growth of what John M. Blum has dubbed "Democratic liberalism." Smith and his nephew, James R. Nugent, were slower to respond, but they gradually became more receptive. Smith and Davis endorsed Wilson for the governorship in 1910, hoping to enhance the Democrat's reputation as the party of reform. Although Wilson later broke with Smith over the issue of "the latter's" reelection to the Senate, he continued to depend upon the urban machine Democrats for the bulk of his legislative support, especially in labor, welfare, taxation and regulatory issues. Wilson's biographer Arthur S. Link has acknowledged that the Jersey City delegation "had been among his most loyal supporters."[21]

Wilson's victory in 1910 gave Democrats control of the lower house but not the Senate, spelling defeat for the income tax amendment in 1911. Wilson urged ratification upon the legislature, declaring it to be necessary because of a "decision of the Supreme Court based upon erroneous economic reasoning" and insisting that "liberal opinion throughout the county clearly expects and demands the ratification of the amendment." To the Republican-dominated Senate, Wilson stressed the Republican origins of the measure, challenging New Jersey to join those states that did not put their own interests ahead of those of the nation. The Assembly responded by passing the ratification resolution, introduced by Charles O'Connor Hennessy, an Irish immigrant lawyer from Paterson, and managed by Democratic floor leader Egan. The vote was 42-0, with nine of Newark's eleven Democrats and ten of Jersey City's twelve providing the bulk of the support. The Senate, however, defeated the resolution on an 8-12 vote that saw only one Republican join the Democrats.[22]

The 1912 election resulted in a sweeping victory for the Democrats, paving the way for ratification. With Wilson heading the national ticket, the Democrats gained control of the lower house by a 50-10 count and the Senate by a 13-8 margin. Hennessy again introduced the resolution, arguing that "only the rich will pay". It passed on a purely partisan

49-8 vote. The entire Newark and Jersey City delegations voted in the affirmative, with all the negative votes cast by Republicans from Atlantic City, Camden, Trenton and Ocean and Burlington Counties. In the Senate Democrat Peter McGinnis of Paterson introduced the resolution, taking the floor to block Republican attempts to table the measure and substitute a state income tax. McGinnis denounced the Republican ploy as a ruse, arguing that it would simply result in the wealthy moving to another state. The vote was 12-9 with only one Democrat, James F. Fielder, a Wilsonian from Jersey City, joining the Republicans in opposition.[23]

In Massachusetts, the major impetus for ratification came from the Democrats, a party heavily dominated by the Boston Irish. The Irish had entered politics there, as elsewhere, because the dominant Yankees had choked off most other avenues of advancement. Since the Republican Party was controlled by Yankees, the Irish became Democrats. By 1910 they dominated the party hierarchy. The party was essentially an alliance of several powerful Boston ward bosses, such as Martin Lomasney, John F. Fitzgerald, and James Michael Curley, in union with such non-Boston Irishmen as David I. Walsh of Clinton. Although they often ran Yankees for state-wide office, the Democrats were an Irish party, as surely as the Republicans of Henry Cabot Lodge, Winthrop Murray Crane, Calvin Coolidge, and Eben Draper were a Yankee one. With the influx of newer immigrants from French Canada and from southern and eastern Europe, the two parties were in serious competition for the loyalty of the newcomers. Generally speaking, the Republicans were more successful in such mill towns as Lynn, Haverhill, Lowell, New Bedford, Fall River and Lawrence, while the Democrats made significant gains in metropolitan Boston. The Republicans owed their good fortune largely to the efforts of the "labor legislators," union officials of the older American stock who represented the immigrant districts. The leadership of the party generally viewed them with suspicion, though, and the labor legislators were often forced to make common cause with those Democrats who also represented working-class districts. Although Massachusetts produced influential middle-class reformers, typified by Louis D. Brandeis, far-reaching social reforms such as the federal income tax amendment and the state income tax passed in 1917, resulted largely from pressure by Irish Democrats and the Republican labor legislators.[24] As Richard Abrams had concluded:

> In Massachusetts, the truly "insurgent" groups--that is those who sought to break through the deep crust of tradition--did not derive from the middle-class businessmen and professionals whom George Mowry and Richard Hofstadter, and other historians, have identified as the vital elements at the core of the Progressive Movement. They came instead primarily from the large Irish-American segment of the population, who purported to represent the newer Americans generally, and, to a lesser extent, from the growing class of labor unionists. The high tide of reform in the state came in the second decade of the century, under the leadership of Democratic Governors Eugene Foss and Walsh, backed by Fitzgerald and Lomasney and their allies.[25]

When the amendment was first considered in 1910, the Republicans were still firmly in control of both houses and they disposed of it with little effort. The opposition was led by Republican Thomas Brown who stigmatized it as a plot to despoil Massachusetts for the benefit of the western states. The Committee on Federal Relations recommended its defeat and the Senate concurred 23-11, with eight Democrats and three labor legislators favoring the amendment. The House also endorsed the committee report 126-101, in preference to the ratification resolution of Thomas Riley of Cambridge. All but one of Boston's twenty-nine Democrats and nine of Cambridge's ten voted for the amendment, as did three-fourths of the Democrats and one fourth of the Republicans in the body. Only six of Boston's twenty-one Republicans voted to ratify and the bulk of G.O.P. lawmakers from other districts were also opposed.[26]

In 1910 the Democrats captured the governorship and made great gains in the legislature. Eugene Foss, a former Republican Congressman, was elected with the strong backing of Lomansney and Fitzgerald, beginning the first of three terms notable for the passage of reform legislation. During the campaign Foss had strongly attacked the state's Republicans for their support of a high protective tariff, blaming it for the increased cost of living. "The people need protection", he charged, "protection from Payne-Aldrich." Although Foss was an old-stock, good government reformer, he was heavily dependent upon machine Democrats for support and leadership and Lomansney became minority leader in the House. In 1911 the amendment passed the lower house, managed by Lomansney and Thomas Meany of Blackstone, Foss' floor leader. The majority vote was a coalition of the Democrats and labor legislators, with fifty-two of metropolitan Boston's fifty-six Democrats voting for ratification. The same was true in the Senate, but the Regular Republicans managed to defeat the measure there by a narrow 11-10 vote, with all thirteen Democrats either voting yes or being paired in favor. They were joined by labor legislators Samuel Ross of the Spinners Union and New Bedford, Arthur Nason of Haverhill, George Newhall of Lynn, and John Schoonmacher of Taunton.[27]

Foss was reelected in 1911 and the Democrats made more gains in the House, but Republican control of the Senate again spelled defeat for the amendment. This time the lower house voted for ratification by a solid 116-95 count. Once again, ratification was supported by a Democratic-labor legislator coalition, although Andrew Doyle of New Bedford, a colleague of Ross in the Spinners Union and leader of the group in the House, voted in the negative. The Senate again rejected the measure 14-17, with the Democrats joining Ross, Newhall, Schoonmacher, and Nason in favor of ratification. The stalemate was finally broken by the election of 1912. Wilson carried the state and Foss was reelected, while David I. Walsh became the first Irish-American lieutenant-governor. The apportionment system denied the Democrats the Senate, but they and the insurgent Republicans were the dominant forces. Even the G.O.P. Regulars were too shaken to oppose the amendment again. Massachusetts finally ratified the measure in 1913 on a voice vote. Although there was no recorded tally, the previous history of the issue, coupled with the election returns, leaves no doubt that ratification owed itself primarily to the efforts of the Democrats and their labor legislator allies. After the final vote, Boston City Association President Edward B. Dailey acknowledged the stake that Boston's more affluent citizens had had in the struggle. Dailey estimated that even a flat one percent tax would cost Boston residents over one million dollars and that, with .7 percent of the nation's population, city residents would pay 1.3 percent of the proposed tax. "The figures prove Boston to be a city of exceptional wealth," Dailey laconically concluded.[28]

The Republican disarray in 1912 also reached into Delaware, dividing party strength and paving the way for ratification in the ensuing legislative session. Under the influence of the DuPont family, the G.O.P. dominated the state's politics, producing so salubrious a climate for business development that many corporations crossed over the Delaware River following the passage of Woodrow Wilson's Seven Sisters laws in neighboring New Jersey. In 1912, however, the Regulars and Insurgents split, and the situation "changed materially," according to Wilson Lloyd Beran. The majority party's factions did agree on a gubernatorial candidate, Charles R. Miller, and elected him over Democrat Thomas M. Monaghan of Wilmington, but produced Regular and Insurgent candidates for most other positions. The result was the election of a Democratic Congressman and a 21-14 Democratic edge in the lower house, while the Republicans kept control of the Senate by a slim 9-7 margin. The ratification resolution, introduced in the Senate by Democrat Thomas Gormley of Wilmington, passed the upper chamber by acclamation and the lower house by a 27-0 count. Part of this enthusiasm was due to Delaware's engagement in a race with New Jersey, New Mexico, and Wyoming to be the thirty-sixth and last necessary state to ratify, a contest that it eventually won. The most compelling reason, though, was the gains made by Insurgent Republican and Democratic forces in 1912, after the Regular Republicans had delayed consideration for nearly three years.[29]

The disintegration of the Regular Republicans also led to the ratification of the amendment by New Hampshire and Vermont in 1913, after long struggles. Unlike Massachusetts, New Jersey, and Delaware, the two New England states were predominantly rural and without any great concentrations of wealth or income. Only about 1.5 percent of the income receivers made over $5,000, taking in just over eleven percent of the total, while the one-half percent over $10,000 accounted for just over 6.5 percent of the states income. Under the circumstances, only Vermont and New Hampshire's strong ties to the G.O.P. can account for its slowness to ratify. The New Hampshire G.O.P. had strong connections with railroad and timber companies, especially the Boston and Maine Railroad, and it was generally recognized that they actually ran the legislature from the Eagle Hotel. Democratic strength was centered in such industrial towns as Manchester and Nashua, especially among Irish and French Canadian laborers, but the apportionment system kept the legislature safely in Republican hands. Reform elements eventually emerged in the majority party, led by the Farm Bureau, novelist Winston Churchill, and Robert P. Bass, a wealthy businessman who generally styled themselves "Lincoln" Republicans. This dual challenge shook the dominant organization severely, leading to Bass' election as governor in 1910. The Concord Evening Monitor rejoiced that "the Republican standard still floats over the granite peaks of New Hampshire, untouched by the landslide that buried almost the entire East under Democratic debris," but Bass had received the nomination by primary election and was not the candidate of the Regular organization. The governor suported many reform measures, including tax equalization, the regulation of campaign expenditures, an anti-pass law, a direct primary, protective legislation for women and children, and ratification of the income tax amendment. In his first address to the legislature, he urged ratification because "an income tax is the most equitable form of taxation because it draws upon citizens directly in proportion to their ability to bear the burden." The predominantly Republican legislature, however, was still dominated by Regulars and failed to act on many of Bass' recommendations, including ratification. Democratic state Senator Henry Hollis, soon to be elected to the U.S. Senate, wrote to Bass that "various interests have been at work upon various Senators, and for various reasons they have allowed their personal interests to prevail over the declarations of the platform." The Senate twice defeated the ratification on votes of 14-9 and 14-8, while the House approved it by a 249-60 count.[30]

The 1912 election produced a Democratic governor, Samuel D. Felker, and a legislature in which the Democrats and Bull Moose Progressives constituted a majority. Governor Felker declared his party's support for the direct election of Senators, workmen's compensation, and a better primary law in his inaugural speech, also urging the legislature to ratify the Sixteenth Amendment and "rectify the mistake made two years ago." He argued that a tax levied "without reference to the number of inhabitants a state has will make it bear more lightly upon our people." The ratification resolution was introduced by the Democratic floor leader, passing the House without a recorded vote. In the Senate, where Democrats had a 14-10 edge, the amendment was ratified 20-2, with Regular Republicans from Canaan and Somersworth forming the opposition.[31]

The Republicans were not quite so uprooted in neighboring Vermont, but were shaken enough to make concessions to their own dissidents.

The most old-stock of the New England states, Vermont was also the most consistently Republican. The Democrats, as political scientist Duane Lockard has suggested, were "more notable for their persistence than for their ultimate political significance." The almost impregnable Republican organization had been constructed and maintained by the Proctor family, owners of the state's largest marble extracting company, and served industrial and financial interests while keeping spending low and social services at a minimum. During the Progressive Era, an insurgent bloc began to develop within the party, emanating largely from farm and professional groups. It did not succeed in capturing either the governorship or the legislature, but did force some concessions from the Proctor machine.[32]

In 1911, the Regular Republicans were still sufficiently vigorous to bury the income tax amendment, on a decisive vote of 143-45 in the House and on a 14-10 one in the Senate. A big factor in the success of the opposition was a speech by former U.S. Senator George Edmunds, a Proctor stalwart, member of the Aldrich inner circle, and one of the attorneys who argued against the income tax in the Pollock case. Among those Senators who cast his vote against ratification was John C. Coolidge of Plymouth, whose son was to preside over the Republican prosperity of the Twenties. In the lower house, the bulk of the affirmative votes were cast by the body's forty-seven Democrats, but the Senate was composed entirely of Republicans. The 1912 election found the Proctor candidate for governor, Allen M. Fletcher, losing votes to both the Progressive and Prohibition candidates, preventing him from achieving a majority and necessitating his election by the legislature. This narrow escape forced Fletcher and the organization to accept a factory inspection law and other reform legislation, including the ratification of the income tax amendment. There can be little doubt that Fletcher's motive, in the opinion of Winston Flint, the most thorough student of Vermont reform, "was to gain control of the rebellious progressives rather than to serve the progressive cause."[33]

Within a few months after the decisive election of 1912, then, the vast majority of northeastern states had ratified the Sixteenth Amendment. Some of these ratifications came after the required number of states had acted favorably, but the political upheaval that preceded the about-faces in New Jersey, Massachusetts, and New Hampshire strongly indicates that ratification owed itself to the triumph of different forces than those that normally controlled those states. Moreover, no ratification was achieved, even after adoption of the amendment, in the three states where the Regular Republicans maintained effective control. Pennsylvania was second only to New York in total income and in concentration at the highest levels, having five men with incomes over $2,000,000 and nineteen with intakes in excess of $1,000,000. Nearly 750 others made over $100,000 and the state's figures for people making over $5,000 were exactly the national average. Connecticut and Rhode Island had only three income receivers each over $1,000,000, but were significantly above the national figures in the over $5,000 and $10,000 categories. Still, none of the three were as wealthy as New York and none significantly more affluent than Massachusetts, New Jersey, Delaware, Illinois or Maryland, all of which ultimately ratified the measure. The difference lay in the greater staying power of their Regular Republican organizations.[34]

In Rhode Island, Republican stability was the result of legislative malapportionment, combined with the political legerdemain of General Charles R. Brayton. In the Senate, each of the state's thirty-nine towns were entitled to one Senator, regardless of population, meaning that West Greenwich, population 481, had the same representation as Providence which had 224,326 people in 1910. The twenty smallest towns, with a combined total of 7.5 percent of the population, were able to control deliberations. Even in the lower house, Providence was legally limited to one-fourth of the seats although having nearly forty percent of the state's population. "The senate," Democratic state Senator and future Congressman George O'Shaunessy once asserted, "is a strong power exercised by the abandoned farms of Rhode Island." The lower house more accurately reflected population distribution but still left the major cities with considerably less proportional representation than the small towns. It was upon this foundation that Brayton had built his machine, "on the good old American stock out in the country," as Lincoln Steffens put it. By 1910 about two-thirds of Rhode Island's population were immigrants or their children, most of whom resided in metropolitan Providence, Woonsocket, and Pawtucket. By staunchly defending the political and cultural hegemony of the Yankees against these new arrivals, Brayton was able to gain the former's support for the protection of the state's industries. By virtue of malapportionment, the retention of property qualifications for local elections, and the passage of "Brayton's law," which gave the gerrymandered legislature virtual independence from the popularly elected governor, the General was able to control the state's business, even though he was blind. Brayton was also astute enough to make overtures to some immigrant groups, especially the French-Canadians, by picking such candidates as Emery San Souci and Aram Pothier for state-wide office, but his basic appeal was to old-stock, small town Rhode Island. Brayton was chief lobbyist for the New Haven Railroad, on a retainer of $10,000 a year, chief counsel for the Consolidated Street Railroad and, in partnership with Nelson Aldrich, the main stockholder in the Providence Electric Car Company. His organization reportedly openly bribed small town lawmakers and purchased elections. "Bribery," said Steffens, "is a custom of the country." On April 25, 1910 Republican State Central Committeeman Nathan M. Wright of Providence wrote to Aldrich that "I have canvassed the situation with General Brayton in regard to registration and it seems that $2000 is as little as we can get along with for Providence. He expects that you will see him about the amount needed in other places. If you will send me the above amount I will go ahead with the ward work in this way with special reference to the new Assembly districts." Brayton insisted that he did not bribe anyone, but rather just helped them get elected, and "when they are in a position to repay me they are glad to do so." For fees as little as $500, the General guaranteed passage of bills for interested businessmen. "I never solicit any business," he told Steffens, "it all comes to me unsought and if I can handle it I accept the retainer." If a legislator crossed him, the General had the power to end his political career with a simple "that man shant come back." Brayton died in 1911, but the organization conducted business as usual, under the direction of Charles Wilson, "a figurehead in the Republican Party for the vested interests of big business and manufacturers in Rhode Island," according to historian Erwin L. Levine.[35]

In this situation, the Irish-Americans in metropolitan Providence were able to establish a virtual monopoly on the hierarchy of the Democratic Party, holding the vast majority of party positions from the state level down to precinct chairmen by 1910. In addition, the Irish sought to act as the spokesmen for the Italians, French-Canadians, and Eastern Europeans, sponsoring legislation to better their economic and political position and defending their cultural heritage. By the second decade of the twentieth century, the Irish-dominated Democrats emerged as the most consistent exponents of reform in Rhode Island, working for virtually all the recognizable progressive causes. Specifically, they pressed for corporation and inheritance taxes, a tax commission, and for levies on intangible property. They were generally unsuccessful, but enjoyed some notable victories, such as the ratification of the Seventeenth Amendment, the regulation of working hours for women and children, and woman suffrage. They also made a serious, but unfruitful, fight for ratification of the income tax amendment.[36]

In 1910, the Democrats undertook responsibility for the amendment, with future Congressman George O'Shaunessy, an Irish immigrant from Providence, moving for ratification. The pro-Democratic Providence _Evening News_, later expressed the party's attitude toward the notion of income taxation in a cartoon that portrayed the income tax collector as a policeman visiting "Mr. Common People" and "Mr Rich Man." The latter was shown hiding behind the chimney of his plush mansion concealing his bulging money bags, while the former proclaimed, "You ain't got nothing on me - I ain't afraid of you - that for you". Speeches in support of the measure were made by fellow Democrats James Nolan, Dennis Shea, and George Geddes, but the Republicans were able to bury the resolution in committee. The same fate attended Democrat- sponsored resolutions in 1911 and 1912, as the Republicans, thanks to the apportionment system, were able to maintain a nearly two to one majority in both houses. Not even the election of 1912 seriously threatened Republican control and, although the G.O.P. was forced to agree to the ratification of the Seventeenth Amendment in 1913, it refused to go along with the Sixteenth. In 1910, the pro-Democrat Providence Bulletin charged that Aldrich had proposed the amendment "only as a means of staving off the immediate enactment of an income tax law," while tax expert K.K. Kennan, a close observer of events in Rhode Island, attributed the defeat to devotion to the protective tariff, insisting that Aldrich made absolutely no effort to secure ratification. Throughout the 1910 session, Aldrich and Brayton kept in close communication regarding the fate of the amendment. On Febraury 19, Brayton informed Aldrich that "there is no talk, whatever, in regard to the proposed amendment to the U.S. Constitution." He provided the Senator with the names of the members of the joint committee considering the measure and assured him that "I think it will not pass." On April 23, Brayton informed Aldrich that the legislature would adjourn the following Friday and that "we hope to kill the amendment to the Constitution of the U.S., known as the income tax, before recess and dispose of the tax bills in some form." On the last day of the session he triumphantly telegraphed Aldrich that "the Assembly voted not to ratify income tax amendment to the U.S. Constitution."[37]

A similar set of circumstances accounted for the defeat of the amendment in Connecticut. Malapportionment of the legislature was again a significant factor, especially in the lower house. The existing rules in 1910 provided that each town was entitled to a maximum of two representatives, based upon the population that had existed in 1818. This meant that Warren and Union, with respective populations of 412 and 322, had the same number of representatives as New Haven, Hartford, and Bridgeport, whose populations were at or above the 100,000 mark. It was estimated that twelve percent of the electorate could choose a majority. The Senate reflected population distribution more accurately, but it still took only about one-third of the voters to elect a majority. The most populous senatorial district contained seven times the people of the least inhabited. The small town and rural areas that benefited from this distortion were primarily Yankee Protestant enclaves in the midst of a population rapidly becoming new stock and Catholic. By 1910 sixty-nine percent of New Haven's population was composed of first or second genertion Americans, as was seventy-four percent of Waterbury's, percentages that were approximated in the other major cities of the state. The distortion was so gross that a frustrated Waterbury Assemblyman once described himself as "one of the less than twenty members who represent collectively more than one half the population of Connecticut."[38]

Another enterprising political entrepreneur had exploited the willingness of small town Yankee Protestants to protect the political and cultural *status quo*, in the service of the economic establishment. J. Henry Roraback ruled the Republican Party for over thirty years, as chairman and treasurer of the state central committee and national committeeman. From his suite in the Allyn House, he reportedly dictated the actions of the majority in the Assembly, frustrating the efforts of any dissident group. Himself a small town boy who had risen to be president of the Connecticut Power and Light Company, five other utilities, chief lobbyist for the New York, New Haven and Hartford Railroad, and president of four insurance companies and one bank, Roraback was the personal embodiment of the alliance that ran the Republican Party and the state. His strength rested on his ability to join the rural Republican base with increasingly powerful utilities and manufacturing interests. The latter provided him with the funds he needed in campaigns and expected in return only government pledged to meeting their business needs. Roraback, according to a close ally, "was the one person who could untangle legislative kinks, work out suggestions applying to state financing . . . in short when the boys got stuck, he helped them find the right answer." The organization's control was so strict that a rebellious newspaper editor once told a Republican governor that "I have as much right to my opinion as you have to J. Henry Roraback's." Unlike Brayton, Roraback did not trouble himself with petty corruption, but worked to create a favorable climate for large-scale enterprise. "Rather than stealing small things," the editor of the Manchester Evening Herald charged, "he stole the entire state of Connecticut." Under his direction, the Regular Republicans ran the state for nearly four decades, losing power only when failing health and revelations of corruption caused Roraback to take his own life in 1937.[39]

The Democrats were the "party of the outs, the immigrants, the Catholics and the poor," and it was the Irish who controlled the party machinery by 1910. The party was a loose alliance of city machines, headed by such Irish Americans as Thomas J. Spellacy of Hartford and Davey Fitzgerald of New Haven, aided by lieutenants from more recent ethnic groups such as Herman Koppleman and Tony Zazzara. The bulk of the party's legislators were also Irish, with other nationalities occasionally represented. Although these machines were allegedly captives of the Roraback Republicans, ignoring their constituents' interests in return for patronage and other favors, the Democrats in the legislature were again the major force for change in the state. As in Rhode Island, they worked for substantial political reform, regulation of business, fairer taxation, economic security, the recognition of the rights of labor unions, and cultural pluralism. On the tax front, the urban Democrats joined with the state's labor unions and several prominent Socialists to seek repeal of the personal tax, a flat rate on each person regardless of wealth or income that businessmen passed along to the consumer. Small-town Republicans generally defended the tax as the "only way to get money from aliens who work here and send money home". They defeated it several times in the lower house after it passed the Senate. The Democrats also sponsored a corporation tax that the state's industrialists successfully opposed, as well as specific levies upon banks, trust funds, insurance companies, and trolley car operators. By the same token, they became almost the sole supporters of the income tax amendment.[40]

Their task was especially difficult because Governor Simeon Baldwin, an old stock Democrat nominated to appeal to the small-town vote, questioned the wisdom of ratification. Echoing Charles Evans Hughes, Baldwin urged the legislature to wait and see how the courts ruled on the issue of taxing state securities. The Republicans went even further. Floor leader Stiles Judson reminded the legislators that Connecticut had just issued ten million dollars worth of securities and that "you, as businessmen, ought readily to see the impairment of the state's resources by the taxation of these bonds on the part of Congress." Later he added that Connecticut would pay an unjust share of the tax to finance "the billion-dollar projects of the west." Another Republican senator argued that "it would be a different question if Connecticut got the benefit from the tax." The pro-ratification Hartford Courant despaired over the fatuous nature of these arguments, insisting that this was to be a tax on individual income, not on a state, and that "the bigger a man's income, the greater the amount of protection he received from the government and the greater his obligation to sustain it." Only a few Republicans agreed, however, such as John Brinsmade, a school teacher from Washington, who declared that he was in favor of ratification because the tax would not be levied on incomes less than $5,000 per year.[41]

The Democrats, despite the qualms of Governor Baldwin, worked for ratification in 1911, with Lester Peck of Danbury leading the debate in the Senate. When the measure failed, 6-19, in the upper house, the six votes in favor were cast by Democrats from New Haven, Hartford, Waterbury, Bridgeport, Norwalk and Danbury. Four Democrats joined the Republicans in opposition, allegedly responding to Baldwin's objections. Included in the pro-income tax votes was that of Hartford Boss Spellacy, the Democratic floor leader. In the lower house, the measure was introduced by Joshua Meltzer, a Russian immigrant Democrat from Bridgeport, and the main argument in favor was made by Charles Murphy of the same city. Ultimately, the unfavorable recommendation of the Committee on Federal Relations was adopted by an 89-74 vote, with the Democrats contributing the bulk of the pro-income tax votes. The Democrats made gains in the 1912 election, with Wilson carrying the state and Baldwin being reelected, but the malapportioned legislature remaained in Republican hands. The ratification resolution, again introduced by a Bridgeport Democrat, died in committee.[42]

The situation in Pennsylvania was different because there was no viable Democratic Party to challenge the entrenched Republicans. Begun by Simon Cameron during the Civil War, developed by Matthew Quay in the late nineteenth century, and perfected by Boies Penrose in the early twentieth century, the Pennsylvania Republican organization was truly state-wide, exercising effective control not only in the rural and small town areas, but also in Philadelphia and Pittsburgh. By a judicious use of patronage and graft, the machine reduced the Democrats to a shadow party with little power or ambition, "nationally notorious for its alliance with the Republicans," according to historian Wayland Dunaway. Pennsylvania, accordingly, remained second only to Vermont in its loyalty to the G.O.P. and no Democrat was elected governor or U.S. Senator between 1894 and 1936. Moreover, the organization's urban adjutants, the Vare brothers in Philadelphia and Christopher Lyman Magee and William S. Flinn in Pittsburgh, had beaten the Democrats at their own game by absorbing the various ethnic groups through patronage, recognition, and economic favors. Penrose's real strength, though, continued to "lay between these two metropolitan areas in the rural districts" and in his connection with the economic interests represented by the Pennsylvania Manufacturers Association, as J. Roffe Wike has demonstrated. "Callous, cynical and indifferent to measures designed to lessen the burdens of the toiling masses," Robert Bowden has charged, "he served the vested interests with unceasing devotion." Penrose handpicked governors and directed the deliberations of the legislature, through such lieutenants as James "Sunny Jim" McNichol, a jovial Irishman who would have seemed more at home in the Democratic Party almost anywhere but Pennsylvania.[43] So complete was his control of the legislaure that the Philadelphia Public Ledger alleged that:

> For some time Boies Penrose has ruled Pennsylvania as absolutely as the Sultan of Sulu ruled his distant domain and with almost as much tender regard for the interests of his subjects. It is several generations since the people of Pennsylvania have known independence except as a Fourth of July tradition. Men who have known Harrisburg in recent decades have spoken of the legislature as pawns . . . they have been puppets automatically obedient to the will of the Sultan of Sulu. There have been periods when the legislature had to mark time and the governor look sublime in enforced idleness until McNichol could discover the will of his sovereign overlord in Washington.[44]

In time, though, the party's urban minions pressed for greater influence by appealing to the needs of their largely ethnic, working class constituents. In Philadelphia the Vare brothers openly challenged the machine in 1911 when William ran for mayor against the Penrose candidate. Although he lost, his older brother Edwin, "the Duke," was rapidly becoming the most powerful politician in the city, in addition to exercising considerable influence as a state Senator. At his highest point, it was estimated that Ed Vare controlled three-fourths of Philadelphia's delegation in the lower house and one-half its Senators. Although voting with the Penrose organization much of the time, Vare and his people clashed with it on such issues as woman suffrage, the direct election of Senators, and election reform. In 1914, they precipitated an open break by threatening to endorse Progressive gubernatorial candidate Gifford Pinchot, eventually forcing Penrose to accept a Vare man, Dr. Martin Brumbaugh, for the position. During Brumbaugh's administration, Ed Vare became the governor's leading spokesman while the Penrose forces worked openly to defeat several gubernatorial proposals. In Pittsburgh similar pressures led Flinn to seek an even clearer separation from the state organization. Like the Vares, Flinn often supported reform legislation, especially if it benefited his constituents or hurt Penrose. By 1912 the differences between the Pittsburgh boss and the state machine were so great that Flinn threw in his lot with the reformers, helping to form the Washington Party that backed Theodore Roosevelt for the presidency. Roosevelt carried the state and the Washington Party held the balance of power in the lower house, but the Regulars retained control of the Senate. The Vare and Flinn forces successfully guided several reform measures through the house but the upper chamber generally prevented their enactment.[45]

On May 10, 1911 the lower house ratified the amendment by a 139-4 margin. Thirty of Philadelphia's forty-one representatives voted in the affirmative, including John R.K. Scott, the Vare leader in the lower house, and only one against. Sixteen of Pittsburgh's twenty-four representatives also declared in favor with only two in opposition. The number of abstentions was significant, indicating that the Penrose machine was reluctant to attack the measure too openly in the face of its demonstrated popularity, especially in the two urban centers. Instead, the Regular Republicans sought to kill the measure by having it referred to the Committee on Judiciary Special, sarcastically deemed the "morgue" and the "strangler of the senate" by the Harrisburg Patriot, because it was dominated by such Penrose stalwarts as McNichol, William Crow, Sterling Catlin, William Sproul and John Fox. Vare was also a member, but was outnumbered by Penrose men even if he had been willing to oppose them on the issue. For almost two years, the committee sat on the ratification resolution, reporting it out only after the Roosevelt victory in 1912. The committee report recommended rejection of the measure, characterizing the income tax as "little short of reckless and foolish," and went on to chastize the federal government for seeking revenue to make "unnecessary expenditures under the guise of progress." It concluded by stating that ratification would endanger the protective tariff system, penalize all those who made over $5,000 per year and make them feel like criminals and "because, as one of the wealthy states, she (Pennsylvania) would bear far more than her proper share of the burden." The Senate endorsed the committee report without a recorded vote, despite the action of the lower house and, if Vare or Flinn disagreed, they made no overt attempt to resist. Thus the Regular Republicans, having retained control fo the Senate even in the face of the upheaval of 1912, added the income tax amendment to the list of progressive measures rejected by that body.[46] The reaction of many Pennsylvanians was best expressed by the Philadelphia Evening Bulletin:

> Notwithstanding the fact that only two more states are needed and that they will be found among the ten states that have not acted makes it idle for Pennsylvania to say "aye" or "nay" to the proposition, and that such states as Illinois, New York and Ohio which share with Pennsylvania and Massachusetts the great bulk of the tax, have approved it, yet your committee has recommended that the legislature, as a matter or principle, shall refuse to ratify the amendment.[47]

Despite the defeats in Rhode Island, Connecticut, and Pennsylvania, however, the industrial Northeast responded to the income tax amendment with an enthusiasm that was unexpected by friends and foes alike. This, in turn, helped insure the ratification of an amendment that few observers thought had much chance of success. Even though a few of the northeastern states ratified after the necessary number of states had acted, most of them responded in time to provide the crucial margin of victory. The cause of this unexpected development was the temporary breakup of the Regular Republican organizations that controlled these states as late as 1909, organizations that produced the standpat Republican Senators who had opposed the federal income tax in 1909. Pressure from dissatisfied elements in their own party eventually led to a rift that culminated in the electoral disaster of 1912, opening the door for control of the legislature by Democrats and Progressives.

Concurrently, the Democrats underwent a metamorphosis that prepared them to function as a vehicle for progressive reform. The urban Democratic machines responded to pressure from constituents, to the insights of younger, better-educated men in their own ranks, to increased demands upon their coffers, and to the general popularity of reform to become instruments of change. Democratic administrations in such urban, industrial states as Illinois, Ohio, New Jersey, New York, and Massachusetts ranked as the high point of progressive reform there. Even where they did not achieve power, as in Connecticut and Rhode Island, Democrats were clearly the most consistent supporters of forward-looking legislation. It was totally in character, then, for the urban Democracy to emerge as the most noticeable champion of the federal income tax amendment in the industrial states. Uniting with the representatives of other discontented groups who sought to create a system of taxation based upon the ability to pay, they effected the ratification of the amendment in most of the states that were expected to spell its doom.

CHAPTER VIII

THE END OF THE ROAD

The enactment of the present system of income taxation followed the ratification of the Sixteenth Amendment by less than eight months. True to predictions, the nation's first permanent income tax proved to be one of low rates, modest graduation, a high exemption, and a minimum of deductions. At most, it directly affected only about three per cent of the country's income receivers. The measure's final form resulted from the interaction of three reasonably distinct groups - the leadership Democrats, a small but influential group of dissenters within the majority commonly styled as "radicals," and the Insurgent Republicans. While the Democratic leadership sought to construct a tax with modest rates that would affect only the nation's most affluent citizens in order to guarantee its acceptance and raise the necessary revenue, the radical Democrats and Insurgents pressed for much higher rates at the upper levels. Although their major cry was for tax equity, some of the Insurgents proposed such stiff rates as to define the income tax as an instrument for the redistribution of wealth. In the end, the radical Democrats and the Insurgents forced the Democratic leadership to adopt a higher rate schedule. Having failed to prevent ratification and clearly unable to head off the enactment of the tax, the greatly depleted Regular Republicans had to content themselves with attempts to delay the effective date, to lower the exemption, to decrease the rates, and to exempt a variety of special interest grouups. Since most of these efforts ultimately failed, the Regulars were forced to witness the adoption of a tax system that realized most of their worst fears. Because the tax was voted upon as a section of the Underwood-Simmons Tariff and not as a separate item, they were denied even the consolation of recording their opposition. Their frustration was perhaps best expressed by Elihu Root, who had defied his closest collegues in the hope that the tax would have minimum impact and only be used in an emergency, when he charged that the income tax had been drawn by men "who did not understand American ways of doing business."[1]

Long before the Sixteenth Amendment had been officially ratified, the most ardent advocates of a federal income tax were clearly proclaiming their intention of utilizing the power that was to be vested in Congress. As early as May of 1911, Franklin Escher, financial expert of Harper's Weekly, was assuring readers that once the federal government was empowered to do so, "the speedy enactment of some sort of an income tax is sure to follow." Even while some of the amendments' backers, such as Taft and Root, were assuring worried colleagues that the tax would only be resorted to in wartime or in other emergency situations, leading Democrats were paving the way for the immediate introduction of an income tax law. Once the Supreme Court upheld the validity of the corporation excise tax of 1909, in the case of Flint v. Stone Tracy (1911), Cordell Hull and the Democratic majority on the House Wage and Means Committee attempted to apply the principle to individuals and partnerships in an effort to reach all incomes over $5000. The difference between such a tax and an income tax, Hull later observed, was the difference between "tweedledum and tweedledee." The committee report acknowledged the desirability of an income tax, but advanced two reasons for not recommending one: 1) because the states were still considering a constitutional amendment to meet the Supreme Courts objection in the Pollock Decision that the tax had not been apportioned according to population, and 2) because the Court, had, in Flint v. Stone Tracy, held that the corporation excise tax did not require apportionment. Extending this latter interpretation to individuals, the committee argued, "will accomplish in the main all the purposes of a general income tax law and at the same time escape the disapproval of the Supreme Court, as it keeps well within the principles laid down by that court in sustaining the constitutionality of the Corporation Tax Act." The measure passed the House by an overwhelming 250-40 vote, but a Republican-controlled Senate added a number of amendments, "none of which affected the body of the Democratic measure," according to the New York Times. The Democrats and Regular Republicans combined to defeat an attempt by Borah to substitute a flat two per cent income tax. On July 29 the House refused to accept the Senate amendments and the measure, already under the threat of presidential veto, died. Some Democrats candidly admitted the semantical nature of the measure and acknowledged that it was a master political stroke designed to impale Taft on the horns of a dilemma. If the tax had passed and Taft signed it into law, the Democrats could have claim credit for enacting the only form of income tax possible. If Taft and the Senate Republicans had killed it, the action would put Taft "in the hole," and "hamper him sadly if he is the Republican nominee for the Presidency next November." The pro-income tax New York World led the praise for measure, while such anti-income tax papers as the New York Times, New York Sun, Albany Journal, Boston Advertiser and Transcript, Milwaukee Sentinel, Philadelphia Press, and Brooklyn Eagle roundly denounced it. The Sun stigmatized it as "an evasion and a subterfuge and quibble," and demanded that the income tax question be settled on its merits. Hull, on the other hand, credited the 1912 excise tax proposal with providing a boost to ratification and deemed the latter "an event of fundamental importance to me" and "fruition to my work and study of twenty years."[2]

The Democratic sweep of 1912 removed any possible doubt that the victorious party would attempt to exercise its prerogative just as soon as it become constitutional to do so. The party's platform "congratulated the country" upon the proposal of the two pending constitutional amendments "demanded in the last national platform" and called upon "the people of all the States to rally to the support of the pending propositions and secure their ratification." The Progressive Party also favored ratification of both amendments, while the G.O.P. ignored the two proposals that many historians have judged to be among the most important achievements of the Taft Administration. As the Washington correspondent of the Philadelphia North American astutely observed, the income tax, "knocked out of a Democratic tariff bill by the Supreme Court eighteen years ago, thus in the Whirligig of time, comes back from the grave in which it has rested ill and taps again at the door of a Democratic Administration. Once ratification was accomplished, few would have quarrelled with the prediction of the Independent that "it appears to be the settled purpose of the dominant party in Congress to pass an income tax bill at the special session."[3]

The Sixty-third Congress was a far different body than the Sixty-first. The most obvious and significant difference was the transformation from Republican to Democratic control. Whereas the G.O.P. had had a 219-172 edge in the House and a 60-32 one in the Senate in 1909, the Democrats now enjoyed a 290-172 margin in the lower chamber and a 51-45 advantage in the upper house. The Democrats' resurgence was primarily based upon spectacular gains in the industrial Northeast, the stronghold of the regular Republicans. In 1909 the G.O.P. had controlled eighty-three of the one-hundred and seven seats in the House of Representatives allotted to the New England and Middle Atlantic states; by 1913 the Democrats occupied seventy-three of them. In the eastern half of the Midwest, the Republican's 73-29 advantage in 1909 had been supplanted by a 58-44 one by the Democrats.[4]

1910 and 1912 were among the greatest loss years for congressional seats ever suffered by the Republican Party in the Northeast, ranking with 1932, 1934 and 1964. In 1910, they lost 24.1 per cent of their New England and Middle Atlantic seats. The Democrats gained twelve seats in New York, eight in Ohio, five in Illinois, and four each in Pennsylvania, Missouri, New Jersey and West Virginia. All told the party gained fifty-nine seats, nearly all of them in states east of the Mississippi and north of the Ohio and Potomac rivers. Two years later, the G.O.P. sustained an even more decisive loss of 40.1 per cent. The entire five man Connecticut delegation had changed from Republican to Democratic hands while New York City voters returned only one Republican to Congress out of twenty-five in 1913, in contrast to a near-even split in 1909. The number of Republicans in the ten man Chicago delegation had declined from seven to three and a seven to three G.O.P. edge in New Jersey had become a nine to four Democratic bulge.[5]

Democratic gains in the Senate were less spectacular, but again were most evident in the industrial Northeast. New Jersey and Indiana each elected two Democrats to replace their two Republicans of 1909, while New York, Ohio, Illinois, New Hampshire, and Maine all supplanted one of their G.O.P. solons. Moreover, the Republican total did not reflect the party's actual voting strength, especially on the income tax, because of the large number of Insurgents who had deviated sharply from the party leadership on the issue in 1909 and who were, if anything, even more militant on the subject in 1913.[6]

Furthermore, deaths, retirements, and electoral defeats had removed many of the income tax's most implacable foes, including the dean of the Standpat Republicans, Nelson Aldrich. Gone too from the Senate was Winthrop Murray Crane, along with as Shelby Cullom, Eugene Hale, Stephen Elkins, Morgan Bulkeley, and Chauncey DePew. Of the seven Senators who had abstained from giving their assent to the 1909 compromise proposal, only two, Henry Cabot Lodge and Frank Brandegee, remained, joined by John W. Weeks of Massachusetts, who had voted against the amendment in the House of Representatives. In the lower chamber, too, many 1909 opponents were no longer present, including John Dalzell, Nicholas Longworth, Ebeneezer Hill, Samuel McCall, Charles Southwick, and William Calderhead. Of the fourteen regular Republicans who had voted "nay" on the submission of the amendment, only three were left, Andrew Barchfeld, Augustus Gardner, and Joseph Fordney. What roles their opposition to the income tax played in their defeats is difficult to determine, but it is almost certain that their overall Standpat record had been repudiated and more clear that their absence did the measure's chances no harm in 1913.[7]

There were, of course, many influential people, both within Congress and without, who still opposed the income tax, but few of them proved willing to challenge the idea on its merits by 1913. Only on rare occasions did overt attacks on the principle of income taxation surface, either in the press or in the halls of Congress. Newspapers that had opposed the tax consistently for several decades still assailed it editionally from time to time. The New York Sun found it socialistic and objected to taxing the few for the benefit of the many, while the New York Herald, St. Louis Globe-Democrat and the Journal of Commerce denounced the tax as "wrong in principle and un-American in spirit." The protectionist American Economist and the Wall Street Journal also continued to voice their displeasure. Even the New York Times occasionally betrayed its longheld view that the tax would punish the honest and let the dishonest escape and, in an April 12 editorial, came out in favor of a stamp tax instead.[8]

Letters to the Times also periodically got down to fundamentals. W.B. Mitchell of Chattanooga, Tennessee, on June 7, characterized the proposed levy as "extortion," a penalty on "ability and intelligence" and an imposition on a "small class powerless to defend itself." On September 13, Karl P. Harrington charged that the income tax would wipe out any small gain which might result from tariff reduction, at least for those with taxable incomes, while former U.S. Senator George Gray of Delaware saw the levy as "double taxation" and "espionage," odious in practice even if fair in theory. Congressman Jefferson Levy of New York City, in a speech before a businessmen's association, deemed the tax unnecessary unless there was a fiscal emergency and predicted the defeat of the party that enacted it, despite the fact that, as a Democrat, he was bound to vote for it. Congressman J. Hampton Moore, Philadelphia

Republican, termed the income tax a penalty "upon the earning power of people" and insisted that the voters did not mandate "the tax of abominations" in 1912. Republican Senators, such as Jacob Gallinger, William Dillingham, and Henry Cabot Lodge, also flayed the tax directly on the floor of the chamber, with Lodge stigmatizing it as "confiscation of property in the guise of taxation."[9]

The principle of a graduated tax also drew much fire from conservative critics and some of the measure's sponsors were reluctant to include a graded scale, lest it raise possible constitutional objections. Once the pro-graduation Democrats forced its acceptance by the House Ways and Means Committee, though, it was obvious that the tax would be scaled and the point was scarcely raised during the Congressional debates. The Republican Regular's sense of resignation to the inevitability of a graduated income tax was well expressed by George Graham of Philadelphia when he acknowledged that "the time for debate upon the question as to whether or not we shall have an income tax has long since passed," and that opponents must "put away their private views and promise not to hinder, obstruct or interfere."[10]

Despite such exhortations, the most diehard opponents of the tax did make a few desperate efforts to head off passage of the income tax section or to include provisions of questionable constitutionality, in an apparent hope that the Supreme Court might once again come to their rescue. A handful of Republican conservatives voted for some of the highest possible rates proposed by the Insurgent wing of their party, with the transparent aim of making the tax so odious that the Democrats might be forced to slay their own creation. Most of their cohorts, though, refused to play this dangerous game for fear that it might prove as counter-productive as had Aldrich's acceptance of the income tax compromise four years earlier.[11]

In the same vein, Senators Gallinger and Dillingham proposed to substitute a revenue-sharing scheme with the various states, but were unable to muster even all the votes of the party Regulars. More serious were the efforts of several Republicans to raise the issue of taxation of state and municipal securities that had caused so much controversy in New York and elsewhere when raised by Governor Hughes. By proposing the taxation of incomes of state and municipal employees and the revenue from their bonds, conservatives seemingly hoped to lay the ground work for possible invalidation by the Supreme Court, an eventuality that would either end the income tax agitation altogether or necessitate another constitutional amendment. Along the same lines, the Regular Republicans also injected the question of taxing the salaries of the president and federal judges.[12]

Unsuccessful in these efforts, the traditional opponents of the income tax sought to introduce a number of extraneous issues designed to distract the attention of the measure's supporters and delay collection of the tax as long as possible. Chief among these were objections that newly created collectors were to be placed, at least temporarily, outside the civil service system. The National Civil Service Reform League, headed by such good government advocates as President Charles W. Eliot of Harvard, Seth Low, Moorfield Storey and Charles G. Bonaparte and head-quartered at 79 Wall Street, petitioned Congress on the matter, as did the Municipal League of Los Angeles and a variety of similar organizations.

The New York Times also backed the argument editorially, but the sincerity of the objection was seriously compromised because the case in Congress was made by such consistent advocates of patronage as Lodge and Penrose. Since it was estimated that it would take two years to empower enough Internal Revenue agents under the civil service regulations, the intent of the regular Republicans to delay the effective date of the tax appeared obvious.[13]

No more effective were the periodic attempts of Elihu Root and others to argue over the effective starting time of the tax. They first objected because the Democrats proposed to tax all income earned from January 1, 1913, since Congress allegedly did not receive the authority until the amendment was officialy ratified in February. When the Democrats accommodated this objection and moved the starting date to March 1, Root and his supporters insisted that no income could legitimately be taxed unless it was earned after the actual passage of the law, a change that would have protected incomes from taxation until October. This latter tack failed to sway the Democrats and its introduction merely serves to illustrate the desire of the Regular Republicans to delay the impact of the tax as long as possible.[14]

Recognizing that arguments over civil service and starting time were delaying tactics at best, the anti-income tax forces in Congress concentrated their attention upon creating a tax structure that would minimize the impact of the levy upon those interests that they had traditionally fostered. There is no evidence as to how much coordination of effort existed, but the striking similarity of the activities of Regular Republicans in both houses suggests strongly the existence of some central direction. At any rate, conservative spokesmen in both chambers pursued two basic strategies: 1) to design the rates in such a manner as to place the tax burden primarily upon the lower and middle classes, and 2) to write in preferences for those engaged in certain categories of business enterprise. The first aim was evident primarily in the myriad attempts to lower the amount of the exemption. The Democrats proposed that no single person who earned under $3,000 a year, nor married person earning less than $4,000, would have to pay any tax, a circumstance that placed the burden on less than three per cent of the population.[15]

Responding to memorials from such groups as the Investment Bankers Association, the National Association of Manufacturers, and the Real Estate Exchange, the Regular Republicans sought to lower the minimum to $1,000 or less, thus including the bulk of the middle class and many wage earners. This tactic would not only spread the burden, but might also lead to widespread unpopularity for the tax, since one of the strongest arguments in favor had always been that "only the rich will pay." At the same time, it would produce so much revenue that rates in the upper income brackets could be kept relatively low, thus undercutting the argument that higher rates were needed for fiscal reasons. Naturally, the Standpatte consistently resisted all attempts to raise the rates in the upper brackets as well, except for those few who occasionally did so with an intent to embarrass. Periodicals that had consistently opposed the income tax were most vocal in their denunication of higher rates, especially the New York Tribune and Times, the San Francisco Chronicle, The Nation, and The Commercial and Financial Chronicle. By lowering the minimum and keeping the maximum rates as small as possible, the operation of the law could prove entirely different from the aim of its sponsors, and be, at worst, a minor nuisance for the well-to-do.[16]

The same design animated attempts to provide preferential treatment for those individuals and corporations who derived their incomes from certain types of enterprises. The Regular Republicans received plenty of ammunition in the petitions and memorials directed at Congress from various industries. Investment bankers and holding companies asked for preference on the grounds that their shareholders would also have to file individual returns and that this amounted to double taxation. They also argued that taxing foreign bond holders would discourage the sale of U.S. securities, and severely damage the balance of trade. New York exporters argued that taxing their income would amount to the taxation of exports and thus be unlawful. Real estate corporations requested that they be allowed to deduct all the interest paid on their indebtedness. Insurance companies were particularly active, with New York Life, for one, asking its policyholders to write their Congressmen to gain considerations of various sorts. Between April 26 and May 22, 1913, Bristow alone acknowledged the receipt of 173 letters from constitutents asking that mutual life insurance companies receive preferential treatment. His Kansas Republican colleague, Congressman Victor Murdock, also received numerous letters from insurance company exectives, insurance agents, and policy holders asking for similar consideration. Darwin P. Kingsley, president of the New York Life Insurance Company, was particularly active on behalf of his industry, testifying before Congressional committees, writing letters to the editor of major newspapers, and organizing letter writing campaigns of policy holders. On February 4, 1913, he even wrote to Oscar W. Underwood insisting that the Democrats adopt the provision in the British income tax law "excepting from the burden of the tax a limited portion of the income which the taxpayer applies to the purchase of insurance for the protection and support of his family." One big bone of contention was the provision to tax insurance companies on their undistributed dividends -- funds marked for disbursement to policyholders but not actually paid. The companies argued that this was actually the policyholder's money and hence not subject to the corporate income tax. Mutual insurance companies presented themselves as non-profit organizations, a status belied by their impressive intake.[17]

In addition, business enterprises of all descriptions objected to the principle of collection at the source that the Democrats included in the corporate income tax section. This provision, used extensively in England, stipulated that, in the payment of various kinds of income such as interest on bank accounts, stock dividends, and rent, the payee must withhold the amount of the tax and send it on to the Internal Revenue Service. This applied only if there was a reasonable expectation that the recipient would earn enough income to be covered by the tax. If it turned out differently, the receiver could apply for a refund. However awkward this procedure may have been, it commended itself to many income tax proponents because it eliminated the need to evaluate intangible property.

Because it put the bookkeeping burden on banks and corporations rather than the I.R.S. or the individual, there was a multitude of protests on the question. The heads of all the prominent New York banks objected to the procedure, as did the city's Chamber of Commerce. They were joined by the American Bankers Association, the Massachusetts Realty Exchange, the Investment Bankers Assocation, and similar organizations. Their cause and that of all the other enterprises seeking preferential treatment were generally espoused by the Regular Republicans in both houses, as part of their overall plan of blunting what they could no longer prevent. Ironically, Franklin Escher, the investment columnist for Harper's Weekly, staunchly defended the income tax against charges that it would have a deletorious effect on those who derived their income primarily from investments. "If the tax is an influence on bond prices at all," Escher argued, "it is an influence so slight and exerted on so small a part of the market that it can be regarded as negligible." Indeed, Escher argued that lowering the tariff would leave middle class people more money to invest, thereby serving as "an influence of incalculable benefit not only to the big corporations, but to the general business of the country."[18]

The proponents of the income tax law divided into three fairly distinct groups. Most visible were the Republican Insurgents, the same westerners and midwesterners who had combined with the Democrats in 1909 and who were only too anxious to do so again. The latter party was sizeable a majority firmly committed to enactment of the tax, but the apparent unanimity insured by the caucus pledge served to hide a deep and growing bifurcation. The leadership and its supporters favored a moderate course that would exempt most of the population without unduly antagonizing the wealthy. A number of more "radical" (to quote the New York Times and Washington Post) senators and representatives sought higher rates for the upper income brackets, a position that moved them even closer to the Insurgent Republicans. Their numbers cannot be precisely gauged, and their caucus pledge to support the official version prevented them from making a floor flight, but their insistence eventually caused the leadership to agree to a compromise that nearly doubled the rates in the upper brackets.[19]

On most of the objections raised by income tax opponents, the three pro-income tax groups were in virtual agreement. They combined to prevent the injection of possibly thorny constitutional questions, such as taxing the income of state and municipal employees. They united to defeat Regular Republican efforts to postpone the effective date of the tax. The three groups divided along partisan lines, though, on the issue of civil service, with the Insurgents generally joining the Republican Regulars, since the issue involved patronage. Both Democratic groups rallied to defeat the attempt to require immediate civil service status for tax collectors, partly because it was an attempt to delay but mostly because they agreed with Senator James Martine of New Jersey that ninety-five per cent of current federal employees were Republicans frozen into their jobs by G.O.P. manipulation of the merit system.[20]

Divisions within the pro-income tax coalition were somewhat more apparent on the question of preferences for special business interests, but there was general agreement to oppose most of them. Some Democrats, such as Walter McCoy of New Jersey and Joseph Goulden of New York, endorsed special consideration for insurance companies because they were insurance men themselves. The big city Democrats produced a serious crisis in the ranks by seeking a special exclusion for the profits that cities derived from the operation of transportation and utility companies.

Provisions to this effect were introduced by Democrats J. Hamilton Lewis of Chicago and James O'Gorman of New York in the upper house and by Republican William Calder of Brooklyn in the lower one, a situation that bespoke the unanimity of big city representatives in both parties on the question. The issue alienated many eastern Democrats from their southern and western allies. Otherwise, all three segments of the pro-income tax coalition were unified against the creation of special preference.[21]

The major issue of contention for the proponents of the tax was the rate schedule. There was general agreement that the \$3,000 exemption should remain, although a few Insurgents, such as LaFollette, Borah and Bristow, felt it should be even higher, and others, such as George Norris, wanted to introduce additional exemptions for children. The Democrats were firmly committed to the \$3,000 figure, though, both out of conviction and political expediency. Most doubtless agreed with the justice of Congressman Clyde Tavenner of Ilinois contention that those wealthy crying "class legislation" were "never heard to complain, however, of the existing class legislation which taxes the hats, coats and shirts of the masses almost seventy-one per cent, and does not require men like Rockefeller and Carnegie to pay a single cent." They would also probably have agreed with the answer given to a man signed "M" by another New York Times correspondent calling himself "C.E.A.," when the former complained that only one in twenty-five would have to pay. The latter countered that the important thing was that "M" would still have considerably more disposable income after he paid the tax on his \$8,000 than would those who made only \$3,000 and escaped taxation. The issue, as Oklahoma Democrat William "Alfalfa Bill" Murray put it, was that a man "should be taxed upon the surplus that he makes over and above the amount necessary for a good living." The tax, said Andrew Peters of Boston, should be levied "on the incomes of those who derived the greatest assistance from the government in protecting their property and who are most favorably situated to meet this expense."[22]

In addition to the justice of exempting those already heavily burdened by the tariff and other federal levies, the Democrats were also well aware of the political implications. The New York Times reported with horror that Congressman A. Mitchell Palmer of Pennsylvania had opposed lowering the exemption to $1,000 because it would upset the voters. "Formerly laws were commended by the equality and generality of their application," the paper editorialized in righteous indignation. Congressman Richard Austin of Tennessee echoed Palmer when he asked rhetorically if lowering the exemption to $1,000 would not result in the defeat of every member who voted for it, while President Wilson favored the higher exemption "in order to burden as small a number of persons as possible with the obligations involved in the administration of what will at best be an unpopular law." This view was echoed by such staunch income tax advocates as Seligman and the Springfield Republican.[23]

The greatest division in the ranks of the income tax forces, as previously noted, came over the upper limits of the tax. The Democratic leadership in both houses was dominated by economic moderates, mostly from the South, who believed that the nation should inaugurate the new system of taxation on a relatively modest scale, increasing the rates only as the need developed and the country became accustomed to the idea. Some were even dubious about the merits of a graduated tax. Their views were very well expressed by the chairman of the Senate Finance Committee's subcommittee in charge of the income tax, John Sharp Williams of Mississippi. Williams had supported the 1894 tax, but preferred prudence at first. "We cannot revolutionize things too rapidly," he cautioned rebels of both parties, "we must have some regard to existing conditions." On another occasion, he accused Bristow of using the tax to punish the rich by high rates. The Insurgents viewed this as a hopelessly conservative view and expressed their dissatisfication by introducing a large number of rate-raising amendments in both houses. Bristow assured one constituent that, although he favored an income tax, he thought that "it ought be drawn along entirely different lines from the present bill." Specifically, he favored a higher exemption, credit for each child and deductions for mortgage payments and rent. Bristow was so concerned about the issue that he corresponded with Seligman even though the latter was in France. The political economist urged Bristow to insist upon "stoppage at the source" and higher rates for "unearned" income, positions that the Insurgents generally advocated. Continuing his unpredictable stance, Theodore Roosevelt demanded "a much heavier progressive tax on incomes" in an article in The Outlook. The radical Democrats, for their part, leaned toward the Insurgents but, rather than join them openly, put pressure on the leadership to compromise and, in the end, threatened to bolt if changes in the rates were not made.[24]

As it had been in 1909, the question of the income tax was almost inextricably bound up with the issue of tariff revision and the attendant need for additional revenue. The Democrats made tariff reform the primary plank in their 1912 platform, declaring "it to be the fundamental principle of the Democratic party that the Federal government, under the Constitution, has no right or power to impose or collect tariff duties, except for the purpose of revenue." The platform identified the "high Republican tariff" as the principal cause of the unequal distribution of wealth, and favored "the immediate downward revision of the existing high, and in many cases prohibitive, tariff duties," insisting that material reductions be speedily made upon the "necessaries of life." The Democrats also demanded that imported goods in competition with "trust controlled products and articles of American manufacture which are sold abroad more cheaply than at home should be put upon the free list." The platform denounced President Taft for vetoing the "pop gun" tariff bills of 1912 that reduced rates on various items and scored the G.O.P. for being "faithless in its pledges of 1908." In a related plank, the Democrats specifically identified the high protective tariff and the trusts created by it as the major reason for the high cost of living that seemed to be the voter's major economic concern. They concluded that no substantial relief from inflation was possible "until import duties on the necessaries of life are materiallly reduced and these criminal conspiracies broken up." Doing the former, the Democrats freely acknowledged elsewhere, would drastically reduce federal revenues by as much as $70,000,000, a deficit that a federal income tax could supposedly neutralize.[25]

The Republicans, conscious of the furor aroused by the Payne-Aldrich Tariff and its association with the high cost of living, contented themselves with a reaffirmation of their "belief in the principle of protection as having been of the greatest benefit to the country, developing our resources, diversifying our industries, and protecting our workmen against competition with cheaper labor abroad." To replace that system with a tariff for revenue only, the Republicans warned, would destroy many industries and create serious unemployment. Acknowledging that some existing duties were too high and in need of reduction, the G.O.P. platform insisted that duties should be high enough to protect industries and wages while raising the necessary revenue. Insisting upon the need to acquire sufficient information to revise the tariff scientifically, the Republicans lauded themselves for establishing the Tariff Board and condemned the Democrats for ignoring its findings. Finally, it attacked the "pop-gun" tariff bills "as sectional, as injurious to public credit, and as destructive to business enterprise." Emphatically denying that the high cost of living was due to the protective system, the party pledged itself to support a "prompt scientific inquiry" into the real causes and to act upon the information yielded. Interestingly enough, the Progressive Party platform proclaimed the "true principle" of the 1908 Republican platform that a protective tariff should "equalize conditions of competition between the United States and foreign countries." Affirming their orientation toward the best interest of laborers and consumers, the new party pledged to seek "an immediate downward revision of those schedules wherein duties are shown to be unjust or excessive." Going the Republicans one better, the Progressives urged the establishment of a "non-partisan scientific tariff commission" that would establish the cost of production, the potential revenue yield, and the effect of rates on prices. Echoing the Democrats, they condemned the Payne-Aldrich Tariff "as unjust to the people." Echoing the Republicans, they damned the Democrats for espousing a tariff for revenue only, "a policy which would inevitably produce widespread industrial and commercial disaster." Attacking both, they demanded immediate repeal of the Canadian Reciprocity Act. The Progressive position on the high cost of living was a bit more complex, attributing it "partly to world-wide and partly to local causes" partly to material and partly to artificial causes, "and claiming that their stands on the tariff, the trusts, and conservation "will of themselves remove the artificial causes." Emulating the Republicans, the Progressives pledged themselves "to such full and immediate inquiry and to immediate action to deal with every need such inquiry discloses."[26]

In reality, the Democrats did not attempt to enact a tariff for revenue only, but rather a "competitive" one that would set rates low enough to compel American producers to compete with foreign manufacturers. This meant establishing duties high enough to produce the desired revenue but low enough to discourage monopolies and trusts from making excessive profits. The resultant competition, the Democrats believed, would yield a "reasonable profit" to both domestic and foreign producers. More specifically, the Democrats promised to equalize the burden of customs duties by placing higher rates on luxuries than on "necessaries." Secondly, they pledged to remove all forms of protection from domestic monopolies and trusts, a Democratized version of the Insurgent's "Iowa Idea." By reducing the duties on "necessaries" or by placing them on the free list, the Democrats hoped to lower the cost of consumer goods and reduce the cost of living. Inplicit in all of this, as Ralph L. McBride has argued, was the conviction that these actions would induce American industries and workers to increase their efficiency in order to compete effectively with foreign competition. Rather than following the "scientific" method, advocated by Republicans and Progressives alike, of determining rates based upon data concerning relative costs of production, the Democrats proposed to lower as many existing rates as possible in order to stimulate competition without utterly eliminating the needed revenue. Such a method was clearly less "scientific" than the one advocated by the Republicans and Progressives, as they and most modern day observers have insisted. The Democrats turned a deaf ear to Republican-Insurgent pleas to delay action until the necessary data had been acquired. "Their time had come," Taussig has observed, "and to have waited would have been politically suicidal."[27]

Nearly all of the important Democratic decisions regarding both the tariff and its income tax section were made and agreed to in party caucus, with each member pledging himself to support that position on the floor. This was done because of the unique situation in each chamber. In the House, where the Democrats had a top heavy majority, there were an unusually large number of first term (and, in all likelihood, single term) members who were almost totally dependent upon the administration and the leadership. In the Senate, on the contrary, the party's margin was so narrow that any slippage would imperil key administration measures. Presenting a united front and enforcing stringent party discipline were considered absolutely vital conditions for success. This meant that most of the discussions were held behind closed doors, but there were plenty of Democrats who were willing to discuss the proceedings with newspaper reporters and other interested parties. Thus organized and disciplined, the Democrats were able to realize their general goal of lowering a significant number of tariff rates and enacting an income tax to cover the anticipated revenue loss. As McBride has astutely observed, the party had four general aims in tariff revision: 1) to place high duties on luxury items, 2) to lower the rates on goods produced by domestic trusts in order to encourage foreign competition, 3) to place the "necessaries" of life on the free list or, at least, to significantly reduce the duty, and 4) to place raw materials on the free list. Since the Democrats generally used ad valorem rates instead of the specific ones used in the Payne-Aldrich Tariff, it was difficult to judge how many specific reductions in rates were achieved or how much revenue loss would occur. It was clear, however, that there were many significant reductions and that many major items, such as sugar, wool, crude iron, and agricultural implements, were added to the free list. Frank Burdick, in his study of Wilson's involvement in tariff reform, has estimated that the average duty was reduced from 40 per cent to 29 per cent and that almost all food and raw materials were put on the free list. Burdick also argues that, contrary to his intention, Wison's actions fostered the growth of trusts in some industries by placing the rates so low that large companies could significantly undersell their domestic competitors. Senator Bristow, spokesman for the Insurgents, called the Underwood-Simmons bill worse than the Payne-Aldrich Tariff and called for "honest protection" that "will actually give to the American laboring man that which it pretends to give him." He also termed the Democratic argument that the tariff caused inflation "ridiculous," assigning that role to American trusts. Even though William Allen White tried to convince him that a vote against the Underwood-Simmons Tariff was a vote to continue the Payne-Aldrich rates, Bristow joined nearly all of his fellow Insurgents and the Regular

Republicans in opposition. In the end, only Robert La Follette and Miles Poindexter voted with the Democratic majority in the Senate, while the two Louisiana Senators were the only Democrats to defy the party caucus.[28]

The Democrats' initial income tax proposal was drafted in the House Ways and Means Committee under the chairmanship of Oscar W. Underwood of Alabama. The Republican members of the Ways and Means Committee, headed by Sereno Payne, wrote a minority report damning both tariff reduction and the income tax, and urging retention of the 1909 schedules. Of the G.O.P. members, only Victor Murdock of Kansas, the lone Insurgent on the committee, refused to sign the minority report. The income tax section was prepared by Cordell Hull and reviewed by the Democratic members of the committee. Hull and Underwood were reluctant to jeopardize the future of the tax before the Supreme Court by including a provision for graduation, but other Democrats forced their hand. Adolph Sabath of Chicago introduced a graduated tax proposal on April 7, while John Nance Garner of Texas and Dorsey W. Schackelford of Missouri worked internally for the principle and eventually carried the day Garner argued that seventy-five per cent of Congress favored graduation. The committee members also wrangled over a suggestion that the president be given discretion to adjust the rates according to fiscal needs, but finally discarded the idea, with Hull leading the opposition.[29]

With simultaneous control of both houses of Congress and of the Presidency for the first time in two decades, the Democrats were determined not to allow factionalism on any issue to destroy their opportunity to enact an entire program. One half of the Senate Democrats and forty per cent of those in the House were southerners and the seniority system gave representatives of that section twelve of the fourteen committee chairmanships in the upper house and eleven of the thirteen in the lower one. For most of these, tariff revision was the crucial issue and they were concerned not to let potential arguments over income tax rates threaten party unity. Many prominent southern Democrats, such as Williams, were also basic economic conservatives, with a firm belief in the sanctity of property and a deep-seated distaste for federal tax collections of any sort. Most southerners wanted to enact a federal income tax because it would be a party victory, a blow at Wall Street and eastern Republicanism, and a justification for tariff reduction, but they had no intention of permitting a drastic assault upon wealth or of raising more revenue than was necessary to offset anticipated losses in customs receipts. The "radical" Democrats were less committed to the panacea of tariff reduction, more serious about taxing incomes, and less fearful of higher rates. Some of these were southern agrarians of Populist leanings, such as Vardaman, Robert Henry and Garner of Texas, Claude Kitchin of North Carolina, and Otis Wingo of Arkansas. Others were westerners, such as Gilbert Hitchcock of Nebraska, who shared the Insurgent Republicans' regional outlook. James Reed of Missouri, one of the most outspoken radicals, was an ally of Joseph Folk and a spokesman for "rural reform Democracy," even though he was from Kansas City, a "wet," and an advocate of organized labor. He had close ties to Missouri corporations but was a harsh critic of eastern colonialism who favored "an equalization of burden and opportunity." Others were urban representatives with large working and middle class constituencies by now highly sensitized to the isue of tax equity. For a large part of the Congressional session, the southern Democratic leadership, with President Wilson's sanction, was able to hold these restive elements in check through the party caucus. A few Democrats, such as Vardaman, Hitchcock, and Tavenner, expressed sympathy for higher rates on the floor and even cast an occasional vote for rate-raising amendments, but the bulk of the Democrats, kept in line by the leadership, combined with the Regular Republicans to defeat all such proposals. Only when an eleventh hour revolt threatened to shatter party unity on the tariff did the Democratic leadership agree to accept somewhat higher income tax rates.[30]

These demands for significantly higher rates by Insurgents and some radical Democrats proceeded, to some degree, from a belief that an income tax could be used as an device to redistribute wealth. LaFollette, according to David P. Thelen, had decided as early as 1905 "that an income tax was the only politically effective way to reach invisible wealth," and that his goal in 1913 was to redistribute wealth. Bristow also received letters from constituents advocating rates as high as fifty per cent to serve as a "practical tendency toward the decentralization of wealth." Certainly the proposals of LaFollette and Poindexter in the Senate and those of Ira Copley and others in the House involved such high rates in the upper brackets as to indicate a desire for redistribution. Outright advocacy of such intentions, as John Hillje has argued, was very rare, limited to only a "handful" of members of Congress who were "more concerned with social reform." According to his tabulation of the content of speeches on the floor, Hillje estimates that while sixty Congressmen stressed some form of tax equity argument and another dozen called the income tax the fairest tax possible, only four cited it as a remedy for the concentration of wealth. There were slightly more opponents of the income tax who "accused" its proponents of advocating redistribution, but these charges were usually vehemently denied by the pro-income tax forces. Root, for example, confided to a close friend that "what these people want to do is to take away the money of the rich, classifying as rich all who have $4000 a year and then to pass laws distributing it among their people at home." The most frequently cited argument for the income tax, that of constructing a system based upon "the ability to pay," was seemingly predicated on the assumption that wealth would remain distributed about as it was and that taxes should reflect that distribution proportionately. At some point, it could be argued, rates designed to promote tax equity could become redistributive if they were sufficiently graduated, but it cannot be proven that anyone in 1913 was trying to promote the redistribution of wealth by indirection. The final rates, while considered drastic by many affluent Americans, were clearly well short of those that would have been necessary to effect any degree of redistribution.[31]

The proposals for higher rates came mostly from Insurgent Republicans and the handful of Progressive Party representatives in the House. Jacob Falconer of Washington sought to raise the surtax on incomes over $100,000 to five per cent, and to require a separate vote on the income tax section, while Victor Murdock of Kansas favored a six per cent rate. Melville Kelly of Pennsylvania suggested a nine per cent rate, while Ira Copley of Illinois presented a steeply graduated scale ranging to a sixty-eight per levy on incomes in excess of $1,000,000. To some extent, the Progressive-Insurgent insistence upon higher rates arose from their regional outlook and their deep suspicion of eastern wealth. They were certainly more economically radical than the southern Democratic leadership was and, unlike Democratic dissenters, had long ago declared their independence of their party's caucus. Their concern, as Laurence J. Holt has argued, "was not with revenue but with the redistribution of wealth and the equalization of burdens." Those convictions, combined with a western "rural, small-town orientation" that abhored "clandestine private interests" accounted for much of the Insurgents' attitude.[32]

Even at that, the Insurgent's motivation was probably as much political as socioeconomic. The 1910 and 1912 elections had convinced them that the policies of the Regular Republicans had been decisively and permanently rejected by the voters. Forty-one incumbent Republicans had been unseated in 1910, "almost every one of them standpatters." At the same time, the Insurgents were unhappy at the tremendous gains made by the Democrats. They abhorred the party of states rights and free trade, of southern Bourbons and urban political machines. As serious as were their disagreements with the Regular Republicans over the tariff, they were minor compared to the dichotomy between free trade and protection. Except for LaFollette and Poindexter, every single Insurgent ultimately voted against the Underwood-Simmons Tariff and Cummins typically described the tariff as a "partisan issue," dismissing Insurgent-Regular disagreements as "intramural." The crucial issue in 1912, the Insurgents believed, was whether they could recast the G.O.P. in their mold and prevent the Democrats from preempting the role of the "progressive" party. To accomplish this, the Insurgents had to carve out positions that were clearly distinct from those of either the Regulars or the Democrats, and to force the Democrats to yield to their pressure. To defeat the Democrats "became an end in itself for many progressive Republicans." LaFollette, the original Insurgent standard-bearer in 1912, "still has Presidential ambitions," the New York Times insisted, "and does not intend to place himself in the position of having to carry out the Demcratic platform." The advanced position taken on income tax rates "provided the Insurgents with a clearly progressive issue on which they could attack the Democrats without the embarrassment of enthusiastic standpat support." The movement for higher rates, Holt has concluded, "was clearly labeled as 'progressive' Republican."[33]

The Regular Republicans, led by Fredrick Gillette of Massachusetts, Martin Madden of Chicago, and William Stafford of Milwaukee, sought to shift the burden downward, rather than upward, by proposing to lower the exemption to $1,000. Democratic spokesmen Austin, Palmer, and Sam Rayburn of Texas led the defense of the higher exemption on the grounds of both equity and political necessity, easily triumphing. Republican Fred Britten of Chicago proposed raising the exemption to $6,000 with an additional immunity of $500 for each child, but since he coupled this with an attack on the principle of graduation in which he was joined by Sereno Payne, it seems likely that his real purpose was to create a reductio ad absurdum. At any rate, the House Democrats easily resisted any and all attempts to spread the burden of the tax downward.[34]

Hull and his fellow Democrats were generally equally successful in parrying the other objections of the Standpatters. Republican James Mann of Chicago and Graham sought to include taxation of the salaries of the president and federal judges, but lost 52-72. Fellow Philadelphian J. Hampton Moore and Calder also failed to include the income from state and municipal bonds and the salaries of government employees. They were effectively answered by Democrat John J. Fitzgerald of Brooklyn who expressed his party's reluctance to raise the perilous constitutional issue involved. John Jacob Rogers of Massachusetts was also unsuccessful in his efforts to exempt charitable organizations and contributions to them, while Madden, Mann, and others raised questions about the taxation of bondholders and real estate companies and concerning collection at the source.[35]

The most protracted debate came over the taxing of insurance companies and their dividends. The Regular Republicans, supported by a few Democrats with insurance company connections, sought to exempt the undistributed dividends from taxation and argued that mutual companies should be considered non-profit organizations, not subject to the levy. Hull, William Borland of Kansas City, John Burke of North Dakota, Michael Phelan of Boston, Rufus Hardy of Texas, and Charles Bartlett of Georgia successfully fended off most of their objections. Borland charged that insurance companies were launching an organized campaign to propagandize their policyholders by misstatements designed to build support for special consideration. Hull insisted that the tax would never touch the money paid to policyholders of life insurance companies, but would fall instead on the large companies that used potential dividends as bait for policyholders but rarely paid them.[36]

Exasperated at all the requests for special consideration, Hull snapped that "it is utterly impossible to write provisions in general law that would specifically apply and govern every phase of the hundreds of thousands of business transactions in the country." Alleging that the insurance companies had been, by their own admission, paying dividends out of actual profits, he insisted that "if the companies persist in mixing the smaller amount of premium savings in the undistributed profits, then no distinction is made." In the end the Democrats agreed to allow mutual insurance companies to deduct premium deposits returned to policyholders but generally resisted other attempts to erode the tax base.[37]

The Ways and Means Committee's income tax section was introduced in the House on April 7. It provided for a one per cent tax on incomes over $4000 with an additional tax of one per cent on that portion of income that exceeded $20,000, two per cent on that over $50,000, and three per cent on that over $100,000. It allowed deductions for business expenses, interest payments, state and local taxes, uninsured losses, worthless debts, and depreciation. It specifically excluded income from state and municipal bonds, the salaries of the president and federal judges (the Constitution prohibited lowering their salaries during their terms of office), and incorporated the one per cent corporation excise tax. It also provided for the principle of collection at the source whenever possible. The Literary Digest surveyed the division of journalistic opinion on the bill and printed material from the New York Tribune that dramatically revealed the unequal distribution of income in the country. In a year when the average family income for a family of five fell significantly short of $1000 per year, John D. Rockefeller would pay an estimated tax of just under $2,000,000 on rates that were graduated only to three per cent on income over $100,000. His son William would owe an estimated $798,260, Andrew Carnegie, an outspoken foe of the tax, $598,260, and George F. Baker, one of the leading opponents in New York, nearly $200,000. The New York Times published a committee estimate of the tax's impact that revealed that there were one hundred people with incomes over $1,000,000 a year and another 350 people with annual intakes over $500,000. All told, the personal income tax was predicted to reach only about 425,000 individuals and to raise about $70,000.000. The one per cent corporation tax was predicted to bring in another $37,000,000 paid by 228,352 corporations. On April 18, the House Democratic caucus accepted a few minor amendments regarding insurance companies, particularly in permitting the taxation of undistributed dividends, and approved the Ways and Means Committee proposal. On April 22, the Committee reported the bill on a strict party vote, with the majority touting the tax as "the fairest and cheapest of all taxes, in order to secure to the largest extent equality of tax burdens, an adjustable system of revenue, and in all respects a modernized fiscal system." In a remarkable two hour speech on April 26 redolent of Bryan's 1894 effort, Hull defended the tax from charges of sectionalism and class legislation and contended that personal property largely escaped taxation, citing Census Bureau data that only about nine billion of the estimated forty-five billion dollars worth of personal property in the nation was actually assessed. Responding to charges of sectionalism, Hull replied indignantly that "it would be monstrous to say that the receivers of great incomes which are drawn from every section of the country may segregate themselves and on the plea of segregation or sectionalism successfully exempt their entire wealth from taxation." On May 7, the Democratic majority beat back the efforts of Regular Republicans to lower the exemption and of the Insurgents to increase the rates. On May 7, the entire House adopted the income tax section without a recorded vote and, on the next day, approved the entire revenue bill on an almost strictly partisan vote.[38]

The Finance Committee, chaired by Furnifold W. Simmons of North Carolina, received the House measure and assigned the income tax section to a subcommittee consisting of Williams, Benjamin Shiveley of Indiana, and Thomas Gore of Oklahoma. Although working in a "committee room piled high with protests and suggestions from many sources," especially insurance companies, railroads, and holding companies, the subcommittee generally endorsed the work of the House. Hull met with the subcommittee on May 29 and defended graduation, the surtax, and the taxing of insurance company dividends, holding them to be "above crticism," and contending that they had been upheld by the federal judiciary. On June 25 the Finance Committee accepted several changes recommended by its subcommittee, the most important one being lowering of the exemption for single persons to $3,000 while leaving that of married couples at $4,000. In addition, the committee opted for the exemption of mutual life insurance companies, in response to a "countrywide protest," by allowing corporations to exempt interest on indebtedness even when in excess of capitalization, if secured by collateral and incidental to business operations, and for immunity for traction companies and utilities on that portion of their profits due to municipalities.[39]

Most of these changes made the Senate version somewhat more conservative than the House one and some reportedly provoked sharp debate in the Democratic caucus. The latter first rejected the exclusion for mutual life insurance companies but voted to restore it. Divisions also were reported over exemptions for children, the taxation of undivided profits, and the proposal of Gilbert Hitchcock to tax the tobacco trust at a much higher rate, but the leadership prevailed in almost all cases. Significantly, though,

Hitchcock and six others -- O'Gorman, Atlee Pomerene of Ohio, Reed, Vardaman, Henry Hollis of New Hampshire, and William Hughes of New Jersey announced that they were opposed to the ruling that all Democrats were bound to support the measure as drafted and not to vote for any Republican amendments. Hughes, an Irish immigrant labor lawyer from Paterson, was "a close friend of the President who has been referred to respectfully as the President's spokesman in the Senate" and his refusal to be bound by the caucus ruling caused some Democrats to feel that they were getting conflicting signals from the White House. The caucus selected Williams and Hughes, as representatives of the two camps, to defend the income tax section on the floor when debate opened on August 26.[40]

The pattern in the Senate was almost an exact replica of the one in the House, except that the proponents of higher rates were eventually more successful. The Regular Republicans again bent their efforts toward lowering the exemption and riddling the tax with loopholes. The efforts of Lodge and his cohorts to raise the civil service question have already been noted, as have those of Root and others to delay the effective date and to introduce the controversy over state and municiapl bonds and salaries. The Regular Republicans were more successful in getting the Democrats to give special consideration to insurance companies and other corporations. Life insurance and mutual fire and marine insurance companies were allowed to deduct premiums paid to policyholders, but only after a ferocious exchange on the question of undistributed dividends in the Finance Committee between Williams and the president of New York Life. Darwin P. Kingsley objected to the taxation of undistributed dividends but admitted under questioning that his company had contributed $250,000 out of that pot to the Republican campaign in 1912, an admission that infuriated Williams, a New York Life policyholder. Apparently, the Mississippian observed, undistributed dividends belong to the policyholder when they were about to be taxed, but otherwise could be used by the company for its own purposes.[41]

In response to the demands of Root and the Republican Standpatters, corporations were allowed to deduct one-half of the interest payments on their indebtedness and state or foreign taxes paid. Beyond that, though, the Regulars were generally frustrated by a solid Democratic-Insurgent front against the introduction of special privilege. The Gallinger-Dillingham revenue sharing scheme got only fourteen votes and the various efforts of the Standpatters to lower the exemption and spread the tax burden all failed decisively. Porter McCumber of North Dakota was unsuccessful in his attempt to begin the tax coverage at $1,000, while Charles E. Townsend of Michigan, strongly backed by Gallinger, was rebuffed in his endeavor to lower the effective rate to one-fourth of one per cent on all incomes, regardless of amount. The last venture of the Regular Republicans in this regard was an eloquent plea by Root to lower the exemption to $1,000, on the grounds that taxing wealth would unfairly damage the industrial states, preventing their legislatures from raising needed revenue. His impassioned oration on behalf of "my people" was interrupted by J. Hamilton Lewis who sarcastically inquired if Root's "people" were "only the brood of gentlemen who nest about Wall Street." The Democrats summarily dispatched the proposal.[42]

On the surface, at least, the Democrats were equally successful at fending off attempts of the Insurgents to magnify the impact of the tax on the upper brackets. Coe Crawford raised a great flurry with his suggestion that the tax distinguish between earned and unearned income, as Seligman had suggested to Bristow. His position was supported by most of the Insurgents, and also by Lodge and Brandegee, but was attacked vigorously by Williams as unworkable and rejected. Insurgent efforts to raise the minimum even higher were also defeated by a combination of Democrats and Republican Regulars, while Norris' effort to add additional exemptions for each child was untracked by a 27-34 vote. A few conservative Republicans, such as Lawrence Y. Sherman of Illinois, supported Norris because they feared "race suicide" unless people were encouraged to have children and because they were committed to almost any type of exclusion for people with high incomes. More typically, Lodge stigmatized efforts to raise the minimum exemption as a "pillage of class."[43]

The major effort of the Insurgents, though, was to raise the rates in the upper brackets. At various times, LaFollette, Bristow, Borah, and Poindexter introduced amendments that would have established the maximum rate anywhere from ten to twenty per cent. The Republican Regulars generally outdid themselves in denouncing these proposals in the strongest possible language. The New York Times stigmatized Bristow and LaFollette as "radical," demanding the defeat of these "drastic amendments" while Lodge pictured the rich as being hunted like animals. In response to Poindexter's twenty per cent rate, Brandegee insisted that he had heard of tithes, but never fifths, while Townsend predicted the destruction of property and unmanageable treasury surpluses. He neglected to add that his proposal to lower the exemption would probably have produced at least as much additional revenue.[44]

Sherman charged that "Socialism is abroad in the land" and that taxing ability went contrary to the concept of Anglo-Saxon individualism, while Dillingham, chairman of the commission on immigration restriction, sounded a nativist note by stressing the danger of allowing "hordes of foreigners" to escape taxation, while giving them the power to tax true Americans. On most of the votes on the Insurgent rate amendments, the Standpatters joined the Democrats to bring about their defeat, with only sixteen or seventeen western Republicans declaring in favor. The final vote on Bristow's proposal to provide a graded scale up to ten per cent for millionaires, however, produced fourteen conservative Republicans in coalition with fifteen Insurgents, in what seemed an attempt to split the pro-income tax forces by making the bill unpalatable to the Democrats. All of these efforts were unsuccessful, though, and the rates remained where they were until an incipient revolt in the ranks of the majority party finally forced them upward.[45]

There were some portents of Democratic dissatisfaction. Seven Senators had refused to pledge their support to the leadership bill after the caucus and numerous Democrats had abstained on the Insurgent amendments. Two events on the floor in late August tolled the alarm bell. Vardaman became the first Democrat to break ranks when he voted for LaFollette's amendment on August 28, while Reed, William Thompson of Kansas, and Henry Ashurst of Arizona announced that they had only withheld their votes in the expectation that the Finance Committee would agree to higher rates.[46]

The same day, Hitchcock introduced his amendment for a graduated surtax on corporations, to be increased according to each unit's share of the market, a combination taxation and anti-trust measure. The leadership refused support and the measure failed, 30-41, without a single Democratic vote save that of the author. The Nebraskan then launched into a bitter tirade against the party leadership and the caucus system, insisting that he and several others had only voted against the Insurgent amendments because they were bound to do so, but that they believed in their essential justice. The air was filled with threats of revolt and the leadership hastily called a new caucus to stem the tide. The "radicals" claimed a majority of twenty-five to twenty-seven and, although their exact identities were obscured by the security of the caucus room, the results suggest the accuracy of their assertion. The only admitted radicals were Vardaman, Reed, Ashurst, Thompson and Hitchcock, but it seems highly likely that Pomerene, O'Gorman, Hughes, and Hollis could be added to the list, since they had refused to take the caucus pledge earlier. The opposition was reportedly led by Williams and Simmons, but the position of most other Democrats is problematic.[47]

The radicals allegedly insisted upon schedules comparable to those proposed by the Insurgents up to a high of ten per cent, but settled for a compromise aggregate of seven per cent for incomes over $500,000, as suggested by Hoke Smith of Georgia. The Senate version provided for a one per cent additional tax on incomes between $25,000 and 50,000 ranging to a six per cent additional levy on those in excess of half a million dollars. Simmons countered radical demands by appealing to Secretary of State William Jennings Bryan who, in turn, contacted the vacationing President Wilson. Wilson responded with a letter to Simmons arguing that "my own opinion is that it is much safer to begin upon somewhat moderate lines, and I think the proposals of the Committee are reasonable and well considered." Reed reportedly continued to press for a ten per cent maximum, but O'Gorman was sufficiently placated to argue vigorously for the compromise figure. The caucus recommended the change to the Finance Committee which quickly accepted.[48] On September 5, the new schedule was introduced on the floor by Hoke Smith and adopted without a recorded vote. The Insurgents made last ditch efforts to increase the maximum rates, but again received no support from the now mollified Democratic rebels. Norris' attempt to graduate the additional tax up to fifty-seven per cent "to break up large fortunes" received only twelve votes. Bristow, LaFollette, and Poindexter were able to muster only eighteen, sixteen, and fifteen votes, respectively, for somewhat more modest proposals. On September 9, the tariff bill, with the income tax section included, passed the Senate 44-37. Although no separate vote was taken on the tax itself, the probable lines of division had been clearly delineated during the legislative process. The only question that a recorded vote might have answered was whether or not the Insurgents would have accepted the Democratic compromise.[49]

Differences between the House and Senate versions, especially on rates, necessitated a conference committee consisting of Williams and Shiveley for the upper chamber and Hull and Kitchin for the lower house. The two versions also differed on exemptions for mutual life insurance companies, on the methods for collecting the tax at the source, on the issue of exemptions for children, on exempting the income received by municipalities from the operation of public utilities, and on the effective date of the tax. The committee generally followed the Senate version more closely, accepting an exemption of $3000 for single persons and

$4000 for married couples. It also agreed to exemptions for the undistributed dividends of mutual life insurance companies, adopted the principle of collection at the source for corporate dividends and moved the effective date to March 1, 1913. The Committee first accepted the motion of additional $500 exemptions for the first two children, but finally rejected the idea. It refused to exempt the interest paid to foreign owners of American securities, despite the protests of the Investment Bankers Association. On September 26, Senator O'Gorman of New York convinced the committee to exempt the income that municipalities received from holders of utility franchises. The proposal engendered a dispute between O'Gorman and fellow radical Democrat James Reed of Kansas City who objected to the wording because his city had a public transit system. An alteration in the language patched up the disagreement. The committee announced on September 27 that the new version was expected to raise $82,066,000 from individual taxpayers and $33,000,000 more from corporations, for a total of $115,000,000. It estimated that the 304,000 who made between $3000 and $10,000 annually would pay about $6,000,000 in taxes, while the 450 people with incomes over $500,000 would provide over $23,000,000 worth of revenue. The committee finished its work on September 27, and the two houses quickly adopted its report. On October 3, President Wilson signed the Underwood-Simmons Tariff Act, thus securing the adoption of the nation's federal income tax system.[50]

The income tax section provided for a "normal" tax of one per cent on all incomes of over $3000 for single persons and $4000 for married couples. It also included a graduated "additional" tax that began at one percent for incomes between $20,000 and $50,000. Over $50,000 the additional tax rose to two per cent, at $75,000 to three per cent, at $100,000 to four per cent, at $250,000 to five per cent, and at $500,000 to six per cent. The tax exempted the interest from state and municipal bonds, the interest on obligations of the United States, and the salaries of the president, federal judges, and state and municipal officals. It allowed deductions for business expenses, interest paid, state and local taxes, losses due to theft, worthless debts, depreciation, and income where the tax had been paid at the source. The income tax section also provided for a flat one per cent tax on corporate net income. Finally, it stipulated the penalities and fines for non-compliance.[51]

Reaction to the final income tax section followed predictable lines. As the Springfield Republican observed, "those who have always opposed this tax are loudest in their criticism of the enforcement of it. "Such periodicals as the Journal of Commerce, Manufacturers Record, and the American Economist attacked the enforcement machinery, while most New York City newspapers stigmatized it as class legislation. The Albany Journal faulted the measure as an act of bad faith on the part of the Democrats. Naturally, those who had consistently supported the tax were just as satisfied as the measure's opponents were unhappy. William Jennings Bryan was ecstatic, noting in The Commoner that he had once been denounced as an "anarchist" for advocating what was now the law of the land. Most economists who expressed a view for publication also rendered generally favorable judgments. The British journal Living Age pronounced the new tax as sensible, elastic, and equitable, and taking issue with many American business spokesman, held that the enforcement machinery was "in almost all respects straightforward and similar to those in other countries."

Finally, Cordell Hull, looking back on the event many years later declared that "if I should live two lifetimes I probably would not be able to render public service equal to my part in the long fight for the enactment of our income tax system."[52]

The nation's first permanent income tax law was the result of the interaction of four fairly distinct groups, each with its own idea of what the levy should be -- the Regular Republicans, the leadership Democrats, the Insurgents, and the Democratic radicals. The Regulars had opposed the tax for decades, but by 1913 were forced to content themselves with attempts to spread out the tax burden and create special havens for a few privileged individuals and corporations. Their Insurgent opponents, for both economic and political reasons, were determined to place the onus even more squarely on those people who had evaded effective taxation for so long. The "radical" Democrats, a mixed bag representing all sections of the country from the rural South to the small town West to the urban industrial East, shared Insurgent attitudes to a large extent but preferred to work within their own party rather than coalesce openly with the maverick Republicans. Caught squarely in the middle, the leadership Democrats were able to fend off attacks from both the left and the right until forced to shift somewhat to the left in order to avoid a split in the party ranks. These lines of division were occasionally blurred when Standpat Republicans supported Insurgent amendments for the purpose of alienating the majority party from its own proposal. The result was probably the strongest measure politically possible in 1913, barring the outright alliance of the Insurgents and the radical Democrats, a prospect virtually unthinkable to any Democrat conscious that his party was working on its first Congressional majority in well over a decade and had many other goals to achieve. Despite their differences, the Insurgents, the leadership Democrats, and the radical Democrats interacted to produce a federal income tax law. Only the regular Republicans could claim no share of the victory. Their frustration was perhaps best expressed by Elihu Root in a letter to a friend who asked what would happen if he ran afoul of the new law. "I guess you will have to go to jail," Root answered, "If that is the result of the income tax law I will meet you there. We will have a merry, merry time for all of our friends will be there." [53]

Chapter IX
The Income Tax and the Progressive Era

The federal income tax, George Mowry has suggested, was "perhaps the most profound reform passed in the course of recent American history." The modern social service state "(as well as the modern day defense establishment), he argues, "probably rests upon the income tax more than upon any other single legislative act," while the absence of a federal income tax "must also have meant the almost complete frustration of any government seeking to redistribute income in any orderly fashion."[1] While not every historian would agree with such a sweeping conclusion, few would deny that the adoption of the tax was one the major achievements of the Progressive Era and that no compilation of the periods' accomplishments could even pretend to completeness without including it. There can be little doubt that its inauguration modernized and rationalized the nation's tax structure by providing a revenue source that was more flexible, productive, and predictable than any politically viable alternative. Nor is there much skepticism that the graduated income tax is, potentially at least, the most equitable means yet devised for placing the financial burdens of government upon those who are proportionally best able to bear them. While there has always been considerable disagreement as to whether the income tax should be or has been an instrument for the redistribution of wealth, there is again little debate that the tax, if drawn to the necessary specifications, could be adapted to that purpose far better than any other mechanism currently available. In contrast to the case with many of the Progressive Era's other reformers, the significance of the income tax as a permanent feature of the national landscape has tended to increase over time.

Moreover, the adoption of the federal income tax between 1909 and 1913 was the culmination of nearly a half century of struggle to reach the vast amounts of wealth generated by the rapid and massive industrialization of the United States, to shift the tax burden from real property and consumption onto financial and industrial assets and the benefits derived from their ownership and employment, and to supply the revenue .ecessary to operate government of the scope appropriate to an urban, industrial world power. The income tax was also one of the few truly nationwide reforms, one that was subject to intense debate and division in Congress and in the legislatures of every single state during a relatively compact four year period. As such, it dramatized as well any other single issue, the validity of the division between "the people" and "the interests" that permeated so much of the rhetoric of the day. Moreover, the income tax issue played a significant, if secondary role, in the major political upheaval of the Era, the temporary disintegration of Regular Republican hegemony and the corresponding resurgence of the Democrats as a "progressive majority."[2] In conjunction with the Payne-Aldrich Tariff, the income tax formed the key symbolic socioeconomic issue that triggered that transformation, one that stigmatized the G.O.P. as a protector of special privilege and as the author of a high cost of living. For all these reasons, an intensive study of the adoption of the federal income tax provides many valuable insights into the nature of the reformist process during the Progressive Era.

Probably the most obvious and valid generalization concerning the process that produced the federal income tax is that it was not the product of the efforts of a single political party, geographical region, socioeconomic class, or reformist organization or movement. Certainly the Democrats took the lead in advocating the measure from the early 1890s, enacted it virtually unaided in 1894, and kept the idea politically alive in the decade after the Pollock Decision. The party's endorsement of a constitutional amendment in 1908 guaranteed its continuation as a topic of national debate, pushed Taft to consider the income tax as a revenue supplement, and forced the issue upon the Sixty-First Congress. During the special session of 1909, Congressional Democrats provided much of the leadership and the lion's share of the votes that convinced Taft and the Regular Republicans to propose the corporation excise tax and the constitutional amendment in order to stave off the enactment of an immediate income tax. During the ratification process, the amendment was endorsed and sponsored by the Democratic parties of nearly every single state, while that party's legislators generally gave it their overwhelming support, except in a handful of southern states. Even there, with the exception of Virginia and Florida, the majority of Democratic lawmakers still voted for ratification. The amendment's triumph in several key northeastern urban, industrial states also owed itself primarily to the temporary capture of those legislatures by resurgent Democrats in 1910 and 1912. Finally, the enactment of the nation's permanent income tax system came at the behest of a Democratic president marshalling the unanimous support of a solidly Democratic Congressional majority through the strict discipline of the party caucus.

Yet, for all that, the income tax was clearly not just a "Democratic" achievement. The Insugent Republicans provided much of the critical pressure and crucial votes to force Aldrich to accept the proposal of the amendment. They also worked hard to promote ratification in their home states, where Democrats exerted very little influence. The Taft Administration was also highly instrumental in forcing the amendment on the hostile Regulars and exerted its influence on Republican legislators in several states on behalf of ratification. Insurgent demands for higher rates in 1913 strenghtened the hand of "radical" Democrats and helped force the majority to accept a more steeply graduated rate schedule. The nascent Progressive Party also materially aided the cause of the tax by endorsing ratification in 1912, by backing it in those legislatures where it established a presence in 1913, and by cooperating with the Insurgents and Radical Democrats in that same year. Over the course of nearly three decades, the income tax was also urged by a variety of minor parties, such as the Populist, Socialist, Socialist Labor, Anti-Monopoly, and Union Labor, who pressed the Democrats to come to grips with the issue. Moreover, appeals to partisanship were not sufficient to compel many state Democratic legislators to vote for ratification, especially in the South. Clearly the triumph of the income tax was not a partisan victory, despite the significant contribution made by the Democrats.

Nor was the income tax primarily a sectional issue, despite the generally overwhelming support that it consistently enjoyed in both the West and the South and regardless of the persistent efforts mde by the measure's opponents to label it a sectional plot by which those two regions planned to despoil the Iron Rectangle. Western and southern representatives introduced all of the income tax bills and resolutions introduced in Congress right up through 1913, and their regional colleagues generally provided the bulk of the support for those measures. During the ratification process, eighteen out of the possible nineteen western states and twelve out of the possible thirteen southern ones lent their support. In 1913, representatives of the two regions again gave their overwhelming backing but the two sections were by no means unanimous in their enthusiasm. The amendment was rejected by Utah, Virginia, and Florida, and encountered significant resistance in Kansas, Wyoming, Georgia, Kentucky, West Virginia, Arkansas, and Louisiana. Moreover, the support of the South and West, however powerful, would have been ineffectual without the backing of sizeable segments of the population in the urban, industrial Northeast. The endorsement of prominent academics and tax experts was crucial in erasing the reputation of the income tax as a nostrum of radicals and disturbers of the peace. The support of urban political organizations with their roots in working and middle class neighborhoods provided much of the impetus to achieve ratification in key northeastern states. In the end, thirteen of the possible sixteen northeastern states ratified the measure, a far higher percentage than either proponents or opponents predicted in 1909. In 1913, the representatives of those same "machines" were virtually unanimous in their support. Clearly sectionalism failed as both on explanation of support and as a rationale for opposition to the income tax. Nor did the success of the income tax owe itself primarily to the efforts of a single socioeconomic class. It is very difficult to establish class divisions with any accuracy, but they are rooted in the intersection between income level and occupational status. Moreover, the widespread belief in social mobility, ethnocultural and geographical divisions, and other factors generally inhibited the development of class consciousness. If anything, the great majority of Americans have usually regarded themselves as part of a large, amorphous, middle class that embraces nearly everyone who is self-supporting, save for the very wealthy. Since the income tax, by definition, was designed to reach the upper two to three per cent of income receivers, there is little reason to doubt that the vast majority of the rest of society realized its stake in the measure's enactment. Because the tax exempted everyone who made under $3000 a year in an age when $827 was the average household income, it was certainly a cause around which nearly every income and occupational group could rally. Naturally the emerging "new class" of technicians, intellectuals, bureaucrats, managers, and "tax experts" took the lead in promoting and publicizing the tax because that was their social function and orientation. Yearley especially stresses their contribution to the "revolution in taxation" in the northeastern states and correctly observes that the members of the National Tax Association were largely people of respectable, native, Protestant, "middle class" backgrounds who argued the need for a rational, modern tax system. The N.T.A. was peopled largely by the same types of individuals who graced the good government associations, the Progressive Party, the National Child Labor Committee, the American Association for Labor Legislation, the National Consumers Union, and a myriad of other activist groups during the Progressive Era. Yearley states flatly that tax reform in the states of the Iron Rectangle "owed surprisingly little to the inspiration or practical consequences of working-class movements, populism, socialism or radialism despite some vocal champions in all of these camps."[3]

Yet, without denying the critical role played by the articulate and activist new middle class, it is clear that they did not effect either the state level "revolution in taxation" or the adoption of the federal income tax without considerable aid from agrarian organizations, organized labor, and politicians representing essentially working and lower middle class constituencies. As demonstrated in Chapter VI, the tax reforms in New York that were adopted at the behest of the N.T.A. were enacted in a legislature dominated by Tammany Democrats, the supposed antithesis and favorite bete moire of most "government by expert" intellectuals and activitists. Nor would the income tax amendment have been ratified in New York and the other northeastern states without the organizational skills and the votes of Tammany - like Democrats. In all these states, too, the measure enjoyed the almost universal support of organized labor and of leftist radicals urging its adoption much more on the grounds of equity or redistribution. In the West and South, the urban middle class generally had to work in concert with the representatives of agrarian movements to effect ratification. These were generally the longest standing and most consistent supporters of the tax and there is no evidence that their enthusiasm was in way diminished by 1909, even if their influence had been somewhat eroded in those states that were becoming more urban and commercial-industrial. Although charges that the income tax was an agrarian - radical plot were patently false and often contrived, their frequency accurately reflected the critical role that agrarian America played in its adoption. Even Yearley, for all his emphasis on the centrality of the articulate new middle class in the "revolution in taxation" in the northeastern states, acknowledges that "in part the federal income tax could be considered the "popular" measure of Southern and Western farm spokesmen."[4] Clearly the federal income tax did not flow primarily from the efforts of the new middle class, agrarians, the urban working class, or any other single socioeconomic segment, however vaguely one might choose to define that term to make it sufficiently inclusive.

Nor can the adoption of the tax be explained sufficiently by reference to any of the conceptual frameworks or syntheses that historians have devised over the years to interpret the Progressive Era, although nearly all of these provide a partial explanation. The earliest interpretations of the Era's reformist activity viewed it as a continuation of Populism, to agrarian radicalism that had grown up, shaved off its whiskers, and moved to the city, as William Allen White phrased it. That view was first popularized by former Populist Mary Ellen Lease who exulted that "the Progressive party has adopted our platform, clause by clause, plank by plank," and given its fullest scholarly expression by John D. Hicks over fifty years ago when he insisted that "many of the reforms that the Populist demanded, while despised and rejected for a season, won triumphantly in the end." As recently as the mid-1960s, Wayne Fuller still argued that "the majority of those who did become reform leaders came from the farms and small towns of rural America" and that "in thought and feeling the majority of them belonged to rural America where they had their roots." It is certainly true that the income tax was a favorite cause of the Populists and other agrarian radicals, that rural based representatives from the South and West were the measure's chief advocates during its least popular period, and that they provided an almost solid phalanx of support between 1909 and 1913. But during the last critical period, the tax received much of its most crucial backing from areas that had been traditionally hostile to agrarian radicalism and to its lineal descendant, William Jennings Bryan. Many of the tax's most dedicated and influential advocates were city born and bred and some of them had even been born outside of the United States. Much of the pressure for the "revolution in taxation," as Yearley has effectively demonstrated, arose out of municipal fiscal crises and the burgeoning demands of urban, industrial life. As with everything else that the Populists had proposed, the income tax's enactment awaited the cooperation of more urban-oriented forces.[5]

Nor can the adoption of the income tax be attributed primarily to the efforts of any of the urban middle class groups about whose origins and motives historians of the Progressive Era have debated so furiously for the past three decades. There is no disputing the contention that most reform movements of any era are generally led by an articulate urban elite situated in strategic positions that enable them to recruit and motivate large numbers of people, especially those who are actively literate and who share many of the same values. Nor is it particularly surprising that the members of such elites in the early twentieth century United States tended to be of old American stock, well-fixed financially, and "touched by the long religious hand of New England," to quote Mowry. But the same can generally be said of those organizations and groups committed to resisting reform, as numerous scholars have demonstrated. For several years, historians debated the assertion of Mowry and Richard Hofstadter, that "progressivism, in short, was to a very considerable extent led by men who suffered from the events of their time not through a shrinkage in their means but through the changed pattern in the distribution of deference to power."

In 1967, however, Robert Wiebe shifted the focus from old elites responding to a revolution in status to "a dynamic and optimistic new middle class, deliberately attempting to substitute an entirely new set of values for traditional, but outmoded, American beliefs." This new middle class consisted of managers, bureaucrats, technicians, intellectuals, and professionals whose values reflected "the regulative, hierarchical needs of urban, industrial life," and included such desiderata as "continuity and regularity, functionality and rationality, administration and management." The "Progressive movement," according to the widely accepted view, "was the triumph of this new middle class with bureaucratic mentality."[6]

More specifically, Yearley has assigned the crucial role in the revolution in taxation to the "new strategic elites "of urban experts, middle class acamedicians, businessmen, politicians and administrators. Reflecting the values of the new middle class they sought to fashion a tax structure that was efficient, predictable, productive, and flexible, by separating state and local revenues, equalizing rates, and exacting income, inheritance, and corporate levies. Such leadership was clearly visible in the enactment of the federal income tax, as such organizations as the National Tax Association and the American Economic Association and such individuals as Seligman, MacVeagh, Kennan, and Kinsman played critical roles. Arguments endorsing the tax as a highly lucrative and flexible fiscal instrument were common both in the press and in legislative halls. But such arguments were relatively rare compared to those urging the income tax on the grounds of equity, and they hardly stirred up the same kinds of passion among politicians and their constituents. Moreover, the tax was also supported by farmers, small businessmen, urban political machines, humanitarians, and southerners, people who were generally resisting the forces of modernization and bureaucratization with all the power that they could muster. The arguments of the experts provided these other groups with the aura of respectability and plausibility that they needed to press for the income tax, but the utterances of their own representatives reflect little confluence of basic values. For these other groups, the issue was "justice" or an urge to punish the rich, not the erection of an efficient, modernized, rationalized tax structure.[7]

Nor can the success of the income tax be explained primarily in terms of "urban liberalism," the upward thrust of the urban, ethnic working and lower middle class operating through "urban political machines." Prior to the publication of J. Joseph Huthmacher's article "Urban Liberalism and the Age of Reform," most interpretations of the Progressive Era generally dismissed the urban lower class as part of "the potent mass that limited the range and achievements of American progressives." Indeed, Yearley assigns them such a role in the "revolution in taxation," limiting their participation to making clamorous demands upon urban politicians for increased public services and expenditures. "Incapable of being a constructive force," Yearly argues, "they were witnessly both a corrupting and a reformist force." It is certainly true that the urban masses did not make the same type of contribution to the income tax coalition that political economists and members of the National Tax Association did, but their votes sustained the "urban political machines" whose representatives played such a crucial role in the ratification process in the major industrial states of the Northeast. They were among the most avid readers of the mass circulation newspapers, such as those of Hearst and Pulitzer, that consistently advocated the tax, and numerous studies have demonstrated that the urban lower classes demanded and responded favorably to organization sponsored candidates who advocated, at least for public consumption, the augmentation of urban lower class political power, and a determined opposition to legislated morality. In the area of taxation, that involved shifting the burden off laborers, small businessmen, and consumers onto the financial and industrial elite, insofar as possible.[8]

As already noted Democratic machine politicians were the most consistent supporters of ratification in key northeastern states, and the major Republican backers were generally those with urban lower and lower middle class constituencies. In New York in 1911, over half the favorable votes were cast by Tammany - dominated Democrats of Irish, Jewish, or German extraction who repreented inner city districts in New York or Buffalo. In New Jersey, thirty of the forty-nine favorable votes were cast by Irish, German, and Slavic-Americans from similar constituencies in highly industrialized north Jersey, while ratification in Massachusettes owed itself to the cooperation of Irish-American Democrats and Republican "labor legislators," both of whom represented heavily Irish, Italian, Jewish, Slavic, and French Canadian constituencies in Boston and in the industrial cities and mill towns of the state. In Rhode Island and Connecticut, urban, working class Democrats were the only identifiable political force advocating ratification. In most northeastern states, the ratification contest closely approximated Huthmacher's observation that "effective social reform of the Progressive Era and in later periods seems thus to have depended upon constructive collaboration, on specific issues, between reformers from both the urban lower class and the middle class (with the further cooperation, at times, of organized labor)." Yet, for all that, such an explanation has almost no relevance for the situation in most states of the South and West where the critical elements of urban liberalism were generally lacking. It also cannot account for the overwhelming support of the tax in Congress by hundreds of representatives from rural, agrarian backgrounds and constituencies.[9]

But if the various agrarian, urban middle class, and urban lower class interpretations provide, at best, only a partial explanation for the enactment of the federal income tax, the perspective that the Progressive Era was essentially a "triumph of conservatism" seems to be totally at odds with the circumstances of the measure's adoption. Relying largely upon an examination of the process that produced federal regulation of big business through such agencies as the Federal Trade Commission, Gabriel Kolko called for a complete reinterpretation of the period "labeled the 'progressive' era by virtually all historians" as "an era of conservatism" brought about not by "any impersonal mechanistic necessity" but by "the conscious needs and decisions of specific men and institutions." In virtually every case involving government and the economy, Kolko charged, national political leaders "chose those solutions to problems advocated by the representatives of concerned business and financial interests." Such proposals, he continued, "were usually motivated by the needs of the interested businesses and political intervention in the economy was frequently merely a response to the demands of particular businessmen." Overall, Kolko concluded, "conservative solutions to the emerging problems of an industrial society were almost universally applied" between 1910 and 1916. Modifying that view somewhat, James Weinstein conceded that reform proposals often originated with "those suffering under intolerable conditions," but that "success in the sense of legislation enacted, followed upon the adoption of particular reform programs by big business leaders."[10]

Whatever the validity of such interpretations when applied to other socioeconomic issues of the period, they are clearly contradicted by the case of the federal income tax. Seldom has any measure enjoyed such almost universal and categorical opposition from big business. Newspapers and periodicals sympathetic to that viewpoint consistently denounced the tax as the first step in the confiscation of property with a passion that often burdened on hysteria. Nearly all of the overt opposition to the measure in Congress and in the halls of the state legislatures was led by politicians and party organizations with long standing and openly acknowledged ties to the business community. Nearly all of the lobbying and the testimony in committees against the tax came from the representatives of big business. When the Regulars yielded to political realities in 1909 and accepted the corporation tax and the amendment proposal at Taft's hand, they freely admitted that they did so only "to beat the income tax." Even at that, business spokesmen and publications almost universally denounced the corporation tax and many businesses participated in an organized nationwide campaign of litigation in order to have the tax invalidated. The Regular's steadfast resistance to having the amendment considered by popular convention was a tacit, but eloquent, admission both of the income tax's overwhelming popularity and of the power that their business-oriented allies wielded in key state legislatures. By 1913, business leaders were powerless to prevent the enactment of the income tax by the Democrat-Insurgent controlled Congress, but they labored feverishly to minimize its impact through lowering the exemption, keeping the rates moderate, and by seeking special exemptions for their lines of endeavor. Once the law had been enacted, as Wiebe noted in the first chapter, it was denounced by businessmen and their publication outlets as the most destructive act in the nation's history. As late as 1924, Jules Bache, president of the National Association of Manufacturers, still denounced the enactment of the tax as the work of "special sections of our people, numerically strong," who, "through unequal and unwise taxation, in a spirit of envy," imposed "an unfair burden upon those more fortunate than themselves."[11]

Looking backward a half century later and being conscious of the recent history of the income tax, especially of the various "loopholes" for tax avoidance by the wealthy that have been devised, it would be easy to conclude that the tax was a conservative plot designed to dupe middle and working class taxpayers into thinking that the rich were paying their fair share. If one assumed that the major purpose of the tax was the redistribution of wealth, then it would also be tempting to judge it to be a conservative palliative since most available data provides little evidence that significant redistribution has occurred in the past half century. Kolko, in Wealth and Power in America, argues that "the impact of Federal income taxes on the actual distribution of wealth has been minimal, if not negligible." To begin with, the original income tax, as we have already seen, was not designed to redistribute wealth or income and only a handful of Insurgents and "radical" Democrats advanced the argument that it ought to be so constructed. Whatever reputation the tax acquired between 1909 and 1913 as a redistributive mechanism came largely from the charges of opponents who were trying to discredit the measure. Moreover, the men of 1909-1913 tried, within the constraints imposed by legislative politics, to construct a tax that rested almost exclusively on the affluent, that contained a minimum of exemptions and deductions, and that was simple to administer. Some of them even tried to tax income from stocks, bonds, and securities at a higher rate than that from salaries and wages.[12]

Whatever the tax may have become later, it was clearly designed by people who wanted to tax income "from whatever source derived" according to the "ability to pay" of the recipients, and to do it with a minimum of bureaucratic obfuscation. That is what they meant by tax equity - that each should contribute according to his or her capacity as measured by income. As Hillje has demonstrated, this concern for equity in taxation was still sufficiently viable to enable "progressive, farmer, organized labor, and low income groups" to prevail upon Congress to rely largely upon the income tax to finance the war effort between 1916 and 1919. Even though the exemption was lowered to $1000 for single persons and $2000 for married couples in 1917, the tax still only affected an estimated seven per cent of the population while levies on individual and corporate income and on excess profits yielded anywhere from forty to seventy-five percent of government revenues during the war. Indeed, Kolko argues that the tax was not extended to middle and lower income receivers until World War II and that most of the present methods of tax avoidance flowed from a response to the theoretically high rates of the "soak-the-rich" tax structure instituted by the Roosevelt Administration. Whatever later developments, the original income tax was designed to promote tax equity and to produce additional revenue to allow for tariff reduction, not to redistribute wealth or income. Those motives were sufficiently powerful and widely shared to sustain the original concept of the tax system at least through World War I.[13]

The most striking observation about the enactment of the federal income tax is that it was the product of disparate groups acting from compatible, but by no means identical, perspectives. Acting independently, at least initially, each came to regard the tax as an partial solution to the economic problems that plagued the nation in general and themselves in particular. Although none of those socioeconomic groups or sections was a monolith with regard to the income tax or to any other issue of the era, their members generally shared a reasonably common outlook on questions of taxation that set them apart from people who were not of their occupational, income, and geographical characteristics. Farmers, for example, were acutely aware that they were generally failing to keep pace on several fronts in a rapidly industrializing and urbanizing country. Agricultural assets had risen only about one-fifth as much as had intangible ones during the last four decades of the nineteenth century and, by 1913, farm income was but seventy-five per cent that of non-farm intake. The farmer's share of national income dropped nearly fifty per cent in the first decade of the new century. Only one-fourth of the nation's farmers were touched by the 1913 tax and they accounted for but three percent of the nation's taxpayers. Moreover, farmers generally saw great advantage in shifting the burden off real property and onto intangible wealth since their assets were mostly in land, buildings, and implements, items virtually impossible to conceal from the assessor. Their money income, on the other hand, was difficult to calculate and far easier to underestimate. The country's impressive wealth was largely in "machinery, credits, securities, mortgages, savings, exchange values, 'going concerns,' and personal possessions," affects that most farmers had very little of and that could be reached most effectively by income and inhertance taxes. In addition, federal customs duties and excise taxes fell upon "farmers as consumers" without supplying "farmers as producers" with any real protection from foreign competition. These considerations combined to convince most farmers that tax revision, and a federal income tax in particular, was both just and in their own best interests.[14]

Generalizing about the urban middle class is obviously much more hazardous. In terms of occupation their ranks included businessmen, managers, professionals, intellectuals, bureaucrats, clerks, and technicians, people whose incomes derived largely or entirely from salaries, professional fees, or business receipts as opposed to interest, dividends, and rent. In terms of income, most fell somewhere between the $827 a year average family income and the $3000-$4000 a year minimum for income tax liability. As already noted, seventy-nine per cent of bankers, eighty-one per cent of lawyers, eighty-two per cent of mine owners, eight-nine per cent of engineers, ninety per cent of manufacturers, ninety-five per cent of realtors and merchants, ninety-six per cent of teachers, and ninety-eight per cent of saloon keepers fell below the minimum. Beyond their incomes, their resources generally consisted of real and personal property that bore most of the brunt of state and local taxation. Their own desires for better municipal services in education, transportation, and recreation contributed significantly to escalating urban budgets and they were among the major consumers of those products whose prices were increased by customs duties and excise taxes. They were the major readers of the muckraking novels and journals that exposed the machinations of wealthy industrialists and financers.[15]

As Yearley and other have observed, many urban, middle class Americans saw themselves as the victims of "two predatory constituencies," the one consisting of "vulgar hordes of working men and immigrants with no stake in society" and the other of the "corporate rich and their 'unproductive' retinues." Many middle class people blamed these two constituencies for increasing government expenditures through welfare demands and graft, conveniently ignoring the fact that their own escalating demands for social services contributed to the same condition. Many saw themselves, as Yearley demonstrates, as financing "both the revels of the new wealth and the bread and circuses of the new democracy." Although middle class people partly sought the remedy for this situation in retrenchment, most realized that costs would continue to rise and that the answer lay in constructing a system that would produce adequate and predictable revenue and shift the burden upward. On the state and local level of government, this generally translated into tax equalization, more accurate accounting systems, and a reliance upon income and inheritance taxes with "tolerable rates and generous exemptions." On the federal level, it meant a disposition in favor of tariff revision and income and inheritance taxes.[16]

The perspective of the blue-collar wage-earner was different from that of farmers or middle class Americans, but it was equally favorable to income taxation. Only one-half of one per cent of the nation's income tax payers in 1913 were wage earners. For the most part, blue collar workers owned little real property but, to the extent that landlords passed the property tax onto renters, they were adversely affected by the rising rates. Since they spent a higher proportion of their income on the necessities of life, wage earners were injured by the rising cost of living even more than were middle class persons and they paid out a correspondingly greater share of their intake on customs and excise taxes. As a rule, they were even more dependent upon social services than were more affluent Americans, although the nature of those services was often significantly different. To the middle class, these were the "vulgar hordes of working men and immigrants with no stake in society" who raised the costs of government by demands for "bread and circuses." Although their comprehension of the complexities of federal tax policy may not have been too sophisticated, they had little difficulty in apprehending claims that present federal tax policies promoted inflation, placed the burden on them as ultimate consumers. They also realized that they would not have to pay a federal income tax.[17]

Professional politicians had yet another perspective on tax reform, one that was an amalgam of those of the new middle class and of the urban wage earner. Yearley painstakingly delineates that perspective and stresses that the urban professional politician was part of the "new strategic elite" of managers, bureaucrats, technicians, intellectuals, and experts. In reality, however, the politico functioned as a broker, a conduit, or a mediator between that world and the universe of the urban, usually immigrant stock, working and lower middle classes. While the new middle class expert typically proceeded out of native-stock, Protestant, middle class origins and earned his position through education or training, the professional politician was much more likely to have his roots in the ethnic, non-Protestant, working and lower middle class. Harold Zink, for example, found that of twenty prominent urban bosses of the early twentieth century, five were immigrants and ten were second generation Americans and that "there seems to be some relationship between the racial stock of municipal bosses and the dominant racial stock of foreign origin in their cities." A similar study of Chicago precinct captains revealed that over eighty per cent were "from the second generation foreign stocks in the city, while an analysis of party organizations in Providence revealed that Irish Americans held over eighty percent of Democratic positions in 1910, with Italians, French Canadians, and eastern Europeans pushing from below. Most of these had working or lower middle class backgrounds, ties to organized labor, and had risen through the organization ranks largely through experience. The typical professional politician was a "marginal man" who stood with one foot in the neighborhoods and precincts and the other in the urban, industrial mainstream, trying to explain and represent the one to the other and to harmonize their often conflicting demands in a manner that would redound to his own continuation in power. On some matters, such as business regulation and welfare legislation, that was a relatively simple task. On others, such as structural political reform or legislated morality, it strained the powers of even the most accommodating politician. For the most part, the income tax fell into the former category.[18]

Party organizations, as Yearley has demonstrated insightfully, had developed their own informal system of tax collection that included assessments of office holders, kickbacks from beneficiaries of government contractors and franchises, and "protection" paid by proprietors of illegal enterprises. Although widely attacked, especially by the new middle class, for its undeniable graft and corruption, this informal system actually reached accumulated wealth much more effectively than did the official structure and provided much more of the revenue needed to meet escalating demands for services. But these increasing demands were matched by an insistence upon honesty, efficiency, and economy in government, especially from the urban middle class. Caught between these conflicting pressures and trying to protect their own instrumental positions, many professional politicians recognized the need to alter the official tax structure in order to meet the needs previously served by the unofficial levies that were now under such heavy fire by "reformers." "The parties' assessment of jobholders and political candidates, the political levies against corporations and certain criminal business on the basis of their ability to pay." Yearley has concluded, "in effect, have been formally incorporated into state income taxes or into a variety of special taxes." Ironically, this ultimately constituted another major step in making government responsive and accessible primarily to organized and sophisticated interest groups and to reducing the effectiveness of the party organization as a conduit to the disorganized and powerless. Although the wealthy constituents of most political organizations undoubtedly put pressure upon them to oppose an income tax, the politicians themselves were generally more responsive to two other imperatives, the need to remain in power by acceding to the demands of the working and middle class for tax equity and the requirement to guarantee more productive and predictable revenue sources.[19]

Different geographical sections also viewed the federal income tax differently, but largely compatibly. People in the West and the South frequently saw the issue in sectional terms and identified their target as the entire population of the northeast. Such expressions generally alienated the middle and working classes of that region and enabled the affluent residents of those states to obfuscate the issue by portraying the tax as a sectional plot to despoil everyone in the area. Such tactics were apparently successful in 1895, but had lost much of their impact by 1909. Income tax advocates in all three regions successfully cast the argument in non-sectional terms, identified the same targets of taxation, and easily refuted appeals to sectional solidarity and states rights. The three sections also viewed the relationship of tariff revision to income taxation in somewhat different, though not necessarily antagonistic, terms. The South was theoretically committed to a tariff for revenue only, whatever the reality, that made the tax a desirable revenue supplement. Westerners generally sought less drastic tariff reduction, making the revenue argument for the income tax less compelling. Insurgent contentions along this line often seemed strained and contrived, compared to their insistence upon equity or redistribution. The residents of the northeastern states were more divided along socioeconomic and partisan lines over the relationship between the tariff and the income tax, with most manufacturers and Regular Republicans ardently opposed to both lowering rates and enacting a revenue supplement. But the majority of people in those states eventually subscribed to the notion that tariff reduction was the best cure for inflation and that the income tax was the ideal substitute, for reasons of both productivity and equity. Even the traditional rationales of full employment and an expanding market for foodstuffs failed to prevent laborers and farmers from joining the revolt and the success of the Democrats in linking the two issues to the high cost of living made inroads into normally Republican voting patterns. The details of which rates to lower and of how much revenue needed to be raised by the income tax caused many strains, both within and between sections, but the consensus that an income tax was necessary, whatever the outcome of tariff revision captured a majority in all three sections.[20]

Finally, the three regions differed in their perception of the relationship between income tax revenues and increased federal expenditures. The West clearly had the greatest expectations of increased federal expenditures on internal improvements, as their success in acquiring federal aid, both before and after the enactment of the tax, demonstrated. Such sentiments were much slower to develop in the South because of the region's historical resistance to intervention by the federal government in nearly every aspect of life. Advocates of the tax rarely argued that the South would benefit in any special fashion beyond tariff reduction and tax equity and concentrated on the almost negligible impact that the tax would have on residents of their states. Opponents of the tax generally conjured up visions of money being extracted from the South to be spent elsewhere and these contentions apparently carried weight in several states. In the northeastern states, advocates of the income tax made no claims that increased federal expenditures would result there. In fact, the measure's opponents insisted that the additional revenue would be spent west of the Mississippi, reenforcing their portrayal of the income tax as a western plot to despoil the northeast. That which was a major pro-income tax argument in the West was a liability in the northeast and little better than that in the South.[21]

Between 1895 and 1909, a broad-based national income tax consensus emerged out of these differing, but compatible, socioeconomic and sectional perspectives. Although those differences persisted, and surfaced at every stage of the process between 1909 and 1913, they were temporarily subsumed by general agreement on several interrelated premises. One was the belief that the rising cost of living was due primarily to the protective tariff system that added substantially to the cost of most items of consumption and fostered trusts that extracted inordinate profits. The second was that the existing federal tax structure of customs duties and excise taxes, as well as the state and local tax system of real and personal property taxes, placed the burden squarely upon the productive working and middle classes and allowed the very wealthy to avoid paying their fair share of the costs of government. The third was that the rising costs of government, and the fall-off in revenue that followed the Panic of 1907, mandated a need for new revenue sources and that any new taxes ought to meet the tests of productivity and equity, both of which dictated the taxation of the wealthy. These three perceptions, whatever their validity as an explanation of reality, dovetailed into an operating consensus that a federal income tax would fall exclusively upon those with the "ability to pay" and that it would tap sources of wealth that had heretofore escaped taxation.[22]

This consensus was nurtured in the growing anti-special privilege atmosphere that characterized the onset of the Progressive Era. Muckraking journalists and novelists set much of the tone by their exposes of financial and political corruption, of the contrast between the idle rich and the suffering poor, and of shoddy products sold at high prices. The mood was intensified by the frequent rhetorical tongue lashings given to the "malefactors of great wealth" by Theodore Roosevelt and his imitators. According to Richard L. McCormick, it reached its zenith right after the "crisis of 1905-06" with the simultaneous "discovery that business corrupts politics" in nearly every state. During those two years investigatory commissions in dozens of states revealed, in sensational detail, the corrupt alliances between various enterprises and party organizations. In 1906, reform candidates promising to end business control of politics wee elected in dozens of states and called for a myriad of remedial measures, including the regulation of lobbyists, the banning of free railroad passes for legislators, the abolition of campaign contributions by corporations, and primary elections. Most typically, they called for the creation or expansion of commissions to regulate railroads, public utilities, and other businesses. Between 1905 and 1907 alone, according to McCormick, fifteen states created railroad commissions and the powers of at least that many others were significantly expanded. "What had hitherto been scattered and isolated movements for state reform," he concludes, "became a nationwide crusade." As already noted, such widespread public indignation at what David Thelen has called "corporate arrogance" persisted throughout the elections of 1910 and 1912, contributing mightily to the downfall of the Regular Republicans and to another spate of reform legislation in 1911 and 1913. The main bone of contention between Roosevelt's New Nationalism and Wilson's New Freedom was the issue of how to deal with the "trusts." Since these were generally owned and operated by the very people who were to be the targets of the federal income tax, the latter could hardly have failed to benefit from this attack on corporate privilege and corruption.[23]

This emerging consensus sustained the formation of a pro-income tax coalition that embraced most socioeconomic groups, except for the well-to-do, and claimed a majority in each of the three geographic regions. Even Yearley acknowledges that "there was some coalescence of previously hostile forces; if there had not been, of course, the final establishment of state and federal income taxation on a broadening scale and as a permanent feature of the money machines of the country during the Progressive Era would have been highly improbable." Despite the leadership exercised by intellectual elites, Yearley continues, fiscal reform's constituency was "democratic because of the pluralism of the total situation; over time each of the many minorities through arguments and appeals which reached every significant element of the populace, urban and rural, managed to gain something." Yearley exempts only the very rich and the very poor from participation in this process, but, as previously mentioned, adds that the latter contributed "wittlessly" by demanding increased social services.[24]

Pressure for the tax was applied partly through the efforts of a variety of interest groups that proliferated during the Progressive Era, because they believed that it squared with the other measures that they were advocating to advance their members'self-interest while serving the "public interest." The American Federation of Labor endorsed the income tax in 1906, along with proposals to permit collective bargaining and picketing, to regulate health and safety in factories, and to curtail child and female labor. The National Farmers Union backed the tax along with demands for parcels post, postal savings banks, federally - secured farm loans, and agricultural extension programs. The National Tax Association pushed the measure along with a myriad of other proposals to rationalize and modernize the tax structure, such as tax equalization, state commissions, inheritance levies, the separation of state and local funds, and the freeing of municipal tax rate schedules from restrictive state charters. The National Municipal League also favored the tax as part of its program to improve the quality of life in American cities. Some of these organizations were primarily what David P. Thelen has designated as "producer-oriented" interest groups primarily concerned with advancing measures of benefit to their own members, whether farmers, laborers, businessmen, or professionals. Others were more reflective of what Thelen has described as a "new citizenship", a growing awarenes on the part of millions of Americans that their common roles as consumers, taxpayers, and citizens transcended their narrower ethnic, socioeconomic, and geographical identifications and united them against corrupt alliances of big businessmen and politicians. Many of these organizations served both purposes to a greater or lesser degree and most Americans felt themselves pushed and pulled back and forth between both sets of consciousness, depending on the nature of the issue being raised.[25]

There can be little doubt that the national debate over tariff revision and the income tax heightened most people's sense of their roles as consumers and taxpayers, but it is problematical whether that recognition involved a corresponding decline in their sense of identification with others of the same socioeconomic, ethnocultural, or geographical backgrounds.

The coalition that produced the income tax arose largely out of the internal logic of the issues that the measure raised and purported to resolve. The matter, by its very nature, divided society along income lines, pitting those who made over a certain amount against those who did not, regardless of occupational, ethnocultural, or geographical backgrounds. Few, if any, other measures broached during the era divided people along those same lines. Even tariff revision, a question inextricably intertwined with the income tax in 1909 and 1913, produced a somewhat different alignment, both within and without Congress. Farmers generally favored an income tax but opposed putting raw materials on the free list. Importers generally favored downward rate revision but opposed an income tax if they would be reached by it. Many working class people who favored an income tax continued to believe that a protective tariff insured full employment. Pro-income tax Democrats frequently voted with Regular Republicans in 1909, if the products of their state or region were involved. The Insurgents generally voted with the Regulars against their income tax allies on the Underwood-Simmons Tariff. The income tax coalition was similar to those that produced other reforms raising related socioeconomics issues and it clearly benefited from its popular association with other measures aimed at eliminating special privilege and business-government collusion. It also, according to Hillje, sustained itself through the debates over financing World War I, maintaining the principle of "ability to pay." But it was, in no sense, a "movement" with a relatively stable membership and a reasonably well defined program that produced a variety of reform efforts.[26]

The National Tax Association and the other organizations that advocated the income tax were typical of the many emerging interest groups of the Progressive Era in that they usually endorsed individual candidates, regardless of party affiliation, if they espoused desired legislation. If they were able to get a political party committed to such legislation, they might endorse its entire slate of candidates, but such partisan behavior alienated office holders of the opposite party and jeopardized the interest group's primary purpose - to enact legislation favorable to its members' interests and ideology. Similarly, they generally followed a non-partisan approach in lobbying legislators in the various state houses and in Congress. Even the American Federation of Labor attempted to be non-partisan before Republican intransigence and Democratic receptivity mandated their endorsement of the latter party. As interest groups organizations proliferated and escalated their activities, they found that political parties, by their nature, were beholden to many constituencies and viewed their function as that of broker among competing demands. As a result, interest group organizations rarely were satisfied with the results of their attempts to secure party backing and many resolved to change the rules of the game in order to weaken the power of the professional politicians and to facilitate interest group access to government. Accordingly, they sponsored a series of political reforms, such as the secret ballot printed by the state, direct primaries, initiative, referendum, and recall, at-large, non-partisan elections, the separation of local elections from state and national ones, civil service, and the short ballot.[27].

Whenever many of these reforms were adopted, they tended to create a "new politics" that was non-partisan, issue-oriented, and candidate-centered and that gradually shifted the locus of power from professional politicians to organized interest groups and "political action committees." Historians strongly debate the ultimate effect of this "new politics," with one school contending that it transferred power from the businessman-professional politician alliance to consumers, taxpayers, and citizens and shifted the focus from irrational, irrelevant ethnocultural issues to rational, relevant, socioeconomic ones. The other school contends that the ultimate gainers were the most powerful interest groups, generally big business, and that the new politics led to a "class-oriented skewing of participation" with a "heavy curtailment of the leverage previously exercised in the political arena by the class-ethnic infrastructure and its representatives," according to Walter Dean Burnham. In any event, the new politics resulted in a dramatic decline in voter turnout during the Progressive Era that has generally continued to the present day.[28]

There is little evidence that these alterations in the political process had much effect on the enactment of the federal income tax. Most of these changes had their initial impact on municipal politics and gradually worked their way upward through the system. They also seemed to have more effect upon electoral than upon legislative politics during the Progressive Era. Party organizations generally remained too powerful to ignore or bypass. Interest group organizations that favored the income tax apparently took a bipartisan, rather than non-partisan, approach, working through whichever party structure would pledge its support. Those organizations opposed to the tax relied heavily upon the Regular Republican organizations in Congress and in the northeastern states and upon Bourbon Democratic factions in the southern states. The great mass of unorganized supporters of the tax had little choice but to depend upon what Burnham has characterized as "the only devices thus far invented by the wit of western man which with some effectiveness can generate collective countervailing power on behalf of the many individually powerless against the relative few who are individually or organizationally powerful." These unorganized masses generally had to express whatever preference they had for an income tax through the medium of one of the two major parties or by supporting the Socialist or Progressive parties in 1912.[29]

Since American political parties have always been essentially pluralistic coalitions of diverse socioeconomic, ethnocultural, and geographical groups "without program and without discipline," to quote Morton Grodzins, it is not surprising that votes on the income tax were rarely along strict partisan lines. The remarkable thing is that, everywhere outside of a few southern states, the Democrats were able to maintain an almost solid front. Even during the convoluted course of events in 1909, they exhibited a remarkable degree of voting cohesion. In 1913, the disagreements over rates and other details between the "radicals" and the administration Democrats were thrashed out in caucus and supported with virtual unanimity on the floor. By contrast, the income tax issue wreaked havoc upon any semblance of Republican solidarity. Large numbers of Insurgents deserted the Congressional ranks in both 1909 and 1913, and there were numerous defections to the income tax forces, especially among urban Republicans, in most northeastern legislatures. In most midwestern and western states, where Insurgent forces generally dominated the party, Republican legislators and leaders supported ratification in impressive numbers. By all indications, the federal income tax resulted from interplay between traditional partisan politics and the emerging issue-oriented, interest group "new politics," with the former being more important inside the various legislative chambers and the latter instrumental primarily in mobilizing popular support.[30]

In the legislative arena, the enactment of the tax resulted from the politics of coalition, compromise, and consensus at every stage of its evolution. During the special session of 1909, the Democrat-Insurgent coalition forced the issue upon the Regulars and frightened them into accepting President Taft's compromise proposal of a corporation excise tax and a constitutional amendment. Presidential intervention forced all three groups to compromise their positions, with the Regulars generally moving to an position of grudgingly accepting the lesser of two evils and the Insurgents and Democrats reluctantly concluding that a partial loaf was the only bread that they could salvage. The Regulars' indignation was modified by a determination to invalidate the corporation tax and to prevent ratification, while the frustration of the Insurgents and Democrats was tempered by a corresponding determination to secure ratification. Even Taft had to accept modifications in the provisions of the corporation tax and worked for the adoption of an amendment whose authority he planned to use only in an emergency. There was no room for compromise in the ratification process, but, except in one party states, coalition politics was the order of the day. In single party states, cooperation between two or more distinct factions was usually necessary to effect ratification. In 1913, a similar Democrat-Insurgent coalition, this time constituting an overwhelming majority of both houses, easily carried the day, but not without conflict and compromise. The demands of the Insurgents for higher rates and fewer exemptions and deductions emboldened a faction of "radical" Democrats who challenged their party leadership on the same grounds. The Regular Republicans were reduced to pushing for smaller rates, a lower starting point, and exemptions and deductions for special interest groups. The resultant compromise produced a tax that was less than the Insurgents and radical Democrats desired, but more drastic than the administration Democrats originally envisioned.

Given the limitations imposed by the structure and values of American Society, the adoption of the federal income tax constituted the best effort that the people of the Progressive Era were able to muster in dealing with the critical dilemma posed by economist Irving Fisher in 1919:

> Our society will always remain an unstable and explosive compound as long as political power is vested in the masses and economic power in the classes. In the end one of these powers will rule. Either the plutocracy will buy up the democracy or the democracy will vote away the plutocracy.[31]

Notes

CHAPTER I
Building a National Consensus

1. Sidney Ratner, American Taxation: Its History As a Social Force in Democracy, (New York, 1942), 51-53; Kossuth Kent Kennan, Income Taxation: Methods and Results in Various Countries, (Milwaukee, 1910), 203-205; Paul Studenski and Herman Krooss, Financial History of the United States, (New York, 1963), 20-21; Randolph E. Paul, Studies in Federal Taxation, (Cambridge, Massachusetts, 1940), 3.

2. National Industrial Conference Board, State Income Tax, vol. 1 Historical Development, (New York, 1930), 1-89; Ratner, American Taxation, 54-56; Delos R. Kinsman, The Income Tax in the Commonwealth of the United States, (New York, 1903), 10-111; Delos R. Kinsman, "The Present Period of Income Tax Activity in the United States," Quarterly Journal of Economics, XXXIII (February, 1909), 296-303; E. R. A. Seligman, The Income Tax, (New York, 1911, 388-412; Kennan, Income Taxation, 209-234; R. Paul, Studies in Taxation, 64.

3. Ratner, American Taxation, 56-235; Studenski and Krooss, Financial History, 49-225; Seligman, Income Tax, 430-510; Roy and Gladys Blakey, The Federal Income Tax, (New York, 1940), 2-15; U.S., Department of the Treasury, Report of the Secretary of the Treasury, 1938, (Washington, 1938), 410-412; U.S., American State Papers, VI, 885-887; Harry Smith, The United States Federal Internal Tax History from 1861 to 1871, (Boston, 1914),

4. Ratner, American Taxation, 181-210; Alfred Kelly and Winfred Harbison, The American Constitution, (New York, 1963), 562-569; Arnold M. Paul, Conservative Crisis and the Rule of Law: Attitudes of Bar and Bench, 1877-1895, (New York, 1969), 160-212, Blakey, Income Tax, 21-22.

5. National Industrial Conference Board, State Income Tax, 36-101; Kinsman, Income Tax in the Commonwealth, 113-302; Clifton K. Yearley, The Money Machines; (Albany, 1970), 229-239; Seligman, Income Tax, 427; ________, "Two Constitutional Amendments," The Chautauquan, 63(July, 1911): 110- 112.

6. Smith, Federal Internal Tax History, 94, 282-296; Kennan, Income Taxation, 237-255; Ratner, American Taxation, 132-143; Yearley, Money Machines, 138-229.

7. Elmer Ellis, "Public Opinion and the Income Tax," Mississippi Valley Historical Review, XXVII (September, 1940), 225-242; Yearley, Money Machines, 188-189; Ratner, American Taxation, 152-159.

8. Ellis, "Public Opinion," 238; Yearley, Money Machines, 230; Ratner, American Taxation, 193-214; A. Paul, Conservative Crisis, 160-196; R. Paul, Studies in Taxation, 4-26.

9. Yearley, Money Machines, 184-190.

10. Studenski and Krooss, Financial History, 222-223; Kennan, Income Taxation, 255-260; Blakey, Income Tax, 9; U.S. Congress, 64th Congress, 2nd Session, House Document 5, Statistics of Income, (Washington, 1916), 12-13. For arguments on western demands for federal spending see Chapters IV, VI, and VII below.

11. House Document 5, 1916, Statistics of Income, 12-13; Joseph Hill, "The Civil War Income Tax," Quarterly Journal of Economics, VIII (July, 1894) 416-452. For Southern "states-rights" arguments see Chapter V, VI and VII below.

12. Kelly and Harbison, American Constitution, 562-571; A. Paul, Conservative Crisis, 186-210; Edward C. Corwin, Court Over Constitution, (Princeton, 1938), 182-3, 190-197; Smith, Federal Internal Tax History, 414; Ellis, "Public Opinion," 233.

13. Robert W. Wiebe, Businessmen and Reform, (Cambridge, 1963), 10-15; Yearley, Money Machines, 123-124, 152; David Rothman, Power and Politics: The United States Senate 1869-1901, (New York, 1969), 37-38;

14. U.S. Congress, 41st Congress, 2nd Session, Congressional Globe, 1869-1870, 4023; Ratner, American Taxation, 69-82, 139-144, 178; Ellis, "Public Opinion," 226-227; R. Paul, Studies in Taxation, 27-29; Seligman, Income Tax, 455; Wayne MacVeagh, "The Graduated Taxation of Income and Inheritances," North American Review, 18(1906), 824-828; Wiebe, Businessmen and Reform, 196-203, 213; American Economist, 43(April 23, 1909): 286; New York Times, March 24, 1910; Literary Digest, 39(August 14, 1909): 118.

15. Wiebe, Businessmen and Reform, 196-203; Herbert L. Griggs to Cordell Hull, February 21, 1913, Cordell Hull Papers, Library of Congress; House Document 5, 1916, Statistics of Income, 31.

16. Rothman, Politics and Power, 37, 112-121, 185-212; Yearley, Money Machines, 123-154; Wiebe, Businessmen and Reform, 101-126.

17. Rothman, Politics and Power, 191-218.

18. Ellis, "Public Opinion," 239-240; Kennan, Income Taxation, 265-266; Kelly and Harbison, American Constitution, 562-569; Ratner, American Taxation, 196, 323; Edward Martin, Joseph Hodges Choate, (New York, 1920), 7.

19. Kennan, Income Taxation, 262-263; Studenski and Krooss, Financial History, 50-51; Kelly and Harbison, American Constitution, 564-567; A. Paul, Conservative Crisis, 162-198; Corwin, Court Over Constitution, 182-183.

20. Martin, J. H. Choate, 9; A. Paul, Conservative Crisis, 160-193; Ratner, American Taxation, 217; Kelly and Harbison, American Constitution, 564-567; Corwin, Court over Constitution, 181-182.

21. Seligman, Income Tax, 572-580; Kennan, Income Taxation, 226-227; A. Paul, Conservative Crisis, 185-196; Robert McCloskey, American Conservatism in the Age of Enterprise, 1865-1910, (New York, 1951), 17; Corwin, Court Over Constitution, 196.

22. Kelly and Harbison, American Constitution, 568; Corwin, Court Over Constitution, 186-190; R. Paul, Studies in Taxation, 44-67; A. Paul, Conservative Crisis, 210.

23. Corwin, Court Over Constitution, 197, 206; Ratner, American Taxation, 209-210, Kelly and Harbison, American Constitution, 565; Robert McElroy, Grover Cleveland, (New York, 1923), 669-670.

24. 158 U.S., Pollock v. Former's Loan and Trust Company, 638, 672, 685; Kelly and Harbison, American Constitution, 556-573; A. Paul, Conservative Crisis, 209-212; Seligman, Income Tax, 589.

25. U.S. Bureau of the Census, Historical Statistics of the United States, From Colonial Times to 1957, (Washington, 1960), Yearley, Money Machines, 258-260; Studenski and Krooss, Financial History, 4-5, 165, 212, 267; George F. Warren and Frank A. Pearson, Prices, (New York, 1933), 1-27, 326-364.

26. Yearley, Money Machines, xii, 3, 25, 127-273; Oscar Handlin, The Uprooted, (New York, 1951), 221-225.

27. Studenski and Kroos, Financial History, 4-5, 212, 267; Samuel Hays, Response to Industrialism, 1885-1914, (Chicago, 1957), 83,111.

28. Yearley, Money Machines, 10-76; Andrew Carnegie to Charles Evans Hughes, April 21, 1910, Chaarles Evans Hughes Papers, Library of Congress; G. P. Watkins, "The Growth of Large Fortunes," Publications of the American Economic Association, 3rd Series, 8, no. 4(1907).

29. Studenski and Krooss, Financial History, 4-5, 57, 165; U.S. Congress, 63rd Congress, 1st Session, House Reports, vol. 2, Tariff Duties and Revenues, 1913, xxxvi - xxxvii; F. W. Taussig, The Tariff History of the United States, (New York, 1964), with an introduction by David M. Chalmers, vi; ________, "American and the Income Tax," The Nation, 92(January 26, 1911): 84-85.

30. Historical Statistics, 167; House Document 5, 1916, Statistics of Income, 20; Willford I. King, et. al., National Bureau of Economic Research, (New York, 1922), Income in the United States: Its Amount and Distribution, 1909-1919, 307-308, 332-335, 379-381; Maurice Leven, H. G. Moulton, and Clark Warburton, Brookings Institution, America's Capacity to Consume, (Washington, 1934), 29, 105-106; Robert C. Gallman, "Trends in the Size Distribution of Wealth in the Nineteenth Century: Some Speculations," in Lee Soltow (ed.), Six Papers on the Size Distribution of Wealth and Income (New York, 1969), 11-15; U.S. Internal Revenue Service, 1916, Personal Income Tax Imposed and Collected Under the Act of October 3,

1913, (1916); Yearley, Money Machines, 226; R. Paul, Studies in Taxation, 87. For contemporary accounts of concentration of wealth see Watkins. "Growth of Large Fortunes," passim., Thomas G. Shearman, "The Owners of Wealth," Forum, (November, 1889): 262-273; George K. Holmes, "The Concentration of Wealth," Political Science Quarterly, 8(1893): 589-600; Charles B. Spahr, The Present Distribution of Wealth in the United States, (New York, 1896); Willford I. King, Wealth and Income of the People of the United States, (New York, 1915); Robert Hunter, Poverty, (New York, 1904); Thorstein Veblen, Theory of Business Enterprise, (New York, 1904); J. H. Underwood, Distribution of Ownership, (New York, 1907); Gustavus Myers, History of Great American Fortunes, (New York, 1909); F. H. Streighthoff, Distribution of Income in the United States, (New York, 1912). For a more recent discussion see Sidney Ratner, (ed)., New Light on the History of Great American Fortunes: American Millionaries of 1892 and 1902, (New York, 1953).

31. House Document 5, 1916, Statistics of Income, 7.

32. Historical Statistics, 150-157, 589, 626, 674; Gallman, "Trends in Size Distribution," 6-7.

33. Yearley, Money Machines, 6-10, 27-30, 60-66; Studenski and Krooss, Financial History, 4-5, 57.

34. Studenski and Krooss, Financial History, 165; Seligman, Income Tax, 498.

35. Ratner, American Taxation, 308-309; Shearman, "Owners of Wealth," 262-273; Ellis, "Public Opinion," 237-242; Historical Statistics, 180. One is reminded here of J. Kenneth Galbraith's observation that the rich do not consume great quantities of bread. See his The Great Crash, (Boston, 1961), 162.

36. Kirk Porter and Donald Johnson, National Party Platforms, (Urbana, Illinois, 1961), 168-175; House Reports, II, 1913, Tariff Duties and Revenues, xxxvii - xxxix.

37. National Bureau of Economic Research, v. 24, Retail Prices After 1850, Ethel D. Hoover (Comp.), (New York, 1933), 142; Historical Statistics, 97-128; U.S. Congress, 61st Congress, 2nd Session, 1910, Senate Select Committee Report, Wages and Prices of Commodities, 37-50; House Reports, II, 1913, Tariff Duties and Revenues, 1-50; Warren and Pearson, Prices, 13-15, 158, 350-357.

38. Warren and Pearson, Prices, 197-217; Senate Select Committee Report, 1910, Wages and Prices of Commodities, 52-55; Ratner, American Taxation, 254; Blakey, Income Tax, 73; King, et al., Income in the United States, 335.

39. Warren and Pearson, Prices, 357; Senate Select Committee Report, 1910, Wages and Prices of Commodities, 52, 112-126; Wiebe, Businessmen and Reform, 95-96.

40. Studenski and Krooss, Financial History, 90-92; Seligman, Income Tax, 494-499.

41. Wiebe, Businessmen and Reform, 90-95; House Report, II, 1913, Tariff Duties and Revenue, xv, Studenski and Krooss, Financial History, 270-271; Kenneth Hechler, Insurgency, (New York, 1940), 96-104; Tom C. Terrill, Tariff, Politics and American Foreign Policy, (Westport, Connecticut, 1975), 213; Taussig, Tariff History, 367.

42. New York Times, November 9, 1910; New York World, May 17, 1910; Studenski and Krooss, Financial History, 270-271; Hechler, Insurgency, 106-108; Wiebe, Business men and Reform, 14-15, 56-57; Carl Chrislock, The Progressive Era in Minnesota, (Minneapolis, 1971), 26-28; House Report, 1913, II, Tariff Duties and Revenue, xvi-xviii; Porter and Johnson, National Party Platforms, 146-147, 158.

43. Hechler, Insurgency, 96-144; James L. Holt, Congressional Insurgents and the Party System, 1909-1916, (Cambridge, 1967), 29-45; Taussig, Tariff History, 363-370.

44. Arthur W. Machen, Jr., A Treatise on the Federal Corporation Tax Law of 1909, (Boston, 1910), 2; U.S. Congress, 61st Congress, 1st Session, Congressional Record, v. 44, 3487; American Economist, 44(July 30, 1909): 54; 44(September 3, 1909): 113; 44(November 5, 1909): 218; 46(November 4, 1910): 221.

45. Yearley, Money Machines, xvi, 150, 183-185; Studenski and Krooss, Financial History, 167; E. R. A. Seligman, "The Theory of Progressive Taxation," Political Science Quarterly, (1893), 223-225. See also Max West, "The Income Tax and National Revenue," The Journal of Political Economy, 8(1900): 437-451; __________, "Prospects of the Federal Income Tax Amendment," World's Work, 22(May, 1911): 14310; and Ratner, American Taxation, 303-305.

46. Kinsman, Income Tax in Commonwealths, 111-116, 306; Ellis, "Public Opinion," 237; R. Paul, Studies in Taxation, 31-35, 93-97, 102, Porter and Johnson, National Party Platforms, 147; House Reports, 1913, II, Tariff Duties and Revenue, xxxvi-xxxvii; Yearley, Money Machines, xvi.

47. David P. Thelen, The New Citizenship: Origins of Progressivism in Wisconsin, 1885-1900, (Columbia, Missouri, 1972), 205; Seligman, "The Theory of Progressive Taxation," 22-221; E. R. A. Seligman, Essays in Taxation, (New York, 1895), 362-363; MacVeagh, "Graduated Taxation," 827; Kennan, Income Taxation, 218-219, 318.

48. Studenski and Krooss, Financial History, 274-275; Roy Blakey, "The Income Tax Exemption," The Outlook, CVI(1914): 259; John W. Hillje, "The Progressive Movement and the Grauated Income Tax," Ph.D. dissertation, University of Texas, 1966, 69-71, 370-371. For a view that redistribution of wealth was a major motive for the income tax agitation of the Progressive Era see Thelen, New Citizenship, 204-205. For a revisionist view that holds that even the New Dean "soak-the-rich" taxes were intended to

produce no meaningful redistribution, see Gabriel Kolko, Wealth and Power in America, (New York, 1962).

49. Leven, et. al., Capacity to Consume, 38-49; Maurice Leven, Income in the Various States, 57-74; Richard A. Easterlin, "Inter-regional Differences in Per Capita Income, Population and Total Income," in National Bureau of Economic Research, v. 24, Trends in the American Economy in the Nineteenth Century, (Princeton, 1960), 92-95; Hays, Response to Industrialism, 116-136; Nash, American West, 34.

50. Hays, Response to Industrialism, 136; Paola Colletta, William Jennings Bryan: Political Evangelist, 1860-1908, (Lincoln, Nebraska, 1964), 56-60, 105, 333-334; Cordell Hull, The Memoirs of Cordell Hull, v. I. (London, 1948), 45-74; Blakey, Income Tax, 7; Kennan, Income Taxation, 266-267; Ellis, "Public Opinion," 237-238; Yearley, Money Machines, 234.

51. For the positions of the various state Democratic and Republican parties in the Northeast toward the income tax amendment, see Chapters VI and VII below. The attitudes of Roosevelt, Taft, and Root are discussed later in this chapter and in Chapters II and VIII below.

52. Yearley, Money and Machines, 193-252. For examples of efforts to substitute a state income tax for a federal one, see Chapters VI and VII below.

53. Ellis, "Public Opinion," 235-263; Kirk Porter and Donald Johnson, National Party Platforms, (Urbana, Illinois, 1961), 98, 131-132, 147; Harvey Wish, "Altgeld and the Progressive Tradition," American Historical Review, 46(1941): 813-831; Richard E. Becker, "Edward Dunne: Reform Mayor of Chicago, 1905-1907," Ph.D. dissertation, University of Chicago, 1971, 147-183; Blakey, Income Tax, 11; Melvin G. Holli, Reform in Detroit: Hazen S. Pingre and Urban Politics, (New York, 1969), 157-184.

54. ______________., "Now For the Income Tax," Hearst's Magazine, 23 (April, 1913): 672-674; New York Times, May 18, 1911; Ellis, "Public Opinion," 237-238; Blakey, Income Tax, 7; William P. Koscher, "The Springfield Republican in the Progressive Era: A Guardian of American Values," Ph.D. dissertation, University of Illinois, 1975, 129-151.

55. Ellis, "Public Opinion," 235-236; Yearley, Money Machines, 167-192; Hillje, "The Progressive Movement," 12-15.

56. Yearley, Money Machines, 167-191; New York Times, April 13, 1909.

57. Randolph E. Paul, Taxation in the United States, (Boston, 1954), 86-89; Ratner, American Taxation, 259-261; New York Times, April 15, 1906.

58. Elting E. Morison (ed.)., The Letters of Theodore Roosevelt, (Cambridge, Massachusetts, 1954), v. V, 217, 261, 344, 366, v. VII, 884; Henry Cabot Lodge, Selections from the Correspondence of Theodore Roosevelt and Henry Cabot Lodge, (New York, 1925), v. II, 341-346. ______________., "The Income Tax," The Outlook, 93(October 16, 1909): 328-329.

59. R. Paul, Taxation in the United States, 90-91; Ratner, American Taxations, 266-270; New York Times, July 29, 1908.

60. Edwin Maxey, "The Democratic Convention," The Arena, 40(September, 1908): 152-153; __________., "The Democratic Convention," The Outlook, 89(July, 1908): 645-654; Colletta, Bryan, Political Evangelist, 334-405. Bryan's Des Moines speech is quoted in Ratner, American Taxation, 269 and Aldrich's remark in the New York Times, April 13, 1909. On the adoption of the income tax plank, see Democratic Party, U.S., National Convention, Denver, 1908. Official Report of the Proceedings of the National Convention Held in Denver, Colorado, 1908, 29-31, 159-174. The committee that unanimously approved the income tax plank consisted of U.S. Senators William Stone of Missouri and Francis Newlands of Nebraska, ex-Senator James Smith of Newark, New Jersey, future Senator Thomas J. Walsh of Montana, Governors Austin Lane Crothers of Maryland, John Burke of North Dakota, and J.C.W. Beckham of Kentucky, Congressman George Fred Williams of Masssachusetts, and Judges Sameul Altschuler of Chicago and Alton B. Parker of New York, an indication of the widespread support that the measure enjoyed.

CHAPTER II
An Amendment of Curious Origins

1. U.S. Congress, Biographical Dictionary of the American Congress, 1774-1971, (Washington, 1971), 297-302; __________, Who Was Who In America, 1897-1942, (Chicago, 1968), 55, 292, 746, 767, 797, 1158, 1217.

2. Claude Bowers, Beveridge and the Progressive Era, (Boston, 1931), 334; Ratner, American Taxation, 275; William MacDonald, "Joseph Gurney Cannon," Dictionary of American Biography, III, (New York, 1929), 476-477; William Hard, "Uncle Joe Cannon," Colliers, 41 (May 23, 30, 1908); Blair Bolles, Tyrant From Illinois; Uncle Joe Cannon's Experience With Personal Power, (New York, 1951), 51-194; Hechler, Insurgency, 11-91; Holt, Congressional Insurgents, 3-31.

3. Biographical Directory, 297-302; Who Was Who, 163-164, 273-316, 324-325, 365; Rothman, Power and Politics, 167; Ratner, American Taxation, 275, 281; Blakey, Income Tax, 23-24; David Graham Phillips, "the Treason of the Senate," Cosmopolitan Magazine, 40 (April, 1906), 628-638; Ernest Crosby, "The House of Dollars," Cosmopolitan Magazine, 40 (March, 1906), 485; Richard W. Leopold, Elihu Root and the Conservative Tradition, (Boston, 1954), 20.

4. Who Was Who, 200, 493-494, 900, 960, 1151; Biographical Directory, 297-302.

5. Rothman, Power and Politics, 123-125, 161, 203-216.

6. Washington Post, June 28, 1909; New York Times, April 10, 1909; Rothman, Power and Politics, 44-55.

7. David W. Detzer, "The Politics of the Payne-Aldrich Tariff of 1909," Ph.D. dissertation, University of Connecticut, 1970, 55-68; Charles R. Brayton to Nelson W. Aldrich, April 17, 1909, Nelson W. Aldrich Papers, Library of Congress; Stanley D. Solvick, "William Howard Taft and the Payne-Aldrich Tariff," Mississippi Valley Historical Review, 50 (1968), 430; Illinois State Register, (Springfield), October 19, 1909.

8. Hechler, Insurgency, 11-91; Holt, Congressional Insurgents, 3-31.

9. Idem.

10. Joseph L. Bristow to James A. Troutman, April 29, 1913, Joseph L. Bristow Papers, Kansas State Historical Society.

11. Mowry, Era of Theodore Roosevelt, 227-229, 259-273; Paul Schlichting to Robert M. LaFollette, November 10, 1909, Robert M. LaFollette Papers, Library of Congress; William Howard Taft to Charles H. Heald, December 25, 1907; William Howard Taft Papers, Library of Congress; Detzer, "Politics of Payne-Aldrich Tariff," 237; Alfred Dick Sander, "The Political and Social Views of William Howard Taft," Ph.D. dissertation, The American University, 1955, 11; Paolo E. Coletta, The Presidency of William Howard Taft, (Lawrence, Kansas, 1973), 255-257.

12. Coletta, Presidency of Taft, 17-18; Sander, "Political and Social Views," 31-50; New York Times, March 5, 1909; Bristow to Gifford Pinchot, June 30, 1911, Bristow Papers.

13. Donald F. Anderson, William Howard Taft: A Conservatives' Conception of the Presidency, (Ithaca, New York, 1973), 108-110; Horace Dutton Taft, Memories and Opinions, (New York, 1942), 116; Sander, "Political and Social Views," 14; Taft to E. N. Huggins, August 11, 1908, Taft to Philander C. Knox, October 24, 1909, Taft Papers of New York Times, April 11, 1909; Detzer, "Politics of Payne-Aldrich," 189-191.

14. Detzer, "Politics of Payne-Aldrich Tariff," 189; Taft to Elihu Root, Novembere 25, 1908, Taft to William D. Foulke, March 12, 1909; Taft to Helen H. Taft, July 7, 1909, Taft Papers; Horace Samuel Merrill and Marion Galbraith Merrill, The Republican Command, (Lexington, Kentucky, 1971), 277-299; Solvick, "Taft and Tariff," 431; Coletta, Presidency of Taft, 61.

15. Taft to Charles P. Taft, April 19, 1910; Taft to John L. Wilson, May 16, 1910; Taft to Horace Taft, June 6, 1909; Taft to Elbert Gary, July 12, 1909, Taft Papers; Taft to Root, August 15, 1908, Special Correspondence of William Howard Taft and Elihu Root, Elihu Root Papers, Library of Congress.

16. Solvick, "Taft and Tariff," 433-437; Coletta, Presidency of Taft, 65; Bristow to Frank B. Bristow, February 13, 1911, Bristow Papers; Jonathan Dolliver to Robert M. LaFollette, October 13, 1909, LaFollette Papers.

17. Coletta, *Presidency of Taft*, 61, 71, 139; Mowry, *Era of Theodore Roosevelt*, 262-265; Anderson, *William Howard Taft*, 110; Taft to Roosevelt, May 26, 1910, *Taft Papers*.

18. *Biographical Dictionary*, 295-302; Ratner, *American Taxation*, 276-277; Claude E. Barfield, "'Our Share of the Booty': The Democratic Party, Cannonism, and the Payne-Aldrich Tariff," *Journal of American History*, LVII (September, 1970): 308-322. The best studies of Congressional Democrats in this era are Jerome V. Clubb, "Congressional Opponents of Reform, 1901-1913," Ph.D. dissertation, University of Washington, 1963; Claude E. Barfield, "The Democratic Party in Congress, 1909-1913," Ph.D. dissertation, Northwestern University, 1965; David Sarasohn, "The Democratic Surge, 1905-1912: Forging on Progressive Majority," Ph.D. dissertation, University of California at Los Angeles, 1976; and Edward M. Silbert, "Support for Reform Among Congressional Democrats, 1897-1913," Ph.D. dissertation, University of Florida, 1966.

19. Ratner, *American Taxation*, 276; *Biographical Directory*, 295-302; Hays, *Response to Industrialization*, 129.

20. *Biographical Directory*, 295-302; Sarasohn, "Democratic Surge," 117-172; Silbert, "Support for Reform," 69-90.

21. John D. Buenker, *Urban Liberalism and Progressive Reform*, (New York, 1973), 1-41; Clubb, "Congressional Opponents," 211, 284; Sarasohn, "Democratic Surge," 117-165; J. Joseph Huthmacher, *Senator Robert F. Wagner and the Rise of Urban Liberalism*, (New York, 1968), 12-37; Nancy Joan Weiss, *Charles Francis Murphy, 1858-1924: Respectability and Responsibility in Tammany Politics*, (Northampton, Massachusetts, 1959), 69-91; John Morton Blum, *Joe Tumulty and the Wilson Era*, (Boston, 1951) 1-27; Silbert, "Support for Reform," 78-90.

22. Solvick, "Taft and Tariff," 424-428; Taussig, *Tariff History*, 361-70; Sidney Ratner, *The Tariff In American History*, (New York, 1972), 41-43; Detzer, "Politics of Payne-Aldrich," 1-2, 41-45, 70-96, 145-154; Hechler, *Insurgency*, 96-145.

23. See note 22 above.

24. Ratner, *American Taxation*, 267-269; Detzer, "Politics of Payne-Aldrich," 41-45; Solvick, *Taft and Tariff*, 424-427; Hechler, *Insurgency*, 146-153.

25. Porter and Johnson, *National Party Platforms*, 158.

26. Nathaniel W. Stephenson, *Nelson W. Aldrich*, (New York, 1930), 348-354, 478; Solvick, "Taft and Tariff," 430-433; Mowry, *Era of Theodore Roosevelt*, 54; Detzer, "Politics of Payne-Aldrich," 1-2, 41-45, 70-96, 145-154; Merrill and Merrill, *Republican Command*, 290.

27. E. E. Schattschneider, *Politics, Pressure and the Tariff*, (New York, 1935), 283; Taussig, *Tariff History*, 361-408; Rothman, *Power and Politics*, 91-95; Detzer, "Politics of Payne-Aldrich," 70-96.

28. Taussig, Tariff History, 363-366; Solvick, "Taft and Tariff," 426-428; Detzer, "Politics of Payne-Aldrich," 145-154.

29. Hechler, Insurgency, 100-106; Taussig, Tariff History, 375; Chrislock, Progressive Era in Minnesota, 26-29; U.S. Congress, Congressional Record, 61st Congress, 1st Session, 1909, 1846. Hereinafter referred to as C.R. 44. Bristow to A. C. Mitchell, May 21, 1909, Bristow to Harold T. Chase, May 22, 1909, Bristow to J. H. Stavely, May 31, 1909, Bristow to W. A. Dawson, June 18, 1909, Bristow to T. C. Leland, Jr., June 7, 1909, Bristow Papers.

30. Hechler, Insurgency, 98-99; Taussig, Tariff History, 284-320, 374-383, 409-445; Holt, Congressional Insurgents, 10-12, 29-43, 81-94; Terrill, Tariff Politics and Foreign Policy, 212-213; Detzer, "Politics of Payne-Aldrich," 1-32, 70-96; Solvick, "Taft and Tariff," 427-428; Clubb, "Congressional Opponents," 134-135.

31. Solvick, "Taft and Tariff," 425-427; Merrill and Merrill, Republican Command, 278-291; Taft to Roosevelt, July 31, 1907; Taft to William Burgess, August 24, 1908, Taft Papers.

32. Solvick, Taft and Tariff, 433-437. Solvick's observations are a faithful reflection of Taft's views expressed in his correspondence. See especially Taft to Horace White, March 25, 1909 and Taft to Edward Colston, June 24, 1909, Taft Papers. Taft's utterances as a presidential candidate have already been discussed in Chapter I above.

33. Barfield, "'Our Share of the Booty,'" 308-315; Porter and Johnson, National Party Platforms, 146.

34. Barfield, "'Our Share of the Booty,'" 308-315; Taussig, Tariff History, 382; Ratner, American Taxation, 271-274; Sarasohn, "Democratic Surge," 134-135. See also U.S. Congress, 61st Congress, 1st Session, The Democrats and the Tariff: Speech of Augustus Bacon, Senate Document 109, 1909.

35. C.R. 44: 1429, 1702, 2102-2104, 3965-3985, 4005-4008, 4037, 4108, 4390-4396, 4400-4414; Marian McKenna, Borah, (Ann Arbor, Michigan, 1961), 106.

36. C.R. 44: 36, 105, 194-195, 266-267, 1300, 1379, 3487, 4403; Lodge, Roosevelt and Lodge, v. II, 338-339; Robert M. LaFollete, "How Aldrich Killed the Income Tax," La Follette's Magazine, 1 (July 10, 1909), 5.

37. New York Times, March 5, 1909; Solvick, "Taft and Tariff," 427-428.

38. Solvick, "Taft and Tariff," 433-437; Ratner, American Taxation, 268-269; Sander, "Political and Social Views," 37-43. See also the sources in note 32.

39. ______________________., "The Income Tax and the Constitution," Current Literature, 47 (August, 1909): 129-133; James C. German, Jr., "Taft's Attorney General: George W. Wickersham," Ph.D. dissertation, New York University, 1969, 200-210.

40. New York Times, March 16, 17, 1909; Solvick, "Taft and Tariff," 427; Ratner, American Taxation, 270-271; Detzer, "Politics of Payne-Aldrich," 46-54, 145-154; Barfield, "'Our Share of the Booty,'" 301-315.

41. Ratner, American Taxation, 270-274; Taussig, Tariff History, 368-373; Detzer, "Politics of Payne-Aldrich," 46-54, 70-150; C.R. 44, 139-142, 194-197, 532-536; __________, "Income Tax and Constitution," Current Literature, 129-133; German, "Taft's Attorney-General," 200-210.

42. C.R. 44: 532-536, 1301; Ratner, American Taxation, 272-274; Solvick, "Taft and Tariff," 428-429; Taft to Marcus M. Marks, June 29, 1909, Taft to Helen H. Taft, July 11, 1909, Taft Papers; Barfield, "'Our Share of the Booty,'" 312-314; U.S. Congress, 61st Congress, 1st Session, 1909, House Wages and Means Committee, To Provide Revenue, Equalize Duties and Protect Industries of the United States, 10-12.

43. Root to Whitelaw Reid, April 3, 1909, Root Papers; Merrill and Merrill, Republican Command, 284; Solvick, "Taft and Tariff," 429-433; Barfield, '" Our Share of the Booty,'" 314-322; Solvick "Taft and Tariff," 430-433; Taft to Helen H. Taft, July 11, 1909; Taft to Charles P. Taft, July 13, 1909, Taft to Wickersham, July 13, 1909, Taft to William Dudley Foulke, July 15, 1909; Taft to Helen H. Taft, July 16, 1909, Taft to Mrs. Charles P. Taft, July 18, 1909, Taft to Helen H. Taft, July 25, 1909, Taft to John Warrington, July 26, 1909, Taft to Elbert F. Baldwin, July 29, 1909, Taft to Aldrich, July 29, 1909, Taft Papers.

44. Taussig, Tariff History, 373-376; Hechler, Insurgency, 99-132; Holt, Congressional Insurgents, 29-33; Ratner, American Taxation, 276-278; New York Times, April 12, 13, 15, 17, 22, 1909; The Charge of "addition, multiplication, and silence," is from Robert M. La Follette, "How the Tariff Bill Is Going Through," La Follette's Magazine, 1 (May 11, 1909): 5-6.

45. Hechler, Insurgency, 99-132; Merrill and Merrill, Republican Command, 284-291; Holt, Congressional Insurgents, 31-33; Mowry, Era of Theodore Roosevelt, C.R. 44: 4301-4316.

46. Taussig, Tariff History, 405-407; Merrill and Merrill, Republican Command, 292-298; Barfield, "'Our Share o f the Booty,'" 314-321; Solvick, "Taft and Tariff," 441-442; Ratner, American Taxation, 280, New York Times, July 8, 1909; C.R. 44: 4305-4316.

47. Ratner, American Taxation, 274-282; New York Times, March 18, 24, April 12, 13, 16, 18, 19, 20, 22, 1909; C.R. 44: 1351, 1420-1428, 1533-1542, 1558-1566; Sam Hanna Acheson, Joe Bailey: The Last Democrat, (New York, 1932), 41-278; Lewis L. Gould, Progressives and Prohibitionists: Texas Democrats in the Wilson Era, (Austin, Texas, 1973), 16-24; Hechler, Insurgency, 86-87, 146-153.

48. C.R. 44: 2443-2457; New York Times, April 19, 21, May 19, 1909; Hechler, Insurgency, 148; Ratner, American Taxation, 284-285; Henry Pringle, The Life and Times of William Howard Taft, (New York, 1939), I, 434;

Ralph M. Sayre, "Albert Baird Cummins and the Progressive Movement in Iowa," Ph.D. dissertation, Columbia University, 1958, 332-339.

49. C.R. 44: 2454-2457, 3135-3138; New York Times, May 28, 29, June 9, 10, 11, 12, 1909; Ratner, American Taxation, 285; Hechler, Insurgency, 146-149; Sayre, "Albert Baird Cummins," 332-339.

50. __________., "Income Tax and Constitution," Current Literature, 129-133; Lodge to Roosevelt, June 21, 1909; Lodge, Roosevelt and Lodge, v. II, 338-339; Stephenson, Aldrich, 359; Taft to Horace Taft, June 27, 1909, Taft to Theresa McCagg, June 26, 1909, Taft to Albert Douglas, July 21, 1909, Taft Papers; Francis Leupp, "President Taft's Own View," The Outlook, 99 (December 2, 1911): 816; New York Times, June 9, 15, 1909; Ratner, American Taxation, 285-287; Hechler, Insurgency, 148-149.

51. New York Times, June 9, 10, 11, 12, 16, 1909; C.R. 44: 3135-3138; George van Lengerke Meyer, The George van Lengerke Meyer Diary, Library of Congress, June 15, 16, 18, 1909.

52. New York Times, June 17, 1909; U.S. Congress, 61st Congress, 1st Session, Senate Document 98, Message of President Recommending Amendment to Tariff Bill For Tax Our Net Income of Corporations, 1909, 1-5.

53. Senate Document 98, Message of President, 3-5; New York Times, June 17, 1909.

54. Taft to J. D. Brannan, June 1909, Taft to Edward Colston, June 24, 1909, Taft to Frederick P. Fish, June 28, 1909, Taft to Therese McCagg, June 28, 1909, Taft Papers; Solvick, "Taft and Tariff," 435; ________., "Income Tax and Constitution," Current Literature, 130-132; New York Times, September 22, 1909; Archibald W. Butt, Taft and Roosevelt: The Intimate Letters of Archie Butt, (Garden City, New York, 1930), v. I, 133-134.

55. Taft to Rollo Ogden, July 20, 1909, Taft to Fish, June 28, 1909, Taft to General Felix Angus, June 29, 1909, Taft to Theodore Roosevelt, May 26, 1910, Taft Papers; Butt, Taft and Roosevelt, v. I, 262-263.

56. German, "Taft's Attorney-General," 201-208; C.R. 44: 2569, 4002-4007, 4690; William E. Chandler to Root, July 10, 1909, Root Papers; Philip C. Jessup, Elihu Root, v. II, (New York, 1964), 226-228, 532; Richard Leopold, Elihu Root and the Conservative Tradition, (Boston, 1954); 76-79; Taft to Horace Taft, August 27, 1909, Taft Papers; Barfield, "Democratic Party in Congress," 126-127.

57. Stephenson, Aldrich, 353-356; New York Times, June 18, 20, 21, 22, 23, 24, 1909; Lodge to Roosevelt, June 21, 1909, Lodge, Roosevelt and Lodge, vol. II, 338-339; C.R. 44: 3929; Butt, Taft and Roosevelt, I, 123-133; Taft to Horace Taft, June 27, 1909, Taft Papers. See also Root to Jefferson Levy, June 29, 1909, Root Papers.

58. C.R. 44: 4066, 4108, 4121, 4228, 4316; New York Times, July 6, 13, 1909.

59. Root to Wickersham, July 28, 1909, Root Papers.

60. Stephenson, Aldrich, 355; John D. Rockefeller, Jr. to Aldrich, June 21, 1909; E. G. Buckland to Aldrich, June 24, 1909, Aldrich Papers; Taft to E. G. Buckland, June 26, 1909, Taft Papers; Butt, Taft and Roosevelt, V. I, 130-131; C.R. 44: 4690; New York Times, August 1, 1909.

61. New York Times, August 1, 6, 1909; Ratner, American Taxation, 293-294.

62. New York Times, June 23, 24, July 1, 3, 8, 10, 11, 1909; __________., "Income Tax and Constitution," Current Literature, 129-133.

63. New York Times, July 3, 8, 10, 11, September 29, November 16, 29, 1909; January 6, 15, 16, 22, 24, 27, 30, March 4, 13, 16, 20, 31, June 1, 7, October 21, 1910; Ratner, American Taxation, 294-295.

64. New York Times, March 14, 1911; U.S. Congress, 62nd Congress, 2nd Session, House Document 601, Decisions of the United States Supreme Court in Corporation Tax Cases and Income Tax Cases with Dissenting Opinions, March 5, 1912, 3-7; Ratner, American Taxation, 295-297. Powell is quoted in Ratner, American Taxation, 296 and in Paul, Taxation in the United States, 96.

65. Hechler, Insurgency, 149-50; Barfield, "Democratic Party in Congress," 121-131; Bristow to Harold T. Chase, June 19, 1909; Bristow to Fred C. Trigg, June 21, 1909, Bristow Papers; Robert M. LaFollette, "How Aldrich Killed the Income Tax," La Follette's Magazine, 1 (July 10, 1909): 5

66. Taft to Horace Taft, June 27, 1909, Taft to Albert Douglas, July 1, 1909, Taft Papers; Butt, Taft and Roosevelt, v. I, 175; Bristow to Harold T. Chase, June 19, 1909, Bristow Papers; Sayre, "Albert Baird Cummins," 332-339.

67. William E. Chandler to Root, July 10, 1909, Root Papers; Roosevelt to Lodge, September 10, 1909, Lodge, Roosevelt and Lodge, v. II, 346.

68. Bristow to Fred C. Trigg, June 21, July 2, 1909, Bristow Papers; Machen, Treatise on the Federal Corporation Tax, 7-16.

69. Bristow to Harold T. Chase, June 19, 1909, Bristow to Henry J. Allen, July 3, 1909, Bristow to T. B. Brown, June 29, 1909, Bristow to E. A. Mize, June 29, 1909, Bristow to J. B. Dawson, June 28, 1909, Bristow to W. S. Guyer, June 29, 1909, Bristow to E. B. Jewett, June 18, 1909, R. W. Sutton to Bristow, July 7, 1909; Bristow Papers; Albert J. Beveridge to Charles F. Remy, June 21, 1901, Albert J. Beveridge Papers, Library of Congress.

70. John Braeman, Albert J. Beveridge: American Nationalist, (Chicago, 1971): 155-157, 195; A. C. Bartlett to Beveridge, July 7, 1909, Beveridge to A. C. Bartlett, July 9, 1909, Albert B. Cummins to Beveridge, September 13, 1909, Taft to Beveridge, July 13, 1909, Beveridge to Charles F. Remy, June 21, 1909, Beveridge to M. W. Schultz, June 22, 1909, Beveridge Papers.

71. Washington Post, June 17, 1909; Clubb, "Congressional Opponents," 121-125; Hull, Memoirs, 60-63; C.R. 44: 4006, 4228, 4316, 4364, 4725, 4755; Ratner, American Taxation, 287-303; Acheson, Joe Bailey, 256-275; William Jennings Bryan to La Follette, July 6, 1909, La Follette Papers; Barfield, "Democratic Party," 121-131; New York Times, June 17, 1909; C.R. 44: 4006-4228.

72. C.R. 44: 3345-3377; Ratner, American Taxation, 298-303; New York Times, June 18, 1909.

73. C.R. 44: 3377, 4067, 4105-4109; Ratner, American Taxation, 298-300; New York Times, June 29, 30, 1909.

74. Ratner, American Taxation, 293; C.R. 44: 4108-4121, 4228, 4390-4440; New York Times, July 3, 6, 13, 1909.

75. C.R. 44: 3900-4007; New York Times, June 29, 30, July 1, 1909; Ratner, American Taxation, 288-289.

76. C.R. 44: 4002-4007, 4036-4041, 4066, 4228, 4316; New York Times, July 2, 3, 8, 9, 1909; Ratner, American Taxation, 289-291; Bristow to W. H. Pratt, July 5, 1909, Bristow Papers.

77. C.R. 44: 3446, 4108-4128; New York Times, July 2, 3, 4, 6, 1909; Ratner, American Taxation, 301-302; Thomas Richard Ross, Jonathan Prentiss Dolliver, (Iowa City, Iowa, 1958), 259-260.

78. C.R. 44: 4364-4384; New York Times, July 10, 1909; Ratner, American Taxation, 291-292.

79. C.R. 44: 4390-4440; New York Times, July 13, 1909; Ratner, American Taxation, 302.

80. Solvick, "Taft and Tariff," 437-442; Detzer, "Politics of Payne-Aldrich," 209-229; New York Times, July 12-15, July 30-31, 1909; Ratner, Tariff in American History, 42-43; Taussig, Tariff History, 376-408; Taft to Helen H. Taft, July 12, 13, 22, 27, 28, 29, 30; Taft to Albert J. Beveridge, July 13, 1909; Taft to John Warrington, July 26, 1909; Taft to Charles P. Taft, August 1, 1909; Taft to Horace Taft, August 11, 1909, Taft Papers; Merrill and Merrill, Republican Command, 292-295.

81. Bristow to Fred C. Trigg, June 21, 1909, Bristow Papers; Ratner, Tariff in American History, 42; Solvick, "Taft and Tariff," 440-442; Taussig, Tariff History, 408; Taft to Helen H. Taft, August 1, 1909, Taft Papers; Merrill and Merrill, Republican Command, 294-295.

82. C.R. 44: 4725-4755, 4877-4949; New York Times, August 1-6, 1909; Ratner, American Taxation, 290-292; Detzer, "Politics of Payne-Aldrich," 215-229.

CHAPTER III
The Chronology of Ratification

1. For an overview of the ratification process, see U.S. Congress. Senate. 71st Congress, 3rd Session, Data on the Ratification of the Constitution and Amendment by States, Senate Document 240, 1930, 10-11. It was also given very thorough coverage in the New York Times between July, 1909 and February, 1913.

2. For a thorough discussion of the situation in New York, see Chapter VI below. For that in Vermont, Massachusetts, New Jersey, New Hampshire, Maine, see Chapter VII below. For that in Kentucky and Arkansas, see Chapter V below.

3. Birmingham Age-Herald, July 6, 1909; ____________., "The Small for the Income Tax," World's Work, II (April, 1910): 1275-12758; Kennan, Income Taxation, 306; Current Literature, XLVII (August, 1909): 131.

4. James Woodburn, "Amending to Constitution," Independent, LXVII (December 30, 1909): 1437-1501.

5. New York Times, August 15, 1909.

6. Idem.

7. Ibid., August 2-10, 1909.

8. Senate Document 240, Data on Ratification, 10-11; New York Times, January 26, 27, February 16, 19, 23, March 1, 9, 10, 26, 29, April 7, 8, 15, May 4, July 26, August 16, 1910.

9. Ibid. January 5, March 1 - May 18, 1910. For a full discussion of the 1910 defeat in New York, see Chapter VI below and John D. Buenker, "Progressive in Practice: New York State and the Federal Income Tax Amendment," New York Historical Society Quarterly, LII (April, 1968): 139-160.

10. New York Times, November 5, 1910.

11. Ibid., November 8, 9, 1910. For a fuller discussion of the 1910 elections in New York and other key northeastern states, see Chapters VI and VII below.

12. Ibid., November 8, 9, 1910.

13. ____________., "Maine and After," The Nation. 91 (September 15, 1910): 232-233; Holt, Congressional Insurgents, 41-43; Kansas City Star, November 8, 9, 10, 1910.

14. Senate Document 240, Data on Ratification, 10-11; New York Times, January 19, 20, 23, 26, 30, 31, February 8, 11, 15, 16, March 16, 18, 21, 30, April 6, 7, 8, 17, 18, 19, 22, 24, May 3, 18, 16, 26, 1911.

15. For a fuller discussion of New York's ratification, see Chapter VI below and Buenker, "Progressive in Practice," 157-160. See also the New York Times from March 18 to July 3, 1911.

16. ____________., "Prospects of the Federal Income Tax Amendment," World's Work, 22 (May, 1911): 14309-14311; ____________., "The Income Tax and the States," The Outlook, 98 (July 22, 1911): 600-601. See also ____________., "Two Constitutional Amendments," The Chautauquan, 63 (July, 1911): 110-112.

17. Senate Document 240, Data on Ratification, 10-11; New York Times, March 6, 13, April 6, 16, 25, June 6, 28, 1912.

18. New York Times, November 5, 6, 1912; Sarasohn, "Democratic Resurgence," 237-293; Mc Inerney, "Election of 1912," 321-376. For a more detailed discussion of the 1912 election in key northeastern states, see Chapter VII below.

19. New York Times, November 6, December 5, 1912; __________., "The Democratic Victory and After," Living Age, 275 (November 30, 1912): 572-574; William Sullivan, (ed.), Edward F. Dunne; Judge, Mayor, Governor, (Chicago, 1916), 490.

20. Senate Document 240, Data on Ratification, 10-11.

21. New York Times, January 31, February 3, 4, 5, 7, 18, 19, March 4, May 21, 1913.

22. Ibid., April 24, 1911, November 6, December 5, 1912; __________., "The Sixteenth Amendment," The Outlook, 103 (February 15, 1913):330-331.

23. New York Times, January 29, February 1, 4, 5, 19, 20, 28, March 5, May 28, 1913; Senate Document 240, Data on Ratification, 10-11.

CHAPTER IV
Triumph in the West

1. In discussing the West I have excluded Arkansas and Texas because, despite their physical locations, their economies, social systems, political cultures, climates and settlement patterns qualify them much more for the inclusion in the chapter on the South. That leaves nineteen states to constitute the West, eighteen of which voted to ratify the Sixteenth Amendment. Thirty-Six states were necessary to secure adoption after the admission of Arizona and New Mexico.

2. U.S., Congress, 42nd Congress, 3rd Session, Executive Document No. 4 1872-1874, 115; U.S. Bureau of the Census, Abstract of the Thirteenth Census of the United States, 1910, (Washington, 1911), 445-60; U.S., Bureau of the Census, Wealth, Debt, and Taxation, (Washington, 1907), 30-3; King, et al., Income in the United States, 56-61.

3. Leven and King, Income in the Various States, 287-94; House Report 5, 1916, Statistics of income, 26-7, 223, 276, 295.

4. Leven and King, Income in the Various States, 290-94.

5. House Report 5, 1916, Statistics of Income, 223-276; King, et al. Income in the United States, 56-61.

6. Nash, The American West in the Twentieth Century, 3-42; Hays, Response to Industrialism, 116-138; Russell B. Nye, Midwestern Progressive Politics, (East Lansing, 1959), 11-223; Theodore Saloutos and John D. Hicks, Agricultural Discontent in the Midwest, 1900-1939, (Madison, 1951), 9-25; Frank Jonas (ed.), Politics in the American West, (Salt Lake City, 1969), 3-6; Bureau of the Census, Abstract of the Thirteenth Census, (Washington,1911), 445-60.

7. Nash, American West, 6-10, 51; Hays, Response to Industrialism, 116-38; Chrislock, Progressive Era in Minnesota, 33-36. See also Gene M. Gressley, "Colonialism, A Western Complaint," Pacific Northwest Quarterly, 54 (1963): 1-8.

8. Nash, American West, 44-5; Elwyn B. Robinson, History of North Dakota, (Lincoln, 1966): 256-7, 332-3; Holt, Congressional Insurgents, 10-12; Lewis L. Gould, Progressives and Prohibitionists: Texas Democrats in the Wilson Era, (Austin, 1973), 31-7, 285-6; Kinsman, Income Tax in the States, 99.

9. Rothman, Power and Politics, 172-3; Nye, Midwestern Progressive Politics, 11-223; Saloutos and Hicks, Agrarian Discontent, 52-3; Earl Pomeroy, The Western Slope, (New York, 1966), 191-215.

10. Quoted in Chrislock, Progressive Era in Minnesota, 36.

11. Quoted in Holt, Congressional Insurgents, 9-10.

12. Nash, American West, 22-3; 41-4; Hays, Response to Industrialism, 116-121, 126-139; Holt, Congressional Insurgents, 10-11; Jonas (ed.), Politics in American West, 6-10, 42, 69, 229, 233, 259, 385; William Allen White to James Bryce, February 19, 1917, White Papers. Eastern concern over federeal spending in the West is reflected below in Chapters VI and VII.

13. House Report 5, 1916, Statistics of Income, 49, 59, 73, 74, 75, 88; Nye, Midwestern Politics, 217-9; Saloutos and Hicks, Agrarian Discontent, 51-2; Jonas (ed.), Politics in the American West, 43-70, 181-95, 203-29; James C. Olson, History of Nebraska, (Lincoln, 1966), 232-48; Calvin Perry Armin, Coe I. Crawford and the Progressive Movement in South Dakota, (Lincoln, 1968), 260-7; Pomeroy, Western Slope, 206; Idaho Statesmen (Boise) January 20, 1911; Gilman Ostrander, Nevada: The Great Rotten Borough, (New York, 1966), viii-xiii, 97-202; Fred L. Israel, Nevada's Key Pittman, (Lincoln, 1963), 21-5; Odie Faulk, Arizona: A Short History, (Norman, 1970), 199-201; Nebraska, General Assembly, House Journal, 1911,

170; Senate Journal, 1911, 227; South Dakota, General Assembly, House Journal, 1911, 347-8; Senate Journal, 1911, 196; Nevada, General Assembly, Assembly Journal, 1911, 33; Senate Journal, 1911, 39; Montana, Legislature, House Journal, 1911, 285; Senate Journal, 1911, 74; Arizona, General Assembly, House Journal, 1912, 134; Senate Journal, 1912, 127.

14. Robert W. Larson, New Mexico's Quest for Statehood, 1846-1912, (Albuquerque, 1968), 275-302, Harry P. Stumpf and T. Phillip Wolf, "New Mexico: The Political State." in Jonas, Politics in the American West, 258-70; House Report 5, 1916, Statistics of Income, 78, 107-8; New Mexico, General Assembly, House Journal, 1913, 64; Senate Journal 1913, 59; Jack E. Holmes, Politics in New Mexico, (Albuquerque, 1967), 145-161; Victor Westphal, Thomas Benton Catron and his Era, (Tucson, Arizona, 1973), 308-348.

15. Faulk, Arizona, 199-201; Ross Rice, "Arizona: Politics in Transition," in Jonas, Politics in the American West, 43-70; Arizona, General Assembly, House Journal, 1912, 134; Senate Journal, 1912, 127.

16. House Report 5, 1916, Statistics of Income, 62, 101-2; Nye, Midwestern Politics, 299-300; Saloutos and Hicks, Agrarian Discontent, 41; Sayre, "Albert Baird Cummins," 304-321; Iowa, General Assembly, House Journal, 1911, 690; Senate Journal, 1911, 566-7.

17. Nye, Midwestern Politics, 217; Saloutos and Hicks, Agrarian Discontent, 52; Robinson, North Dakota, 255-346; North Dakota, General Assembly, House Journal, 1911, 177; Senate Journal, 1911, 685.

18. House Report 5, 1916, Statistics of Income, 83, 109-10; Leven and King, Income in the Various States, 287-94; Edwin C. McReynolds, Oklahoma: A History of the Sooner State, (Norman, 1964), 322-5; Edward Everett Dale and Morris L. Wordell, History of Oklahoma, (Englewood Cliffs, N.J., 1948), 323; Keith L. Bryant, Jr., "Kate Barnard, Organized Labor and Social Justice in Oklahoma During the Progressive Era," Journal of Southern History, 35 (May, 1969), 145-64; Kinsman, "Present Period of Income Tax Activity," 302; Oklahoma, General Assembly, House Journal, 1910, 466; Senate Journal, 1910, 465.

19. House Report 5, 1916, Statistics of Income, 70; 104-5; Leven and King, Income in the Various States, 287-94; Nye, Midwestern Politics, 213-16; Saloutos and Hicks, Agrarian Discontent, 41; Theodore Blegen, Minnesota: A History of the State, (Minneapolis, 1963), 450-9; Chrislock, Progressive Era in Minnesoat, 1-36.

20. Blegen, Minnesota, 425-56; Chrislock, Progressive Era in Minnesota, 7-18; Minnesota, General Assembly, House Journal, 1912, 24; Senate Journal, 1912, 53.

21. Edwin C. McReynolds, Missouri: A History of the Crossroads State, (Norman, 1962), 315-23; Louis Geiger, "Joseph W. Folk v. Ed Butler: St. Louis, 1902," Journal of Southern History, 28 (November, 1962), 438-49; Lyle Dorsett, The Pendergast Machine, (New York, 1968), 1-40; John Fenton, Politics in the Border States, (New Orleans, 1937), 126-55; Nicholas C. Burckel, "Progressive Governors In the Border States: Reform Governors of Missouri, Kentucky, West Virginia, and Maryland, 1900-1918," Ph.D. dis-

sertation, University of Wisconsin, 1971, 131-151; Jack David Muraskin, "Missouri Politics During the Progressive Era, 1896-1916," Ph.D. dissertation, University of California, Berkeley, 1969, 258-259, 371-377; House Report 5, 1916, *Statistics of Income*, 72, 105-6; Missouri, General Assembly, *House Journal, 1911*, 1117; *Senate Journal, 1911*, 606.

22. Leroy R. Hafen, *Colorado and Its People*, (New York, 1948), 311, 508-12; Percy Stanby Fritz, *Colorado: The Centennial State*, (New York, 1941), 353-403; Curtis Martin and Ralph Gomez, *Colorado Government and Politics*, (Boulder, 1964), 139-40; Colin B. Goodykoontz (ed.), *The Papers of Edward P. Costigan Relating to the Progressive Movement in Colorado, 1902-1917*, (Boulder, 1941), 148-61; Fred Greenbaum, *Fighting Progressive: A Biography of Edward P. Costigan*, (Washington, 1971), 1-53; Roland L. De Lorme, "The Shaping of a Progressive: Edward P. Costigan and Urban Reform in Denver, 1900-1911," Ph.D. dissertation, University of Colorado, 195, 198-216, 236-245; *Denver Post*, February 8, 1911; Colorado, General Assembly, *House Journal, 1911*, 483; *Senate Journal, 1911*, 331.

23. House Report 5, 1916, *Statistics of Income*, 51, 98; Leven and King, *Income in the Various States*, 287-94; Oscar Lewis, *The Big Four*, (New York, 1966), 400-12; George Mowry, *The California Progressives*, (Berkeley, 1951), 1-23; Walton Bean, *Boss Reuf's San Francisco: The Story of the Union Labor Party, Big Business and the Graft Prosecutions*, (Berkeley, 1952), passim; Nash, *American West*, 45; R. Hal Williams, *The Democratic Party and California Politics, 1880-1896*, (Stanford, California, 1973), 233-268.

24. Alexander Saxton, "San Francisco Labor and the Populist and Progressive Insurgencies," *Pacific Historical Review*, 34 (1965), 421-37; Michael P. Rogin and John L. Shover, *Political Change in California*, (Westport, Connecticut, 1969), 35-85.

25. Mowry, *California Progressives*, 121, 131; California, Legislature, *Assembly Journal, 1911*, 323; *Senate Journal, 1911*, 323; *San Francisco Chronicle*, January 24, 1911.

26. Oscar O. Winther, *The Great Northwest: A History*, (New York, 1948), 395-410; Pomeroy, *Western Slope*, 191-215; Warren M. Blankenship, "Progressives and the Progressive Party in Oregon, 1906-1916," Ph.D. dissertation, University of Oregon, 1966, 3-73; Albert Pike, Jonathan Bourne, Jr., Progressive," Ph.D. dissertation, University of Oregon, 1957, 37-75, 128-131; Carl Smith and H. P. Edward, *Behind the Scenes at Salem*, (Salem, Oregon, 1911), 15-24. Hendrick is quoted in the article entitled "Oregon: Political Experiment Station," written by Swarthout and Gervais in Jonas, *American West*, 299-300.

27. Oregon, General Assembly, *House Journal, 1911*, 126-127; Smith and Edward, *Behind the Scenes*, 15-24; Allen H. Eaton, *The Oregon System: The Story of Direct Legislation in Oregon*, (Chicago, 1912), 1-160; *Daily Oregon Statesman*, (Salem), January 19, 24, 1911; Oregon, General Assembly, *Senate Journal, 1911*, 53; *Portland Oregonian*, January 18, 1911.

28. Mary W. Avery, Washington: A History of the Evergreen State, (Seattle, 1965), 217-224; Pomeroy, Western Slope, 205-206; Winther, Great Northwest, 403-411; Washington, General Assembly, House Journal, 1911, 160; Senate Journal, 1911, 229; Robert D. Saltvig, "The Progressive Movement in Washington," Ph.D. dissertation, University of Washington, 1966, 66-87, 116-139, 476-485; Hermas J. Bergman, "Progressive on the Right: Marian E. Hay, Governor of Washington, 1909-1913," Ph.D. dissertation, Washington State University, 1967, 1-13, 97-121.

29. House Report 5, 1916, Statistics of Income, 63, 91, 97, 102-103, 111-113; Leven and King, Income in the Various States, 287-294.

30. Nye, Midwestern Politics, 219-200; Soloutos and Hicks, Agrarian Discontent, 51; William Zornow, Kansas, (Norman, Oklahoma, 1957), 201-220; Emporia Gazette, January 20, 1911; Robert L. La Forte, Leaders of Reform: Progressive Republicans in Kansas, (Lawrence, Kansas, 1974), 77-96, 107-108, 164, 244, 312-314; Fred S. Jackson to Bristow, February 18, 1911; Cyrus Leland to Bristow, January 21, 24, 1911; Bristow to Fred C. Trigg, January 31, 1911, Bristow Papers.

31. Kansas, General Assembly, House Journal, 1911, 493; Senate Journal, 1911, 11, 12, 13, 69, 84, 105, 117, 172, 220, 224, 261, 275, 309, 313, 318, 405, 506; Emporia Gazette, January 20, 1911; Topeka Daily Capitol, January 1, 11, 12, 20, February 10, 13, 18, 19, 1911; Wichita Eagle, February 12, 15, 1911; Carl Cooper to Victor Murdock, February 14, 1911, William Allen White to Murdock, February 6, April 11, 1911, Victor Murdock Papers, Library of Congress; La Forte, Leaders of Reform, 128-129.

32. T. A. Larson, Wyoming, (Lincoln, Nebraska, 1965), 317-387; Lewis L. Gould, Wyoming: A Political History, 1868-1896, (New Haven, Connecticut, 1968), 264-268; Rothman, Power and Politics, 172-173.

33. Larson, Wyoming, 349-387; Wyoming, General Assembly, House Journal, 1913, 145; Senate Journal, 1913, 117; The State Leader (Cheyenne), February 4, 1913.

34. House Report 5, 1916, Statistics of Income, 91, 111-2; Leven and King, Income in the Various States, 287-294; Census Bureau, Wealth, Debt and Taxation, 791; Frank H. Jonas, "Utah: The Different State," in Jonas, Politics in the American West, 327-41; Jan Shipps, "Utah Comes of Age Politically: A Study of the State's Politics in the Early Years of the Twentieth Century," Utah Historical Quarterly, 35 (1967), 91-111; Kent Sheldon Larsen, The Life of Thomas Kearns, an unpublished thesis in the University of Utah, 1964; Milton Merrill, Reed Smoot: Utah Politician, (Logan, Utah, 1953), 1-30; Ephraim Edward Erickson, The Psychological and Ethical Aspects of Mormon Group Life, (Chicago, 1922), 22-79; R. J. Snow, "The American Party in Utah: A Study of the Political Struggle During the Early Years of Statehood", M.A. Thesis, University of Utah, 1964. I am also indebted to Professor Snow for additional information gained through correspondence. The statement of the 1903 Senatorial Committee is quoted in J. Leonard Arrington, Great Basin Kingdom: An Economic History of the Latter-day Saints, 1830-1900, (Cambridge, Massachusetts, 1958), 405-411.

35. Shipps, "Utah," 95-7; Snow, "American Party," 85-91; William L. Roper and Leonard J. Arrington, William Spry: Man of Firmness and Governor of Utah, (Salt Lake City, Utah, 1971), 53-103.

36. Shipps, "Utah," 97-100; Snow, "American Party," 25-40, 85-118; Jonas, "Utah," 327-41.

37. Merrill, Smoot, 8-32; Shipps, "Utah," 99-111; Snow, "American Party," 270-300; Jonas, "Utah," 327-41, 364-373.

38. Utah, General Assembly, House Journal, 1911, 10, 37-8, 65, 606-7; Senate Journal, 1911, 256; Salt Lake Tribune, January 2, 11; March 11, 12, 17, 1911.

CHAPTER V
Unexpected Trouble in the South

1. Thirteenth Census, 1910, VIII, 57, 542, Leven and King, Income in the Various States, 223, 264-267; U.S. Department of Commerce, Statistical Abstract of the United States, 1914, 603-604; 1933; 259; C. Vann Woodward, The Origins of the New South, (Baton Rouge, 1951), 318-319; King, et. al., Income in the United States, 25-29; Hays, Response to Industrialism, 116-129.

2. Leven and King, Income in the Various States, 288-293; House Report 5, 1916, Statistics of Income, 98-113; Jackson (Mississippi) Daily News, January 27, 1910.

3. Hays, Response to Industrialism, 116-129.

4. Ibid., 129-139.

5. Birmingham (Alabama) Age-Herald, August 1, 1909; Arkansas Gazette (Little Rock), April 25, 1911; William Shelton, "The Income Tax in Georgia," Journal of Political Economy, 18, (1910) 610-627.

6. See, for example, the Arkansas Gazette, April 13, 1911, and the Atlanta Constitution, January 19, 1910; Terrill, Tariff Politics and Foreign Policy, 211-217.

7. New Orleans, Times-Picayune, June 28, 1912; Louisiana, General Assembly, House Journal, 1910, 205-206; Senate Journal, 1910, 147-149, 167-169, 207.

8. Charleston News and Courier, February 17, 1910; Richmond Times-Dispatch, February 26, March 2, 1910; Louisville Courier-Journal, January 27, 28, 1910; Arkansas Gazette, April 6, 12, 13, 23, 1911; Knoxville Daily Journal and Tribune, April 7, 8, 1911.

9. Simkins, South, Old and New, 381-385; Hesseltine and Smiley, The South, 435-474; Woodward, New South, 291-320; Jasper B. Shannon, Towards

A New Politics in the South, (Knoxville, 1949), 38-53, House Report 5, 1916, Statistics of Income, 98-113; Leonard Reissman, "Urbanization in the South," in John C. McKinney and Edgar T. Thompson, The South in Continuity and Change, (Durham, 195), 81.

10. Jack Temple Kirby, Westmoreland Davis, (Charlottesville, 1968), 46-50; Raymond H. Pulley, Old Virginia Restored, 1870-1930, (Chapel Hill, 1967), 15-50; Allen W. Moger, Virginia: From Bourbonism To Byrd, 1870-1925, (Charlottesville, 1968), 268-351; Sidney Walter Martin, Florida's Flagler, (Athens, Georgia, 1948), 225-239; William T. Cash, History of the Democratic Party in Florida, (Tallahasse, 1936), 94-124; Thomas D. Clark, A History of Kentucky, (Lexington, 1960), 419-435; Fenton, Politics in the Border States, 12-46; New York Times, April 15, 1909.

11. Woodward, New South, 1-23; Sheldon Hackney, From Populism To Progressivism in Alabama, (Princeton, 1969), 212-326; Wilbur J. Cash, The Mind of the South, (New York, 1941), 145-188; Thomas D. Clark and Albert Kirwan, The South Since Appomatox, (New York, 1967), 53-60; Hesseltine and Smiley, The South, 422-493; Simkins, South, Old and New, 220-445; Dewey Grantham, The Democratic South, (Athens, 1963), 23-49; John Ezell, The South Since 1865, (New York, 1963), 101-114.

12. C. Vann Woodward, The Strange Career of Jim Crow, (New York, 1957), 67-110; U.S. Census Bureau, Abstract of the Twelfth Census of the United States, 1900, 40; Andrew Buni, The Negro in Virginia Politics, 1902-1965, (Charlottesville, 1967), 24-25; George B. Tindall, "The Campaign for the Disfranchisement of the Negro in South Carolina, Journal of Southern History, 15, (May, 1949), 212-234; Frank B. Williams, "The Poll Tax as a Suffrage Requirement in the South," Journal of Southern History, 18 (November, 1952), 469-496; Hackney, Populism to Progressivism, 178-229; Woodward, New South, 330-344, Clark and Kirwan, South Since Appomatox, 73-117; Hesseltime and Smiley, The South, 431-434; V.O. Key, Southern Politics in State and Nation, (New York, 1949), 533-644; Shannon, Towards A New Politics, 16-37.

13. William Nisbet Chambers, Political Parties in a New Nation, (New York, 1963), 1-17; Key, Southern Politics, 3-18. See also the discussion Everett Carll Ladd, Jr., Where Have All The Voters Gone?: The Fracturing of America's Political Parties, New York, 1978, xii-xxiv and Walter Dean Burnham, Critical Elections and the Mainsprings of American Politics, New York, 1970, 1-33, 91-193.

14. Allan P. Sindler, "The South in Political Transition," in McKinney and Thompson, South in Continuity and Change, 300-302.

15. Arkansas Gazette, March 8, April 6, 12, 23, 1911; Louisiana Senate Journal, 1910, 167-169.

16. Jackson Daily News, Janury 27-February, 1910; Arkansas Gazette, March 8, 1911; Atlanta Constitution, July 7, 8, 11, 12, 13, 24, 1910; Louisiana, House Journal, 1910, 147-149; Louisiana, Senate Journal, 1910, 167-169; Birmingham Age-Herald, August 8, 1909. For a discussion of the Hughes argument see Chapter VI below.

17. Richmond Times-Dispatch, March 8, 1910; T. Harry Williams, "The Gentlemen From Louisiana: Demagogue or Democrat?", Journal of Southern History, XXVI (February, 1960), 13-14.

18. Paul M. Gaston, The New South Creed, (New York, 1970), 221; Rothman, Politics and Power; 171.

19. Kenneth Stampp, The Era of Reconstruction 1865-1877, (New York, 1967), 182; John Hope Franklin, Reconstruction After The Civil War, (Chicago, 1961), 115-142; Hays, Response to Industrialism, 129-139.

20. Theodore Saloutos, Farmer Movements in the South, (Lincoln, 1964), 152-212; Hackney, Populism To Progressivism, 98-129; Ezell, South Since 1865, 171; Grantham, Democratic South, 45; Hesseltine and Smiley, The South, 490; Clark and Kirwan, South Since Appomatox, 117; Woodward, New South, 355-372.

21. Simkins, South, Old and New, 440; Grantham, Democratic South, 57-58; Hesseltine and Smiley, The South, 484-489. See also the individual studies on Watson, Tillman, Bilbo, and Vardaman referred to in the discussion of their respective states. Atlanta Constitution, July 10, 1910; Jackson Daily News, January 27, 29, February 3, 1910; Jackson Clarion Ledger, March 10, 1910.

22. Atlanta Constitution, July 7, 8, 11, 12, 13, 24, 1910; Alabama, General Assembly, House Journal, 1909, 156; Senate Journal, 1909; 220; South Carolina, General Assembly, House Journal, 1910, 698; Louisiana, General Assembly, House Journal, 1910, 205-206; Tennessee, General Assembly, House Journal, 1911, 192-193, Virginia, House of Delegates, House Journal, 1910, 854.

23. Consult the same sources as those in n. 22. For a more thorough discussion see the section on the appropriate state below.

24. Data on Ratification of the Constitution and Amendments by States, 10-11.

25. David Duncan Wallace, A History of South Carolina, (New York, 1934) IV, 219-220, 335, 356, 671-673, 682; Emily Bellinger Reynolds and Joan Reynolds Faunt (comp.), Biographical Directory of the Senate of South Carolina, 1776-1964, (Columbia, 1964), 197, 231, 234, 248, 253, 269, 309, 312, 323, 326; South Carolina, House Journal, 1910, 698, Senate Journal, 1910, 685; Arkansas Gazette, March 8, April 6, 12, 18, 23, 25, 1911; Arkansas, General Assembly, House Journal, 1911, 346; Senate Journal, 1911, 394. For a more detailed discussion of the Virginia situation, see below.

26. Alabama, General Assembly, House Journal, 1909, 156; Senate Journal, 1909, 220; Hackney, Populism to Progressivism, 210-213; Birmingham Age-Herald, August 1, 1909; David Alan Harris, "Racists and Reformers: A Study of Progressivism in Alabama, 1896-1911," Ph.D. dissertation, University of North Carolina, 1967, 275-382; New York Times, August 3-11, 1909;

Texas, House Journal, 1911, 51; Austin Statesman, August 5, 1911; Robert Cotner, James Stephen Hogg: A Biography, (Austin, 1959), 169-321; Gould, Progressives and Prohibitionists, 25-45; James A. Tinsley, "The Progressive Movement in Texas," Ph.D. dissertation, University of Wisconsin, 1954, 1-54, 311-335.

27. North Carolina, General Assembly, House Journal, 1911, 127; Senate Journal, 1911, 106; Hugh T. Lefler and Albert R. Newsome, North Carolina: The History of a Southern State, (Chapel Hill, 1963), 507-538; Woodward New South, 474-475, 532-538; Grantham, Democratic South, 60-61; Key, Southern Politics, 58-82, 208-223; Knoxville Daily Journal and Tribune, April 2, 6, 1911; Tennessee, House Journal, 1911, 769-770; Tennessee, Senate Journal, 1911, 529.

28. Mississippi, General Assembly, House Journal, 1910, 214-215; Senate Journal, 1910, 215-219, 521-522; Jackson Weekly Clarion - Ledger, March 10, 1910; Jackson Daily News, January 27, 29, February 3, 1910; Albert D. Kirwan, The Revolt of the Rednecks, (Gloucester, Mass., 1964), 136-210; William Holmes, The White Chief: James Kimble Vardaman, (Baton Rouge, 1970), 81-229; A Wigfall Green, That Man Biblo, (Baton Rouge, 1963), 19-24; Charles Granville Hamilton, Progressive Mississippi, (Aberdeen, Mississippi, 1978), 27-93.

29. South Carolina, House Journal, 1910, 698; Senate Journal, 1910, 658; The State, February 5-19, 1910; Charleston News and Courier, February 17, 1910; Wallace, History of South Carolina, IV, 219-220, 335, 356, 671-673, 682; Reynolds and Faunt (Comp.), Bibliographical Directory of Senate of South Carolina, 197, 231, 234, 248, 253, 269, 309, 312, 323, 326; Ernest McPherson Lander, Jr., A History of South Carolina, 1865-1960, (Chapel Hill, 1960), 35-50; Doyle W. Boggs, "John Patrick Grace and the Politics of Reform in South Carolina, 1900-1931;" Ph.D. dissertation, University of South Carolina, 1977, 4, 40, 82-85; John J. Duffy, "Charleston Politics in the Progressive Era," Ph.D. dissertation, University of South Carolina, 1963, 32-78, 155-205, 286-341.

30. C. Vann Woodward, Tom Watson: Agrarian Rebel, (New York, 1955), 129-395; Dewey Grantham, Hoke Smith and the Politics of the Old South, (Baton Rouge, 1958), 50-212; Atlanta Constitution, July 8, 9, 10, 11, 12, 13, 24, 1910; Atlanta Journal, July 7, 11, 13, 1910; Birmingham Age Herald, August 8, 1909; Alton D. Jones, "Progressivism in Georgia, 1898-1918," Ph.D. dissertation, Emory University, 1963, 162-182, 165-285; New York Times, August 1-6, 1909.

31. Georgia House Journal, 1910, 755-736; Senate Journal, 1910, 281-282; Atlanta Constitution, July 10, 11, 12, 13, 1910; Atlanta Journal, July 10, 11, 12, 13, 1910; New York Times, July 12, 1910. Slaton was elected governor in 1912 and became famous for his pardon of Leo Frank, a Jewish mill manager accused of the rape-murder of a young girl. Frank was lynched, largely due to the urgings of Watson's paper, and Slaton had to flee the state for a time.

32. Thomas D. Clark, A History of Kentucky, (Lexington, 1960), 419-435; Fenton, Politics in the Border States, 12-46; Nicholas C. Burckel, "William Goebel and the Campaign for Railroad Regulation in Kentucky, 1888-1900," Filson Club Quarterly, 48 (January, 1974), 43-60; Burckel,

"Progressive Governors in Border States," 218-223; James C. Klotter, William Goebel, The Politics of Wrath, (Lexington, Kentucky, 1977), 10-51, 100-125.

33. Kentucky, House Journal, 1910, 228, 568; Senate Journal, 1910, 315, 1704; Louisville Courier-Journal, January 27, 28, February 24, 25, March 16, 1910; Data on Ratification of the Constitution and Amendments by States, 10-11; New York Times, February 26, 1911.

34. Arkansas Gazette, March 8, April 6, 12, 1911; Arkansas, House Journal, 1911; Senate Journal, 1911; John Gould Fletcher, Arkansas, (Chapel Hill, 1947), 289-315; David Thomas, Arkansas and Its People, (New York, 1930), 283-286; Key, Southern Politics, 184-21; Joe T. Seagraves, "Arkansas Politics, 1874-1918," Ph.D. dissertation, University of Kentucky, 1973, 324-340; Richard L. Niswonger, "Arkansas Democratic Politics, 1896-1920," Ph.D. dissertation, University of Texas, 1974, 274-282, 366-375; John M. Wheeler, "The People's Party in Arkansas, 1891-1896," Ph.D. dissertation, Tulane University, 1975, 525-564.

35. Arkansas Gazette, April 12-25, 1911; Arkansas House Journal, 1911, 346-394; Senate Journal, 1911; Stuart Towns, "Joseph T. Robinson and Arkansas Politics," Arkansas Historical Quarterly, (Winter, 1965), 295-302; C.R. 45: 1726.

36. Allan P. Sindler, Huey Long's Louisiana, (Baltimore, 1966), 19-31; Frank T. Hair, Bourbonism and Agrarian Protest, (Baton Rouge, 1969), 24, 111, 268-269; Grady McWhiney, "Louisiana Socialism in the Early Twentieth Century: A Study of Rustic Radicalism," Journal of Southern History, XX, (August, 1954), 315-319; Perry Howard, Political Tendencies in Louisiana, (Baton Rouge, 1957), 107-112; Key, Southern Politics, 123; Hays, Response To Industrialism, 123; Louisiana, House Journal, 1910, 205-206; Senate Journal, 1910, 147-149, 167-169, 297, Kennan, Income Taxation, 300-301; Matthew J. Schott, "The New Orleans Machine and Progressivism," Louisiana History, 24 (1983): 141-153.

37. Louisiana, House Journal, 1912, 177; Louisiana, Senate Journal, 1912, 551-554; New Orleans Times-Picayune, June 28, 1912.

38. Carolyn Karr, "A Political Biography of Henry Hatfield," West Virginia History, 28 (October, 1966): 36-53, 28 (Janury, 1967): 137-170; Virginia D. Malcomson, William E. Glasscock: Governor of the People, unpublished thesis, University of West Virginia, 1950, 35-85; Charles H. Ambler and Festus P. Summers, West Virginia: The Mountain State, (Englewood Cliffs, 1958), 376-382; Rothman, Power and Politics, 95, 161, 179, 208-9; Dictionary of American Biography, VI, 83-84; Fenton, Politics in the Border States, 82-111; Burckel, "Progressive Governors in Border States," 336-406; Neil Shaw Penn, "Henry D. Hatfield and Reform Politics: A Study of West Virginia Politics from 1908 to 1917," Ph.D. dissertation, Emory University, 1973, 25-202.

39. West Virginia, House Journal and Bills, 1911, 39, 138, 368; Senate Journal and Bills, 1911, 368; Charleston Daily Mail, February 3, 16,

17, April 16, May 15, 16, 1911; Burckel, "Progressive Governors in the Border States," 261-262.

40. Karr, "Henry Hatfield," 47-62, 165-167; Malcolmson, William E. Glasscock, 35-85; House Journal and Bills, 1913, 368; Senate Journal and Bills, 1913, 209; Charleston Daily Mail, February 1, 1913; Burckel, "Progressive Governors in the Border States," 373-415.

41. Martin, Florida's Flagler, 103-244; Cash, Democratic Party in Florida, 94-124; Key, Southern Politics, 182-105; Samuel Proctor, Napoleon Bonaparte Broward: Fighting Florida Democrat, (Gainsville, 1950), 55-95, 159-310; Kathryn Trimmer Abbey, Florida: Land of Change, (Chapel Hill, 1941), 337-350; George Green, "The Florida Press and the Democratic Primary of 1912," Florida Historical Quarterly, (January, 1966): 169; Edward N. Akin, "Southern Reflection of the Gilded Age: Henry M. Flagler's System, 1885-1913," Ph.D. dissertation, University of Florida, 1975, 164-185, 222. For Gilchrist's reaction to the Hughes argument, see the New York Times, January 7, 1910. See also Arnold M. Pavlovsky, "We Busted Because We Failed: Florida Politics, 1880-1908," Ph.D. dissertation, Princeton University, 1974, 315-356.

42. Florida, General Assembly, House Journal, 1911, 15-16, 397, 1263; Senate Journal, 1911, 594, 903, 1097-1101, 1193; Florida Times-Union (Jacksonville), May 13, 19, 23, June 1, 1911.

43. House Journal, 1913, 1686; Senate Journal, 1913, 1097-1099.

44. Kirby, Westmoreland Davis, 46-54; Pulley, Old Virginia Restored, 15-50; Moger, Bourbonism to Byrd, 166-180, 268-351; Key, Southern Politics, 19-36; Paschal Reeves, "Thomas S. Martin: Committee Statesmen," Virginia Magazine of History and Biography, 68 (1960): 344-364.

45. Moger, Bourbonism to Byrd, 155, 268; Richmond Times-Dispatch, March 2-10, 1910.

46. Virginia, House Journal, 1910, 854; Senate Journal, 1910, 651; Richmond Times-Dispatch, March 9-10, 1910; Petersburg Index-Appeal, March 9, 1910; New York Times, March 7, 1912.

47. Arkansas Gazette, April 12, 1911; Richmond Times-Dispatch, March 11, 1910.

CHAPTER VI
Toppling the Keystone: The Amendment in New York

1. Census Bureau, Wealth, Debt and Taxation, 797; Census Bureau, Thirteenth Census, 1910, 57-61; U.S. Department of Commerce, Statistical Abstract of the United States, 1933, 259-60; Leven and King, Distribution of Income, 22-30; House Report, 5, 1916, Statistics of Income, 18-20; Ratner, American Taxation, 307-310.

2. Leven and King, Income Distribution, 22-30, 223-87; House Report 5, 1916, Statistics of Income, 22-7; Ratner, American Taxation, 307-10; Census Bureau, Wealth, Debt and Taxation, 797. The term "iron rectangle" was coined by C.K. Yearley in Money Machine, 8-9.

3. Elmer E. Cornwell, Jr., "Bosses, Machines and Ethnic Groups," Annals of the American Academy of Political and Social Science, 353 (May, 1964), 28-30; Duane Lockard, New England State Politics, (Princeton, 1959), 136-48, 173-90, 243-57, 305-20; Harold F. Gosnell, Boss Platt and His New York Machine, (Chicago, 1924), 1-72, 150-181, 219-261; Buenker, Urban Liberalism, 12-22; David Patton, "Our Rhode Island," Providence Journal, February 13, 1956.

4. Cornwell, "Bosses, Machines and Ethnic Groups," 28-33; Buenker, Urban Liberalism, 12-25, 163-97.

5. Chester Jones, "The Rotten Boroughs of New England," North American Review, 97, (April, 1913), 485-90; Lockard, New England Politics, 178, 272-75; Joseph I. Lieberman, The Power Broker, (Boston, 1966), 19-21; Buenker, Urban Liberalism, 13-15; Providence Journal, February 28, 1910; John M. Blum, Joe Tumulty and the Wilson Era (Boston, 1951), 11-14, 34-38; Warren Moscow, What Have You Done For Me Lately?, (Englewood Cliffs, New Jersey, 1967), 7-55; Illinois State Register, (Springfield), May 11, 1911.

6. Charles Glaab and A. Theodore Brown, A History of Urban America, (New York, 1967), 167-99; William Riordan, Plunkitt of Tammany Hall, (New York, 1948), 28; Clifford Patton, The Battle for Municipal Reform, Washington, 1940), 17, 70; Ransom E. Noble, New Jersey Progressivism Before Wilson, (Princeton, 1946), 22; Lincoln Steffens, The Autobiography of Lincoln Steffens, (New York, 1931), 443; Buenker, Urban Liberalism, 15-6. Brayton and Aldrich were business partners in the state's largest traction company. Often the organization reserved one senate seat for each of the state's largest cities, e.g. Hanna was from Cleveland and Foraker from Cincinnati, Penrose was from Philadelphia and George Oliver from Pittsburgh.

7. Buenker, Urban Liberalism, 22-5, 34-41; Sarasohn, "The Democratic Surge," 117-293. The possible relationship between Republican losses and the income tax amendment in New York is discussed later in this chapter.

8. Arthur Mann, Yankee Reformers in the Urban Age, (Cambridge, 1954), 242; Robert H. Wiebe, The Search for Order, 1877-1920, (New York, 1967), 133-95; Mowry, California Progressives, 86-104; Richard Hofstadter, The Age of Reform, (New York, 1955), 131-73; Clarke A. Chambers, Seedtime of Reform: American Social Service and Social Action, 1918-1933, (Minneapolis, 1963), 1-27; Alfred D. Chandler, Jr., "The Origins of Progressive Leadership," in The Letters of Theodore Roosevelt, vol. 8, Appendix III, Elting E. Morison, editor, (Cambridge, 1954).

9. Chicago Tribune, March 21, 1919; Joel A. Tarr, A Study in Boss Politics: William Lorimer of Chicago, (Urbana, Illinois, 1971), 26-48;

Holli, Reform in Detroit, 157-184; Raymond Wolfinger, "The Development and Persistence of Ethnic Voting," American Ethnic Politics, edited by Lawrence H. Fuchs, (New York, 1968), 165-93; Buenker, Urban Liberalism, 9-12, 21.

10. Hays, Response to Industrialism, 149; Cortez Ewing, Congressional Elections, 1896-1944, (Norman, Oklahoma, 1947), 53-60; Buenker, Urban Liberalism, 34-41; Sarasohn, "The Democratic Surge, 117-29.

11. Hays, "Response to Industralism," 149; J. Joseph Huthmacher, "Urban Liberalism and the Age of Reform," Mississippi Valley Historical Review, 44 (September, 1962): 231-241; Huthmacher, Senator Robert F. Wagner, 18-24; Buenker, Urban Liberalism, 31-34; Noble, New Jersey Progressivism, 61, 98, 148-149; Weiss, Charles Francis Murphy, 69-91; Frances Perkins, The Roosevelt I Knew, (New York, 1946), 9-27; Blum, Tumulty and Wilson Era, 1-25; Herbert G. Gutman, "Class Status and the Gilded Age Radical: A Reconsideration of the Case of a New Jersey Socialist," Many Pasts: Readings in American Social History, (Englewood Cliffs, New Jersey, 1973), vol. II, 125-151, edited by Herbert G. Gutman and Gregory S. Kealy; Allen B. Davis, Spearheads For Reform: The Social Settlements and the Progressive Movement, (New York, 1970), 148-217; James L. Crooks, Politics and Progress: The Rise of Urban Progressivism in Baltimore, 1895-1911, (Baton Rouge, Louisiana, 1968), 77, 121.

12. Buenker, Urban Liberalism, 34-41; David M. Ellis, James A. Frost, Harold C. Syrett, and Harry J. Carman, A Short History of New York State, (Ithaca, New York, 1957), 376-389; Sarasohn, "Democratic Surge," viii-ix.

13. For a discussion of the formation of "reform coalitions" see Thelen, New Citizenship, 55-175 and John D. Buenker, John C. Burnham, and Robert M. Crunden, Progressivism, (Cambridge, Massachusetts, 1977); 31-70. See also Yearley, Money Machines, 234-260 and Sarasohn, "Democratic Surge," 117-293.

14. __________., "The Income Tax and the States," The Outlook, 98 (July 22, 1911): 600-601; _________., "Governor Hughes and the Income Tax," Review of Reviews, 41 (March, 1910): 272.

15. Leven and King, Distribution of Income, 25-30; House Report 5, 1916, Statistics of Income, 18-48; Census Bureau, Thirteenth Census, 1910, 57-61; Commerce Department, Statistical Abstract, 1933, 259-260.

16. Leven and King, Distribution of Income, 223-290; House Report 5, 1916, Statistics of Income, 79-80; Census Bureau, Wealth, Debt, and Taxation, 777-778.

17. Gosnell, Boss Platt, 6-73, 262-290; Warren Moscow, Politics in the Empire State, (New York, 1948), 70-75; Moscow, What Have You Done For Me Lately?, 7-55; Robert K. Wesser, Charles Evans Hughes: Politics and Reform in New York, 1905-1910, (Ithaca, New York, 1967), 1-18; Rothman, Power and Politics, 164. For Platt's personal assessment of his political impact, see Thomas C. Platt, The Autobiography of Thomas Collier Platt, (New York, 1910): 367-515.

18. Census Bureau, Thirteenth Census, 186-245; Gosnell, Boss Platt, 2-9; Cornwell, "Bosses, Machines, and Ethnic Groups," 28-30.

19. Gosnell, Boss Platt, 352; Moscow, Politics in the Empire State, 70-71; Moscow, What Have You Done For Me Lately?, 53-54.

20. Wesser, Charles Evans Hughes, 252, 309; Merlo J. Pusey, Charles Evans Hughes, (New York, 1951), vol. I, 254.

21. Moscow, What Have You Done For Me Lately?, 54; J. Joseph Huthmacher, "Charles Evans Hughes and Charles Francis Murphy: The Metamorphosis of Progressivism," New York History, XLVI (January, 1965): 25-40; Weiss, Charles Francis Murphy, 25-92; Perkins, Roosevelt I Knew, 24-26; Huthmacher, Senator Robert F. Wagner, 19-37.

22. Huthmacher, "Metamorphosis," 25-40; Weiss, Charles Francis Murphy, 69-92; Huthmacher, Senator Robert F. Wagner, 24-37; McInerney, "Election of 1912," 154-215. For a somewhat more skeptical analysis of Tammany's "conversion to reform" and its political impact, see Thomas M. Henderson, Tammany Hall and the New Immigrants: The Progressive Years, (New York, 1976), 92-125, 268-296.

23. New York Times, January 6-10, 1910; State of New York, Senate, Special Message from the Governor Submitting to the Legislature Certified Copy of a Resolution of Congress Entitled "Joint Resolution Proposing an Amendment to the Constitution of the United States, January 5, 1910, 3-8.

24. Idem.

25. Ibid.; New York Tribune, January 5, 1910; Albany Evening Journal, January 5, 1910; New York World, January 5, 1910.

26. Nicholas Murray Butler to Charles Evans Hughes, January 6, 1910, Hughes to Butler, January 9, 1910, J. Warren Green to Hughes, January 7, 1910, John Minor to Hughes, January 10, 1910, W. John Bigelow to Hughes, January 13, 1910, Frederick D. Colson to Hughes, February 3, 1910, Charles Evans Hughes Papers, Library of Congress.

27. Ratner, American Taxation, 304-307; U.S. Congress, 61st Congress, 2nd Session, 1910, Senate Document 365, Message of Governor of New Jersey on Proposed Income Tax,; New York Times, February 8, 1910.

28. U.S. Congress, 61st Congress, 2nd Session, 1910, Senate Document 398, The Proposed Income Tax Amendment: Letter of Elihu Root to the New York Legislature, 4.

29. New York Times, February 11, 1910; Taft to Josiah Newcomb, March 4, 1910, Root Papers; Root to Hughes, March 25, 1910, Hughes Papers, Wickersham's letters to Senate President J. Mayhew Wainwright and Speaker James W. Wadsworth on April 26, 1910 are quoted in German, "Taft's Attorney General," 205. The report of Taft's telegrams to New York legislators is in the New York World, April 28, 1910.

30. C.R. 45: 1698.

31. Ibid., 1699, 2254-2257; U.S. 61st Congress, 2nd Session, December 14, 1910, Senate Document 705, Shall The Income Tax Be Ratified?, 3-9.

32. Seligman, The Income Tax, 595-610; Seligman, "The Income Tax Amendment," Political Science Quarterly, 25 (1910): 193-219; U.S. Congress, 61st Congress, 2nd Session, February 16, 1910, Senate Document 365, Message of the Governor of New Jersey, 3-5; Yearley, Money Machines, 244.

33. Providence Evening Bulletin, January 28, 1910.

34. Earl Ketcham, The Sixteenth Amendment, (Urbana, Illinois, 1926), 10; Hartford Courant, February 17, 1910; Boston Daily Globe, March 10, 1910; Charleston New and Courier, January 18, 1910; Louisiana Senate Journal, 1910, 147-9; Congressional Record (1910), 1957-8; New York Times, February 26, 1911.

35. Brushaber v. Union Pacific Railroad, 240 U.S. 1 (1924); New York Times, January 25, 1916; Pusey, Charles Evans Hughes, 254; American Taxation, Ratner, 205; Corwin, Court Over Constitution, Dexter Perkins, Charles Evans Hughes and American Democratic Statemanship, (Boston, 1956), 260.

36. New York World, January 6, 1910.

37. Albany Evening Journal, February 18, 1910.

38. Ratner, American Taxation, 256; New York World, March 8, 1910; New York Tribune, February 3, 1910; Joseph Choate, et. al., The Proposed Sixteenth Article of Amendment to the Constitution of the United States, (Albany) 1910; Kennan, Income Taxation, 292-3. Former Senator Edmunds' letter is quoted in the New York Times, February 15, 1910. See also U.S. Congress, 61st Congress, 2nd Session, Income Tax, Senate Document 367, February 17, 1910.

39. Choate, et.al., Proposed Sixteenth Amendment, 13-7.

40. Wiebe, Businessmen and Reform, 196; Herbert L. Griggs to Cordell Hull, February 21, 1913, Cordell Hull Papers, Library of Congress.

41. Albany Evening Journal, February 20, 1910; New York Times, April 20, 1911.

42. Frederick Davenport, "The Income Tax Amendment," Independent, LXVII, (May 5, 1910), 969; Albany Evening Journal, May 15, 1910; Yearley, Money Machines, 201, 244; Lawson Purdy, "The Income Tax Amendment Should Be Ratified," Journal of Accountancy, X, (May, 1910): 13-26.

43. Albany Evening Journal, May 15, 1910.

44. Ibid., April 19, 1910.

45. *New York World*, May 17, 1910.

46. *Ibid*., January 6, 1910; New York, General Assembly, *Assembly Journal, 1910*, I, 468; Root, 5; Philip Jessup, *Elihu Root*, (New York, 1938), 412; Richard W. Leopold, *Elihu Root and the Conservative Tradition*, (Boston, 1954), 76-9, 92-3; *New York Times*, February 22, March 1, 1910.

47. William Borah, "The Income Tax: Sound in Law and Economics," *Journal of Accountancy*, X, (May, 1910), 31; *New York Times*, March 25, 1910.

48. *New York Times*, March 30, April 14, 21, 1910; New York, Legislature, *Assembly Journal*, II, 1786.

49. *Ibid*., April 22, 26, 28, 29; May 3, 4, 1910; *Assembly Journal*, II, 2392.

50. *Ibid*., April 21, 26, 28, May 4, 5, 7, 18, 1910; New York, Legislature, *Senate Journal, 1910*, II, 1563; ______________., *National Cyclopedia of Biography*, (Ann Arbor, Michigan, 1967), v. 20, 124-125.

51. *Ibid*., May 26, 1910; *Assembly Journal*, III, 2392.

52. Ratner, *American Taxation*, 306; *New York World*, April 28, 1910; Austin Fox to Hughes, May 4, 1910, *Hughes Papers*; *New York Times*, June 1, November 16, 1910; Pusey, *Charles Evans Hughes*, 253-254; *Chicago Tribune*, May 2, 1910; *Elmira* (New York) *Advertiser*, May 7, 1910.

53. Gosnell, *Boss Platt*, 315; *New York Times*, November 9, 1910; Morison (ed.), *Letters of Theodore Roosevelt*, v. VII, 140-141; *National Cyclopedia of Biography*, v. 23, 226-227.

54. Wesser, *Charles Evans Hughes*, 275-276; Taft to Root, September 24, 1910, *Root Papers*; Taussig, *Tariff History*, 409-410; *New York Times*, November 9, 1910.

55. James MacGregor Burns, *Roosevelt: The Lion and the Fox*, (New York, 1956), 37; Huthmacher, *Senator Robert F. Wagner*, 24-38; Weiss, *Charles Francis Murphy*, 69-100; Yearley, *Money Machines*, 238.

56. *New York Times*, January 5, 1911; Burns, *Roosevelt: Lion and Fox*, 37; Weiss, *Charles Francis Murphy*, 48-49.

57. *New York Times*, April 6, 7, 15, 1911.

58. *Ibid*., April 20, 1911; *Arkansas Gazette*, April 18, 1911; *Senate Journal, 1911*, I, 618; *Albany Evening Journal*, April 19, 1911.

59. *New York Times*, May 11, 12, 13, 17, 1911.

60. *Ibid*., May 18, 20, 21, 1911.

61. *Ibid*., May 21, 24, 1911.

62. *Ibid*., May 25, 27, 28, 30, June 1, 4, 6, 8, 1911.

63. *Ibid*., June 14, 1911; *Assembly Journal, 1911*, IV, 3724.

64. *Ibid*., November 7, 1911, January 17, 24, 31, February 2, March 7, 12, 14, 16, 19, 12; McInerney, "Election of 1912," 216-287; Henderson, *Tammany Hall*, 92-126.

65. McInerney, "Election of 1912," 321-374; Sarasohn, "Democratic Surge," 237-293; Huthmacher, *Robert F. Wagner*, 24-56.

CHAPTER VII
Breaking the Iron Rectangle: The Northeastern States

1. Leven and King, *Incomes in the Various States*, 288-93.

2. House Report 5, 1916, *Statistics of Income*, 98-113.

3. Porter and Johnson, *National Party Platforms*, 169, 181; Frank Kelly, *The Fight for the White House, 1912*, (New York, 1912), 3; Sullivan, *Edward F. Dunne*, 490; *New York Times*, November 9, 1910, November 6, 1912; *Baltimore Sun*, November 9, 1910; *Wilmington Every Evening*, November 9, 1910; *Philadelphia Evening Bulletin*, November 9, 1910; *Chicago Tribune*, November 9, 1910; *Trenton True American*, November 9, 1910; Hays, *Response to Industrialism*, 149; Sarasohn, "Democratic Surge," 237-293. On the "revolution in taxation" in the northeastern states, see Buenker, *Urban Liberalism*, 103-117 and Yearley, *Money Machines*, 137-252. For a detailed analysis of the Republican disintegration in a key state, see McInerney, "Election of 1912," 1-26, 154-375.

4. Duane Lockard, *New England State Politics*, (Princeton, 1959), 173-208, 228-276.

5. Leven and King, *Income in the Various States*, 288-93; David P. Thelen, *The New Citizenship: Origins of Progressivism in Wisconsin, 1885-1900*, (Columbia, Missouri, 1972), 204-7, 288; Kenneth C. Acrea, "Wisconsin Progressivism: Legislative Response to Social Change," Ph.D. dissertation, University of Wisconsin-Madison, 1968; Wisconsin, Legislature, *House Journal, 1911*, 193-4; *Senate Journal, 1911*, 713; Indiana, General Assembly, *House Journal, 1911*, 658; *Senate Journal, 1911*, 126.

6. Lockard, *New England Politics*, 98-101; Maine, General Court, *House Journal, 1911*, 902; *Senate Journal, 1911*, 697; Kennan, *Income Taxation*, 306; Portland, *Evening Express and Advertiser*, March 28, 31, April 1, 1911; *Daily Kennebec Journal* (Augusta), March 28, 31, 1911; *New York Times*, March 31, 1911; Elizabeth Ring, *The Progressive Movement of 1912 and Third Party Movement of 1924 in Maine*, Orono, Maine, 1933, 20-25; ____________., "Maine And After," *The Nation*, 91 (September 15, 1910): 233; Bangor *Daily News*, September 3, 1910.

7. Leven and King, Income in the Various States, 288-93; House Report 5, 1916 Statistics of Income, 69, 82; Hoyt L. Warner, Progressivism in Ohio, 1897-1917, (Columbus, Ohio, 1964), 3-41; Zane L. Miller, Boss Cox's Cincinnati, (New York, 1968), 163-238.

8. Warner, 23-70, 128, 191-251; Glaab and Brown, History of Urban America, 213-5; Fredrick Howe, Confessions of a Reformer, (New York, 1925), 91-9; Wellington G. Fordyce, "Nationality Groups in Cleveland Politics," The Ohio State Archaeological and Historical Quarterly, 46 (1937), 125; John D. Buenker, "Cleveland's New Stock Lawmakers and Progressive Reform," Ohio History, 78 (Spring, 1969), 116-38.

9. Warner, Progressivism in Ohio, 211-440; Buenker, "Cleveland's Lawmakers," 116-138; Ohio, General Assembly, House Journal, 1911, 436; 1913, 1031-32; 1917, 53-4; 1919, 660, 969; Senate Journal, 1911, 598; 1913, 482, 710; 1917, 39-40; 1919, 350, 644.

10. George Mowry, The Era of Theodore Roosevelt, (New York, 1958), 236; Ohio, General Assembly, Senate Journal, 1911, 48; House Journal, 1911, 80; James K. Mercer, Ohio Legislative History, 1909-1913, (Columbus, 1913), 440-640; Ohio State Journal, (Columbus), January 20, 1911; Cleveland Plain Dealer, January 19, 1911, Kennan, Income Taxation, 306; New York Times, Taft to G.W. Mooney, January 3, 1910; Taft to Albert Douglas, January 14, 1910, Taft Papers.

11. Stephen B. and Vera H. Sarasohn, Political Party Patterns in Michigan, (Detroit, 1957), 3-15; Milo M. Quaif and Sidney Glazer, Michigan, (New York, 1948), 267-283; Willis F. Dunbar, Michigan: A History of the Wolverine State, (Grand Rapids, 1965), 525-544; F. Clever Bald, Michigan in Four Centuries, (New York, 1954), 339; Holli, Reform in Detroit, 157-184.

12. Holli, 185-219; Dunbar, 540-4; Sarasohn and Sarasohn, Political Party Patterns, 9-15.

13. Michigan Legislature, House Journal, 1911, 62, 204; Senate Journal, 1911, 307.

14. Leven and King, Income in the Various States, 288-93; House Report 5, 1916, Statistics of Income, 60, 100-1; Harold F. Gosnell, Machine Politics: Chicago Model, (Chicago, 1937), 148; Charles Merriam, A More Intimate View of Urban Politics, (New York, 1929): 90-133, 222-267; Zink, City Bosses, 275-90; Tarr, Boss Politics, 3-114.

15. Edward F. Dunne, History of Illinois, (Chicago, 1933), Zink, City Bosses, 61, 299; John D. Buenker, "Edward F. Dunne: The Urban, New Stock Democrat as Progressive," Mid-America, 50 (January, 1968): 3-21; John D. Buenker, "Urban Immigrant Lawmakers and Progressive Reform in Illinois," in Donald F. Tingley, editor, Essays in Illinois History, (Carbondale, 1967), 52-7; James W. Fullenwider, "The Governor and the Senator: Executive Power and the Structure of the Illinois Republican Party, 1880-1917," Ph.D. dissertation, Washington University, 1974, passim; Donald F. Tingley, The Structuring of the State: The History of Illinois, 1899-1928, (Urbana,

Illinois, 1980), 150-195; Robert P. Howard, *Illinois: A History of the Prairie State*, (Grand Rapids, Michigan, 1972), 417-436; Ralph A. Straetz, "The Progressive Movement in Illilnois, 1900-1916," Ph.D. dissertation, University of Illinois, Urbana, 1951, 67-100, 404-467.

16. *Chicago Tribune*, February 3, 1910; Illinois, General Assembly, *Senate Journal, Special Session, 1909-1910*, 23, 129, 199; *House Journal*, 76; Illinois, Secretary of State, *Blue Book*, 1909-1910, 196-226.

17. Illinois, *House Journal, 1909-1910*, 318; Blue Book, 1909, 196-226.

18. Fenton, *Politics in the Border States*, 171; Crooks, *Politics and Progress*, 77, 121; Leven and King, *Income in the Various States*, 288-93; House Report 5, 1916, *Statistics of Income*, 67, 104-5; Burckel, "Progressive Governors in the Border States," 45-507; Raymond S. Sweeney, "Progressivism in Maryland, 1900-1917," Ph.D. dissertation, University of North Carolina, Chapel Hill, 1971, 85-103, 270-287.

19. Maryland, House of Delegates, *Assembly Journal, 1910*, 956-7; *Senate Journal, 1910*, 36-7, 1461, 2097.

20. Leven and King, *Income in the Various States*, 288-93; House Report 5, 1916, *Statistics of Income*, 54, 68, 77; Ransom E. Noble, *New Jersey Progressivism Before Wilson*, (Princeton, 1946), 3-25; Arthur S. Link, *Wilson: The Road to the White House*, (Princeton, 1947), 93-205.

21. Noble, *New Jersey Progressivism*, 4-5; Link, *Wilson*, 135-7; Blum, *Joe Tumulty*, 1-50; James Kerney, *The Political Education of Woodrow Wilson*, (New York, 1926), 27-114, Rudolph Vecoli, *The People of New Jersey*, (Princeton, 1965), 165-70.

22. New Jersey, General Assembly, *Assembly Minutes*, 1911, 815; *1912*, 1407, *Senate Journal, 1911*, 639-40, 401; New Jersey, General Assembly, *Manual of the Legislature, 1911*, 286-339; Link, *Wilson*, 266-8.

23. New Jersey, *Assembly Minutes, 1913*, 93, 107; *Senate Journal, 1913*, 107; *Manual, 1913*, 320-65; *Newark Evening News*, January 20, February 4, 1913.

24. J. Joseph Huthmacher, *Massachusetts People and Politics, 1919-1933*, (New York, 1969), 1-18; Lockard, *New England Politics*, 121-48; Richard Abrams, *Conservatism in a Progressive Era*, (Cambridge, 1964), 50-2; Donald B. Cole, *Immigrant City: Lawrence, Massachusetts, 1845-1921*, (Chapel Hill, 1963), 78, 88-9.

25. Abrams, *Conservatism*, 132; Huthmacher, *Massachusetts People*, 61-9.

26. Massachusetts, General Court, *House Journal, 1910*, 1115; *Senate Journal, 1910*, 952; Massachusetts, Secretary of State, *Manual of the General Court, 1910*, 423-43; *New York Times*, May 5, 1910.

27. Abrams, Conservatism, 217-88; Richard B. Sherman, "Foss of Massachusetts: Demagogue v. Progressive," Mid-America, 43 (April, 1961), 88-90; House Journal, 1911, 1076, 1092; Senate Journal, 1911, 1001; Bangor Daily News, 1910.

28. Massachusetts, House Journal, 1912, 1365; 1913, 740; Senate Journal, 1912, 1219; 1913, 575; Springfield Daily Republican, November 6, 1912; New York Times, February 10, 1913.

29. Wilson Lloyd Beran, ed., History of Delaware: Past and Present, II (New York, 1929), 883-5; Delaware, General Assembly, House Journal, 1913, 303; Senate Journal, 1913, 512; Wilmington Every Evening, February 3, 1913; Marquis James, Alfred I Dupont, The Family Rebel, (Indianapolis, 1941), passim.

30. Lockard, New England Politics, 45-69; Concord Evening Monitor, November 9, 1910, January 19, March 23, 1911; New Hampshire, General Court, House Journal, 1911, 44-5; Leven and King, Income in the Various States, 288-93; House Report 5, 1916, Statistics of Income, 76, 92; Jewel Bellush, "Reform in New Hampshire: Robert Bass Wins the Primary," New England Quarterly, 35 (1962): 469-488; Thomas R. Agan, "The New Hampshire Progressive Movement," Ph.D. dissertation, State University of New York, Albany, 1975, IV, 103-188, 201-211, 272-275.

31. New Hampshire, House Journal, 1913, 59, 68, 430-1; Senate Journal, 1913, 176.

32. Lockard, New England Politics, 10-43; Winston Flint, The Progressive Movement in Vermont, (Washington, 1941), 5-60.

33. Burlington Free Press, February 18, 1913; U.S. Congress, 61st Congress, 2nd Session, Senate Document 367, Letter of George F. Edmunds Relating to Income Tax, 1910; Vermont, General Assembly, Senate Journal, 1911, 415; Flint, Progressive Movement in Vermont, 60; House Journal, 1913, 1017; Senate Journal, 1913, 823.

34. For ratification dates see U.S., Congress, Data on Ratification of the Constitution and Amendments by States. 71st Congress, 3rd session, Senate Document 240, 10-1. For income statistics, see Leven and King, Income in the Various States, 53, 85-6.

35. Cornwell, "Bosses, Machines and Ethnic Groups," 29; Lockard, New England Politics, 174-208; Lincoln Steffens, The Autobiography of Lincoln Steffens, (New York, 1931), 464-9; Providence Evening Bulletin, January 20, 1909, January 5, 10, 13, 18, February 28, April 1, 1910; Jones, "Rotten Boroughs of New England," 488; Lincoln Steffens, The Struggle for Self Government, (New York, 1906), 130-9; Erwin L. Levine, Theodore Francis Green, The Rhode Island Years, (Providence, 1963), 1-40, 58-9; Patten, "Our Rhode Island," Providence Journal, February 13, 1956; Nathan M. Wright to Nelson W. Aldrich, April 25, 1910, Nelson W. Aldrich Papers, Library of Congress. O'Shaunessy was quoted in the Providence Journal, February 28, 1910.

36. Cornwell, "Party Absorption," 205-10; Murray S. and Susan W. Stedman, "The Rise of the Democratic Party of Rhode Island," New England Quarterly, 24, (September, 1951), 329-39; John D. Buenker, "The Emergence of Urban Liberalism in Rhode Island, 1909-1919," Rhode Island History, (Spring, 1971), 35-51, "The Politics of Resistance: The Rural-Based Republican Machines of Connecticut and Rhode Island," New England Quarterly, 47 (1974): 214-215 and Urban Liberalism, 107-108.

37. Providence Evening Bulletin, April 29, 1910; February 2, May 4, 1911; February 14, March 22, 1912; March 26, April 9, 1913; Providence Daily Journal, January 7, 10, 1910; Rhode Island, Secretary of State, Manual with Rules and Orders for the Use of the General Assembly of Rhode Island, 1911, 382-405; 1912, 386-408; 1913, 385-410; Ratner, American Taxation, 305; Kennan, Income Taxation, 305; Providence Evening News, March 4, 1915; Charles R. Brayton to Nelson W. Aldrich, February 19, April 23, April n.d., 1910, Aldrich Papers.

38. Jones, "Rotten Boroughs," 489-90; Lieberman Power Broker, 19-21; Lockard, New England Politics, 299-75; Hartford Courant, February 12, 1910.

39. Lockard, New England Politics, 239-65; Lieberman Power Broker, 19-31; Buenker, "Politics of Resistance," 213-229. Alan Olmstead, editor of the Manchester Evening Herald and the Roraback ally are quoted in Lieberman, Power Broker, 29-30. The rebellious newspaper editor's reply to the Connecticut governor is quoted in Lockard, New England State Politics, 248.

40. Lockard, New England Politics, 239-50; Lieberman, Power Broker, 25-48; Raymond E. Wolfinger, "The Development and Persistence of Ethnic Voting," in Lawrence H. Fuchs, editor, American Ethnic Politics, (New York, 1968), 167-75; John D. Buenker, "Progressivism in Connecticut: The Thrust of the Urban, New Stock Democrats," Bulletin of the Connecticut Historical Society, 35 (October, 1970), 97-109; Buenker, Urban Liberalsim, 108.

41. Hartford Courant, June 29, 1911; Hartford Times, June 28, 1911; Connecticut, General Assembly, Senate Journal, 1911, 55, 67-8.

42. Senate Journal,1911, 1346-7; House Journal, 1911, 225; 1913, 965; William Harrison Taylor, editor, Legislative History and Souvenir of Connecticut, 1911-1912, (Hartford, 1912), 12-288.

43. Wayland F. Dunaway, History of Pennsylvania, (Englewood Cliffs, New Jersey, 1935), 573-577, 594-598; Robert Bowden, Boies Penrose, (New York, 1937), 163-188, 203-245; Walter Davenport, The Power and the Glory, 65-197; J. Roffe Wike, The Pennsylvania Manufacturers Association, (Philadelphia, 1960), 10-20; Philips S. Klein and Ari Hoogenboom, A History of Pennsylvania, (New York, 1973); 371-394.

44. Philadelpha Public Ledger, February 7, 1911.

45. Zink, City Bosses, 175-230; William S. Vare, My Forty Years in Politics

(Philadelphia, 1933), 20-107; Bowden, Boies Penrose, 241; Harrisburg Patriot, February 1, 10, April 3, 16, 23; May 1, 1913.

46. Pennsylvania, General Assembly, House Journal, 1911, 2690; Senate Journal, 1911, 2162; Harrisburg Patriot, May 2, 1911; Herman P. Miller, (comp.), Smull's Legislature Hardbook and Manual of the State of Pennsylvania, 1911, (Harrisburg, 1911), 729-54; New York Times, January 29, 1913.

47. Philadelphia Evening Bulletin, January 28, 1913.

CHAPTER VIII
The End of the Road

1. Root to Ben Johnson, November 21, 1913, Root Papers; Jessup, Elihu Root, 229.

2. Hull, Memoirs, 65-67; __________., "An Indirect Direct Tax," Literary Digest, 44 (March 30, 1912): 629-630; U.S. Congress, House, Committee on Ways and Means, 62nd Congress, 2nd Session, The Excise Tax, July 29, 1912, House Report 1039; New York Times, July 27-30, 1912.

3. Porter and Johnson, National Party Platforms, 168-185; __________., "Income Tax Legislation," Independent, 74 (February 13, 1913): 84. The statement of the Washington correspondent of the North American is quoted in Paul, Taxation in the United States, 103.

4. Cortez Ewing, Congressional Elections, 1896-1944, (Norman: 1947), 9-85.

5. Ibid., 53-60; Congressional Directory, 295-312; Holt, Congressional Insurgents, 47-48.

6. Congressional Directory, 295-312.

7. Idem.

8. New York Times, April 12, June 7, 21, September 13, 1913; C.R. 50: 3840, Appendix, 89; Hillje, "Progressive Movement," 44-45.

9. New York Times, June 7, 21, September 13; C.R. 50: 3840, Appendix 89.

10. Blakey, Income Tax, 75-83; Marquis James, Mr. Garner of Texas, (Indianapolis, 1939), 68.

11. Blakey, Income Tax, 89; New York Times, August 29, 1913.

12. C.R. 50: 505, 1261-1263, 4420.

13. C.R. 50: 2720, 3874-3876; New York Times, April 15, August 7, 1913.

14. C.R. 50: 1304, 2467; New York Times, July 19, August 27, 1913.

15. The original Democrat proposal began at $4,000 but the Senate changed it to $3,000 for single taxpayers and $4,000 for married ones. See Ratner, American Taxation, 326-329 and Blakey, Income Tax, 76, 86. In 1913 about 1.3 million people made over $3,000 a year. About 50 per cent of all taxpayers fell in the $2,000-$3,000 category, a major reason for the Democrats not to lower the exemption. See King, et. al., Income, 249-268.

16. C.R. 50: 1247, 3771, 3801, 3810-3814, 3836, 3848, 4067, 4611: New York Times, May 4, 7, 18, 19, 26, 30, June 23, September 2, 3, 28, 1913; Hillje, "Progressive Movement" 56-57.

17. New York Times, April 13, 15, 16, May 4, 8, 11, 17, 18, 21, 27, June 5, 28, July 6, 14, 20, 27, August 3, September 18, 1913; C.R. 50: 506-513, 1131, 1235, 1241, 1257, 1299, 1304-1306, 2016, 2239, Appendix 9, 13-15, 60-61. The letters from Bristow to the 173 constituents between April 26 and May 22, 1913 are found in Bristow Papers. See also Henry Allen Ware to Victor Murdock, April 18, 1913; H. W. Allen to Murdock, August 30, 1913; P. H. Albright to Murdock, April 19, 1913; Floyd N. Anderson to Murdock, April 17, 1913; Charles Aylesbury to Murdock, April 28, 1913; Victor Murdock Papers, Library of Congress and Darwin P. Kingsley to Oscar W. Underwood, February 4, 1913 in U.S. Congress, 62nd Congress, 3rd Session, Tariff Hearings, 1912-1913," House Document 133, 1913.

18. New York Times, May 2, 3, 6, 7, 8, 18, 25, June 6, July 8, September 18, 1913; C.R. 50: 4379; Blakey, Income Tax, 79; Franklin Escher, "The Income Tax and The Investor," Harper's Weekly, 55 (May 13, 1911): 22 and "The Income Tax and the Market," Harpers Weekly, 57 (February 22, 1913): 20.

19. Washington Post, August 29, 1913; New York Times, August 29, 1913.

20. C.R. 50: 505, 1261-1263, 1304, 2467, 2720, 3874-3876, 3886-9.

21. C.R. 50: 1306-1307, 1241, 1258; New York Times, May 3, June 21, September 6, 27, 1913.

22. New York Times, May 1, 7, July 23, 1913; C.R. 50: 399, 1247-1251.

23. New York Times, May 7, 1913; C.R. 50: 1247-1251; Ray Stannard Baker, Woodrow Wilson: Life and Letters, IV (Garden City: 1927), 111-112; Hillje, "Progressive Movement," 68-69; Seligman, "Federal Income Tax," 12.

24. C.R. 50: 3771, 3805, 3819, 3848. It will be remembered from Chapter IV that several Southern Democrats, such as Williams and Furnifold W. Simmons, were the leaders of the conservative factions at home. See also Theodore Roosevelt, "A Premium on Race Suicide," The Outlook, 105 (September 27, 1913): 163-164: and Bristow to L. M. Jones, May 1, 1913; Bristow to M. B. McNair, May 2, 1913; Seligman to Bristow, May 6, 1913, Bristow Papers.

25. Porter and Johnson, National Party Platforms, 168-169.

26. Ibid., 180-185.

27. Taussig, Tariff History, 409-446; Ralph L. McBride, "Conservatism on the Mountain West: Western Senators and Conservative Influences in the Consideration of National Progressive Legislation, 1906-1914," Ph.D. dissertation, Brigham Young University, 1976, 241-244.

28. McBride, Conservatism in the Mountain West," 241-245; Taussig, Tariff History, 415-446; Frank Burdick, "Woodrow Wilson and the Underwood Tariff," Mid-America, 50 (October, 1968): 275-286; Tindall, Emergence of New South, 10-12; Bristow to W. A. White, May 22, 1913; Bristow to W. H. Wilson, May 22, 1913; William Rockhill Nelson to Theodore Roosevelt, June 27, 1913, Bristow Papers.

29. C.R. 50: 87; James, Garner: 68-69; Blakey, Income Tax, 75-80; Ratner, American Taxation 325-6, New York Times, April 3, 1913; Studenski and Krooss, Financial History, 273; House Reports, II, 1913; Tariff Duties and Revenues, iv.

30. Morton Sosna, "The South in the Saddle: Racial Politics During the Wilson Years," Wisconsin Magazine of History, 54 (Autumn, 1970), 30-49; Tindall, Emergence of the New South, 1-32. On Reed, see Muraskin, "Missouri Politics," 319-325.

31. David P. Thelen, Robert M. La Follette and the Insurgent Spirit, (Boston, 1976), 47, 101-102; J. H. Leader to Bristow, August 5, 1913, Bristow Papers; Hillje, "Progressive Movement," 69-71, 370-371; Root to Clara S. Hay, April 21, 1913, Root Papers.

32. C.R. 50: 1245-1257; Holt, Congressional Insurgents, 10-11.

33. Holt, Congressional Insurgents, 45-48, 85-93; New York Times, May 26, 1913.

34. Blakey, Income Tax, 77-80; Ratner, American Taxation, 325-326; C.R. 50: 503-514, 1245-1257; J. S. Seidman, Legislative History of Federal Income Tax Laws, (New York: 1938) presents a detailed analysis of the various phases of the 1913 and the Congressional debates relating to the major issues, but gives no hint as to the political forces involved.

35. Ibid., 505, 1258, 1261-1263, 1306, 2339; New York Times, May 7, 1913.

36. C.R. 50: 507-510, 1235, 1241, 1257-1261, 1304, 2016; Blakey, Income Tax, 80-81; New York Times, May 5, 1913.

37. C.R. 50: 513-14, 1422-1424.

38. Hillje, "Progressive Movement," 27-38, 70-71; New York Times, March 8 - May 7, 1913; __________., "The Income Tax Plan," Literary Digest, 46 (April 19, 1913): 877-878; __________., "Prospects of the Federal Income Tax," Journal of Political Economy, 21 (March, 1913): 263-265; __________., "Effectiveness of the Income Tax," The Nation, 96 (April 17, 1913): 381-382; __________., "Details of the New Income Tax," The Outlook, 103 (April 19, 1913): 848-851.

39. New York Times, May 23, 29, June 20, 25, July 1, 2, 1913; Blakey, Income Tax, 84-87; Ratner, American Taxation, 329-330.

40. New York Times, June 4, 21, July 8, 1913; Ratner, American Taxation, 330; Blakey, Income Tax, 83-87.

41. New York Times, May 27, 1913; C.R. 50: 4381; Blakey, Income Tax, 89.

42. C.R. 50: 3774, 3797, 3810, 3813, 3834, 4067, 4420; New York Times, September 3, 1913.

43. C.R. 50: 3771, 3776, 3815, 3837, 3842-3843, 3847-52; New York Times, July 23, August 29, 1913.

44. C.R. 50: 3772, 3805, 3819, 3831, 3834, 3836, 4067; New York Times, August 27, 28, 1913.

45. C.R. 50: 3802, 3818, 4417.

46. Washington Post, August 29, 1913; C.R. 50: 4611-4613; Holmes, The White Chief, 274-275; Arthur S. Link, Wilson: The New Freedom, (Princeton: 1956), 192-193.

47. C.R. 50: 2020, 3860-3863; Washington Post, August 30, 1913; New York Times, August 28, 1913. O'Gorman, Reed, and Hitchcock later continued their revolt against the administration over currency reform and patronage. Several Democrats abstained on all the Insurgent rate amendments but all of the professed "radicals" voted with the leadership on one or more of those occasions, making it difficult to use that as a criterion.

48. New York Times, August 29, September 2, 6, 1913; Blakey, Income Tax, 89; Ratner, American Taxation, 332; Grantham, Hoke Smith, 249; Link, The New Freedom, 193.

49. C.R. 50: 4611-4612; New York Times, September 6-10, 1913, Washington Post, September 6, 1913.

50. New York Times, September 22-30, 1913; Ratner, American Taxation, 333; Blakey, Income Tax, 94-95; Hillje, "Progressive Movement," 63-66.

51. Blakey, Income Tax, 96-100; Ratner, American Taxation, 333-336; U.S. Congress. 63rd Congress, 1st Session, Income Tax: Extract From a Bill to Reduce Tariff, 1913, Senate Document 4.

52. Hillje, "Progressive Movement," 67-68; ____________., "Tangles and Snarls of the Income Tax," Current Opinion, 55 (December, 1913): 452-453.

53. Root to Ben Johnson, November 21, 1913, Root Papers; Jessup, Elihu Root, 229.

CHAPTER IX
The Income Tax and the Progressive Era

1. Mowry, Era of Theodore Roosevelt, 263-264.

2. See the discussion above in Chapters VI and VIII and in Sarasohn, "Democratic Surge," 117-173.

3. The classic statement is Wiebe, The Search for Order, 111-163. See also Yearley, Money Machines, 167-192.

4. Yearley, Money Machines, 238, 248.

5. John D. Hicks, The Populist Revolt: A Hitory of the Farmer's Alliance and the People's Party, (Minneapolis, 1931), 404-422; Wayne E. Fuller, "The Rural Roots of the Progressive Leaders," Agricultural History, 42 (1968): 1-13.

6. George E. Mowry, The California Progressive, (Chicago, 1963), 86-105; Mowry, Era of Theodore Roosevelt, 85-105; Hofstadter, The Age of Reform, 131-173.

7. Yearley, Money Machines, 167-192.

8. Hofstadter, The Age of Reform, 182; Huthmacher, "Urban Liberalism and the Age of Reform," 231-241; Yearley, Money Machines, 270-271.

9. Huthmacher, "Urban Liberalism," 240.

10. Gabriel Kolko, The Triumph of Conservatism: A Reinterpretation of American History, 1900-1916, (New York, 1967); 1-4; James Weinstein, "Big Business and the Origins of Workmen's Compensation," Labor History, VIII (Spring, 1967): 156-174.

11. Wiebe, Businessmen and Reform, 10-15; Jules Bache, "Upholding of Business Dependent upon Future Taxation Policy," Proceedings of the National Association of Manufactures, (1921): 64-65. See also Julius Barnes, The Genius of American Business, (New York, 1925), 6-13.

12. Kolko, Wealth and Power in America, 30-45.

13. Hillje, "Progressive Movement," 366-377; Kolko, Wealth and Power in America, 30-35.

14. Yearley, Money Machines, 39-45; King, et. al., Income in the United States, 335, Norman Pollock, The Populist Response to Industrial America, (New York, 1966), 11-12, 43-67.

15. Kelly, Fight for the White House, 3; Yearley, Money Machines, XV, 147, 167, 191, 247, 248; Thelen, New Citizenship, 136-139, 183-188; 203-211.

16. Yearley, Money Machines, 3-35.

17. Ibid., 250.

18. Ibid., xii, 3, 25, 127, 183; Harold Zink, City Bosses in the United States, 69-85, 218-230; Sonya Forthal, Cogwheels of Democracy: A Study of the Precinct Captain, (New York, 1946), 19-45; Elmer E. Cornwell, Jr., "Party Absorption of Ethnic Groups: The Case of Providence, Rhode Island," Social Forces, 38 (March, 1960), 205-210.

19. Yearley, Money Machines, 26-30, 101-110, 270-273; Monte Calvert, Technical Decision Making in a Political Context: The American City, 1880-1924," Urban Bosses, Machines, and Progressive Reformers, (Boston, 1972), 45-55, edited by Bruce M. Stave; Burnham, Critical Elections, 91-134; Edgar Litt, Beyond Pluralism: Ethnic Politics in America, (Glenview, Illinois, 1970), 39-74.

20. Hillje, "Progressive Movement," 1-73; Ratner, American Taxation, 145-168; Hays, Response to Industrialism, 132-139; Taussig, Tariff History, 361-370.

21. Hays, Response to Industralism, 129-131; Nash, American West, 18-50.

22. For a more complete discussion of this consensus see Chapter I above and Hillje, "Progressive Movement," 1-25, 366-377.

23. Richard L. McCormick, "The Discovery That Business Corrupts Politics: A Reappraisal of the Origins of Progressivism," American Historical Review, 86 (1981): 247-74. The anti-special interest atmosphere seemed to permeate discussions in most state legislators and to dominate much of the rhetoric in the 1910 and 1912 elections.

24. Yearley, Money Machines, 234-235, 270.

25. Ibid., 187-191; 194-204; Marc Karson, American Labor Unions and Politics, (Carbondale, Illinois, 1958), 28-29; Hays, Response to Industrialism, 62-63; Thelen, New Citizenship, 1-4, 33-85; Frank M. Stewart, A Half-Century of Municipal Reform: The History of the National Municipal League, (Berkeley, California, 1950), 113-114, 123-126, 207.

26. For a discussion of the growing emphasis on the diversity of Progressive Era reform see Daniel T. Rodgers, "In Search of Progressivism," Reviews in American History, 10 (December, 1982): 113-132.

27. For a discussion of the "New Politics," see Rodgers, "In Search of Progressivism," 113-117; Thelen, New Citizenship, 130-175; Buenker, Burnham, and Crunden, Progressivism, 31-70, 112-125; Richard L. McCormick, From Realignment to Reform: Political Change in New York State, 1893-1910, (Ithaca, New York, 1981) passim; David Paul Nord, Newspapers and New Politics: Midwestern Municipal Reform, 1890-1900, (Ann Arbor, Michigan, 1981), 1-20, 113-130; Burnham, Critical Elections, 91-174.

28. The differences in the impact of the "New Politics" are apparent from a comparative reading of the sources cited in note 27.

29. Burnham, Critical Elections, 133.

30. Morton Grodzins, The American System: A New View of Government in the United States, (Chicago, 1966), 254-289, edited by Daniel Elazar.

31. Irving Fisher, "Economists in the Public Service," The American Economic Review, IX (March, 1919): 16, supplement.

BIBLIOGRAPHY

Manuscript Collections

The Nelson W. Aldrich Papers. Library of Congress.
The Albert J. Beveridge Papers. Library of Congress.
The Joseph L. Bristow Papers. Kansas State Historical Society.
The Charles Evans Hughes Papers. Library of Congress.
The Cordell Hull Papers. Library of Congress.
The Robert M. LaFollette Papers. Library of Congress.
The Elihu Root Papers. Library of Congress.
The William Howard Taft Papers. Library of Congress.
The George van Lengerke Meyer Diary. Library of Congress.
The William Allen White Papers. Library of Congress.
Link, Arthur S. (ed.). The Papers of Woodrow Wilson, vol. 27 and 28. Princeton, New Jersey, 1978.

Memoirs, Correspondence, and Autobiographies

Bryan, William Jennings. The First Battle. Chicago, William B. Company, 1896.
Butt, Archie. Taft and Roosevelt, the Intimate Letters of Archie Butt. Garden City, New York, 1930.
Clark, Champ. My Quarter Century of American Politics. New York, 1920.
Debs, Eugene. Writings and Speeches. New York, 1948.
Hennessey, Michael. Twenty-Five Years of Massachusetts Politics. Boston, 1917.
Hicks, Fredrick (ed). Arguments and Addresses of Joseph H. Choate. St. Paul, Minnesota 1926.
Hull, Cordell. Memoirs. New York: Macmillan Company, 1948.
LaFollette, Robert. Autobiography. Madison, Wisconsin, 1913.
Lodge, Henry Cabot. Selections from the Correspondence of Theodore Roosevelt and Henry Cabot Lodge. New York, 1925.
Morison, Elting E., ed. The Letters of Theodore Roosevelt. Cambridge, Mass., 1954.
Sherman, John. Selected Speeches. New York, 1879.
Taft, Horace D. Memories and Opinions. New York, 1942.
Roosevelt, Theodore. Presidential Addresses and State Papers. New York 1910.

State Documents

Alabama. Legislature. House Journal. 1909.
Alabama. Legislature. Senate Journal. 1909.
Arizona. Legislature. House Journal. 1910-1912.
Arizona. Legislature. Senate Journal. 1912-1913.

Arkansas. General Assembly. *House Journal*. 1910-1912.
Arkansas. General Assembly. *Senate Journal*. 1910-1912.
California. Legislature. *House Journal*. 1910-1912.
California. Legislature. *Senate Journal*. 1910-1912.
Colorado. General Assembly. *House Journal*. 1910-1912.
Colorado. General Assembly. *Senate Journal*. 1910-1912.
Connecticut. General Assembly. *Legislative Record*. 1910-1913.
Delaware. General Assembly. *House Journal*. 1910-1913.
Florida. Legislature. *House Journal*. 1910-1913.
Florida. Legislature. *Senate Journal*. 1910-1913.
Georgia. General Assembly. *House Journal*. 1910.
Georgia. General Assembly. *Senate Journal*. 1910.
Idaho. Legislature. *House Journal*. 1910-1911.
Idaho. Legislature. *Senate Journal*. 1910-1911.
Illinois. General Assembly. *House Journal*. 1910.
Illinois. General Assembly. *Senate Journal*. 1910.
Illinois. Secretary of State. *Blue Book*. 1909.
Indiana. General Assembly. *House Journal*. 1910-1911.
Indiana. General Assembly. *Senate Journal*. 1910-1911.
Iowa. General Assembly. *House Journal*. 1910-1911.
Iowa. General Assembly. *Senate Journal*. 1910-1911.
Kansas. Legislature. *House Journal*. 1910-1912.
Kansas. Legislature. *Senate Journal*. 1910-1912.
Kansas State Historical Society. *The Annals of Kansas*. 1956.
Kentucky. General Assembly. *House Journal*. 1910-1911.
Kentucky. General Assembly. *Senate Journal*. 1910-1911.
Louisiana. Legislature. *House Debates*. 1910-1912.
Louisiana. Legislature. *Senate Debates*. 1910-1912.
Maine. Legislature. *House Journal*. 1910-1913.
Maine. Legislature. *Senate Journal*. 1910-1913.
Maryland. General Assembly. *Journal of the Proceedings*. 1910-1912.
Massachusetts. General Court. *House Journal*. 1910-1913.
Massachusetts. General Court. *Senate Journal*. 1910-1913.
Michigan. Legislature. *House Journal*. 1910-1911.
Michigan. Legislature. *Senate Journal*. 1910-1911.
Minnesota. Legislature. *House Journal*. 1910.
Minnesota. Legislature. *Senate Journal*. 1910.
Mississippi. Legislature. *House Journal*. 1910.
Mississippi. Legislature. *Senate Journal*. 1910.
Missouri. General Assembly. *House Journal*. 1910-1911.
Missouri. General Assembly. *Senate Journal*. 1910.1911.
Montana. Legislative Assembly. *House Journal*. 1910-1911.
Montana. Legislative Assembly. *Senate Journal*. 1910-1911.
Nebraska. Legislature. *House Journal*. 1910-1911.
Nebraska. Legislature. *Senate Journal*. 1910-1911.
Nevada. Legislature. *House Journal*. 1910-1911.
Nevada. Legislature. *Senate Journal*. 1910.1911.
New Hampshire. General Court. *House Journal*. 1910-1913.
New Hampshire. General Court. *Senate Journal*. 1910-1913.
New Jersey. Legislature. *House Minutes*. 1910-1913.
New Jersey. Legislature. *Senate Minutes*. 1910-1913.
New Mexico. Legislature. *House Journal*. 1912.

New York. General Assembly. *Assembly Journal*. 1910-1911.
New York. General Assembly. *Senate Journal*. 1910-1911.
New York. Legislature. *Red Book*. 1910-1911.
New York. Senate. "Special Message from the Governor submitting to the Legislature Certified Copy of a Resolution of Congress Entitled 'Joint Resolution Proposing An Amendment To The Constitution of the United States,' January 5, 1910."
New York. Legislature. "The Proposed Income Tax Amendment: Letter of Senator Elihu Root to the New York Legislature, 1910."
New York. Legislature. "The Proposed Sixteenth Article of Amendment to the Constitution of the United States: Arguments of Joseph H. Choate, et. al., 1910.
State of New York. In Senate. "Special Message from the Governor Submitting to the Legislature Certified Copy of a Resolution of Congress, Entitled 'Joint Resolution Proposing An Amendment To The Constitution of The United States,' January 5, 1910."
North Carolina. General Assembly. *House Journal*. 1910-1911.
North Carolina. General Assembly. *Senate Journal*. 1910-1911.
North Dakota. Legislative Assembly. *House Journal*. 1910-1911.
North Dakota. Legislative Assembly. *Senate Journal*. 1910-1911.
Ohio. General Assembly. *House Journal*. 1910-1911.
Ohio. General Assembly. *Senate Journal*. 1910-1911.
Oklahoma. Legislature. *House Journal*. 1910-1911.
Oklahoma. Legislature. *Senate Journal*. 1910-1911.
Oregon. General Assembly. *House Journal*. 1910-1911.
Oregon. General Assembly. *Senate Journal*. 1910-1911.
Pennsylavania. General Assembly. *The Legislative Journal*. 1910-1913.
Rhode Island. General Assembly. *House Journal*. 1910-1913.
Rhode Island. General Assembly. *Senate Journal*. 1910-1913.
South Carolina. General Assembly. *House Calendar*. 1910-1911.
South Carolina. General Assembly. *Senate Journal*. 1910-1911.
South Carolina. Senate. *Biographical Directory of the Senate of South Carolina, 1776-1964*. Emily Bellinger Reynolds and Joan Reynolds Faunt, (Comp.). Columbia, South Carolina, 1964.
South Dakota. Legislature. *House Proceedings*. 1910-1911.
South Dakota. Legislature. *Senate Proceedings*. 1910-1911.
Tennessee. General Assembly. *House Journal*. 1910-1911.
Tennessee. General Assembly. *Senate Journal*. 1910-1911.
Texas. Legislature. *House Journal*. 1910-1911.
Texas. Legislature. *Senate Journal*. 1910-1911.
Utah. Legislature. *House Journal*. 1910-1912.
Utah. Legislature. *Senate Journal*. 1910-1913.
Vermont. General Assembly. *House Calendar*. 1910-1913.
Vermont. General Assembly. *Senate Calendar*. 1910-1913.
Virginia. General Assembly. *House Journal*. 1910-1912.
Virginia. General Assembly. *Senate Journal*. 1910-1912.
Washington. Legislature. *House Journal*. 1910-1912.
Washington. Legislature. *Senate Journal*. 1910-1912.
West Virginia, Legislature. *House Journal*. 1910-1912.
West Virginia, Legislature. *Senate Journal*. 1910-1913.
Wisconsin. Legislature. *House Journal*. 1910-1911.
Wisconsin. Legislature. *Senate Journal*. 1910-1911.

Wyoming. Legislature. House Journal. 1912-1913.
Wyoming. Legislature. Senate Journal. 1912-1913.

Other Official Publications

American Federation of Labor. Convention Proceedings, 1906.
American Federeation of Labor. Textbook of Labor's Political Demands. Washington, D.C., 1906.
Brookings Institution. America's Capacity to Consume. Leven, Maurice, H.G. Moulton and Clark Warburton, (comps.). Washington, 1934.
Democratic Party, U.S. National Convention, Denver, 1908. Official Report of the Proceedings of the National Convention Held in Denver, Colorado, 1908.
Legislative Voters League of the State of Illinois. Candidate for the Forty-seventh General Assembly. 1910.
National Association of Manufacturers. Industrial Education. 1912.
National Bureau of Economic Research. Income in the United States. 1912.
National Bureau of Economic Research. Trends in the American Economy in the Nineteenth Century. Princeton, New Jersey, 1960.
National Bureau of Economic Research. Retail Prices After 1850. Hoover, Ethel D. (comp.). New York, 1933.
National Bureau of Economic Research. Income in the Various States, 1919, 1920, 1921. Leven, Maurice and Willford I. King., (comp.). New York, 1924.
National Bureau of Economic Research. Wealth and Income of the People of the United States. King, Willford I., (comp.). New York, 1915.
National Bureau of Economic Research. Shares of Upper Income Groups in Income and Savings. Kuznets, Simon, (Comp.). New York, 1953.
National Industrial Conference Board. State Income Taxes: Historical Development. New York, 1930.
Progressive Party. Progress. 1912.
Progressive Party of New York. Official Proposal of the National Progressive Party of the State of New York. 1912.
Republican Executive Congressional Committee. Revenue and Expenditures: Speech of Senator John Sherman. 1860.
__________. Dictionary of American Biography. New York, 1929.
__________. Who Was Who in America, 1897-1942. Chicago, 1968.
__________. The National Encylopedia of American Biography. Ann Arbor, Michigan, 1967.

United States Documents

U.S. American State Papers, VI.
U.S. Bureau of the Census. Herman Miller, (comp.). Income Distribution in the United States. Washington, 1966.
U.S. Bureau of the Census. Historical Statistics of the United States: From Colonial Times to 1957. Washington, 1960.

U.S. Bureau of the Census. *Statistical Abstract*. 1933.

U.S. Bureau of the Census. *Wealth, Debt and Taxation*, 2 vols. Washington, 1913.

U.S. Bureau of the Census. *Thirteenth Census of the United States*. 1910.

U.S. Bureau of the Census. *Special Report on Wealth, Debt and Taxation*. 1907.

U.S. Bureau of the Census. *Utah: Vital Statistics*. 1910.

U.S. Congress. *Biographical Directory of the American Congress, 1774-1971*. Washington, 1971.

U.S. Congress. *Congressional Globe*. 1860-1872.

U.S. Congress. *Congressional Record*. Vol. XLIV-XLVIII (1909-1913).

U.S. Congress. *Congressional Record*. Vol. XXVI (1894).

U.S. Congress. *Official Congressional Directory*. 1909.

U.S. Department of Commerce and Labor. *Income and Inheritance Taxes*.

U.S. Department of the Treasury. *Report of the Secretary of the Treasury, 1938*. Washington, 1939.

U.S. Internal Revenue Service. 1916. *Personal Income Tax Imposed and Collected Under the Act of October 3, 1913*.

U.S. *Report of the Secretary of the Treasury*. 1938.

U.S. Conference Committee. *Tariff Act of 1909*. 61st Congress, 1st Session.

U.S. Congress, 61st Congress, 1st Session, House Report 15, *To Amend Constitution of U.S. Relative To Income Tax*, 1909.

U.S. Congress. House. Committee on Ways and Means. *Statement of the Proposed Changes in the Tariff Laws*. 61st Congress, 1st Session, House Report 34.

U.S. House. 61st Congress, 1st Session, *The Payne-Aldrich Tariff: Speech of Samuel McCall*. House Document. 56, 1909.

U.S. Congress. *Comparison of the Tariff Act of 1909 with the Dingley Tariff Law*. 61st Congress, 1st Session, House Document 109.

U.S. Congress. House. Committee on Ways and Means. *To Provide Revenue, Equalize Duties and Protect the Industries of the United States*. 61st Congress, 2nd Session, House Report 231.

U.S. Congress. 61st Congress, 2nd Session, House Document 691, *Records In Connection With Collection of Corporation Tax*, 1910.

U.S. Congress. 62nd Congress, 2nd Session, House Document 601, *Decisions of the United States Supreme Court In Corporation Tax Cases And Income Tax Cases, with Dissenting Opinions*, 1912.

U.S. Congress. House. Committee on Ways and Means. 62nd Congress. 2nd Session, House Report 1093, *Special Excise Tax On Corporations Extended To Individuals*, 1912.

U.S. Congress. House. 63rd Congress, 1st Session. House Reports: Tariff Duties and Revenues. 1913.

U.S. Congress. 63rd Congress, 3rd Session, Senate Document 632, *Income Tax Collected During 1914*.

U.S. Congress. 64th Congress, 2nd Session. House Document 5: Statistics of Income. 1916.

U.S. Congress. Senate. Committee on Finance. *The Tariff and Internal Customs Acts of 1894*. 53rd Congress, 1st Session, Senate Document 118.

U.S. Congress. 61st Congress, 1st Session, Senate Document 98, Message of President Recommending Amendment To Tariff Bill For Tax On Net Income of Corporations. 1909.

U.S. Congress. Senate. 61st Congress, 1st Session, The Democrats and the Tariff: Speech of Augustus Bacon, Senate Document 109. 1909.

U.S. Congress. Senate Reports, Vol. 3. Report of the Select Committee on Wages and Prices of Commodities, Part 1. 61st Congress, 2nd Session. 1910.

U.S. Congress. 61st Congress, 2nd Session, Senate Document 365, Message Of Governor Of New Jersey On Proposed Income Tax. 1910.

U.S. Congress. 61st Congress, 2nd Session, Senate Document 367, Letter Of George F. Edmunds Relating To Income Tax. 1910.

U.S. Congress. 61st Congress, 2nd Session, Senate Document 398, Letter From Elihu Root On Proposed Income Tax. 1910.

U.S. Congress. Senate Committee on the Judiciary. Amendment to the Constitution. 61st Congress, 3rd Session, Senate Document 198. 1910.

U.S. Congress. Senate. Shall Income Tax Amendment Be Ratified? 61st Congress, 3rd Session, Senate Document 705. 1910.

U.S. Congress. 62nd congress, 3rd Session, Senate Document 956, Profits and Business Of Certain Corporation. 1912.

U.S. Congress. Senate. Income Tax Collected During 1914. 63rd Congress, 3rd Session, Senate Document 623.

U.S. Congress. Senate. Data on the Ratification of the Constitution and Amendments by States. 71st Congress, 3rd Session, Senate Document 240, 1930.

U.S. Congress. 63rd Congress, 1st Session. Senate Document 4, Income Tax Reduce Tariff Duties and Provide Revenue for Government, 1913.

U.S. Congress, Senate. 62nd Congress, 1st Session, Senate Document 171, Opinions Relative To Income Tax Amendment, 1913.

U.S. Supreme Court. Income Tax Cases: Arguments of the Honorable Joseph H. Choate Before the Supreme Court in the Pollock Case. 1895.

Newspapers

Albany Evening Journal. 1909-1913.
Arizona Republican (Phoenix). 1909-1912
Arkansas Gazette (Little Rock). 1909-1910.
Atlanta Constitution. 1909-1912.
Augusta Chronicle (Georgia). 1909-1910.
Austin Statesman. 1911.
Baltimore Sun. 1909-1912.
Bangor (Maine) Daily News. 1910.
Birmingham Age Herald (Alabama). 1909-1911.
Boston Daily Globe. 1909-1913.
Burlington Daily Free Press (Vermont). 1909-1913.
Charleston Daily Mail (West Virginia). 1911-1913.
Charleston News and Courier. 1909-1911.
Chicago Daily News. 1909-1910.
Chicago Tribune. 1909-1913.
Christian Science Monitor (Boston). 1909-1913.

Cincinnati Enquirer. 1909-1912.
Cleveland Plain Dealer. 1909-1912.
Concord Evening Monitor (New Hampshire).
Daily Kennebec Journal (Augusta, Maine), 1911.
Daily Oklahoma (Oklahoma City). 1909-1910.
Des Moines Register. 1909-1911.
Denver Post. 1911.
Elmira Gazette (Kansas). 1910-1911.
Florida Times-Union (Jacksonville). 1910-1913.
Harrisburg Patroit. 1909-1913.
Hartford Courant. 1909-1913.
Hartford Times. 1909-1913.
Idaho Statesman (Boise). 1911.
Illinois State Register (Springfield). 1909-1910.
Jackson Weekly Clarion Ledger (Mississippi). 1910.
Jackson Daily News (Mississippi). 1910.
Kansas City Star. 1910.
Knoxville Daily Journal and Tribune. 1911.
Louisville Courier Journal. 1909-1912.
Milwaukee Journal. 1971.
Minneapolis Journal. 1909-1912.
Mobile Register. 1909-1910.
Montgomery Advertizer. 1909-1910.
Montpelier Argus and Patriot. 1909-1913.
Nashville Tennessean. 1911.
Natchez Democrat. 1910.
Nebraska State Journal (Lincoln). 1910-1912.
Newark Evening News. 1909-1913.
Newark Star. 1909-1913.
New Orleans Times-Picayne. 1910-1912.
New York Sun. 1909-1913.
New York Times. 1860-1872, 1894-1895, 1908-1913.
New York Tribune. 1894-1895, 1908-1913.
New York World. 1890-1895, 1908-1913.
Ohio State Journal (Columbus). 1909-1911.
Philadelphia Evening Bulletin. 1909-1913.
Philadelphia Inquirer. 1909-1913.
Philadelphia Public Ledger. 1909-1913.
Portland (Maine) *Evening Express and Daily Adverteger*, 1911.
Portland Oregonian. 1910-1911.
Providence Evening Bulletin. 1909-1913.
Providence Evening News. 1914.
Providence Journal. 1909-1913.
Richmond Times-Dispatch. 1909-1911.
Sacramento Union. 1909-1913.
Salt Lake Tribune. 1909-1913.
San Francisco Chronicle. 1911.
Springfield Daily Republican (Massachusetts). 1909-1913.
Tacoma Daily Ledger. 1909-1912.
The State Leader (Cheyenne). 1913.
The State (Columbia, South Carolina). 1909-1912.
Topeka Daily Capitol. 1911.

Topeka State Journal. 1909-1912.
Trenton Daily True American. 1909-1913.
Tucson Daily Citizen. 1909-1913.
Vicksburg Herald. 1909-1910.
Washington Post. 1908-1910.
Washington Post. 1908-1910.
Washington Star. 1908-1910.
Wilmington Every Evening. 1909-1913.
Wisconsin State Journal. (Madison). 1909-1912.

Unpublished Dissertations

Acrea, Kenneth C. "Wisconsin Progressivism: Legislative Response to Social Change," University of Wisconsin, 1968.
Agan, Thomas Raymond. "The New Hampshire Progressive Movement." State University of New York, Albany, 1975. 359 p.
Akin, Edward Nelson. "Southern Reflection of the Gilded Ages: Henry M. Flagler's System, 1885-1913. University of Florida, 1975.
Armin, Calvin Perry. "Coe I. Crawford and the Progressive Movement in South Dakota." University of Colorado, 1957.
Barfield, Claude. "The Democratic Party in Congress, 1909-1913." Northwestern University, 1965.
Becker, Richard E. "Edward Dunne, Reform Mayor of Chicago, 1905-1907." University of Chicago, 1971.
Bergman, Hermas John. "Progressive On The Right: Marion E. Hay, Governor of Washington, 1909-1913." Washington State University, 1967.
Blankenship, Warren Marion. "Progressives and the Progressive Party in Oregon, 1906-1916." University of Oregon, 1966.
Boggs, Doyle Willard, Jr. "John Patrick Grace and the Politics of Reform in South Carolina, 1900-1931." University of South Carolina, 1977.
Burckel, Nicholas C. "Progressive Governors in the Border States: Reform Governors of Missouri, Kentucky, West Virginia and Maryland, 1900-1918."
Clubb, Jerome. "Congressional Opponents of Reform, 1901-1913." University of Washington, 1963.
De Lorne, Roland L. "The Shaping of a Progressive: Edward P. Costigan and Urban Reform in Denver, 1900-1911." University of Colorado, 1968.
Detzer, David W. "The Politics of the Payne-Aldrich Tariff of 1909." University of Connecticut, 1970.
Duffy, John Joseph. "Charleston Politics in the Progressive Era." University of South Carolina, 1963.
Fullenwider, James W. "The Governor and the Senator: Executive Power and the Structure of the Illinois Republican Party, 1880-1917." Washington University, 1974.
German, James C., Jr. "Tafts' Attorney General: George W. Wickersham." New York University, 1969.
Harris, David Alan. "Racists and Reformers: A Study of Progressivism in Alabama, 1896-1911." University of North Carolina, Chapel Hill, 1967.
Hillje, John W. "The Progressive Movement and the Graduated Income Tax." University of Texas, 1966.

Jones, Alton Dumar. "Progressivism in Georgia, 1898-1918." Emory University, 1963.
Ketcham, Earle. "The Sixteenth Amendment." University of Illinois, 1926.
Koscher, William P. "The Springfield Republican in the Progressive Era: A Guardian of American Values." University of Illinois, 1975.
Larsen, Kent Sheldon. "The Life of Thomas Kearns." University of Utah, 1964.
Link, Arthur S. "The South And the Democratic Campaign of 1910-1912." University of North Carolina, 1943.
Malcomson, Virginia D. "William E. Glasscock: Governor of the People." University of West Virginia, 1950.
McBride, Ralph L. "Conservatism in the Mountain West: Western Senators and Conservative Influences in the Consideration of National Progressive Legislation, 1906-1914." Brigham Young University, 1976.
McInerney, Thomas J. "The Election of 1912 in New York State." University of Denver, 1977.
Muraskin, Jack David. "Missouri Politics During the Progressive Era, 1896-1916." University of California, Berkeley, 1969.
Niswonger, Richard Leverne. "Arkansas Democratic Politics, 1896-1920." University of Texas, Austin, 1974.
Pavlovsky, Arnold M. "'We Busted Because We Failed': Florida Politics, 1880-1908." Princeton University, 1974.
Penn, Niel Shaww. "Henry D. Hatfield and Reform Politics: A Study of West Virginia Politics from 1908 to 1917." Emory University, 1973.
Pike, Albert. "Jonathan Bourne, Jr., Progressive." University of Oregon, 1957.
Ratner, Sidney. "The Income Tax of 1894." Columbia University, 1940.
Saltvig, Robert D. "The Progressive Movement in Washington." University of Washington, 1966.
Sander, Alfred. "The Political and Social Views of William Howard Taft." American university, 1955.
Sarasohn, David. "The Democratic Surge, 1905-1912: Forging A. Progressive Majority." University of California at Los Angeles, 1976.
Sayre, Ralph M. "Albert Baird Cummins and the Progressive Movement in Iowa." Columbia University, 1958.
Scales, James. "Political History of Oklahoma, 1907-1949." University of Oklahoma, 1949.
Seagraves, Joe Tolbert. "Arkansas Politics 1874-1918." University of Kentucky, 1973.
Silbert, Edward W. "Support for Reform Among Congressional Democrats, 1897-1913," University of Florida, 1966.
Snow, R.J. "The American Party in Utah: A Study of the Politics of Party Struggle During the Early Years of Statehood." University of Utah, 1964.
Straetz, Ralph A. "The Progressive Movement in Illinois, 1910-1916." University of Illinois, Urbana, 1951.
Sweeney, Raymond Stanley. "Progressive in Maryland, 1900-1917." University of North Carolina, Chapel Hill, 1971.
Tinsley, James. "The Progressive Movement in Texas." University of Wisconsin, 1954.

Warner, Robert M. "Chase S. Osborn and the Progressive Movement." University of Michigan, 1957.
Wheeler, John McDaniel. The People's Party in Arkansas, 1891-96." Tulane University, 1975.

Articles and Periodicals

Adams, T.S. "Ideals and Idealism in Taxation." American Economic Review XVIII (March, 1928): 1-12.
Allen, Howard W., and Clubb, Jerome. "Progressive Reform and the Political System." Pacific Northwest Quarterly 65 (1974): 103-45.
Bache, Jules. "Upholding of Business Dependent Upon Future Taxation Policy." Proceedings of the National Association of Manufacturers, (1921): 479-491.
Bacote, Clarence A. "Negro Proscription, Protests and Proposed Solutions in Georgia, 1880-1908." Journal of Southern History 25 (November, 1959): 479-491.
Barfield, Claude. "'Our Share of the Booty': The Democratic Party, Cannonism, and the Payne-Aldrich Tariff." Journal of American History LVII (September, 1970): 308-323.
Bascom, John. "Problems of an Income Tax." The Dial LI (September 16, 1911): 196-198.
Bellush, Jewel. Reform in New Hampshire: Robert Bass Wins the Primary." New England Quarterly 35 (1962): 469-88.
Borah, William. "The Income Tax: Sound in Law and Economics." Journal of Accountancy X (May, 1910): 26-32.
______________. "Income Tax Amendment." North American Review CXCI (June, 1910): 775-761.
Braeman, John. "Seven Progressives." Business History Review 35 (Winter, 1961): 581-592.
Brooks, Sydney. "Aspects of the Income Tax." North American Review CXVII (April, 1913): 542-555.
Brooks, Sydney. "The Landslide in America, Living Age 275 (November 30, 1912): 563-565.
Brown, Norris. "The Income Tax Amendment." Outlook XCIV (February, 1910): 215-219.
Bryant, Keith L., Jr. "Kate Barnard, Organized Labor and Social Justice in Oklahoma During the Progressive Era," Journal of Southern History 35 (May, 1969): 145-164.
Buenker, John D. "Cleveland's New Stock Lawmakers and Progressive Reform." Ohio History 78 (1969): 116-138.
Buenker, John D. "Edward F. Dunne: The Urban New Stock Democrat as Progressive." Mid-America 50 (1968):
Buenker, John D. "The Emergence of Urban Liberalism in Rhode Island, 1909-1919." Rhode Island History (1971): 35-51.
Buenker, John D. "The Politics of Resistance: The Rural-Based Republican Machines of Connecticut and Rhode Island." New England Quarterly 47 (1974):
Buenker, John D. "Progressivism in Connecticut: The Thrust of the Urban New Stock Democrats." Bulletin of the Connecticut Historical Society 35 (1970: 97-109.

Buenker, John D. "Urban Immigrant Lawmakers and Progressive Reform in Illinois." Essays in Illinois History, Carbondale, Illinois, 1967, 52-57, edited by Donald F. Tingley.

Bullock, Charles. "Federal Income Tax." Proceedings of the National Tax Association, 1914, 264-279.

Burckel, Nicholas C. "From Beckham to McCreary: The Progressive Record of Kentucky Governors." The Register of the Kentucky Historical Society 76 (1978): 285-306.

Burckel, Nicholas C. "William Goebel and the Campaign for Railroad Regulation in Kentucky, 1880-1900." Filson Club Quarterly 48 (January, 1974), 43-60.

Burdick, Frank. "Woodrow Wilson and the Underwood Tariff." Mid-America 50 (October, 1968): 273-290.

Clubb, Jerome M. and Allen, Howard W. "Party Loyalty in the Progressive Years, The Senate, 1909-1915." Journal of Politics, 29 (August, 1967): 567-84.

Cornwell, Elmer E., Jr. "Bosses, Machines and Ethnic Groups." Annals of the American Academy of Political and Social Science 353 (May, 1964): 28-30.

Cornwell, Elmer E., Jr. "Party Absorption of Ethnic Groups: The Case of Providence, Rhode Island." Social Forces 38 (March, 1960): 205-210.

Crosby, Ernest. "The House of Dollars." Cosmopolitan KL (March, 1906): 485-487.

Cummins, Albert. "The Reason for the Income Tax." Independent LXVII (July 22, 1910): 969-971.

Davenport, Frederick. "The Income Tax Amendment." Independent LXVIII (April 28, 1910): 176-182.

Dillard, J.H. "Taxation and Public Welfare." Proceedings of the National Tax Association 3 (1909): 45-53.

Edmunds, George. "Salutary Results of the Income Tax Decision." Forum XIX (June, 1895): 513-521.

Ellis, Elmer. "Public Opinion and the Income Tax." Mississippi Valley Historical Review XXVII (September, 1940): 225-242.

Escher, Franklin. "Income Tax and the Investor." Harpers Weekly 57 (February 22, 1913): 20.

Escher, Franklin. "Income Tax and the Senator." Harpers Weekly 55 (May 13, 1911): 22.

Filene, Peter. "An Obituary for the Progressive Movement." American Quarterly 22 (1970): 20-34.

Fisher, Irving. "Economists in Public Service." American Economic Review IX (March, 1919): 5-21, supplement.

Fordyce, Wellington G. "Nationality Groups in Cleveland and Politics." The Ohio State Archaeological and Historical Quarterly, 46 (1937): 125-140.

Fox, Austen. "Insert No Ambiguities into the Constitution." Journal of Accountancy X (May, 1910): 2-8.

Geiger, Louis. "Joseph W. Folk v. Ed Butler: St. Louis, 1902." Journal of Southern History 28 (November, 1962): 438-440.

Glad, Paul. "Progressivism and the Business Culture of the 1920's." Journal of American History LIII (June, 1966): 65-82.

Godkin, E.L. "Income Tax." The Nation LX (April 11, 1895): 272.

Godkin, E.L. "Income Tax." The Nation XXVI (May 2, 1891): 287.

Gould, Lewis L. "Western Range Senators and the Payne-Aldrich Tariff." Pacific Northwest Quarterly 64 (1973): 49-56.
Green, George. "The Florida Press and the Democratic Primary of 1912." Florida Historical Quarterly 32 (January, 1966): 157-173.
Gressley, Gene M. "Colonialism, A Western Complaint." Pacific Northwest Quarterly 54 (1963): 1-8.
Guthrie, William. "No Taxation Without Representation." Journal of Accountancy X (May, 1910): 8-13.
Hall, U.S. "The Income Tax: Reasons in its Favor." Forum XVII (February, 1894): 14-19.
Halsell, Willie D. "The Bourbon Period in Mississippi Politics, 1875-1890." Journal of Southern History 11 (November, 1945): 519-537.
Hard, William. "Uncle Joe Cannon." Colliers (May 23, 30, 1908):
Hays, Samuel. "Politics of Reform in Municipal Government in the Progressive Era." Pacific Northwest Quarterly LV (October, 1964): 50-65.
Hill, Joseph. "The Civil Was Income Tax." Quarterly Journal of Economics VIII (July, 1894): 416-452.
Hill, Joseph. "The Income Tax of 1913." Quarterly Journal of Economics XXVIII (November, 1913): 46-68.
Holmes, George K. "The Concentration of Wealth." Political Science Quarterly 8 (December, 1893): 589-600.
Hundley, Norris. "Katherine Phillips Edson and the fight for the California Minimum Wage, 1919-1923." Pacific Historical Review XXIX (August, 1960): 270-285.
Huthmacher, J. Joseph, Hughes, Charles Evans, and Murphy, Charles Francis. "The Metamorphosis of Progressivism." New York History XLVI (Janury, 1965): 25-40.
Huthmacher, J. Joseph. "Urban Liberalism and the Age of Reform." Mississippi Valley Historical Review 49 (September, 1962): 231-241.
Jones, Chester. "Rotten Boroughs of New England." North American Review XCVII (April, 1913): 486-498.
Karr, Carolyn. "A Political Biography of Henry Hatfield." West Virginia History 28 (October, 1966): 35-63; (June-August, 1967): 137-170.
Kinsman, Delos. "The Present Period of Income Tax Activity in the United States." Quarterly Journal of Economics 23 (February, 1909): 296-306.
Kirby, Jack Temple. "Irony and Alcohol: The Campaign of Westmorland Davis for Governor, 1909-1917." The Virginia Magazine of History and Biography 123 (July, 1965): 261-277.
Kirwan, Albert D. "Apportionment in the Mississippi Constitution of 1890." Journal of Southern History 14 (May, 1948): 234-246.
La Follette, Robert M. "How Aldrich Killed the Income Tax. " La Follette's Magazine 1 (July 10, 1909): 5.
La Follette, Robert M. "How the Tariff Bill Is Going Through." La Follette's Magazine 1 (May 1, 1909): 5-6.
Leupp, Francis. "President Taft's Own View." The Outlook XCIV (December 2, 1911): 811-818.
Lewis, A.H. "Now For The Income Tax." Hearst's Magazine 23 (April, 1913): 672-674.
Link, Arthur S. "The Progressive Movement in the South." North Carolina Historical Review 12 (April, 1946): 172-183.

Link, Arthur S. "What Happened to the Progressive Movement in the 1920's?" American Historical Review, LXIV (July, 1959): 836-840.

Lloyd, Henry Demarest. "The Populists at St. Louis." Review of Reviews XIV (September, 1896): 298-303.

McCormick, Richard L. "The Discovery That Business Corrupts Politics: A Reappraisal of the Origins of Progressivism." American Historical Review 86 (1981): 247-274.

Mac Veagh, Wayne, "The Graduated Taxation of Incomes and Inheritances." North American Review 182 (June, 1906): 824-828.

Mallock, W.H. "Is the Income Tax Socialistic?" Forum XIX (August, 1895): 707-723.

Maxey, Edwin. "The Denver Convention." The Arena 40 (September, 1908): 150-154.

McWhiney, Grady. "Louisiana Socialism in the Early Twentieth Century: A Study of Rustic Radicalism." Journal of Southern History 20 (August, 1954): 311-330.

Morrow, Dwight. "The Income Amendment." Columbia Law Review X (July, 1909): 379-385.

Peterson, James. "The Trade Unions and the Populist Party." Science and Society VIII (Spring, 1944): 140-149.

Phelps, William. "The Income Tax." Independent LXXIII (September 12, 1912): 654-656.

Phillips, David Graham. "The Treason of the Senate." Cosmopolitan 40 (March-April, 1906): 487-628.

Purdy, Lawson. "The Income Tax Amendment Should Be Ratified." Journal of Accountancy X (May, 1910): 13-26.

Putnam, Jackson K. "The Persistence of Progressivism in the 1920's: The Case of California." Pacific Historical Review XXXV (November, 1966): 380-840.

Reeves, Paschal. "Thomas S. Martin: Committee Statesman." Virginia Magazine of History and Biography. 68 (July, 1960): 344-64.

Robinson, Clement. "Tax Legislation of 1910." Proceedings of the National Tax Association (1907): 24-49.

Rodgers, Daniel T. "In Search of Progressivism." Reviews in American History 10 (December, 1982): 113-132.

Roosevelt, Theodore. "A Premium on Race Suicide." The Outlook 105 (September 27, 1913): 163-164.

Roper, Charles L. "The Taxes of Incomes." Proceedings of the National Tax Association (1907): 24-49.

Schaper, William A. "Sectionalism and Representation in South Carolina." Annual Report of the American Historical Association 1(1900): 450-462.

Schott, Matthew J. "The New Orleans Machine and Progressivism." Louisiana History 24 (1983): 141-153.

Scott, Ann Firor. "A Progressive Wind from the South, 1906-1913." Journal of Southern History XXIX (February, 1963): 53-71.

Seligman, E.R.A. "Income Tax Amendment." Political Science Quarterly, 25 (June, 1910): 193-219.

Seligman, E.R.A. "Is the Income Tax Constitutional and Just?" Forum XIX (March, 1895): 48-57.

Seligman, E.R.A. "The Theory of Progressive Taxation." Political Science Quarterly (1893): 223-225.

Shearman, Thomas G. "The Owners of Wealth." Forum (November, 1889): 262-273.

Shelton, William. "The Income Tax in Georgia." Journal of Political Economy 18 (1910): 610-627.

Sherman, Richard B. "Foss of Masssachusetts: Demogogue v. Progressive." Mid-America 43 (April, 1961): 88-90.

Shipps, Jan. "Utah Comes of Age Politically: A Study of the State's Politics in the Early Years of the Twentieth Century." Utah Historical Quarterly 35 (October, 1967): 91-111.

Solvick, Stanley. "William Howard Taft and the Payne-Aldrich Tariff." Mississippi Valley Historical Review 50 (1968): 424-442.

Smith, Goldwin. "The Income Tax." Banker's Magazine XX (May, 1866): 870-876.

Sosna, Morton. "The South in the Saddle: Racial Politics During the Wilson Years." Wisconsin Magazine of History 54 (Autumn, 1970): 30-49.

Stedman, Murray S. and Susan W. "The Rise of the Democratic Party of Rhode Island." New England Quarterly 24 (September, 1951): 329-339.

Stone, Clarence. "Bleasism and the 1912 Election." North Carolina Historical Review 38 (Winter, 1963): 54-73.

Tager, Jack. "Progressives, Conservatives and the Theory of the Status Revolution." Mid-America 48 (July, 1966): 162-173.

Thelen, David P. "Social Tensions and the Origins of Progressivism." Journal of American History 56 (September, 1969): 323-341.

Tindall, George B. "The Campaign for the Disfranchisement of the Negro in South Carolina." Journal of Southern History 15 (May, 1949): 212-234.

Towns, Stuart. "Joseph T. Robinson and Arkansas Politics." Arkansas Historical Quarterly 36 (Winter, 1965): 295-302.

Tucker, Rufus B. "The Distribution of Income Among Income Taxpayers in the United States, 1863-1935." Quarterly Journal of Economics 52 (August, 1938): 561-586.

Watkins, G. P. "The Growth of Large Fortunes." Publications of the American Economic Association 3rd Series, 8, v. 4 (1907): 735-904.

Weinstein, James. "Organized Business and the City Commissioner and Manager Movements." Journal of Southern History XXVIII (May, 1962): 166-182.

Weinstein, James. "Big Business and The Origins of Workmen's Compensation." Labor History VIII (Spring, 1967): 156-174.

Wells, David. "The Income Tax: Is it Desirable?" Forum XVII (March, 1894): 1-14.

Wells, David. "The Communism of a Discriminating Income Tax." North American Review CXXX (March, 1880): 236-246.

West, Henry. "Shall Incomes Be Taxed?" Forum XLI (June, 1909): 513-515.

West, Max. "The Inome Tax and the National Revenue." Journal of Political Economy 8 (September, 1900): 433-451.

Whitney, Edward. "Political Dangers of the Income Tax Decision." Forum XIX (June, 1895): 521-523.

Williams, Frank B. "The Poll Tax as a Suffrage Requirement in the South, 1870-1901." Journal of Souothern History 18 (November, 1952): 469-496.

Williams, T. Harry. "The Gentleman From Louisiana: Demagogue or Democrat?" Journal of Southern History XXVI (February, 1960): 1-21.

Willis, H. Parker. "Relation of Federal to State and Local Taxation." Proceedings of the National Tax Association (1907): 201-210.
Wish, Harvey. "Altgeld and The Progressive Tradition." American Historical Review 46 (1941): 813-831.
Wolfinger, Raymond E. "The Development and Persistence of Ethnic Politics." American Ethnic Politics, Lawrence H. Fuchs, ed., New York, 1968: 163-193.
Woodburn, James. "Amending the Constitution." Independent LXVII (December 30, 1909): 1497-1501.
______________. "America and the Income Tax." Living Age CCXXVI (March 5, 1913): 698-701.
______________. "America and the Income Tax." The Nation 92 (January 26, 1911): 84-85.
______________. "The Corporation Income Tax." Chatauquan LXII (May, 1911): 299-301.
______________. "Defeat for the Income Tax." American Economist 46 (November 4, 1910): 221.
______________. "The Democratic Convention." The Outlook 89 (July, 1908): 645-54.
______________. "The Democratic Victory and After." Living Age 275 (November 30, 1912): 572-574.
______________. "Details of the New Income Tax Law." The Outlook 103 (April 19, 1913): 848-851.
______________. "Effectiveness of the Income Tax. The Nation 96 (April, 17, 1913): 381-382.
______________. "Federal Income Tax in the United States." Living Age 277 (June 21, 1913): 761-763.
______________. "From Plaisted to Plaisted." The Outlook XLVI (September, 24, 1910): 139-40.
______________. "Governor Hughes and the Income Tax." The Outlook XCIV (Janury 15, 1910): 109-111.
______________. "Governor Hughes and the Income Tax." Review of Reviews 41 (March, 1910): 272-273.
______________. "Hardships of Income Tax." American Economist 44 (November 5, 1909): 218.
______________. "How Aldrich Killed the Income Tax." LaFollette's Weekly Magazine I (July 10, 1909): 5-8.
______________. "How the Income Tax Strikes Home." Current Opinion 54 (June, 1913): 503.
______________. "An Income Tax." American Economist 43 (April 23, 1909): 286.
______________. "The Income Tax." Commercial and Financial Chronicle XII (April 24, 1909): 32.
______________. "The Income Tax Amendment." Literary Digest XLVI (February 15, 1913): 325-327.
______________. "Income Tax Amendment." The Nation 92 (April 27, 1911): 414.
______________. "The Income Tax Amendment." The Outlook 95 (May 14, 1910): 49-51.
______________. "Income Tax Legislation." Independent 74 (February 13, 1913): 384.

______________. "Income Tax Legislation." Literary Digest LXXIV (February 13, 1913): 382-385.

______________. "Income Tax Plan." Literary Digest 46 (April 19, 1913): 877-878.

______________. "The Income Tax Tangle." The Nation 96 (May 15, 1913) 490-491.

______________. "The Income Tax - Two Questions." The Outlook 104 (May 24, 1913): 140.

______________. "Income Tax Under Fire." Literary Digest 46 (May 24, 1913): 1163-1164.

______________. "The Income Tax and the Constitution." Current Literature 47 (August, 1909): 129-133.

______________. "Income Tax and Protection." American Economist 44 (July 30, 1909): 54.

______________. "The Income Tax and the States." "The Outlook 98 (July 22, 1911): 600-601.

______________. "Income Taxation." Merchant's Magazine and commercial Review LII (January, 1865): 60.

______________. "Indirect Direct Tax." Literary Digest 44 (March 30, 1912): 629-630.

______________. "Justice of an Income Tax." The Outlook 93 (October 16, 1909): 328-329.

______________. "The Landslide in America." Living Age 275 (November 30, 1912): 563-565.

______________. "Life Insurance and the Income Tax." Independent 74 (April 17, 1913): 890.

______________. "Lopsided Income Tax." The Nation 97 (September 11, 1913): 224.

______________. "Maine and After." The Nation XCI (September 15, 1910) 232-3.

______________. "The New Income Tax Bill." The Nation 96 (May 1, 1913): 432.

______________. "Now for the Income Tax." Hearst's Magazine XXVIII (April 22, 1913): 672.

______________. "The Proposed Income Tax: A Poll of the Press." The Outlook 104 (May 10, 1913): 58-60.

______________. "Prospects of the Federal Income Tax." Journal of Political Economy 21 (March, 1913): 263-265.

______________. "Prospects of the Federal Income Tax Amendment." World's Work 22 (May, 1911): 14309-14311.

______________. "Rich Man's Share of the Income Tax." Literary Digest 47 (September 13, 1913): 407.

______________. "Senator Root and the Income Tax Amendment." The Outlook XCIV (March 12, 1910): 552-553.

______________. "The Sixteenth Amendment." The Outlook 103 (February 15, 1913): 330-331.

______________. "The Small Chance for the Income Tax." World's Work XIX (April, 1910): 12757-12758.

______________. "Strange Reasons for Favoring Income Tax." American Economist 44 (September 3, 1909): 113.

______________. "Tangles and Snarls of the Income Tax." Current Opinion 55 (December, 1913): 452.

______________. "Two Constitutional Amendments." Chautauquan 63 (July, 1911): 110-112.

______________. "The Victory of the Democrats." Living Age 275 (November 30, 1912): 565-567.

Books

Aaron, Daniel. Men of Good Hope: A Story of American Progressives. New York, 1960.

Abbey, Kathryn Trimmer. Florida: Land of Change. Chapel Hill, 1941.

Abrams, Richard. Conservatism in a Progressive Era. Cambridge, 1964.

Acheson, Sam. Joe Bailey: The Last Democrat. New York, 1932.

Ambler, Charles and Summers, Festus. West Virginia: The Mountain State. Englewood Cliffs, New Jersey, 1958.

Anderson, Donald F. William Howard Taft: A Conservatives' Conception of the Presidency. Ithaca, New York, 1973.

Armin, Calvin Perry. Coe I. Crawford and the Progressive Movement in South Dakota. Lincoln, Nebraska, 1968.

Arrington, Leonard J. Great Basin Kingdom: An Economic History of the Latter-day Saints, 1830-1900. Cambridge, Massachusetts, 1958.

Avery, Mary W. Washington: A History of the Evergreen State. Seattle, 1965.

Bain, Richard. Convention Decisions and Voting Records. Washington, 1960.

Baker, Ray Stannard. Woodrow Wilson: Life and Letters, Four volumes. Garden City, New York 1927.

Bald, F. Clever. Michigan in Four Centuries. New York, 1954.

Ball, William Watts. The State That Forgot: South Carolina's Surrender to Democracy. Indianapolis, 1932.

Barnes, Julius. The Genius of American Business. New York, 1925.

Bazelon, David. The Paper Economy. New York, 1963.

Bean, Walton. Boss Reuf's San Francisco: The Story of the Union Labor Party, Big Business, and the Graft Prosecutions. Berkeley, California, 1952.

Bean, Walton. California: An Interpretive History. New York, 1968.

Beran, Wilson Lloyd, ed. History of Delaware: Past and Present, II. New York, 1929.

Bernd, Joseph L. Grass Roots Politics in Georgia. Atlanta, 1960.

Blakey, Roy and Gladys. National Tax Association Digest and Index. New York, 1927.

Blakey, Roy and Gladys. The Federal Income Tax. New York, 1940.

Blegen, Theodore. Minnesota: A History of the State. Minneapolis, 1963.

Blum, John M. Joe Tumulty and the Wilson Era. Boston, 1951.

Blum, John Morton. The Promise of America: A Historical Inquiry. Baltimore, 1965.

Bolles, Blair. Tyrant From Illinois: Uncle Joe Cannon's Experience with Personal Power. New York, 1951.

Bowden, Robert. Boies Penrose. New York, 1937.

Bowers, Claude. Beveridge and the Progressive Era. Boston, 1923.

Braeman, John. Albert J. Beveridge, American Nationalist, Chicago.
Buenker, John D., Burnham, John C., and Crunden, Robert M. Progressivism. Cambridge, Massachusetts, 1977.
Buenker, John D. Urban Liberalism and Progressive Reform. New York, 1973.
Buni, Andrew. The Negro in Virginia Politics, 1902-1965. Charlottesville, 1967.
Burnham, Walter Dean. Critical Elections and the Mainsprings of American Politics. New York, 1970.
Burns, James M. Roosevelt: The Lion and the Fox. New York, 1956.
Burton, Theodore E. John Sherman. Boston and New York, 1906.
Carroll, Mollie Ray. Labor and Politics. Boston, 1923.
Cash, Wilber J. The Mind of the South. New York, 1941.
Cash, William T. History of the Democratic Party in Florida.
Caughey, John W. California. New York, 1953.
Chambers, Clarke A. Seedtime of Reform: American Social Service and Social Action, 1918-1933. Minneapolis, 1963.
Chambers, William Nisbit. Political Parties in a New Nation. New York, 1963.
Childs, Lawrence. Labor and Capital in National Politics. Columbus, Ohio, 1930.
Chrislock, Carl. The Progressive Era in Minnesota. Minneapolis, 1971.
Clark, Norman H. Washington: A Bicentennial History. Nashville, Tennessee, 1976.
Clark, Thomas D. A History of Kentucky. Lexington, Kentucky, 1960.
Clark, Thomas D. and Kirwan, Albert D. The South Since Appomattox. New York, 1967.
Cleland, Robert Glass. From Wilderness to Empire: A History of California. New York, 1967.
Cole, Donald B. Immigrant City: Lawrence, Massachusetts, 1845-1921. Chapel Hill, North Carolina, 1963.
Coletta, Paolo F. The Presidency of William Howard Taft. Lawrence, Kansas, 1973.
Coletta, Paolo F. William Jennings Bryan: Political Evangelist, 1860-1908, Lincoln, Nebraska, 1964.
Coletta, Paolo F. William Jennings Bryan: Progressive Politician and Moral Statesman, 1909-1915, Lincoln, Nebraska,
Commons, John R. The Distribution of Wealth. New York, 1893.
Corwin, Edward. Court Over Constitution. Princeton, New Jersey, 1938.
Cotner, Robert. James Stephen Hogg: A Biography. Austin, Texas, 1959.
Coulter, E. Merton. A Short History of Georgia. Chapel Hill, North Carolina, 1960.
Craf, John. Economic Development of the United States. New York, 1952.
Crooks, James B. Politics and Progress: The Rise of Urban Progressivism in Baltimore, 1895-1911. Baton Route, Louisiana, 1968.
Dale, Edward Everett and Wardell, Morris L. History of Oklahoma. Englewood Cliffs, New Jersey, 1948.
Dalton, Hugh. Principles of Public Finance. London, 1934.
Dalton, Hugh. Some Aspects of the Inequality of Incomes in Modern Communities. New York, 1920.
Davenport, Walter. The Power and the Glory. New York, 1931.

Davis, Allen B. Spearheads for Reform: The Social Settlements and the Progressive Movements, 1890-1914. New York, 1970.
Destler, Chester. American Radicalism. New London, 1946.
DeWitt, Benjamin Parke. The Progressive Movement: A Non-Partisan Comprehensive Discussion of Current Tendencies in American Politics. New York, 1915.
Doane, F.C. From South Street to Albany. New York, 1928.
Dorsett, Lyle. The Pendergast Machine. New York, 1968.
Dulles, Foster Ray. Labor in America. New York, 1949.
Dunbar, Willis Frederick. Michigan: A History of the Wolverine State. Grand Rapids, Michigan, 1965.
Dunaway, Wayland. History of Pennsylvania. Englewood Cliffs, New Jersey, 1945.
Dunne, Edward F. History of Illinois. Chicago, 1933.
Eaton, Allen H. The Oregon System. Chicago, 1912.
Ellis, David M., James A. Frost, Harold C. Syrett and Harvy J. Carman. A Short History of New York State. Ithaca, New York, 1957.
Ely, Richard. Taxation in American States and Cities. New York, 1888.
Erickson, Ephraim Edward. The Psychological and Ethical Aspects of Mormon Group Life. Chicago, 1922.
Ezell, John S. The South Since 1865. New York, 1963.
Faulk, Odie. Arizona: A Short History. Norman, Oklahoma, 1970.
Faulkner, Harold Underwood. The Decline of Laissez-Faire. New York, 1951.
Fausold, Martin. Gifford Pinchot and the Progressive Movement. Palo Alto, California, 1953.
Federal Writers Project. Montana: A State Guide Book. New York, 1949.
Federal Writers Project. North Dakota: A Guide to the Northern Prairie State. New York, 1950.
Fenton, John H. Politics in the Border States. New Orleans, 1957.
Fine, Nathan. Labor and Farmer Parties in the United States. New York, 1961.
Finkbeiner, Daniel. Pennsylvania Vote Trends in National and State Elections. Harrisburg, Pennsylvania, 1958.
Fletcher, John Gould. Arkansas. Chapel Hill, North Carolina, 1947.
Flint, Winston. Progressive Movement in Vermont. Washington, 1941.
Foner, Philip. History of the Labor Movement in the United States. New York, 1947.
Forthal, Sonya. Cogwheels of Democracy: A Study of the Precinct Captain. New York, 1946.
Foulke, Roland. The Federal Income Tax. Chicago, 1927.
Franklin, John Hope. Reconstruction After the Civil War. Chicago, 1961.
Fritz, Percy Stanby. Colorado: The Centennial State. New York, 1941.
Frost, Thomas. A Treatise on the Federal Income Tax. Albany, New York 1913.
Fuchs, Lawrence, ed. American Ethnic Politics. New York, 1968.
Galbraith, J. Kenneth. The Great Crash. Boston, 1961.
Galloway, George. History of the House of Representatives. New York, 1961.
Garraty, John. Henry Cabot Lodge: A Biography. New York, 1953.
Gaston, Paul M. The New South Creed. New York, 1970.
Ginger, Ray. The Bending Cross. New Brunswick, New Jersey, 1949.

Glaab, Charles and Brown, Theodore. History of Urban America. New York, 1967.
Gleason, Philip. The Conservative Reformers. Notre Dame, Indiana, 1968.
Gluck, Elsie. John Mitchell, Miner. New York, 1929.
Goldman, Eric. Rendevous with Destiny. New York, 1952.
Gompers, Samuel. The American Labor Movement. Washington, 1913.
Goodykoontz, Colin B. ed. The Papers of Edward P. Costigan Relating to the Progressive Movement in Colorado, 1902-1917. Boulder, Colorado, 1941.
Gore, Samuel. Illinois Votes. Urbana, Illinois, 1959.
Gosnell, Cullen. Government and Politics of Georgia. New York, 1936.
Gosnell, Harold F. Boss Platt and His New York Machine. Chicago, 1924.
Gould Lewis L. Wyoming: A Political History, 1868-1896. New Haven, Connecticut, 1968.
Gould, Lewis L. Progressives and Prohibitionists: Texas Democrats in the Wilson Era. Austin, Texas, 1973.
Graham, Otis L., Jr. An Encore For Reform: The Old Progressives and the New Deal. New York, 1968.
Grantham, Dewey. The Democratic South. Athens, Georgia, 1963.
Grantham, Dewey. Hoke Smith and the Politics of the New South. Baton Rouge, Louisiana, 1963.
Greeley, Andrew. Why Can't They Be Like Us? New York, 1971.
Green, A. Wigfall. The Man Bilbo. Baton Route, Louisiana, 1963.
Greenbaum, Fred. Fighting Progressive: A Biography of Edward P. Costigan. Washington, 1973.
Griffin, Solomon. W. Murray Crane: A Man and Brother. Boston, 1926.
Grimes, Alan P. The Puritan Ethic and Woman Suffrage. Princeton, New Jersey, 1967.
Grodzins, Morton. The American System: A New View of Government in the United States. Chicago, 1966. Edited by Daniel Elazor.
Groves, Harold. Financing Government. New York, 1939.
Gutman, Herbert G. and Gregory S. Kealey. Many Pasts: Readings in American Social History. Englewood Cliffs, New Jersey, 1973.
Haber, Samuel. Efficiency and Uplift: Scientific Management in the Progressive Era, 1890-1912. Chicago, 1964.
Hackney, Sheldon. From Populism to Progressivism in Alambama. Princeton, New Jersey, 1969.
Hafen, Leroy R. Colorado and Its People. New York, 1948.
Hair, Frank T. Bourbonism and Agrarian Protest. Baton Rouge, Louisiana, 1969.
Hamilton, Charles Granville. Progressive Mississippi. Aberdeen, Mississippi, 1978.
Handlin, Oscar. Al Smith and His America. Boston, 1958.
Handlin, Oscar, ed. Immigration as a Factor in American History. Englewood Cliffs, New Jersey, 1959.
Handlin, Oscar. The Uprooted. New York, 1951.
Hanna, Frank A. State Income Differentials, 1919-1954. Durham, North Carolina, 1959.
Havard, William and Beth, Loren. The Politics of Mis-Representation. Baton Rouge, Louisiana, 1962.
Hays, Samuel P. Conservation and the Gospel of Efficiency. Cambridge, Mass., 1959.

Hays, Samuel P. Response to Industrialism, 1885-1914. Chicago, 1957.
Heard, Alexander. A Two Party South? Chapel Hill, North Carolina, 1952.
Heaton, John. The Story of a Page. New York, 1913.
Hechler, Kenneth. Insurgency. New York, 1940.
Hein, Clarence. Kansas Votes. Lawrence, Kansas, 1958.
Henderson, Thomas M. Tammany Hall and the New Immigrants: The Progressive Years. New York, 1976.
Hesseltine, William B. and Smiley, David. The South in American History. Englewood Cliffs, New Jersey, 1960.
Hicks, John D. The Populist Revolt: A History of the Farmer's Alliance and the People's Party. Minneapolis, 1931.
Higham, John. Strangers in the Land: Patterns of American Nativism, 1860-1925. New York, 1970.
Hofstadter, Richard. The Age of Reform. New York, 1955.
Hofstadter, Richard, ed. Great Issues in American History. New York, 1959.
Hofstadter, Richard. The Progressive Movement, 1900-1915. Englewood Cliffs, New Jersey, 1963.
Holli, Melvin. Reform in Detroit. New York, 1969.
Holmes, Jack E. Politics in New Mexico. Albuquerque, New Mexico, 1967.
Holmes, William F. The White Chief: James Kimble Vardaman. Baton Rouge, Louisiana, 1970.
Holt, James. Congressional Insurgents and the Party System, 1909-1916. Cambridge, Massachusetts, 1967.
Howard, Perry. Political Tendencies in Louisiana. Baton Rouge, Louisiana, 1957.
Howard, Robert P. Illinois: A History of the Prairie State. Grand Rapids, Michigan, 1972.
Howe, Frederic. Confessions of a Reformer. New York, 1925.
Huthmacher, J. Joseph. Massachusetts People and Politics, 1919-1933. New York, 1969.
Huthmacher, J. Joseph. Senator Robert F. Wagner and the Rise of Urban Liberalism. New York, 1968.
Hunter, Robert. Poverty. New York, 1904.
Israel, Fred. Nevada's Key Pittman. Lincoln, Nebraska, 1963.
James Marquis. Alfred I. DuPont, The Family Rebel. Indianapolis, 1941.
James Marquis. Mr. Garner of Texas. Indianapolis, 1939.
Jessup, Philip. Elihu Root. New York, 1939.
Johnson, Clauduis, O. Borah. New York, 1936.
Jones, Chester. Readings on Parties and Elections in the United States. Washington, 1942.
Jones, Frank, ed. Politics in the American West. Salt Lake City, 1969.
Karson, Marc. American Labor Unions and Politics, 1900-1918. Boston, 1970.
Kelly, Alfred and Harbison, Winfred. The American Constitution. New York, 1963.
Kelly, Frank. The Fight for the White House, 1912. New York, 1961.
Kennan, Kossuth Kent. Income Taxation: Methods and Results in Various Countries. Milwaukee, 1910.
Kennedy, David M. Progressivism: The Critical Issues. Boston, 1971.
Kent, Frank. The Democratic Party. New York, 1928.

Kerney, James. The Political Education of Woodrow Wilson. New York, 1926.
Key, V.O. Southern Politics. New York, 1949.
Kinsman, Delos. The Income Tax in the Commonwealth of the United States. Madison, Wisconsin, 1900.
Kipnis, Ira. The American Socialist Movement. New York, 1952.
Kirby, Jack Temple. Westmorland Davis. Charlottsville, Virginia, 1968.
Kirwan, Albert D. The Revolt of the Rednecks. Gloucester, Massachusetts, 1964.
Klein, Philip S. and Hoogenboom, Ari. A History of Pennsylvania. New York, 1973.
Kleppner, Paul. The Cross of Culture: A Social Analysis of Midwestern Politics, 1850-1900. New York, 1970.
Klotter, James C. William Goebel: The Politics of Wrath. Lexington, Kentucky, 1977.
Kolko, Gabriel. Wealth and Power in America. New York, 1962.
Kolko, Gabriel. The Triumph of Conservatism. New York, 1963.
Kraus, Michael. Immigration: The American Mosaic. New York, 1966.
Ladd, Everett Corll. Where Have All The Voters Gone?: The Fracturing of America's Political Parties. New York, 1978.
La Forte, Robert Sherman. Leaders of Reform: Progressive Republicans in Kansas, 1900-1916. Lawrence, Kansas, 1974.
Lander, Ernest McPherson. A History of South Carolina, 1865-1960. Chapel Hill, North Carolina, 1960.
Larson, Robert W. New Mexico's Quest for Statehood, 1946-1912. Albuquerque, New Mexico, 1968.
Larson, T.A. History of Wyoming. Lincoln, Nebraska, 1965.
Lefler, Hugh T. and Newsome, Albert R. North Carolina: The History of a Southern State. Chapel Hill, North Carolina, 1963.
Leopold, Richard W. Elihu Root and the Conservative Tradition. Boston, 1954.
Levine, Daniel. Varieties of Reform Thought. Madison, Wisconsin, 1964.
Levine, Edward. Theodore Francis Green: The Rhode Island Years. Providence, 1963.
Lewis, Oscar. The Big Four. New York, 1966.
Lieberman, Joseph. The Power Broker. Cambridge, Massachusetts, 1966.
Link, Arthur. Wilson: The Road to the White House. Princeton, New Jersey, 1954.
Link, Arthur. Woodrow Wilson: The New Freedom. Princeton, New Jersey, 1956.
Litt, Edgar. Beyond Pluralism: Ethnic Politics in America. Glenview, Illinois, 1970.
Lockard, Duane. New England State Politics. Princeton, New Jersey, 1959.
Lubove, Roy. The Struggle for Social Security, 1900-1935. Cambridge, Massachusetts, 1968.
Lubell, Samuel. The Future of American Politics. New York, 1965.
Lundberg, Ferdinand. The Individual Income Tax. Washington, 1965.
Lundberg, Ferdinand. The Rich and the Super Rich. New York, 1968.
Lutz, Harley, Public Finance. New York, 1936.
Machen, Arthur W. A Treatise on the Federal Corporation Tax Law of 1909. Boston, 1910.

Malone, Michael P. and Roeder, Richard B. The Montana Past: An Anthology. Missoula, Montana, 1969.

Marshall, F. Roy. Labor in the South. Cambridge, Massachusetts, 1967.

Mann, Arthur. Yankee Reformers in An Urban Age. Cambridge, Massachusetts, 1954.

Manners, William. TR And Will: A Friendship That Split the Republican Party. New York, 1969.

Martin, Curtis and Gomez, Rudolph. Colorado Government and Politics. Boulder, Colorado, 1964.

Martin, Edward. The Life of Joseph Hodges Choate. New York, 1920.

Martin, Sidney Walter. Florida's Flagler. Athens, Georgia, 1948.

Maxwell, Robert. LaFollette and the Rise of Progressivism in Wisconsin. Madison, Wisconsin, 1956.

McCloskey, Robert. American Conservatism in the Age of Enterprise, 1865-1910. New York, 1951.

McCormick, Richard L. From Realignment to Reform: Political Change in New York State, 1893-1910. Ithaca, New York, 1981.

McElroy, Robert. Grover Cleveland. New York, 1923.

McKenna, Marion. Borah. Ann Arbor, Michigan, 1961.

McKinney, John C. and Thompson, Edger T. The South in Continuity and Change. Durham, North Carolina, 1965.

McReynolds, Edwin C. Missouri: A History of the Crossroads State. Norman, Oklahoma, 1962.

McReynolds, Edwin C. Oklahoma: A History of the Sooner State. Norman, Oklahoma, 1964.

McWilliams, Carey. Brothers Under the Skin. Boston. 1964.

Mercer, James K. Ohio Legislative History, 1909-1913. Columbus, 1913.

Merriam, Charles. Chicago: A More Intimate View of Urban Politics. New York, 1929.

Merrill, Horace S. Bourbon Leader. Boston, 1957.

Merrill, Horace S. and Merrill, Marion Galbraith. The Republican Command, 1897-1913.

Merrill, Morton. Reed Smoot: Utah Politician. Ogden, Utah, 1953.

Merton, Robert K. Social Theory and Social Structure. New York, 1957.

Miller, Herman P. Rich Man, Poor Man. New York, 1964.

Miller, Herman P. Smull's Legislature Handbook and Manual of the State of Pennsylvania, 1911. Harrisburg, Pennsylvania, 1911.

Miller, Zane L. Boss Cox Cincinnati. New York, 1968.

Moger, Allen W. Virginia: From Bourbonism to Byrd, 1870-1925. Charlottesville, Virginia, 1968.

Moos, Malcom. The Republicans. New York, 1956.

Morgan, H. Wayne. Eugene v. Debs. Syracuse, New York, 1962.

Moscow, Warren. Politics in the Empire State. New York, 1948.

Moscow, Warren. What Have You Done for Me Lately? Englewood Cliffs, New Jersey, 1967.

Mowry, George. The California Progressives. Berkley, California, 1951.

Mowry, George. The Era of Theodore Roosevelt. New York, 1958.

Mowry, George. Theodore Roosevelt and the Progressive Era. Madison, Wisconsin, 1946.

Myers, Gustavus. History of Great American Fortunes. Chicago, 1909.

Nash, Gerald B. The American West in the Twentieth Century. Englewood Cliffs, New Jersey, 1973.

Neuberger, Richard and Kahn, Stephen. Integrity, The Life of George Norris. New York, 1937.

Nevins, Allen. Grover Cleveland. New York, 1933.

Noble, Ransom E. New Jersey Progressivism Before Wilson. Princeton, New Jersey, 1947.

Nord, David Paul. Newspapers and New Politics: Midwestern Municipal Reform, 1890-1900. Ann Arbor, Michigan, 1981.

Norris, George W. Fighting Liberal. New York, 1945.

Nye, Russell B. Midwestern Progressive Politics. East Lansing, Michigan, 1959.

Olson, James C. History of Nebraska. Lincoln, Nebraska, 1966.

Orfield, L.B. The Amending of the Federal Constitution. Ann Arbor, Michigan, 1942.

Ostrander, Gilman. Nevada: The Great Rotten Borough. New York, 1966.

Page, Thomas. Legislative Apportionment in Kansas. Lawrence, Kansas, 1952.

Parker, William. Justin Smith Morrill. Boston, 1924.

Patton, Clifford. The Battle for Municipal Reform. Washington, 1940.

Paul, Arnold M. Conservative Crisis and the Rule of Law: Attitudes of Bar and Bench, 1887-1895. New York, 1969.

Paul, Randolph E. Studies in Federal Taxation. Cambridge, Massachusetts, 1940.

Paul, Randolph E. Taxation For Prosperity. Indianapolis, 1947.

Paul, Randolph E. Taxation in the United States. Boston, 1954.

Pechman, Joseph. The Rich, The Poor, And the Taxes They Pay. Washington, 1969.

Perkins, Frances. The Roosevelt I Knew. New York, 1946.

Perry, Arthur L. Political Economy. New York, 1883.

Phelps, Edith. Selected Articles on the Income Tax. New York, 1917.

Platt, Thomas C. The Autobiography of Thomas Collier Platt. New York, 1910.

Pollock, Norman. The Populist Response to Industrial America. New York, 1966.

Porter, Kirk and Johnson, Donald. National Party Platforms. Urbana, Illinois, 1961.

Pringle, Henry. The Life and Times of William Howard Taft. New York, 1939.

Pringle, Henry. Theodore Roosevelt. New York, 1931.

Pulley, Raymond H. Old Virginia Restored, 1870-1930. Chapel Hill, North Carolina, 1967.

Pusey, Merlo J. Charles Evans Hughes. New York, 1951.

Quaif, M.H. and Glazer, Sidney. Michigan. New York, 1948.

Quint, Howard, Albertson, Dean, and Cantor, Milton. Main Problems in American History, II. Homewood, Illinois, 1968.

Ratner, Sidney. A Political and Social History of Federal Taxation. New York, 1942.

Ratner, Sidney, ed. New Light on the History of Great American Fortunes: American Millionaires of 1892 and 1902. New York, 1953.

Ratner, Sidney. The Tariff In American History. New York, 1972.

Ring, Elizabeth. The Progressive Movement of 1912 and Third Party Movement of 1924 in Maine. Orono, Maine, 1933.

Riordan, William, ed. Plunkitt of Tammany Hall. New York, 1948.

Robinson, Elwyn B. History of North Dakota. Lincoln, Nebraska, 1966.

Rogin, Michael Paul and Shover, John L. Political Change in California. Westport, Connecticut, 1969.

Rolle, Andrew. California: A History. New York, 1967.

Roper, William L. and Arrington, Leonard J. William Spry: Man of Firmness and Governor of Utah. Salt Lake City, 1971.

Ross, Thomas Richard. Jonathan Prentiss Dolliver. Iowa City, Iowa, 1958.

Rothman, David. Power and Politics: The United States Senate, 1869-1901. New York, 1969.

Ruskay, Joseph A. and Osserman, Richard A. Halfway to Tax Reform. Bloomington, Indiana, 1970.

Saloutos, Theodore and Hicks, John D. Agricultural Discontent in the Middle West, 1900-1939. Madison, Wisconsin 1951.

Saloutos, Theodore. Farmer Movements in the South, 1865-1933. Lincoln, Nebraska, 1964.

Sarasohn, Stephen B. and Vera H. Political Party Patterns in Michigan. Detroit, 1957.

Schattschneider, E.E. Politics, Pressures and the Tariff. New York, 1935.

Schlesinger, Arthur M., Jr. The Crisis of the Old Order. New York, 1957.

Seidman, Jacob. Legislative History of Federal Income Tax Laws. New York, 1938.

Seitz, Don Carlos. Joseph Pulitzer. New York, 1924.

Seligman, Edwin R.A. The Income Tax: A Study of the History, Theory and Practice of Income Taxation at Home and Abroad. New York, 1911.

Shannon, David A. The Socialist Party of America. New York, 1955.

Shannon, Fred. The Farmer's Last Frontier. New York, 1945.

Shannon, Jasper B. Towards a New Politics in the South. Knoxville, Tennessee, 1949.

Sharkansky, Ira. The Politics of Taxing and Spending. Indianapolis, 1969.

Simkins, Francis B. Pitchfork Ben Tillman: South Carolinian. Baton Rouge, Louisiana, 1944.

Simkins, Francis B. The South, Old and New: A History. New York, 1947.

Sindler, Allan P. Huey Long's Louisiana. Baltimore, 1956.

Smith, Carl and Edward, H.P. Behind the Scenes at Salem. Salem, Oregon, 1911.

Smith, Harry. The United States Federal Internal Tax History From 1861 to 1871. Boston, 1914.

Soltow, Lee, ed. Six Papers on the Size Distribution of Wealth and Income. New York and London, 1969.

Spahr, Charles B. The Present Distribution of Wealth in the United States. New York, 1896.

Stampp, Kenneth. The Era of Reconstruction, 1865-1877. New York, 1967.

Stave, Bruce M. Urban Bosses, Machines, and Progressive Reformers. Boston, 1972.

Steffens, Lincoln. The Autobiography of Lincoln Steffens. New York, 1931.

Steffens, Lincoln. The Struggle For Self-Government. New York, 1906.

Stephenson, Nathaniel. Nelson Aldrich: A Leader in American Politics. New York, 1930.
Stern, Philip. The Great Treasury Raid. New York, 1964.
Stewart, Frank M. A Half-Century of Municipal Reform: The History of the National Municipal League. Berkeley, California, 1950.
Streighthoff, F.H. Distribution of Incomes in the United States. New York, 1912.
Studenski, Paul and Herman Kroos. Financial History of the United States. New York, 1963.
Sullivan, William. Edward F. Dunne: Judge, Mayor, Governor. Chicago, 1916.
Swanberg, W.H. Citizen Hearst. New York, 1961.
Taft, Horace Dutton. Memoirs and Opinions. New York, 1942.
Taft, Philip. The A.F.L. in the Time of Gompers. New York, 1957.
Taussig, F.W. The Tariff History of the United States. New York, 1964.
Tarr, Joel A. A Study in Boss Politics: William Lorimer of Chicago. Urbana, Illinois 1971.
Taylor, William Harrison, ed. Legislative History and Souvenir of Connecticut, 1911-1912. Hartford, Connecticut, 1912.
Tebeau, Charlton W. A History of Florida. Coral Gables, Florida, 1971.
Terrill, Tom L. Tariff, Politics and American Foreign Policy. Westport, Connecticut, 1972.
Thelen, David P. The New Citizenship: Origins of Progressivm in Wisconsin, 1885-1990. Columbia, Missouri, 1972.
Thelen, David P. Robert M. LaFollette and The Spirit of Insurgency. Boston,
Thomas, David. Arkansas and Its People. New York, 1930.
Thompson, Warren S. and Whelpton, P.K. Population Trends in the United States. New York, 1933.
Timberlake, James H. Prohibition and the Progressive Movement, 1900-1920. New York, 1970.
Tindall, George B. The Emergence of the New South, 1913-1945. Baton Rouge, Louisiana, 1967.
Tingley, Donald F. The Structuring of the State: The History of Illinois, 1899-1928. Urbana, Illinois, 1980.
Titus, Charles. Voting Behavior in the United States. Berkeley, California, 1935.
Underwood, J.H. Distribution of Ownership. New York, 1907.
Van Den Haag, Ernest and Ross, Ralph. The Fabric of Society: An Introduction to the Social Sciences. New York, 1957.
Vare, William S. My Forty Years in Politics. Philadelphia, 1933.
Veblen, Thorstein. Theory of Business Enterprise. New York, 1904.
Vecoli, Rudolph. The People of New Jersey. Princeton, New Jersey, 1965.
Wallace, David Duncan. A History of South Carolina. New York, 1934.
Wallace, David Duncan. South Carolina: A Short History, 1520-1948. Columbia, South Carolina, 1966.
Warner, Hoyt L. Progressivism in Ohio, 1897-1917. Columbus, 1964.
Warren, George F. and Pearson, Frank A. Prices. New York, 1933.
Weiss, Nancy Joan. Charles Francis Murphy 1858-1924: Respectability and Responsibility in Tammany Politics. Northampton, Massachusetts, 1959.

Wesser, Robert K. Charles Evans Hughes: Politics and Reform in New York, 1905-1910. Ithaca, New York, 1967.
Westphal, Victor. Thomas Benton Catron and His Era. Tucson, Arizona, 1973.
Weyl, Walter. The New Democracy. New York, 1913.
Wickersham, George W. The Changing Order. New York. 1914.
Wiebe, Robert. H. Business Men and Reform. Cambridge, Massachusetts, 1963.
Wiebe, Robert. H. The Searach For Order, 1877-1920. New York, 1967.
Wike, J. Rofe. The Pennsylvania Manufacturers Association. Philadelphia, 1960.
Wilkinson, J. Harvie. Harry Byrd and the Changing Face of Virginia Politics, 1945-1966. Charlottsville, Virginia, 1968.
Williams, R. Hal. The Democratic Party and California Politics, 1880-1896, Stanford, California, 1973.
Winther, Oscar O. The Great Northwest: A History. New York, 1948.
Woodward, C. Vann. The Origins of the New South. Baton Rouge, Louisiana, 1951.
Woodward, C. Vann. Reunion and Reaction. New York, 1951.
Woodward, C. Vann. The Strange Career of Jim Crow. New York.
Woodward, C. Vann. Tom Watson: Agrarian Rebel. New York, 1955.
Yearly, Clifton K. The Money Machines: The Breakdown and Reform of Governmental and Party Finance in the North, 1860-1920. Albany, New York, 1970.
Yellowitz, Irwin. Labor and the Progressive Movement in New York State, 1897-1916. Ithaca, New York, 1965.
Zink, Harold. City Bosses in the United States. Durham, North Carolina, 1930.
Zink, Harold. Who's Who in State Politics. Boston, 1907.
Zornow, William. Kansas. Norman, 1957.

INDEX